Marketing Madness

A Survival Guide
for a Consumer Society

Michael F. Jacobson

and

Laurie Ann Mazur

Center for the Study of Commercialism

with a Foreword by Ralph Nader

Westview Press

BOULDER • SAN FRANCISCO • OXFORD

Copyright © 1995
by CENTER FOR THE STUDY OF COMMERCIALISM

Published in 1995 in the United States of America by Westview Press, Inc., 5500 Central Avenue, Boulder, Colorado 80301-2877, and in the United Kingdom by Westview Press, 12 Hid's Copse Road, Cumnor Hill, Oxford OX2 9JJ

Design by Scott Frommer

Library of Congress
Cataloging-in-Publication Data

Jacobson, Michael F.

Marketing madness:
a survival guide for a consumer society
Michael F. Jacobson and
Laurie Ann Mazur.
p. cm.

Includes index.

ISBN 0-8133-1980-3 (HC)
ISBN 0-8133-1981-1 (Pbk)

1. Marketing—Social aspects—United States. 2. Advertising—Social aspects—United States. 3. Marketing—United States—Psychological aspects. 4. Advertising—United States—Psychological aspects. I. Mazur, Laurie Ann. II. Title. HF5415.1.J25 1995
658.8—dc20
94—12878CIP

Printed and bound in the United States of America

The paper used in this publication meets the requirements of the American National Standards for Permanence of Paper for Printed Library Materials Z39.48-1984

10 9 8 7 6 5 4 3 2

ette's happiness in a more

commercialized society

el F. Jacobson

memory of my mother,

iet Mazur, with love

rie Ann Mazur

Contents

Foreword

by Ralph Nader

This book is a detailed report on the commercializing of just about every-thing. In area after area that was generally off limits to commercialism, the mercantile juggernaut has moved in or swarmed over—into our schools and colleges, our public media, our amateur sports, our holidays and ritu-als, our arts, our children, our privacy and private sensibilities, our reli-gious institutions, our environment, our language, and our politics. Our historically treasured cultural values are either viewed as marketing imped-iments—such as democratic tools for civic assertiveness—or are comman-deered, coopted, or outright commodified in the service of corporate profits.

BUT DIDN'T PRESIDENT CALVIN COOLIDGE say back in the 1920s that "the business of America is business"? Hasn't the com-mand of commerce, the lure of profits, the sin-gle-minded focus on markets been around since the days of the thirteen colonies? Nothing past is remotely comparable to the pervasive, time-consuming, and flouting of formerly noncom-mercial space and institutions in our country as the hyper-intensity and calculation of the mega-sales pitch that sweeps all prior restraints and functional decorums aside in today's malling of America.

Churches speak more about marketing them-selves than about Mammon. Children demand of their parents what children's television pro-gramming and advertising, which directly bypasses the parents, seduces the youngsters into wanting. And corporate hucksters have even used former Presidents, such as George Washington, Thomas Jefferson, and Abraham Lincoln, as commercial pitchmen for car dealers, furniture stores, and banks. There are almost no limits or boundaries to commercialism, except perhaps beer commercials interrupting presiden-tial speeches or billboards by the Grand Canyon or in front of Mount Rushmore.

It is important to read *Marketing Madness* as a critique of commercialism that goes beyond matters of taste. Commercial dictates have much greater power in their economic, political, and media manifestations than other more basic values such as health, safety, justice, civic voice, and, yes, beauty and truth. In its rampage, commercialism has put these values on a collision course with itself. It is not much of a contest. Public schools allow commercial television—replete with product advertising—into the class-rooms, arguing that they couldn't otherwise afford the donated television equipment. These are the same schools that have turned their mis-sions into vocational training at the expense of the civic training and critical thinking that our society so strongly needs.

How often have you heard politicians say that companies cannot afford to meet modest health and safety standards—the same companies that are paying their executives enormous salaries and are sitting on bloated corporate bureaucra-cies. This pattern occurred in the 1970s and 1980s within the auto industry—the same industry that admitted in its downsizing that billions of dollars a year were being wasted on excess layers of management. The triumph of commercialism is seen every day in Washington, D.C., and state capitals. From political action committee payoffs to government's massive dis-bursement of welfare to corporations, the imper-ative of commercialism surges through our soci-ety. Yet even taken on its own terms—that of fostering greater material comforts for the general population—rampant commercialism has failed to deliver, as the gap between the rich and other Americans grows wider each year.

It does not take too many years of this obsession to institutionalize commercialism not just in the ways of our society but in the minds of its people, starting at a very young age. Teenagers have told reporters that "you are what you buy." The sense of the heroic for pre-teens is almost entirely drawn from celluloid celebrities such as the Ninja Turtles or the Power Rangers. Real history does not exist in their frame of reference, their aspirations, or their dialogue. Soon to come in a big, time-absorbing, and violent manner is virtual reality, which induces the children to take a direct part in the virtual mayhem.

In the Biblical literature and in mandarin China, commerce was told to respect boundaries in order not to contaminate or damage noncommercial practices, traditions, and customs. In old China, merchants were near the bottom of the social status ladder. At the time of Ben Franklin's pronouncements about thrift and moderation, there was concern among the nation's founders about greed and overreaching. During the Civil War, munitions manufacturers, in their avarice to maximize profits, produced defective equipment that took the lives of soldiers. The populist-progressive movements aimed to decentralize power by reclaiming it from the mighty railroads and banks and distributing it to the common people. Call that reform chapter in our history a drive to build a power base for values beyond commerce—democratic values, way-of-life values, family security values—in addition to demanding the power to make a decent living shielded from corporate predators.

Any culture that surrenders its vision and its self-sustaining human values to the narrow judgment of commerce will be neither free nor just. Commercialism does serious damage to the *substance* of democracy, if not to its forms. It leads to censorship or self-censorship of the media, to invisible chains that keep people from speaking out, to the indentured status of politicians, and to an overall coarseness that deprecates the humanitarian impulses and the creative drives of a culture in balance, a culture having commerce without commercialism. Also, the commercialistic cocoon enveloping children with the "entertainment" of violence, addiction, and low-grade sensuality reflects the displacement of more nurturing values by a "marketing madness."

Michael Jacobson and Laurie Ann Mazur have compiled the details and the insights that expose the pretensions of the apologists for commerce without boundaries. They have recommended modes of personal and family rebellion that improve well-being and have proposed broader strategies by constituencies that are expected to protect and nurture other cultural values. But it is the detailed texture of this volume, which is so full of material for family, neighborhood, and community discussions, that may be its most important contribution. Looking at the world through independent thought processes does more than free young women from harming their health through destructive dieting in order to be as thin as the models in the fashion magazines. It is a form of intellectual liberation from the skillfully applied psychology of commercial persuasions that limit human potential and the cultural advancement that views more grandly the purposes of life and the qualities of economies.

Washington, D.C.
December 1994

Acknowledgments

WE WOULD LIKE TO THANK numerous people for their assistance in working on this book. Ronald K.L. Collins, a co-founder of the Center for the Study of Commercialism, played a key role in conceptualizing this book. He also drafted parts of the Prologue, "Making Pawns of the Press," and other passages in Part One. Karen Brown, the stalwart staffer at the Center for the Study of Commercialism, made sure this book happened: She oversaw organizational aspects of the project, contributed to the writing of Part One, took some of the photographs and wrote the photo captions, and provided thoughtful criticisms of the entire book. Research assistant Jenny Manner contributed greatly by conducting library research, inputing edits, taking several photos, and tracking down illustrations and references. We also thank Josh Mader and Susan Monaco for their capable research assistance and Tim Miles for preparing the graphs and performing other computer tasks. ✳ We greatly appreciate the generosity of Pat Aufderheide, Deborah Baldwin, Russell Belk, Steve Brobeck, Peggy Charren, Stanley Cohen, Les Dlabay, Albert J. Fritsch, Henry Geller, George Gerbner, Steve Goldstein, Dan Guttman, George Hacker, Jean Kilbourne, Larry Kirstein, Steve Kostant, Jonathan Kozol, Howard Lenhoff, Alice Tepper Marlin, Ed McMahon, Mark Crispin Miller, Alex Molnar, Katherine Montgomery, Frensch Niegermeier, Robert Parham, Richard Pollay, Marsha L. Richins, Vicki Robin, Jill Savitt, Herbert Schiller, Andrew Jay Schwartzman, Bruce Silverglade, Betsy Taylor, Martin Teitel, and Emanuel Thorne for reading sections of the manuscript, offering useful suggestions, providing specific pieces of information, or helping in other ways. The authors and the Center for the Study of Commercialism are also grateful to the Maximilian O. and Marion E. Hoffman Foundation and the C. S. Fund for their financial assistance, which made this book possible. Other grants from the late Philip Stern, the J. Roderick MacArthur Foundation (for a study of advertiser pressure on the media), New Road Map Foundation, Foundation for Deep Ecology, Ottinger Foundation, L. J. and Mary C. Skaggs Foundation, and Foundation for New Paradigm Thinking provided additional support to the center. ✳ We greatly appreciate the confidence that Gordon Massman of Westview Press had in the authors. We also thank production editor Michelle Asakawa for her gracious and meticulous editing of the book and Scott Frommer for his herculean efforts in designing this book. The entire staff of Westview has been a pleasure to work with. ✳ Finally, Michael Jacobson thanks his wife, Donna Lenhoff, for her excellent last-minute editing assistance and for letting him get away with less than his fair share of diaper-changing and other tasks while writing this book, and Laurie Mazur thanks Russ Haven for his many patient draft readings, insightful criticism, and emotional support.

Michael F. Jacobson
Laurie Ann Mazur

Prologue

Commercialism: The Word and the Philosophy

Commercialism: Ubiquitous product marketing that leads to a preoccupation with individual consumption to the detriment of oneself and society.—Center for the Study of Commercialism

ALMOST FIFTY YEARS AGO, THE BUSINESS MAG-azine *Fortune* observed, "No place on earth is geographically beyond the reach of the hawkers and hucksters; the only oases of peace—the peace that is free of advertising—are the darkened sickrooms of the dying where the customer is not worth bothering about and a few billboardless roads and the depths of the national parks."[1] Today, commercialism—particularly in the form of its chief harbinger and handmaiden, advertising—pervades our society to an extent not dreamed possible several decades ago. Consider just a few recent examples:

- *Commercial billboards are proposed for low-earth orbit.*

- *"Virtual billboards" inserted electronically into telecasts of baseball games simulate signs that don't really exist at the ballparks.*

- *McDonald's spent $2.5 million to produce one ad aired during the 1994 Super Bowl.*

- *The sides of school buses in Colorado Springs, Colorado, are covered with advertising.*

Advertising—exalted by businesses, vilified by muckrakers—is here in a big way and here to stay. Product and service messages have been crafted to appeal to our visual, tactile, olfactory, and aural senses. They talk to our conscious, rational mind, as well as to our subconscious desires and vulnerabilities. They have been placed in everything from books to movies to the bottoms of holes on putting greens. They've been slapped onto everything from beach volleyball nets to ski lifts to bathroom doors to pro athletes' wrists and feet. They are pumped into subway stations and grade school classrooms, snuck into computer programs and arcade games, and zapped through phones and fax machines. Even our clothing carries commercial logos, making us walking billboards. It seems that marketers won't be satisfied until every square inch of space, every moment of time, is filled with the message "Buy."

The bottom line is that in 1994 marketers spent well over *$150 billion* to persuade Americans to buy their products and that the average American will devote almost three full years of his or her waking life just to watching TV commercials! Those ads are amusing, annoying, or boring, but they have effects of far greater import than the transient emotions they elicit.

Advertising is just the tip of the commercialism iceberg. Marketers are aggressively commercializing aspects of life that were once noncommercial. Children used to play in the backyard, the local park, or on the school grounds; for many children today, the playground of choice is the one at the local McDonald's. For outings, many families now go to Disneyland and other commercial theme parks instead of state and national parks. In fact, a large shopping mall, Potomac Mills Mall, is the number-one tourist destination in the state of Virginia. Fifty years ago, Halloween was a time when kids and parents crafted their own hobo, princess, witch, and other costumes; today, trick-or-treaters wear store-bought outfits featuring Aladdin, Batman, or other trademarked commercial characters. Free book readings at the public library are now upstaged by those at major bookstores, where the goal is to sell, not loan. And children's books, as likely as not, feature cartoon characters that were launched as movies, migrated to television, and then showed up on t-shirts, games, and a thousand other products. Even physiognomies are for sale, one and a half million a year, courtesy of your local cosmetic surgeon.[2] Commercialism knows no bounds, engulfing everything from schools to professional sports to scientific research.

The signs of commercialism are so numerous that we risk becoming oblivious to the obvious. Still, many Americans have begun to express their frustrations with the commercial way. As *Business Week* has observed, "Consumers [are] fed up with being bombarded by up to 3,000 marketing messages a day....A consumer revolt against advertising seems to be taking shape."[3]

When confined to appropriate limits, the business side of life can coexist with family, religion, recreation, and other facets. But when unleashed and allowed to grow without restriction, commerce adds an "ism" and becomes a philosophy—"commercialism"—that destroys the previous balance.

Commercialism is founded on an illusion of unlimited resources, an obsession with acquiring ever-more material goods. This *ism* stands in stark contrast to the civic ideal of community, or communitarianism, which was one of the core beliefs of our nation's founders.

The old-fashioned ideals of simple living and moderation in the marketplace are foreign to the modern idea of commercialism. Frugality was a key word in the founders' civic vocabulary. "Commerce without commercialism" is how Benjamin Franklin or John Adams might have put it. They recognized that there are values beyond the marketplace, worthy aspirations beyond profit and pleasure, and joys in the simple life of modest consumption and friendship with others.

Commercialism teaches us a lesson that is at war with the teachings of our founders. And that commercial message is this: To be a *citizen* means no more than being a *consumer*—patriotism and commercialism are one and the same thing. Hunter College professor Stuart Ewen says that the captains of commerce are moving us from a citizen democracy to a "consumer democracy."[4] In such a world, the citizen's most cherished right, indeed his or her *duty*, is to consume.

Commercialism also preaches a lesson at odds with the teachings of moral leaders. The commercial message holds that being a *person* is synonymous with being a *consumer*. That is, "personhood" is defined by what we buy, never mind such traits as honesty, generosity, and loyalty.

We consumers have learned our new lessons well, even to the extent of liberating ourselves from such obsolete values as self-restraint and frugality. Gross excesses of conspicuous consumption[5]—such as $7,100 mink-trimmed, cashmere sleeping bags and $98,000 chinchilla blankets—are offered up in the temples of commerce. Such products are out of reach of most of us, but many of us still buy far more than we need or can afford. And focusing so much of our attention on the marketplace may distract us from the noncommercial aspects of life.

*   *   *

Today, the very quest for a nation in which the public's welfare is paramount is threatened by rampant commercialism. In Part One of *Marketing Madness*, we describe how marketers insinuate sales pitches into every facet of our lives and of our culture, turning us into a country of Black Belt shoppers.

Business executives maintain that commercialism has served the public well, providing unprecedented levels of convenience and material comfort. Marketers maintain that advertising does nothing more than mirror society's mores and values, alert people to new products and bargains, or motivate people to switch brands; at the very worst, they say, it bores or annoys. With all due respect to those advocates, we contend that commercialism—and the spending of over $500 annually for every man, woman, and child in the country on highly sophisticated and carefully targeted commercial messages—has far more damaging effects than goading Joe Six-Pack to buy Miller instead of Budweiser. In Part Two, Chapter 9, we explore some of the ways that living in a society dominated by commercial interests affects us as individuals and as a nation.

Social forces are like biological organisms in at least one regard: Once they occupy a niche, they can be almost impossible to dislodge. And, unlike pigeons or dandelions, the champions of commercialism have lawyers, PAC committees, and other hallmarks of contemporary economic and political power. Still, there is time to right the balance in our lives, and perhaps in our society, if only we open our eyes and raise our voices. Thus, in Part Two, Chapter 10, we present an agenda for controlling the marketers whose ultimate effect is to turn citizens into consumers.

PART ONE

The Face of Commercialism

The American citizen lives in a state of siege from dawn till bedtime. Nearly everything he sees, hears, tastes, touches, and smells is an attempt to sell him something. Luckily for his sanity he becomes calloused shortly after diaperhood; now, to break through his protective shell the advertisers must continuously shock, tease, tickle, or irritate him, or wear him down by the drip-drip-drip or Chinese water-torture method of endless repetition. —Fortune *magazine (November 1947)*[1]

This is the secret of propaganda: Those who are to be persuaded by it should be completely immersed in the ideas of the propaganda, without ever noticing that they are being immersed in it. —*Joseph Goebbels (March 1933)*[2]

MASS COMMERCIALISM'S ASSAULT ON THE public's psyche is spearheaded by incessant thirty-second TV spots, but its scope is far broader. Recent advances in commercialism's all-fronts offensive include:

- *Anheuser-Busch's planting a horse-drawn Budweiser-beer wagon in the middle of President Clinton's 1993 inaugural parade.*

- *Infiltrating schools with daily "Channel One" news shows punctuated by commercials, fast-food outlets in the cafeterias, and curricula produced by major corporations.*

- *Corporations paying $30,000 a pop to put their names on children's gameboards.*

- *Reebok's sponsoring the 1992 U.S. Olympic team—on the condition that medalists wear Reebok outfits on the winner's stand.*

- *Advertisers inserting their "product placement" ads in movies, making a mockery of artistic integrity.*

- *"Noncommercial" public radio and television stations accepting increasingly blatant advertising.*

- *Ink-jet printing with edible inks enabling advertising to be printed on eggs, ice-cream cones, and other foods currently "advertising deficient."*

- *The Catholic Church's selling 100-odd items bearing the pope's likeness during His Holiness's 1993 visit to Denver.*

- *The makers of cigarettes and alcoholic beverages sponsoring African-American, feminist, antipoverty, and environmental organizations, in the process discouraging those groups from criticizing companies whose products are killing their constituencies.*

- *Corporations producing "video news releases" that are aired by local TV stations as genuine news.*

- *Orkin Pest Control donating money to renovate the Smithsonian's Insect Zoo—provided that the museum also displayed the company's logo.*

- *Computer-driven telemarketing that invades the privacy of millions of American homes daily.*

- *Philip Morris's sponsorship of a national tour of the Bill of Rights as part of its effort to invoke the First Amendment to protect cigarette advertising.*

- *Companies advertising on the Internet computer network and setting up an electronic shopping mall on CompuServe.*

Money is one measure of the magnitude of commercialism. From 1935 to 1994, U.S. expenditures on media advertising (newspapers, magazines, direct mail, billboards, television, radio, etc.) and other promotions soared almost eightfold, from $19 billion to $148 billion (adjusted for inflation; 1994 dollars). Those expenditures have doubled since 1971 and risen 50 percent since 1981.[3] On a per capita basis, expenditures for advertising *quadrupled* between 1935 and 1994.[4] (Businesses spend an *additional* $115 billion a year on store displays, coupon redemptions, point-of-purchase materials, trade shows, and the like.[5])

To put that $148 billion advertising figure in perspective, consider that that's more than 2 percent of our nation's entire gross national product. It is equal to what our nation spent on higher education in 1990.[6] It's more than the federal government spends on Medicare and more than the combined budgets of the Departments of Transportation, Justice, Interior, Housing and Urban Development, and Labor.[7]

Businesses are spending more than $565 per person, or over $2,200 per family of four, to encourage us to be consumers. That's almost as much as a family of four spends on medical care and five times what it spends on gasoline and oil.[8] Ultimately, of course, those advertising expenditures are paid for by consumers themselves.

But those figures still fail to capture marketers' influence on our culture because they do not convey the increased pervasiveness and intrusiveness of modern sales techniques. Nor do they reflect the vastly increased sophistication of marketers and the greater seductiveness of modern advertising. Who in 1935 would have even imagined sneaking cigarette ads into video arcade games or selling ad space on computer networks or having battery-operated sound effects in magazine ads?

At times, marketers must feel like pesticide manufacturers: Both must cope with targets, be they television viewers or insects, that develop a resistance or immunity to previous offenses. Both

JUST THE FACTS

Total U.S. Advertising Spending–1993[9]

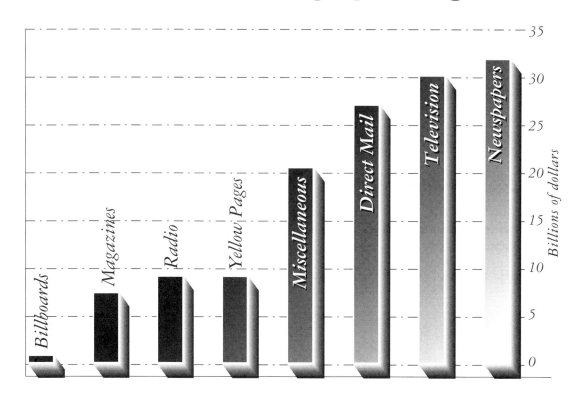

Billboards · *Magazines* · *Radio* · *Yellow Pages* · *Miscellaneous* · *Direct Mail* · *Television* · *Newspapers*

Billions of dollars — 0, 5, 10, 15, 20, 25, 30, 35

must devise new techniques that can overcome the targets' defenses.

It's anybody's guess what the creative geniuses on Madison Avenue will devise for us in the future, but the trends are ominous. Will Domino's Pizza or Disney help fund schools on the condition that school-bus drivers or teachers wear the company's uniform? Will every play, every pitch, every free throw of every sports event be "brought to you" by a sponsor? Will cities allow the "wasted" space on streets to be turned into giant "streetboards" selling goods to office workers looking out of high-rise offices? Will books be peppered with ads? Will phone companies offer free phone calls, provided we listen to a product plug before the connection is made? Will marketers give us discounts if we provide them with personal information that will facilitate their future marketing efforts?

Before you protest that those examples are ludicrous, come with us on a tour of marketing strategies in use *today*. You will discover an America where marketing envelops our lives like smog, where the commercial excesses begin as soon as toddlers learn to turn on a TV set or recognize the Mickey Mouse design on their shirts. The marketing mania continues with pinpoint marketing that focuses on children, women, baby boomers, yuppies, minorities, seniors, factory workers, computer owners, overweight people, dog owners, childless high-income suburban families, and practically every other demographic slice that computers can identify. The individual messages push jeans, soda pop, and mattresses, and a thousand other products. But the common, underlying message is "BUY!" Part One reveals how Americans are trained almost from infancy to be consumers.

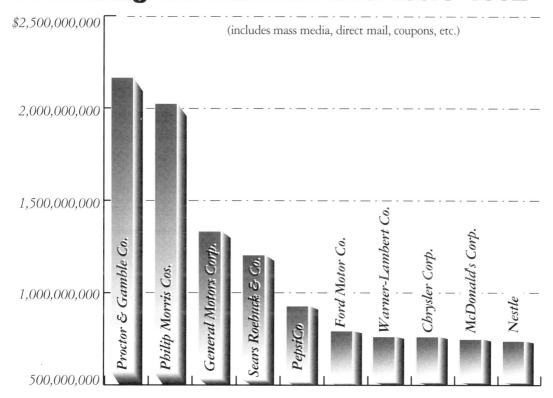

10 Leading U.S. National Advertisers–1992[10]

(includes mass media, direct mail, coupons, etc.)

- $2,500,000,000
- 2,000,000,000
- 1,500,000,000
- 1,000,000,000
- 500,000,000

Proctor & Gamble Co. | Philip Morris Cos. | General Motors Corp. | Sears Roebuck & Co. | PepsiCo | Ford Motor Co. | Warner-Lambert Co. | Chrysler Corp. | McDonald's Corp. | Nestle

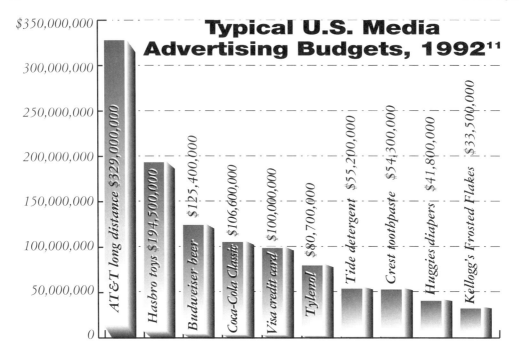

Typical U.S. Media Advertising Budgets, 1992[11]

- AT&T long distance $329,000,000
- Hasbro toys $194,500,000
- Budweiser beer $125,400,000
- Coca-Cola Classic $106,600,000
- Visa credit card $100,000,000
- Tylenol $80,700,000
- Tide detergent $55,200,000
- Crest toothpaste $54,300,000
- Huggies diapers $41,800,000
- Kellogg's Frosted Flakes $33,500,000

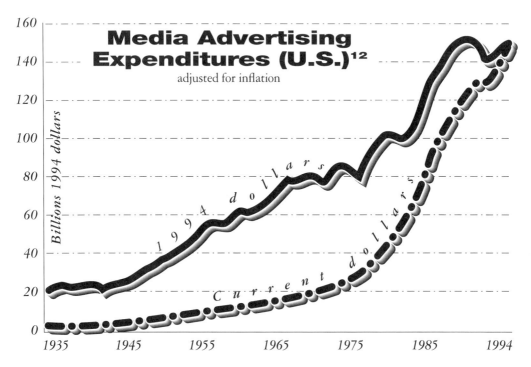

Media Advertising Expenditures (U.S.)[12]

adjusted for inflation

Billions 1994 dollars

1994 dollars

Current dollars

1935 1945 1955 1965 1975 1985 1994

Global Advertising (U.S. $ billions)[13]

	United States	Overseas	Total
1985	94.8	63.3	158.1
1990	128.6	145.9	274.5
1994	148.0	170.3	318.3

Each day, 260 million Americans are exposed to at least[14]

• *18 billion display ads in magazines and daily newspapers* • *2.6 million radio commercials* • *300,000 television commercials* • *500,000 billboards* • *40 million direct-mail pieces and leaflets*

Advertising consumes approximately[15]

• *60 percent of newspaper space* • *52 percent of magazine pages* • *18 percent of radio time* • *17 percent of network television prime time.*

CHAPTER ONE

Targeting Children

Marketers understand well the value of early brand recognition. Introducing a product to a child might provide a company with a customer today—and for the next seventy years. For that reason cereal, toy, snack food, and other companies target children with their advertising. The sophistication of Madison Avenue is pitted against the innocence of children...and guess who wins. Not only do companies succeed in persuading children to buy particular products, they also imbue children with the values of commercialism. Until recently, businesses recognized certain limits when it came to marketing to kids. But now anything goes, and even public schools are used to exploit captive audiences.

The Littlest Consumers

It isn't enough to just advertise on television….You've got to reach kids throughout their day—in school, as they're shopping at the mall…or at the movies. You've got to become part of the fabric of their lives.[1]

—*Carol Herman, senior vice president, Grey Advertising*

IN THE 1990S, MARKETERS ARE weaving their way into children's lives as never before. Ads adorn kids' clothing, lunch boxes, and bed sheets; they beckon from the television screen, lurk in magazines, and masquerade as TV cartoon shows. As we'll see in the next section, they even infiltrate the school curriculum. The bright tapestry of advertising captures kids' imaginations, shapes their dreams, and even influences their values.

In the early days of advertising, marketers rarely targeted their appeals to children. However, in the 1920s a few farsighted advertisers realized that kids could be enlisted to help sell things to their parents. Noting the "difficulty one meets in breaking habits" among adults, advertising psychologist Alfred Poffenberger stressed the "importance of introducing innovations by way of the young."[2] Still, it was not until the 1950s, when the baby boom swelled their numbers, that children became a target market in their own right.

Today, kids are a much-coveted consumer group. They are prized not only for their personal spending power but for their influence on parental purchases as well. In 1992, kids aged four to twelve spent an estimated $9 billion,[3] and teenagers between the ages of twelve and nineteen

Designer clothes manufacturers are developing pre-pubescent lines, like Baby Guess and Baby Gap.

accounted for a whopping $93 billion.[4] Moreover, kids directly influence another $130 billion in family spending.[5] Realizing this, some advertisers seek to deploy the ultimate manipulative weapon: the nagging child. Hyatt Hotels Corporation, for example, collects names and addresses of children who stay at its resorts, then mails them promotional brochures. Why target kids who could not reasonably be expected to pay for resort vacations? "There's nothing like a seven-year-old asking nineteen times, 'When are we going back to that hotel?' to get parents to go back," explains Marc Yanofsky, Hyatt's senior vice president for marketing.[6]

Young people are also attractive to advertisers because they have a lifetime of spending ahead of them, and their brand loyalties are still open to influence. As *Seventeen* magazine promises prospective advertisers, "Reach a girl in her *Seventeen* years and she may be yours for life."[7] Mike Searles, president of Kids 'R' Us, doesn't believe in waiting that long. "If you own this child at an early age," he says, "you can own this child for years to come. Companies are saying, 'Hey, I want to own the kid younger and younger.'"[8]

It may seem odd to aim ads at toddlers, but from a marketing perspective it makes perfect sense. Research indicates that six-month-old babies are already forming mental images of corporate logos and mascots. By the time they are three years old, most children are making specific requests for brand-name products.[9]

Model cars are plastered with corporate logos—in some cases advertising products kids are too young to buy legally.

Marketers know that kids emulate stars from popular TV shows like *Beverly Hills 90210.*

Batteries Not Included

Once kids are old enough to sit up in front of the television, advertisers begin targeting them in earnest. TV is, by far, the favored medium for advertising to children, accounting for over $350 million worth of advertising dollars.[10] Between the ages of two and five, the average American kid watches nearly four hours of TV each day; six- to eleven-year-olds log three and a half hours a day in front of the tube.[11] By the time they are eighteen, most children will have spent more time watching TV than in school. Accordingly, the average child sees about 40,000 TV commercials every year.

Commercials are especially appealing to young children, who are drawn to their bright colors, fast pace, strange sound effects, and animated characters. However, young kids are often unable to separate fact from advertising fiction, or even to understand that a commercial's purpose is to sell a product. In one study, a group of four- to seven-year-olds were shown a commercial for Cocoa Pebbles cereal. Afterward, the kids told interviewers that they wanted the cereal because it had a chocolaty taste, it would make them smile, and Fred Flintstone and Barney Rubble had recommended it. One-third of the kids thought Fred and Barney were experts on nutrition.[12]

Older children also fall for advertising hype, often disregarding disclaimers such as "batteries not included," "some assembly required," or "each sold separately." In one study, 61 percent of parents surveyed bought a toy because their child saw it advertised on TV and later had to cope with the child's disappointment when it differed from the commercial.[13] Children simply do not have the cognitive sophistication and breadth of experience with which to evaluate advertising claims.

Some activists have taken advertisers to task for making misleading, and potentially harmful, claims. In the 1970s, Action for Children's Television (ACT), a consumer-advocacy organization that disbanded in 1992, persuaded the FTC to strictly regulate the way companies advertise vitamins to children. Although vitamins can be poisonous to kids when taken in quantity, ACT founder Peggy Charren said that "drug companies were pushing them like candy."[14]

Recognizing children's vulnerability to advertising appeals, in 1974 the Federal Communications Commission (FCC) set limits on the number of ads allowed during shows aimed at kids. But these regulations were withdrawn in 1984 by Reagan-appointed FCC chairman Mark Fowler. Throughout the 1980s, advocates led by ACT protested the increasing commercialization of kids' TV and succeeded in winning passage of the Children's Television Act in 1990. That legislation limits commercials during kids' shows to ten and a half minutes per hour on weekends and twelve minutes on weekdays and requires stations to broadcast educational programs.

The law's effectiveness remains to be seen. Vague wording gave broadcasters license to sidestep some of its requirements. Charged with providing "educational and informational" programming, broadcasters claimed that cartoons like *The Jetsons* and *G.I. Joe* fulfilled that obligation, according to a study by the Center for Media Education.[15] In 1993 the FCC levied fines against four television stations for exceeding the law's commercial time limits. "I think the stations are still testing. They don't take anything seriously until they see someone is watching," said ACT's Charren.[16]

Program-Length Commercials

Even more insidious than thirty-second pitches are shows that blur the distinction between advertising and programming. Toy-inspired shows like *G.I. Joe, My Little Pony, Strawberry Shortcake*, and *The Care Bears* actually function as program-length commercials. In his book *Children's Television,* ad executive Cy Schneider describes how advertisers joyfully discovered that they could "first design the character as a product, then write a television show starring this character, thereby reversing the traditional process." Kids' shows, he explains, "now contain numerous characters for the obvious reason that this creates multiple purchases by the consumer, rather than a single purchase of a single popular character."[17] (During the first *Care Bears* special, one bear spoke for toy retailers everywhere when he remarked that "ten bears are better than one.") Schneider says kids' shows also deliberately feature lots of "gadgets, gimmicks, hardware, and vehicles—the stuff of which kids' products are made."[18]

The 1980s were the heyday of the "program-length commercial"—by 1986, seventy toys had mutated into TV shows. This strategy was a great boon for toy manufacturers. *He Man and the Masters of the Universe*, for example, enabled Mattel to sell more than 70 million plastic models in three years. And with the help of *The Transformers*, Milton Bradley's Transformer toys raked in $100 million in their first year, making it the most successful toy introduction ever.[19] As advertising critic Eric Clark has pointed out, "At a commercial level it made great sense to both the toymen and the television companies. The toy firms received a literally priceless amount of exposure for their products; the broadcasters got a pre-sold audience for their new programs."[20]

But how are kids served by the cozy symbiosis of toymakers and broadcasters? Action for Children's Television charged that program-length commercials have displaced other kinds of children's shows "in the name of vested-interest commercial speech. . . . Newspaper editors would never dream of turning over their editorial pages to advertisers; yet that's exactly what broadcasters are doing with children's television."[21] Consumer advocates also charge that broadcasters are trying to circumvent the commercial limits of the Children's Television Act.

Now movies are taking their cue from kids' TV. Countless feature films have inspired the manufacture of toys; *Home Alone II: Lost in New York* turned this process on its head by designing the toys *first*. Producer John Harris teamed up with toymaker Tiger Electronics to develop the many nifty gadgets used in the film, with an eye toward marketing them nationwide. Kids who saw the film no doubt clamored for MacCauley Caulkin's handheld radio or "monster foam" soap. Roger Shiffman, an executive vice president at Tiger, acknowledges that this scheme creates desires for unnecessary items. "I have two kids and I'd be hard-pressed to say they need even 1/100 of what I supply them," he says, but shrugs, "We are in the toy business, and we are trying to expose our products in such a way that kids will want them."[22]

Marketers publish children's magazines to showcase their toys and accessories. *Barbie: The Magazine for Girls* contains mainly ads and pseudo-articles promoting Barbie dolls and accessories. *Super Mario Brothers: The Official Movie Magazine* pushes Nintendo videogames and licensed products.

Invasion of the Teenage Mutant Ninja Turtles

Toys make the leap from screen to store with the help of the licensing industry, a thriving enterprise capable of transforming any popular concept or character into a line of salable merchandise. Children are a

ONLY OUR KIDS HAVE THIS MUCH POWER OVER THEIR PARENTS.

Today's kids influence over $130 billion of their parents' spending annually. Kids also spend $8 billion of their own money. That makes these little consumers big business. Kids who watch Turner's animated programming will consume 3/4 of the products purchased across a variety of kids' categories.

So if you need a lift in reaching these powerful consumers, let Turner help support your marketing efforts by calling Stan Weil at 212-852-6980.

CARTOON NETWORK *TBS*

In addition to spending billions of their own dollars, kids influence about $130 billion of their parents' spending. Turner Broadcasting, which owns several networks watched by kids, dangles those dollar amounts before potential advertisers in this trade magazine ad.

prime target for licensed products, perhaps because of their tendency to idolize fictional characters and celebrities—from Davy Crockett to Barney.

Although licensing has been around for years, sales of licensed products grew fivefold in the 1980s, reaching an astonishing $63 billion worldwide by 1993.[23] Licensers acquire the rights to a character, image, or logo, then rent out those rights to manufacturers, who produce and market the product. We have the licensing industry to thank for such products as Looney Tunes frozen dinners, M. C. Hammer pencil cases, Vanna White dolls, Bart Simpson hair gel, and Batman breakfast cereal. By 1993, character licenses made up approximately 64 percent of products advertised to kids.[24]

One of the licensing industry's greatest triumphs is the Teenage Mutant Ninja Turtles (TMNT). The pugnacious, pizza-eating Turtles spawned 200 licensed products, which raked in $1.87 billion in

1990.[25] (In contrast, ticket sales for the *TMNT* movie totaled a mere $135 million.[26]) Theoretically, a child could outfit herself exclusively in licensed TMNT clothing, shoes, and accessories—and subsist (although unhealthfully) on licensed TMNT foods. The Turtles concept was hatched in an advertising agency and launched with a massive multimedia advertising blitz—the ultimate fusion of children's entertainment and marketing. As TMNT producer Andy Heyward candidly admits: "The success of 'Ninja Turtles' was not solely due to the creative merits. There was a five-part miniseries, a toy line, a Burger King video promotion, the movie, and the TV show. By the time it came to CBS there was no part of the kids' market not exposed."[27]

The Turtles have since shared the licensing spotlight with other profit-making phenomena. *Jurassic Park* garnered approximately $1 billion from 5,000 different dinosaur-oriented licensed products (compared to $880 million in world-wide box office sales).[28] Disney's *Beauty and the Beast*, *Aladdin*, and *The Little Mermaid* produced more than $1 billion in sales of related merchandise.[29] And the latest licensing marvel to waddle forth is Barney, a corpulent purple dinosaur whose saccharine persona has been accorded near-cult status by young kids. When he's not filming his show, *Barney and Friends*, Barney makes appearances in shopping malls to promote his extensive line of licensed products, the sales of which totaled more than $200 million in 1993 alone. Some are troubled by the commercialization of Barney because his show appears on non-commercial public television and is subsidized with public broadcasting funds (see Chapter 2, "The Private Life of Public Broadcasting"). Larry Jarvik, who has studied public television, believes it is unethical for a private production company to use public TV as a marketing vehicle. "They pretend they aren't selling to children," he says, "But everyone knows they are."[30]

What Advertisers Are Selling to Kids

Clearly, many advertisers use exploitative *methods* to sell to children. But what, exactly, are they selling? Plenty of kids' products are well-made and useful, but many others are worthless, unhealthful, or dangerous.

Into the benign but worthless category fall such products as Fun 'n' Fresh, a deodorant for children as young as seven years old. Then there are products that cater to the basest instincts of their target market, such as the Savage Mondo Blitzers toy line from Kenner, which featured characters with names like Snot Shot, Barf Bucket, Puke Shooter, Eye Pus, and Knight to Dismember. (In response to a consumer boycott, Kenner changed the names.)

Most of the foods hawked on kids' TV are downright unhealthful. A 1992 study by the Center for Science in the Public Interest found that nine out of ten food ads on Saturday morning TV were for candy bars, sugary cereals, salty chips, or other nutritionally flawed foods. Researchers have discerned links between TV commercials and obesity and elevated levels of cholesterol in children.

Ads also blatantly reinforce gender stereotypes. In the world of children's commercials, boys play with trucks and war toys; girls play with dolls, makeup, and miniature appliances. *Still.* Spurred by ads aimed at little boys, sales of war toys rose by more than 200 percent in the 1980s and now exceed $1 billion per year.[31]

A game called Careers for Girls, created by Hasbro's Parker Brothers division, featured such remunerative positions as "supermom" and secretary (this was in 1991, mind you, not 1951) and was discontinued after it drew protests. But that didn't stop another Hasbro subsidiary, Milton Bradley, from introducing games called Mall Madness and Electronic Mall Madness, which simulate an out-of-control shopping spree. According to *Adweek* reporter Fara Warner, Mall Madness

"makes women out to be bargain-crazy, credit-happy fashion plates."[32] Although the game is ostensibly for boys as well as girls, boys are nowhere to be seen in the game's TV commercials.

Teenage Mutant Ninja Turtles, the movie, has turned into *TMNT*, the TV series. Both help promote the multi-billion-dollar licensing industry of TMNT products.

The Solution to All of Life's Problems

Advertising sells more than products. When kids hunker down in front of the tube to receive their daily dose of commercial messages, they absorb more than the desire for specific items. Taken as a whole, the collective body of advertising sells a vision of the world, a way of life. Each ad is a parable that illuminates the same theme: All of life's problems can be solved and happiness attained by *buying things*.

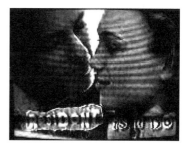

Residont suggests that its acne cream is a prerequisite for young love. Oxy10 threatens horror and ridicule should a teenager discover a pimple on her face.

Perhaps more than any previous generation, today's kids have taken that message to heart. By many indicators, today's young people are an exceptionally brand-conscious and materialistic lot. Selina Guber of Children's Market Research says there are "significant differences" between kids reared in the 1980s and their predecessors. Today's children, she says, "are aware of brands and status items even before they can read."[33]

"If you don't know the taste of Honey-Comb," goes the voice-over in this commercial for Honey-Comb cereal, "get a life!" Each ounce of Honey-Comb contains eleven grams of sugar— one of the highest sugar contents of any cereal on the market.

Advertising may even skew children's values. In one study, four- and five-year-olds were asked if they would prefer to play with a "not so nice" boy who had a toy barn or a "nice" boy who didn't. Kids who had seen the ad chose the "not so nice" playmate and the toy barn two to one as compared to children who had not seen the ad.[34] In a 1993 survey of parents, 92 percent said that commercials are making their kids too materialistic.[35]

Kids are inundated with ads for junk food like M&Ms, while nutrition education on TV is practically non-existent.

Values learned in childhood generally stick. A study of high school seniors by researchers at the University of Southern California found that from the 1960s to the 1990s, making money has become much more important as a life goal. Concurrently, the importance of "finding purpose and meaning in life" has taken a sharp downward turn.[36] Of course, marketers and advertising are not solely to blame for the ascendancy of materialism; myriad forces contribute to the gestalt of a given era. But advertising is the insistent voice of the consumer culture, and the sheer ubiquity of its messages can drown out other voices, other views.

Obsessed with Designer Duds

As ads stoke children's material desires, the cost of satisfying those desires continues to escalate. A Barbie doll mansion goes for up to $400, an Alva skateboard for $150, an Atari Lynx video game for $180. A pair of Killer Loop sunglasses, marketed to teens by Bausch and Lomb, retails for $120. The clothing industry, in particular, has targeted kids with ads for pricey brand-name clothes and shoes. These ads have helped fuel a nationwide obsession with designer duds.

Burger King makes collectible toys that personify burgers, fries, and soda—encouraging frequent visits to the restaurant and creating early attachment to its brand of fast food.

MCI distributes an MCI Kid Card—which closely resembles a regular calling card—on which to keep home and emergency numbers.

Milton Bradley's "Electronic Mall Madness" game cultivates impulse shopping among young girls.

According to a 1993 USA Today-CNN-Gallup Poll, 61 percent of boys and 44 percent of girls considered brand names on clothes "very important" or "somewhat important."[37] As Aime Lorenzo, an eleventh-grader from Miami, told the *Los Angeles Times* in 1989, "When people look at you and you're not wearing something that has a name brand, they'll comment on it." Ten-year-old Darion Sawyer from Baltimore adds, "People will tease you and talk about you, say you got on no-name shoes or say you shop at Kmart."[38] Even the much-hyped "grunge" look, which briefly defied the national preoccupation with designer labels, has been co-opted by the fashion industry. Back-to-school shoppers in fall 1993 encountered such upscale grungewear as $48 prefaded flannel shirts and $135 Doc Marten shoes.[39]

Advertisers cultivate the forces of peer pressure that fuel fashion faddism. Nancy Shalek, an ad agency president, says: "Advertising at its best is making people feel that without their product, you're a loser. Kids are very sensitive to that. If you tell them to buy something, they are resistant. But if you tell them they'll be a dork if they don't, you've got their attention. You open up emotional vulnerabilities and it's very easy to do with kids because they're the most emotionally vulnerable."[40]

Countless ads play on kids' insecurities. For example, one ad for acne medicine shows a boy ostracized because of his bad skin, another depicts a girl's date laughing out loud at her skin problem. An ad for Sega Genesis video games shows a nerdy outcast tormented by his peers; they sit behind him in class, tweaking his

Burger King promotes its Kids Club as the remedy for loneliness and boredom. But this is one club that never meets.

The Super Mario Brothers cartoon doubles as promotion for the corresponding Nintendo video game.

oversized ears. Then the outcast gets Sega Genesis and his torturers appear humbly offering a plate of cookies.

Because it's so expensive to keep a kid in name-brand accoutrements, many parents find themselves embroiled in endless struggles with their children. "Money is always a battle," says Char Christian, a mother from suburban Chicago. "I am torn trying to determine the difference between what she needs and what she wants."[41]

That struggle can subtly undermine parental authority. As kids' material urges are stimulated by advertising, parents become gatekeepers to the world of consumer products. In most households, that means saying no a lot. Parents who try to instill other values in their children—such as conservation and thrift—find their voices drowned out by the onslaught of commercial messages. A rift develops, with parents and children in opposite and often hostile camps. As one child psychologist testified at a Federal Trade Commission hearing on advertising to children: "Mistrust results when legitimate authority figures—such as parents—are implicitly silenced or discredited, as they are if they pit their meager persuasion techniques against the might of television advertising directed at their children."[42]

Advertisers, of course, defend their right to aim ads at kids. In an undeniably commercial world, they argue, kids should be exposed to advertising as soon as possible, so that they may learn to evaluate its claims. But kids are not so much exposed to as *enveloped in* advertising. When ads are woven into the fabric of kids lives, how can they achieve the distance and perspective they need to see them for what they are? Or even if they can reject the claims of a specific ad, can they question the call to consume that is the overarching message of all ads?

Children's special vulnerability warrants protection from the

The Barney the Dinosaur retail craze, based on the popular PBS kids show, has generated hundreds of millions of dollars of sales.

"Biker Mice from Mars" joins the lucrative industry of licensed toys related to TV shows.

Toys advertised on TV frequently promote violent behavior. "Electronic Survivor Shot" toy gun imparts a sensation of being shot.

manipulations of marketers. Ideally, childhood should be an "ad-free zone" where parents, schools, and the child's own imagination are dominant influences. However, it would be nearly impossible to insulate kids from all commercial messages in our advertising-saturated culture. But we could follow the lead of other countries and ban broadcast ads targeted to kids. And we could put a stop to the sneaky tactics used to market goods to children.

Disney's
The Lion King
spawned licensed T-shirts, backpacks, and stuffed animals. Woodward and Lothrop department store employs happy, adorable children to guilt-trip parents into a shopping spree.

Toddlers nurse on brand-name soda bottles, courtesy of Munchkin Bottling, Inc.

What People Have Done

Most Western countries offer kids some amount of protection from advertising. Some have gone even further: Belgium, Denmark, Norway, Sweden, and the Canadian province of Quebec ban all advertising to children on television and radio. In the late 1970s, an effort to pass similar legislation in the United States was squelched by a coalition of food and toy companies, broadcasters, and ad agencies.

On a smaller scale, many parents and kids have campaigned successfully to get rid of particularly deceptive or offensive ads. For example, Jennie Randall, an eleven-year-old from Fort Collins, Colorado, wrote to Consumers Union to protest a TV commercial for Hasbro's Army Ants. The cartoon ad, she argued, could mislead little kids because it created the illusion that the toy insects could move, talk, and fire weapons. Consumers Union forwarded the complaint to Hasbro, which dropped the commercial.

WHAT YOU CAN DO

- *Write to your representatives and tell them you support a ban on broadcast advertising to children.*
- *Pressure your local TV station to comply with the Children's Television Act. The Center for Media Education is coordinating efforts to monitor implementation of the law; contact them for information on how to get your station in compliance:*

    CENTER FOR MEDIA EDUCATION
    1511 K ST. NW, #518
    WASHINGTON, DC 20005
    202 628-2620

- *Protest exploitative ads. Toymakers and broadcasters are sensitive to criticism from parents and may respond to unfavorable attention.*
- *Talk about ads with your kids. Help them understand the purpose of commercials and encourage them to distinguish between the products being sold and the advertising hype. The Children's Advertising Review Unit of the Better Business Bureau publishes a helpful booklet entitled "A Parent's Guide to Advertising and Your Child." You may order the free booklet from*

    CHILDREN'S ADVERTISING REVIEW UNIT
    NATIONAL ADVERTISING DIVISION
    COUNCIL OF BETTER BUSINESS BUREAUS
    845 THIRD AVE.
    NEW YORK, NY 10022
    212-754-1353

- *Teach your kids to be wary consumers. Consumer Reports publishes an excellent magazine for kids aged eight to fourteen—Zillions—which encourages a critical perspective on ads. Subscribe by sending $16 to*

    ZILLIONS SUBSCRIPTION DEPARTMENT
    P.O. BOX 51777
    BOULDER, CO 80321-1777

- *Urge your school system to teach kids about the goals, methods, and tricks of advertising. For materials teachers can use, contact*

    CENTER FOR MEDIA LITERACY
    1962 S. SHENANDOAH ST.
    LOS ANGELES, CA 90034
    STRATEGIES FOR MEDIA LITERACY
    1095 MARKET ST. #617
    SAN FRANCISCO, CA 94103

Schools Go Commercial

Port Angeles, Washington. It's Mary Leinart's first day in sixth grade. As she nervously takes her seat in homeroom class, a TV monitor blinks on. A few announcements, then the pledge of allegiance. Next, with a blast of loud rock music and dazzling graphics, Channel One fills the screen. For the next twelve minutes, Mary and her classmates watch a frenetically paced amalgam of hard news (wars, elections, a solar eclipse) and human interest stories (dating, high school sports) punctuated by two minutes worth of ads for sneakers, junk food, and other products. Sometimes it's hard to tell the ads from the rest of the program: A music review, for example, openly plugs the latest albums by heavy metal bands Megadeth, Slayer, and Anthrax.

WELCOME, MARY, TO PUBLIC EDUCATION in the 1990s, where advertisements fill the hallways and classrooms and ooze their way into the curriculum.

Mary Leinart is one of more than 8 million students across the country who watch Channel One each school day. The brainchild of Christopher Whittle, chairman of Whittle Communications, Channel One is a stroke of marketing genius.[43] In exchange for a loan of video and satellite equipment, schools are required to make the daily "news" program required viewing. Channel One is therefore able to offer advertisers a captive audience of schoolchildren. The scheme works: By 1994, Channel One was raking in approximately $800,000 a day, charging $198,000 for each thirty-second spot.[44] So far, more than 12,000 schools (which account for about 40 percent of U.S. high school students)[45] have bought into Whittle's deal.

Whittle was not the first huckster to get a foot in the classroom door, but he may be the most brazen. Remember those scratchy filmstrips you used to watch in social studies class, with titles like "Aluminum and You"? Those were primitive versions of in-school advertising. Or how about the four food groups? Generations of Americans were force-fed the National Dairy Council's self-serving nutritional guidelines, which called for consuming—you guessed it—hefty amounts of milk, cheese, ice cream, and butter. That, too, was corporate propaganda in the schools.

"Exploiting America's students for brand share is a very old business," writes Laurie Petersen in *Adweek*. "But now that exploitation has reached new — and gluttonous — heights."[46] Corporations have infiltrated schools at every level, ingratiating themselves with teachers by providing free study guides, magazines, posters, and book covers. Such offers are understandably seductive to cash-poor schools; state and city budget cuts have left many school districts scrambling for funds. And harried teachers will often take any help they can get. As one Brooklyn junior high school teacher confessed: "Teachers are so overwhelmed with their total job that they welcome *anything* that will aid them in making their subject area more attractive to the students, easier to grasp, and save teacher time in making up original material. If an industry can offer all of those things, a teacher is just grateful—to hell with where it comes from."[47]

For their part, marketers have always coveted access to children in school. Think of it: impressionable young minds, in an atmosphere relatively free of ad clutter, with the implicit backing of the school system. Enter Chris Whittle *et al.* Despite his professed concern for the quality of American education, Whittle is first and foremost a marketing strategist. Eschewing ads in traditional magazines and TV programs, Whittle pioneered the use of "guerrilla media," narrowly targeted magazines and posters that critics say exist solely as vehicles for advertising.

Over objections from the National Education Association, the National PTA, and other major educational groups, Whittle launched Channel One in 1989, saying the program would boost students' awareness of current events and provide schools with much-needed equipment. Advertising, he said, was the only way to pay for the program. "Schools have a choice," he told *Time* magazine, "either do without, or do it this way."[48] In Mary Leinart's school district, board members were given a hard-sell "now or never" pitch. "They were told if they didn't sign the contract immediately, they'd be put on a waiting list," said Mary's mother, Virginia. Fearful of losing a chance to get "free" equipment, thousands of schools took the bait, usually with no public debate. As a result, students are legally bound to watch commercials for junk food, diet soda, high-priced sneakers, and other products that parents often teach their kids to *avoid*.

Channel One has been particularly attractive to the most budget-strapped school districts. In 1993, a demographic study of Channel One schools, conducted by the University of Massachusetts at Amherst, found that "schools with the greatest concentration of low-income students are *more than twice as likely* as the schools with the wealthiest students to have Channel One. As community income levels drop, the proportion of schools receiving Channel One steadily rises" (emphasis added). The study's authors concluded that the poorest students are unfairly sold to corporate bidders and forced to watch commercials for products they can ill afford.[49]

And what do schools get in return for auctioning off access to their kids? A slick, fast-paced news-entertainment show of

Scholastic produces curriculum packets for major companies: Discovery Credit Card's "Extra Credit" accustoms kids to using a charge card; CBS Records' promotional package for Billy Joel's single "We Didn't Start the Fire" masquerades as a high school history lesson.

negligible educational value. Robert Goldberg of the *Wall Street Journal* describes Channel One this way: "The underlying assumption of Channel One [is] that the news has to be really loud and really REALLY fast for kids to watch. 'Arms negotiations in Vienna,' for example, flies by in fifteen seconds, with two maps and five images—that's a relentless cut every two seconds. Moreover, with wall-to-wall announcing, the program is jampacked, breathless, a sensory overload. By the end of the first three shows, I was exhausted. And what sank in? Not much....It's the *USA Today* disease—a slice-and-dice, Cuisinart approach to news, as if only little morsels were appetizing."[50]

Research confirms that Channel One has limited value as an academic tool. A study conducted at the University of Michigan found that teenagers who had watched the program during the 1990-1991 school year learned only slightly more about current events than students in schools without Channel One. (Ironically, this three-part study was funded by Whittle, but its researchers insisted on complete independence.[51]) The second year of that study found widely varying degrees of current events knowledge among Channel One students, depending on whether teachers incorporated the show into lesson plans or simply used it as a time-out from class.[52] But even when the "news" went right by them, kids watching Channel One displayed near-perfect recall when it came to the commercials. "Kids never fail," said Jerome Johnston, director of the study. "They always know who's promoting it."[53]

Even more ominous, a study of 3,000 students in North Carolina found that most students thought the products advertised on Channel One must be good for them, since they were being shown in school.[54]

Even with the perk of free goods, many school officials find that Channel One is less of a bargain than promised. The "free" video equipment can be taken away if the school fails to deliver its audience. And the "free" satellite dishes are permanently tuned to Channel One, limiting their usefulness for educational purposes. A PTA group in Washington, D.C., one of hundreds nationwide that oppose Channel One, points out that the program wastes student time and taxpayer money. In the course of a year, students spend the equivalent of six school days watching Channel One; a full day is lost to commercials. So each year, D.C. taxpayers spend approximately $108,000 per school for teacher time while students are watching Channel One. That works out to more than three times as much as the estimated value—$30,000, according to Whittle Communications—of the "free" video equipment. Four science teachers in Detroit, who allowed their students to do lab work instead of watching Channel One, were reprimanded by the school for violating their contract; the teachers maintained that the twelve-minute program was eating into the thirty-five-minute class.[55]

Besides, are video monitors in every classroom an unmitigated gain? Kids hardly need further encouragement to watch TV. By age nineteen, the average American has logged 19,000 hours in front of the tube, compared to just 11,000 hours in school. Neil Postman, author of *Amusing Ourselves to Death: Public Discourse in the Age of Show Business,* asserts that "educational" television has actually deformed education by confusing it with entertainment. "No one has ever said or implied that significant learning is effectively, durably, and truthfully achieved when education is entertainment," he writes. Citing several studies showing that TV viewers retain little of what they watch, he concludes, "Television viewing does not increase learning, is inferior to and less likely than print to cultivate higher-order, inferential thinking."[56]

"Perspectives," a curriculum series produced by Procter and Gamble, addresses economic issues in American history. The kits praise corporate America in general and Procter and Gamble in particular.

School Properties pioneered corporate advertising at high school athletic events.

Privatizing Public Schools

Peggy Charren, the founder of Action for Children's Television and a vocal critic of ads aimed at kids, worries that Channel One will lead to greater commercialization of American education. "Soon the portion of classroom time devoted to advertiser-controlled material will be multiplied," she warns, "as corporations with increasingly innovative sweeteners compete for the in-school audience and hard-pressed schools are forced to auction off, bit-by-bit, minutes of access to their pupils."[57]

The auction is already under way. Thousands of American corporations provide curricular and other material for schools, often through marketing companies such as Lifetime Learning Systems of Fairfield, Connecticut. "Let Lifetime Learning Systems bring your message to the classroom, where young people are forming attitudes that will last a lifetime," purrs the company's sales kit, "Whatever your objective, we can help you meet it."[58] Hundreds of companies and other entities have hired Lifetime to peddle their wares (or ideologies) in the schools, including the American Nuclear Society, Coca-Cola Company, the National Frozen Pizza Institute, the Snack Food Association, and the government of Saudi Arabia. Lifetime claims to reach 63 million young people every year.

Lifetime is up front about using the authority of the classroom to benefit advertisers. "Coming from school," promises the sales kit, "all these materials carry an extra measure of credibility that gives your message added weight." Another ad asks potential clients to "IMAGINE millions of students discussing your product in class. IMAGINE their teachers presenting your organization's point of view."[59]

Although Lifetime's promotional literature declares that its materials "combine both strong commercial appeal and sound educational information," the educational value of its curricula is highly suspect.[60] For example, one Lifetime teaching kit, sent to

How to reach puberty.

We can help you deliver a message
to his classroom that he'll carry into young adulthood.
If he's in your target market, call us at **(800) 237-7114**.

✳ Modern

515 Madison Avenue, Suite 500 • New York. NY 10022

Modern Talking Pictures lures advertisers to its in-school product sampling program in this *Advertising Age* appeal: "We can help you deliver a message to his classroom that he'll carry into young adulthood."

Dow Chemical Company advertises its own products in "Recycle This," a pamphlet about the recyclability of plastics.

third-grade teachers, purports to be a "FREE educational program focusing on math, social science, and language arts skills." Entitled "Count Your Chips," the kit is sponsored by the National Potato Board and the Snack Food Association. Its first activity urges kids to "be a chip-e-matician!" by digesting facts about potato chips and solving simple math problems. Students are told that "each person in the United States eats about six pounds of potato chips in one year" and are asked to calculate the number of one-ounce bags of chips that represents. Another activity, "The Chip Story," recounts the glorious origins of the potato chip and asks children to conduct research on which chip flavors people like best. Suggested follow-up activities include interviewing family members to determine the favorite family snack and writing "a humorous family snack story."[61]

Another Lifetime creation, entitled "GUSHERS Wonders of the World," was sent to science teachers at the behest of General Mills, makers of GUSHERS fruit snacks. After a perfunctory lesson on geothermic "gushers"—volcanoes, geysers, and hot springs—Lifetime gets to the real point of the exercise. The teacher is instructed to "distribute the samples of GUSHERS supplied with this program, and suggest that students each place a GUSHER in their mouths. Then discuss the process needed to make these fruit snacks 'gush' when you bite into them."[62] The educational merit of these programs is debatable, but their ingenuity as marketing stratagems is not.

Even preschoolers are subjected to classroom sales pitches. After all, according to Lifetime, "Preschool prepares children to become consumers. . . . Research shows that children begin to make brand decisions at age four."[63] To secure the loyalty of these consumers of tomorrow, Lifetime helped General Mills design sample kits of its Fruit Roll-Ups. Nursery school teachers served as volunteer hucksters, passing out more than a million of the samples to preschoolers.[64]

Lifetime is not the only company to use the classroom as a marketing tool. Scholastic, Inc., publisher of *Scholastic News* and other respected periodicals for students, is now trading on its venerable reputation by courting advertisers and producing corporate propaganda. Scholastic's alliance with the corporate world has produced some odd offspring, such as a nutrition program for fifth- and sixth-graders sponsored by the M&M-Mars candy company.[65] Scholastic specializes in "study guides" keyed to the release of motion pictures. When courting advertisers, Scholastic candidly refers to the guides as "promotion tie-ins."[66] But when addressing teachers, Scholastic touts their educational value. A guide to *Bill and Ted's Excellent Adventure*, for instance, is billed as "a rare opportunity for innovative social studies teaching." Guides to *Teenage Mutant Ninja Turtles II: The Secrets of the Ooze* and *Jetsons: The Movie* are offered up as courses in environmental issues.[67]

The World According to Weyerhaeuser

Once corporations have bribed their way into the classroom, they present their own versions of facts, issues, and history. Take, for example, a teacher's guide to forestry designed by Weyerhaeuser, the timber-industry giant. The guide instructs teachers to divide the class in groups to discuss questions of universal interest and importance, such as:

soft drinks to more nutritious foods. For instance, the poster equates sugar-laden soft drinks to nutrient-rich milk by stating that "a diet of milk alone would result in dietary deficiencies. Likewise, soft drink consumption alone would be unhealthy."69

Channel One requires students to watch ads for junk food and soft drinks.

It goes on to compare soda pop and a peach by stating that "The peach may give you certain vitamins that the soft drink does not, just as the soft drink gives you more liquid than the peach does."70 In an era in which child and teenage obesity rates are soaring, it is remarkable that companies are encouraging teachers to tell students that soft drinks, milk, and fresh fruit are all in the same league.70

- *What major events have occurred in the history of Weyerhaeuser?*
- *What related companies are part of Weyerhaeuser?*
- *How does Weyerhaeuser use a typical dollar from sales?*
- *What innovative practices has Weyerhaeuser introduced in recent years?*68

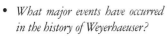

Georgia-Pacific distributes "The Tree Trunk" activities kit, which defends the practice of clear-cutting, underscores the necessity for paper products, and expresses the company's concerns about the environment.

Similarly, the National Soft Drink Association, whose members' products are regularly lambasted by nutritionists, gives teachers a colorful poster suitable for hanging. The poster, entitled "Soft Drinks and Nutrition," compares

Or how about "Coping with Growth," a unit on labor issues in the late 1800s, published by Procter and Gamble Educational Services. If you've read your history, you remember this era as a time when children labored in factories, fourteen-hour workdays were not uncommon, wages approximated slavery, and frequent worker uprisings were brutally quashed by company goons and the National Guard. But, to hear Procter and Gamble tell it, this labor turmoil was little more than a family spat, brought on by insufficient "closeness": "In earlier times, when everything was on a smaller scale, owner and worker had toiled side by side....Now this closeness was ending. The individual worker was losing touch with the man at the top, and the owner was so far removed that he couldn't know what was going on in the factory. Gone, or at least in danger of disappearing, was the feeling that owner and worker were both working toward the same goals. Instead, as they moved apart, differences inevitably arose."[71]

Armed with this eviscerated version of history, students are then invited to assume the role of William Cooper Procter in 1886, a year when P&G's workers went out on strike fourteen times. "Whenever the employees start a walkout you feel there ought to be some way of kindling among the workers a stronger feeling of respect for and loyalty to P&G," the text suggests. "How can they be convinced that their overall interests are truly inseparable from those of Procter and Gamble?"[72]

Clearly, the interests of workers *are* "separable" from those of their employers. The corporate imperative is to maximize profits, a goal that is not always compatible with safe working conditions and decent wages. Procter and Gamble, it seems, suffers from a form of myopia endemic among corporate educators—an inability to distinguish its own bottom line from the larger public interest.

Other companies are training students to support industry in contemporary policy debates. Mobil hired Learning Enrichment, Inc. to produce a series called Critical Thinking About Critical Issues 92-93. One unit in the series addressed the debate surrounding the North American Free

A cartoon commentary on Pepsi's deal with the Toronto school system.

Trade Agreement (NAFTA), which Mobil staunchly supported. The curriculum included a published Mobil editorial on the virtues of NAFTA, with no discussion of the company's commercial bias. The subsequent "questions for a critical thinker" were designed to help the student understand and support the conclusion of the Mobil editorial, not to question it.[73]

Exxon produced a video for classroom use entitled Scientists and the Alaska Oil Spill, which lauded the company's supposed success in cleaning up after the *Valdez* oil-tanker wreck. One teacher who showed the video was alerted to the ruse only when one of her students remarked, "Mrs. Steele, we've just seen a commercial." Steele then took the trouble to go looking through scientific magazines for the opposing argument—but few teachers have time for independent research.[74]

In a well-rounded curriculum, teachers might be expected to counter the corporate message with other views. But can frazzled teachers in underfunded schools really compete with slick, polished business propaganda? And who decides whether these materials are appropriate? Textbooks usually undergo rigorous approval processes; corporate materials typically escape any review by school boards and administrators.

Hucksters in the Hallways

As if dictating the curriculum were not enough, advertisers have been inventing new ways to promote and sell their products in school. A company called Cover Concepts supplies free book covers with splashy plugs for teen-oriented products. Whittle Communications decorated elementary school hallways with giant wall-mounted poster displays called The Big Picture, which mingled advertisements with trendy coverage of youth issues (this particular sales scheme was dropped). A company called School Properties USA, Inc. specializes in arranging sponsorship of high school athletic events, then plastering corporate logos on team uniforms and in gymnasiums. And in Atlanta, the Telephone Advertising Corporation of America has generously installed telephone kiosks in local high schools. The three-sided enclosures are topped with forty-eight-inch video screens that play an endless stream of silent fifteen-second spots for junk food and clothes.[75]

als are punctuated with ads. StudentBody founder Ron Yaros says proudly, "No other program takes a captive audience and ties it to a sponsor message."[76]

That, indeed, is the central problem with advertising to kids in school—exploitation of the ultimate captive audience. Children are required *by law* to attend school; when ads invade the curriculum and facilities, students have no choice but to watch and listen.

Photo courtesy of Colorado Springs School District 11, Office of Public Relations.

Colorado Springs (Colorado) Public Schools sells advertising space on its school buses.

Fast-food chains have managed to introduce both their corporate names and their products, into school lunch programs around the country. By 1994, Taco Bell had outlets in over 3,000 schools, and Pizza Hut was delivering to over 4,000.

Another school marketing scheme is StudentBody, a four-week, multimedia course in health and fitness. Teachers receive free curricular materials to conduct the course, and students are urged to go home and watch a related daily segment on local TV news with their families. Both the TV segment and the classroom materi-

Not-So-Free Equipment

Lots of corporations score public relations points by donating "free" equipment or supplies to schools. But often the gift is contingent on sales of the corporate benefactor's product. Campbell's Soup, for example, will provide schools with a copy of the filmstrip *Boyhood of Abraham Lincoln* in exchange for a mere 5,125 can labels. For 20,000 more labels, the school can get a projector with which to show the filmstrip; another 6,750 labels earns a screen to project it on. Assuming an average cost of 95 cents per can, the students' families would have to spend nearly $30,000 on Campbell's soup before the students could settle in to watch the filmstrip.[77] The Apples for the Students program employs a similar strategy: Schools can earn Apple

NATIONAL PRINCIPLES FOR CORPORATE INVOLVEMENT IN THE SCHOOLS

School-business relationships based on sound principles can contribute to high-quality education. However, compulsory attendance confers on educators an obligation to protect the welfare of their students and the integrity of the learning environment. Therefore, when working together, schools and businesses must ensure that educational values are not distorted in the process. Positive school-business relationships should be ethical and structured in accordance with all eight of the following principles:[1]

• Corporate involvement shall not require students to observe, listen to, or read commercial advertising.

• Selling or providing access to a captive audience in the classroom for commercial purposes is exploitation and a violation of the public trust.

• Since school property and time are publicly funded, selling or providing free access to advertising on school property outside the classroom involves ethical and legal issues that must be addressed.

• Corporate involvement must support the goals and objectives of the schools. Curriculum and instruction are under the purview of educators.

• Programs of corporate involvement must be structured to meet an identified education need, not a commercial motive, and must be evaluated for educational effectiveness by the school and district on an ongoing basis.

• Schools and educators should hold sponsored and donated materials to the same standards used for the selection and purchase of curriculum materials.

• Corporate involvement programs should not limit the discretion of schools and teachers in the use of sponsored materials.

• Sponsor recognition and corporate logos should be for identification rather than for commercial purposes.

computers by encouraging students and their families to shop at a sponsoring store. Typically, one Wisconsin elementary school collected $500,000 worth of cash register receipts in order to be eligible for $3,000 worth of computer equipment.[78] Free-equipment schemes sometimes employ emotional appeals and guilt to get families to participate. The MOM program, created by Computers for Education, asks students to sell magazine subscriptions in exchange for computer equipment. Students are instructed to write plaintive letters to relatives and friends; a sample letter ends with "Please help me if you can....P.S. I love you."[79]

Corporate-School Partnerships

Increasingly, schools are entering into full-fledged partnerships with business. These partnerships can take many forms, including on-the-job training or corporate-sponsored skill-building programs. According to the U.S. Department of Education, corporate-school partnerships more than tripled in number from 42,200 in 1983 to 140,800 in 1988, when the last survey was conducted.[80]

On the surface, it seems harmless enough. Businesses have a legitimate interest in the quality of education, and well-publicized reports of the failure of our school system to produce literate, skilled workers have raised justifiable alarm in the corporate community. Many corporate-school partnerships seem nobler than Channel One's unabashed commercialism or Procter and Gamble's self-serving propaganda. For example, AT&T has launched a school program for teenage mothers and their children in Plainfield, New Jersey—a seemingly laudable effort. The program does not plaster the halls with corporate ads or cajole students into buying AT&T products.

So what's wrong with corporate-school partnerships? A lot, says Alex Molnar, a professor of education at the University of Wisconsin at Milwaukee who has studied commercialism in schools. For one thing, there is an inherent conflict of interest between the imperatives of business and education: "Business and schools do *not* have the same interests—despite what business says. A business's first responsibility is to the people who own it. That usually means making the largest profit as

also reinforce the values of the consumer culture. For example, in Pinellas County, Florida, the county board of education, in cahoots with local corporations, constructed a "school-in-a-mall" called Enterprise Village. The stores in Enterprise Village—a McDonald's, a Blockbuster

quickly as possible. In contrast, public schools belong to us all and exist to promote the public welfare."[81]

Corporate interest in schools is one-dimensional: Companies want to sell products and services. But the public schools have a broader mandate to produce citizens who can think critically and participate in democracy. That includes thinking critically about the advertising messages they are bombarded with daily. In a school where the content and form of education is influenced by advertisers, will students be encouraged to question the means and motivations of business? Will the information that companies want to impart squeeze out more important information?

Even well-designed corporate-school partnerships manage to infuse the curriculum with business ethics and ideology. As Molnar points out, "Corporations are trying to use the schools to secure ideological allegiance to their version of free enterprise. The virtues of the American free enterprise system are arguable propositions, not revealed truths."[82]

Some corporate-school partnerships

Exxon, whose oil tanker *Valdez* caused an environmental catastrophe in Alaska, distributed to schools a misleading video that sidestepped the company's responsibility for the accident while lauding its efforts in the clean-up.

Video, a Century 21 real estate office—are staffed by fifth-graders who prepare for six weeks to be entrepreneur for a day. Not only are students trained for selling and spending but they develop an early affinity for their corporate "employers." And just like West Virginia coal miners in a turn-of-the-century company town, Enterprise students get paid in "scrip" that can only be spent at the mall.[83]

What People Have Done

Are corporate-sponsored schools the wave of the future? Thousands of parents, teachers, and school administrators say *no*.

Channel One has been forcefully opposed by Action for Children's Television, the National PTA, the National Association of Secondary School Principals, Ralph Nader, and dozens of others. At the local level, parent groups have led the fight. Virginia Leinart, the mother of the young girl we met earlier in this chapter, organized a public forum on Channel One in Port Angeles, Washington, that generated intense debate. Her daughter, Mary, was among a handful of students in the district who opted out of watching Channel One (although eventually Virginia took her children out of public school after failing to oust the program). And some educators are using the ads on Channel One to teach media literacy and foster skepticism about marketing techniques.

The New York State Department of Education officially bans Channel One in public schools despite intense lobbying efforts by Whittle that managed to overturn similar bans in other states. California's superintendent of schools Bill Honig publicly denounced the program, though the California Department of Education lost a court battle to ban Channel One in state schools.

Parents and educators are not the only opponents of Channel One; in fall 1990, 650 students in Fargo, North Dakota, marched out of class to protest being forced to watch the daily program, which they said was condescending and dull.[84] And in 1993 several young activists formed an organization named UNPLUG to help students oppose Channel One and commercialization in the classroom.

Grassroots protests may ultimately wound Channel One's Achilles' heel by scaring away advertisers. Indeed, the criticism is already taking a toll. Pepsi and Nike canceled their advertising contracts with Channel One. As a Pepsi spokeswoman explained, "We don't want to be shackled to something that isn't wanted or popular."[85]

In 1990, educators at a meeting hosted by the University of Wisconsin at Milwaukee developed a series of principles for corporate involvement in the schools (see sidebar on p. 36). These common-sense rules have been endorsed by the National PTA, the American Association of School Administrators, the National Education Association, and the National Association of State Boards of Education. If widely adopted, these principles could end many of the exploitative practices described in this chapter. However, these organizations have not yet mustered the political support to enforce the guidelines. That's where *you* come in.

WHAT YOU CAN DO

- *Attend school board or PTA meetings and ask the principal or other officials about corporate-sponsored materials used in your school. Push the board to adopt guidelines on the use of corporate materials. You may want to use the guidelines in the sidebar, or write your own.*

- *Tell the principal at your child's school that you don't want your child taught with corporate materials.*

- *Question your kids' teachers about corporate materials. Talk with your kids about what they learn in school and warn them to be on the lookout for propaganda.*

- *Fight Channel One. If your school board is set on using some sort of video teaching device, there are alternatives to Channel One. CNN, for example, produces a free, adless news program for use in schools. C-SPAN and the Discovery Network have similar projects.*

- *Persuade your school to teach "media literacy" skills in order to enable kids to decode and evaluate the messages of advertising, movies, and TV programs.*

- *Urge your school to start a community volunteer program. Participating in a recycling program or caring for the elderly can be a*

lot more educational than sitting immobile in front of a video screen.

- *Support adequate funding for public education. That could mean shifting resources from rich to poor communities or higher tax rates on corporations and the wealthy. Without proper resources, schools will be eternally doomed to mediocrity or tempted by corporations bearing "free" gifts.*

- *Ask your senators and representative to eliminate tax deductibility for in-school advertising. That would not only raise revenue but also reduce the incentive to advertise in schools.*

CHAPTER TWO

The Private and Public Airwaves

Television is the vanguard of commercialism. Corporations now spend $33 billion on television advertising.[1] Commercials may be clever or annoying, but their sheer volume has made them a dominant cultural force. ✳ *TV may become even more cluttered with commercial fare as home-shopping channels proliferate and interactive television offers us even higher-tech ways to spend our cash. Moreover, noncommercial public television no longer provides a refuge for ad-battered consumers; commercialism threatens the independence and integrity of public TV (and radio).*

The Trojan Horse

Commercial Television

You've heard it all before: Television is turning us into a nation of lazy, violent, mush-brains. So why reiterate this often-repeated theme in a book about commercialism? ✳ *Because TV is, first and foremost, a marketing tool. Television broadcasting is a largely private, for-profit enterprise supported almost entirely by ad revenues. As a result, TV exists largely to serve the interests of advertisers, and it carries their messages far more deeply into our homes and consciousness than any other medium. Just as humor within ads is used to draw attention to the selling proposition, so television programs themselves are used to deliver an audience for commercials. TV works like a Trojan horse: It gains entry into our homes with promises of entertainment and novelty, then delivers its true cargo of commercial messages.*

TELEVISION OFFERS advertisers unparalleled access to potential consumers. American children and adults watch an average of at least three hours of TV each day, or more than twenty-one hours a week.[2] By the time today's teenagers reach the age of seventy-five, they will have devoted a total of *thirteen of those years* watching television. In the United States, more homes have televisions than have indoor plumbing or telephones. Roughly 98 percent of Americans tune in for at least a little while every day.[3]

A Word from Our Sponsors

For those of us who grew up watching corporate-sponsored TV, it's hard to imagine an alternative. "Commercial breaks" every ten or fifteen minutes

may be annoying, but they seem to be part of the natural order of the universe, like thunderstorms or mosquitoes. But corporate-sponsored broadcasting represents only one of many possible systems, and it was not adopted without a struggle.

Back in 1925, before the debut of television, two-fifths of all radio stations were owned by nonprofit institutions, mostly colleges and universities. Indeed, according to communications historian Robert McChesney, "In all public discourse on the matter prior to 1927, there was general agreement that nonprofit broadcasting should play a significant and perhaps even dominant role in the U.S. system and that commercial advertising's potential contributions to the field should be regarded with greater skepticism."[4] The airwaves, many argued, were a public resource, and broadcasting should be regarded as a public utility.

But commercial interests coveted the frequencies of nonprofit stations and pressured the Federal Radio Commission for regulations that favored private, for-profit broadcasters. This advantage enabled commercial stations to squeeze out their nonprofit competitors; by 1934, nonprofit broadcasting accounted for only 2 percent of national airtime.[5] The nonprofits did not go down without a fight. Many be-

In September, our new serials swept the ratings.

NBC's new shows #1

This fall, our favorite cereals sweep the country.

NBC Marketing

TV networks and advertisers jointly promote programs and products.

Special TV events allow advertisers to target specific audiences. The Miss America Pageant provides a yearly showcase for advertisers of beauty products.

lieved they were engaged in a titanic struggle for the hearts and minds of Americans. As Joy Elmer Morgan, director of the National Committee on Education by Radio, told supporters in 1931: "There will probably develop during the twentieth century either chaos or a world-order of civilization. Whether it shall be one or the other will depend largely upon whether broadcasting will be used as a tool of education or as an instrument of selfish greed. So far, our American radio interests have thrown their major influence on the side of greed....There has never been in the entire history of the United States an example of mismanagement and lack of vision so colossal and far-reaching in its consequences as our turning of the radio channels almost exclusively into commercial hands."[6]

Despite impassioned opposition, history clearly came down on the side of greed. The contours of American broadcasting established in the age of radio have survived intact in the age of TV. Yes, there are public, nonprofit TV stations in many cities, but commercial broadcasting dominates the airwaves. And increasingly, even public TV has come under the influence of corporate interests, as we will discuss later in this chapter.

Although television was invented in the 1920s, it did not go into mass production until after World War II. In the early days of TV, advertiser control of programming was direct and total. In fact, many shows were produced by agencies for a single sponsor and had names like *Texaco Star Theater*, *Goodyear TV Playhouse*,

and *Kraft Television Theater*. (Some of those were actually quite good, although they stayed within the bounds of advertiser-approved content.) But as the medium came of age in the 1960s and 1970s, the "big three" networks prospered and seized control of programming. The networks remained dependent on ad revenues, but their shared monopoly of a valuable marketing medium afforded them great power.

By the 1980s, with the advent of cable and video rentals, the networks lost their stranglehold over the viewing audience—and much of their leverage with advertisers. Advertisers cheerfully contemplated the possibilities offered by weakened network control. As ad executive Jack McQueen enthused, "Advertisers have long been interested in regaining control over the programs with which their commercials are associated. . . . It's enormously gratifying for a guy who has seen the evolution from the early days of radio, to the full sponsorship of TV, through the period in the '60s and '70s when the advertisers had no clout in programming, to reach a period when we can not only provide bulk advertising . . . but actually create programming environments that heighten our clients' messages."[7]

In the 1990s, television is increasingly dominated by "programming environments" favorable to advertisers. Faced with falling ratings and declining ad revenues, broadcasters go to great lengths to curry favor with corporate sponsors. In recent years, networks have devoted segments of regular shows to sponsor-chosen themes, conducted joint sweepstakes with retailers, and aired programs that were produced or co-produced by advertisers. ABC's *Good Morning America*, for example, announces "theme weeks" on subjects of interest to sponsors, then sells blocks of ad time to makers of related products. CBS agreed to prominently display a Coke machine in a sitcom that was heavily sponsored by—you guessed it—Coca-Cola.[8] And after brokering a promotion deal with Miller Brewing Company, CBS's *Northern Exposure* featured a scene with characters drinking, and discussing, Miller Lite.

Single-sponsor programs are also making a comeback. Procter and Gamble, for instance, has a deal with Lifetime cable network to produce its own shows for young mothers, who make up a large part of P&G's market. P&G's Luvs diapers, Dreft laundry detergent, and Downy fabric softener are the sponsors of, and advertisers on, Lifetime's long-running *What Every Baby Knows With Dr. T. Berry Brazelton*. Erica Gruen, an executive at Saatchi and Saatchi advertising agency, encourages other advertisers to produce their own TV shows, but only if the programs fulfill certain marketing needs. In an *Advertising Age* article, Gruen recommends that advertisers make a checklist of criteria, including "Does [the program] fit and enhance the brand and the brand's advertising?" "Can guarantees be built in?" and "Does it fit with long-term positioning and corporate objectives?"[9]

Dictating Content

Broadcasters frequently censor the content of their shows to avoid scaring advertisers away. News programs, in particular, avoid biting the hands that feed them (see broader discussion in Chapter 9, "Making Pawns of the Press"). But producers of TV dramas and sitcoms also try to avoid material that would scare advertisers away. And nothing scares advertisers more than *controversy*.

Some standards have loosened since the 1970s, notably those governing sex, violence, and suggestive language; other subjects have now become taboo. For example, in 1973 when Beatrice Arthur's character on *Maude* got pregnant unexpectedly, she chose to have an abortion. But when the unmarried star of the sitcom *Murphy Brown* found herself in the same predicament in 1991, she decided to have the baby. Abortion was not a possibility for Murphy Brown, says Diane English, the show's creator. "If we

had done that," she said, "it would have been lights out."[10]

Even NBC's *Saturday Night Live* (*SNL*), notorious for irreverent parodies of politicians, had to alter the script of one sketch that targeted advertisers. In the original version of the skit, Tall Tales from the

Recession, executives from Ford and General Motors were depicted bragging about massive layoffs. But General Motors, a major advertiser on *SNL*, got wind of the spoof and complained; the final version featured fictitious company names.[11]

Such instances point to a clear double standard in broadcasters' pursuit of "free speech." In the debate over violence on television, broadcasters vehemently object to government regulation of television content, such as Representative Edward Markey's (D–Mass.) proposal to provide computer chips that could block violent television shows. However, producers *voluntarily* soften their approach to avert advertiser pullouts. Fear of advertiser displeasure casts a pall over the creative process and leads writers and producers to censor their own work. "It's censorship based not so much on the direct influence of special interests, social conservatism, or religious fanatics," says producer Barney Rosenzweig. "It's censorship based on economics. It's a real issue in a very different and more ominous way than we've ever confronted it before." And writer

New technologies like interactive TV may keep people glued for even longer periods of time to their sets. *Trivial Pursuit* uses the technology to create its own game show.

Bruce Paltrow notes, "This kind of climate alters the way you think. You find yourself censoring yourself."[12] The result? TV programs that flow seamlessly into commercials, avoiding controversy, lulling us into submission like an electronic tranquilizer.

The Tube and Us

What effect, then, is this electronic tranquilizer having on the 250 million Americans exposed to it each day? Some critics have argued that by bombarding kids with external stimuli, TV drowns out the internal dialogue essential to learning. And the television dream factory of imagery tends to overwhelm and supersede children's own imaginations. Much research supports this view. In one Canadian study, for example, researchers studied children in a small mountain town both before and after the arrival of television. They found that TV helped precipitate a 20 percent drop in creativity and reduced persistence in problem solving.[13]

TV addicts may be ill prepared to creatively solve the world's problems, but they provide an ideal audience for advertisers. Extended television viewing, researchers say, can make a person passive and suggestible. In their book *Television and the Quality of Life: How Viewing Shapes Everyday Experience,* Robert Kubey and Mihaly Csikszentmihalyi report that people concentrate less and feel more passive while watching TV than in any other waking activity. This passivity, they found, can persist even *after* the tube gets turned off. "With prolonged viewing, analytic skills may be less likely to be directed toward the screen, and some people may become less able—or less inclined— to engage in a complex analy-

sis of what they view. This raises the possibility that viewers may be less guarded against, and more susceptible to, certain kinds of persuasive messages the longer they view."[14] Advertisers, of course, do not want you to engage in a complex analysis of their commercials. By rendering its audience passive and open to persuasion, television offers corporate America an unequaled means of influencing our thinking—or at least our spending.

By radically altering our habits of leisure, television has changed our experience of the world. Think again, if you will, of the twenty-plus hours a week Americans spend watching TV. In earlier generations, that time may have been spent talking to friends and family, reading, dancing, playing cards, or just thinking. In any case, leisure usually involved some sort of direct interaction with the world of people and objects. But with the invention of television, everything changed. As Jerry Mander observed, "In one generation...America has become the first culture to have substituted secondary, mediated versions of experience for direct experience of the world. Interpretations and representations of the world were being accepted as experience, and the difference between the two was obscure to most of us."[15]

Nonsense, you may argue. Of course people can tell the difference between truth and fiction on TV. Why, then, did the fictional sitcom doctor on *Marcus Welby, M.D.* receive *250,000* written requests for medical advice? Even those who can usually manage to separate fantasy from reality may have trouble distinguishing between programs and commercials. As we point in Chapter 3, "Blurring the Distinctions," the bound-

Under the guise of celebrity interviews, late-night talk shows promote the latest CDs, books, and movies. Below, Jay Leno plugs a new album by George Benson.

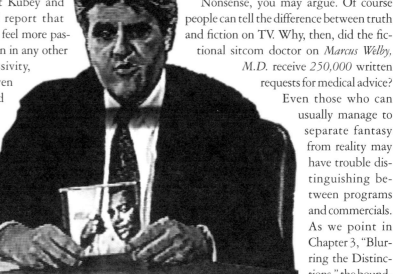

aries between the two have become extremely porous.

As New York University communications professor Neil Postman observed in *Amusing Ourselves to Death: Public Discourse in the Age of Show Business*, television is primarily a visual medium—its reliance on imagery distinguishes it from radio or print. In written discourse, an author makes a series of assertions, which the reader may accept or refute. An image, however, need not make a rational assertion. It simply *is.* We do not reject the evidence of our senses; each image carries its own truth. Many disagreed with Reagan's theory of supply-side economics, but it was harder to reject the emotion-stirring imagery of his "Morning in America" election-year ad campaign.

Emotion-stirring imagery is what television does best. Television commercials make excellent use of that and, as such, are often the most effective shows on TV. They certainly have more lavish production budgets than anything else on the tube—in 1992, the average price tag for a nationally aired commercial was $196,000, according to the American Association of Advertising Agencies[16]. Mander notes that the average production budget for a minute of TV advertising is roughly ten times the cost of a comparable minute of programming.[17] *Harper's* "Index" reported that each *second* of advertising on the hit show *The Simpsons* cost $10,000 just for the airtime.[18]

Contemporary television commercials rarely make propositions about the quality of the goods they sell. Instead, notes Postman, they offer parables about life. A McDonald's commercial, for example, "is a drama—a mythology, if you will—of handsome people selling, buying, and eating hamburgers and being driven to near ecstasy by their good fortune."[19] If a commercial can be said to have a plot, it is usually a simple one: All problems can be solved, and quickly, with the intervention of commodities. Although they say little about the objective specifications of

products, commercials speak volumes about the hopes, fears, and insecurities of the people who may buy them.

Commercial minidramas, with their quick cuts, simple messages, dazzling visuals, and emotional appeals, are perfectly suited to the coarse, visual venue of television. Given that TV exists by the grace of corporate America, it is hardly surprising that commercials should represent the apotheosis of the medium. More chilling, perhaps, is the way the conventions of TV commercials have come to pervade all public discourse. TV commercials are one of the most voluminous forms of public communication in our culture; the average American will watch more than two million by the time he or she turns sixty-five.[20] Because of their sheer ubiquity, TV commercials have emerged as the paradigm for communication in our culture. Where commercials set the standard, other discourse—including politics, news, religion, and education—must be visually appealing, simple, and, above all, brief.

Back when the printed word was the dominant form of communication, attention spans were longer. Consider, for example, a debate between Abraham Lincoln and Stephen Douglas in 1854. Each speaker was granted—and took—*three hours* in which to address his audience, plus rebuttal time.[21] In contrast, the currency of information in the age of the TV commercial is the aptly named "sound bite," a bite-sized nugget of fact, or a pithy saying.

The Brave New World of Home Shopping and Interactive TV

As we have seen, television is a Trojan horse that dazzles us with entertainment in order to deliver its freight of commercial messages. With the advent of home-shopping networks, some marketers dispensed with the Trojan horse entirely. Home-shopping channels broadcast twenty-four-hour-a-day commercials without the periodic distractions of sitcoms or the news. For Barry Diller, the former chairman of Fox Television and

QVC Home Shopping Network promotes 24-hour-a-day shopping from the couch.

a major investor in the QVC home-shopping network, home shopping "is the first successful real translation of the television set from a viewing mode into a transactional mode."[22]

Home shopping got its start on local UHF and cable channels during the 1980s. The first channels featured an odd blend of downmarket goods and high technology: big-haired hosts hawked cubic zirconium jewelry and spray-on vitamins while orders were taken on phone systems capable of handling thousands of calls per minute. Many sneered at their kitschy ambiance and silly products, but home-shopping networks amassed fortunes. By 1993, industry leaders QVC and the Home Shopping Network were

each raking in over $1 billion in sales annually.[23] Total 1993 home-shopping sales reached $3 billion, and analysts predict that could rise to $25 billion by the year 2000.[24] Huge profits have attracted increasingly upscale marketers: Saks Fifth Avenue showcased its wares on QVC, and Macy's hopes to be the first department store to launch its own home-shopping channel.[25] Catalog 1, a joint cable venture of Time-Warner and Spiegel, is going after the highbrow home shopper with merchandise from Eddie Bauer, Williams-Sonoma, Sharper Image, and Neiman Marcus.[26]

Traditional programmers are also taking on the home-shopping format. Joan Rivers, the brassy talk-show host, translated her shtick into a syndicated home-shopping show called *Can We Shop?*[27] Although the show was cancelled due to low ratings, TV stations earned $2 million from their percentage of the merchandise sales.[28] MTV, which has served as a vehicle to advertise recorded music albums, began testing a home-shopping show for music- and entertainment-oriented paraphernalia on MTV, VH-1, and Nick at Nite. "We've already developed environments that are uniquely conducive to the marketing of music," said MTV CEO Tom Freston in a news release.[29]

The home-shopping industry got a major boost in July 1993, when the Federal Communications Commission (FCC) ruled that home-shopping channels can

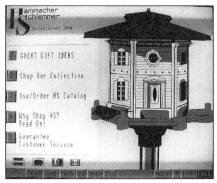

Home shopping has already gone on-line. Hammacher-Schlemmer sells upscale wares on Prodigy.

demand that local cable systems carry their programs. That ruling was based on the "must carry" provision of cable law, which was written to guarantee viewers access to local programming. Many now fear the FCC ruling will force small cable systems to drop public affairs programming, such as the C-SPAN network, in order to carry local home-shopping channels. "It's hard to understand how a home shopping network better serves the public than live coverage of Congress," says Susan Swain, a senior vice president at C-SPAN.[30]

Home-shopping channels make their millions by encouraging viewers to buy on impulse. "Nobody gets up in the morning and says I must buy something from television today," says Alan Gerson, executive vice president for marketing at the Home Shopping Network. "You have to create an impulse which says I *should* buy that."[31] Impulse buying is often the purchase of something you don't really need. Marketers know that impulse buying must be made as effortless as possible. The more steps involved in purchasing an unneeded item, the greater the chance that your rational mind will awaken and seize control. Home shopping successfully removed several layers of difficulty; to make a purchase, you simply pick up the telephone and dial a toll-free number.

Interactive television, a component of the much-hyped "information superhighway," will make impulse buying easier still. In essence, interactive television–the offspring of phone- and cable-company mergers–enables viewers to "talk back" to their TV, using a handheld remote-control device or a relay box that sits atop the console. If it catches on, interactive TV will be a great boon for the home-shopping networks. To make a purchase, you won't even have to find your wallet or dial the phone. A single flick of the remote control will send your credit card number pulsing through the airwaves, and within minutes your new cubic zirconium ring will be on its way to your mailbox. Retail analyst Ful-

ton MacDonald predicts that interactive TV "will change the face of retail [shopping]. Home shopping is going to be a $250 billion business in ten to twelve years, and it will probably represent half of all retail sales in twenty years."[32]

"Virtual reality," a variation of interactive TV, opens even more doors for intrusive advertising. RJR Nabisco pioneered a virtual reality video game in which users strapped on special goggles to take a tour of computer-generated Planet Bubble Yum. General Media Publishing Group has introduced interactive video games that, when dormant for several minutes, prompt a character to jump out at the user and convey a loud message. Advertisers can simply insert their favorite pitchman and slogan into the spot.[33] Who knows, perhaps the Energizer bunny will soon be able to "virtually" beat a consumer into submission until he or she relents to the sales pitch.

Democracy Down the Tube?

The ascension of TV culture, many have argued, does not bode well for democracy. Democracy demands an informed citizenry; TV reduces information to oversimplified factoids. Democracy requires eternal vigilance; TV discourages critical thinking. Democracy demands involvement; television keeps us glued to the couch. Democracy depends on freedom of the press; television is con-

Several self-proclaimed "game shows" incorporate brand-name products into stunts and contests. At left, contestants for *Supermarket Sweep* frantically search the mock supermarket aisles for Comet detergent. Other contestants try to guess brand-name products by giving each other word clues.

Video Jukebox sells a home-shopping service that brings music videos to the home TV screen.

trolled by a handful of private interests. Democracy thrives in strong communities; television keeps us isolated in our separate living rooms.

To what degree are the evils of television the fault of advertising? It's difficult to say, as TV and advertising have helped shape each other's form and content. But corporate sponsors clearly benefit from the control they exert through direct and indirect censorship of programming. And advertisers are also well served by other by-products of television culture: passive, easy-to-persuade consumers with a hazy grasp of reality who think life's problems can be solved by shopping. In this way, commercial TV reflects and perpetuates the consumer culture as it erodes democracy.

Interactive television may enable viewers to make impulse purchases without leaving the couch.

What People Have Done

Several communities have organized "no-TV weeks" to help raise consciousness about the tube's negative effects. Such events can help remind people that there is more to life than television. In Andover, Connecticut, for example, citizens pulled the plugs on their Tvs and engaged in dozens of alternative activities: a fishing derby, a model rocket launch, wine tasting, and a family pizza night.

Several groups have organized to improve the *content* of television. Action for Children's Television, which disbanded in 1992, took the lead in encouraging diverse, high-quality TV fare. The Center for Media Education (CME) is continuing ACT's work by monitoring enforcement of the Children's Television Act of 1990 and organizing citizens in several communities to demand educational broadcasts for kids.

Other organizations are working to provide programming alternatives to corporate-sponsored mediocrity. Deep Dish TV, for one, helps amateur and semiprofessional videomakers produce documentaries that are aired on public-access channels. CME is organizing groups to ensure that the proliferation of cable channels and other high-tech broadcasting options represent the public interest, not just corporate profits.

WHAT YOU CAN DO

- *Turn off the tube! Remember, the average American will spend thirteen years watching TV in his or her lifetime. Think of that time as a prison sentence from which you've just been given a reprieve.*

- *If you must watch, choose specific programs—don't just "watch TV." Use a remote control or VCR to avoid commercials.*

- *Support public television. Urge Congress to increase funding for nonprofit TV and join your local public station.*

- *Teach your kids (and yourself) to be media literate. The Center for*

Media Literacy, a Los Angeles–based advocacy group, publishes a workshop kit that helps parents and kids watch TV with a critical eye. Strategies for Media Literacy also produces a newsletter and teaching kits. You can learn the cost of those materials by writing or calling

CENTER FOR MEDIA LITERACY
1962 SHENANDOAH STREET
LOS ANGELES, CA 90034
310-559-2944

STRATEGIES FOR MEDIA LITERACY
1095 MARKET ST., #617
SAN FRANCISCO, CA 94103
415-621-1613

- *To find out more about making your own "grassroots TV," contact*

DEEP DISH TV
339 LAFAYETTE ST.
NEW YORK, NY 10012
212-473-8933

- *Contact the Center for Media Education for information on how citizens can chart the course of the information superhighway.*

CENTER FOR MEDIA EDUCATION
1511 K ST. NW, #518
WASHINGTON, DC 20005
202-628-2620

The Private Life of Public Broadcasting

A commercial fills the television screen: Soda pours into a tall frosty glass while a narrator lauds "the people who keep you refreshed with the crisp, clean taste of Sprite." You clutch at the remote control, seeking refuge in the noncommercial public television station. ✷ *But wait—this is public TV!*

ONCE UPON A TIME, IT WAS easy to tell the difference between public broadcasting and its commercial counterparts. When the Public Broadcasting Act was signed in 1967, it sought to offer a thinking person's alternative to the mindless, ad-punctuated fare on commercial TV and radio. Journalist Bill Moyers, who served in the Johnson White House at the time, recalls that "the primary idea was to keep one station free of commercial values."[34] But thirty years later, public television and radio are increasingly dominated by corporate sponsors and "commercial values."

President Johnson originally proposed to create an endowment for public broadcasting, financed with a surcharge on sales of television sets. This idea was vigorously opposed by broadcasters, who ensured its speedy demise in Congress. Instead, legislators set up a Byzantine arrangement in which public TV and radio stations rely on a patchwork of federal and state funds, foundation grants, and corporate and individual donations. National programming is produced by the Public Broadcasting Service (PBS) and National Public Radio (NPR), with federal funds channeled through the Corporation for Public Broadcasting (CPB), and corporate and foundation grants. In the 1980s, President Reagan slashed the federal subsidy for public broadcasting,

PBS buys full-page ads in trade magazines to encourage advertising on its "noncommercial" network. The above ad from *AdWeek* states: "Whether your strategy includes being seen in the company of those who influence our time, or tackling issues affecting your bottom line, Public Television delivers what no one else can."

and cash-poor state governments followed suit. Desperate to stay afloat, public broadcasters lunged for the corporate bait.

By 1992, corporations supplied 30 percent of the PBS budget for national programming.[35] Corporate funding may be on the rise; PBS heartily encourages its affiliates to pursue potential sponsors. One PBS study recommended that public TV stations shun local programming in favor of the splashy national programs popular with underwriters.[36] Jennifer Lawson, executive vice president of national programming at PBS, told *Harper's* editor Lewis Lapham, who formerly produced the PBS talk show *Bookmark*, that she had no use for "cheap little half-hour service shows."[37] And at a 1991 seminar, PBS urged its local stations to develop customized marketing packages in order to make sponsorships more attractive. Many have taken the advice: Boston's WGBH, for example, conducted a sweepstakes in which station members called in to win prizes donated by sponsors.[38]

Attracting corporate donations became a lot easier in the 1980s, when Reagan's Federal Communications Commission (FCC) gutted the rules against sponsor identification on public TV. Now, advertisers (or underwriters, as they are delicately referred to in the genteel world of public broadcasting) may mention their products and even display them as long as they don't describe them in flattering terms, reveal their price, or overtly urge anyone to run out and buy them.

Needless to say, this rule is routinely bent to the breaking point. "Extended sponsorship credits" or "enhanced identification credits," as commercials are called when they appear on public broadcasting, are easy to mistake for regular ads. Indeed, deBeers Diamond Corporation ran exactly the same ad on PBS and network TV: a spot showing a beautiful woman emerging from a volcano holding a diamond.[39] Another "identification credit" showed a Citicorp bankcard looming behind the slogan "Anyhow. Anywhere.

Pepsi gets airplay through a long graphic sequence before and after the *MacNeil-Lehrer NewsHour*.

Anytime. Right Now." One of Washington, D.C.'s PBS stations (WETA) runs a spot that shows a Saab tooling along a mountain road. That sort of ad, in which a corporation refines its image rather than describes the specifications of its products, is increasingly the norm for national advertisers in commercial media as well— so the gap between "identification credits" and advertising is mighty thin.

The rules governing identification credits are not stringent, but some sponsors still manage to break them. One PBS affiliate ran this *very* enhanced identification credit for Genessee beer: "Genessee Beer…the great outdoors in a glass, talks with wildlife cameraman Scott Ransom: Working outdoors all the time sounds

At right, Saab ran this 15-second ad of a luxury car cruising along a mountain road—the same kind of image-based advertising common on network TV.

like a perfect life but it does have its disadvantages, like sitting with your camera and the mosquitoes for six hours to get one good shot at a beaver swimming. That's when I start dreaming about a nice campfire, dry clothes and a Genessee beer. Our one brewery makes it best. . . . Genessee, the great outdoors in a glass. Genessee Brewing, Rochester."

The Genessee ad provoked an FCC sanction, but other ad-like broadcasts continue to proliferate. For example, many PBS affiliates fill the afternoon hours with cooking shows that function as infomercials for the featured chef's cookbook. Lou Reda, who produced a cooking show shown on many PBS stations, told one of this book's authors (M.F.J.) that he was paid to mention certain food brands on the air. Jeff Smith of PBS's *The Frugal Gourmet* admitted to having a financial stake in some of the products he mentions on the air.[40] And in a neat merger of sponsorship and programming, Norm Abrams, host of the PBS woodworking show *The New Yankee Workshop*, is shown using tools produced by one of the show's underwriters, Delta International Machinery Corporation.[41]

Some local stations are taking on commercial ventures to supplement their funding base. One PBS station, Chicago's WTTW, tested a home-shopping program that allows viewers to purchase jewelry, toys, and accessories that are produced by—and will benefit—various cultural institutions. Bruce Marcus, WTTW's vice president for corporate marketing and communications, noted that merchants can now "move aggres-

sively into a market niche that likely will be filled by someone else if not by us."[42]

How do such blatantly commercial broadcasts escape the notice of the FCC? In a document explaining its guidelines, the FCC stressed that it "will continue to rely on the good faith determinations of public broadcasters in interpreting our noncommercialization guidelines."[43] In other words, broadcasters are on their own. Considering the sums of money at stake in corporate sponsorship, some public TV and radio stations may be tempted to trade good faith for solvency.

In 1994, PBS announced that it planned to relax its rules even further. To attract more sponsors, PBS proposed allowing company spokespeople to appear in "credits," increasing the time allotment for those credits, and permitting underwriters to use the same advertisements on commercial and noncommercial TV. Moreover, PBS may allow companies to directly promote products, rather than just identify themselves.[44]

Public radio is also sliding down the slippery slope toward commercialization. Fifteen-second ads are routine on some stations. Broadcasts of NPR's *Morning Edition* on Washington, D.C.'s WAMU are sponsored "by the National Agricultural Chemicals Association on behalf of the makers of crop-protection chemicals, who serve mankind with science through agriculture;...by the Compaq Computer Corporation, providing high-performance business, personal computers and systems around the world...by the creators of *Remains of the Day*, opening this Friday at area theaters, and...by *People* magazine, a place to meet the fascinating as well as the famous."

Some stations have gone even further: A Cincinnati public radio station aired a Jiffy Lube ad that offered a "discount on air conditioner recharging with a Pennzoil oil change and a fourteen-point lube check." That proved too much for the FCC, which levied a fine against the station. It was the word "discount,"

apparently, that offended the guardians at the FCC.[45]

At least one ad agency now specializes in producing commercial spots for public broadcasting. In its promotional brochure, Public Broadcast Marketing (PBM) touts public television as "a pristine and uncluttered medium" that is perfect for companies intent on "improving their public image." Advertisers have much to gain through an association with the rarefied atmosphere of public broadcasting, including access to upscale, educated consumers. Herb Schmertz, former marketing director for Mobil Oil, once boasted that sponsorship of *Masterpiece Theater* made Mobil "the thinking man's gasoline."[46] Some who work in the sponsorship business put profits before public service. Daniel Billy of Public Broadcast Marketing says that corporations should view public TV as "a media buy rather than a philanthropic gesture."[47]

And PBS openly sells its audience as a lucrative market. Jan Wilson, PBS director of corporate support, wrote an article for the *Advertiser* called "Public Television: How It Can Fit into Your Marketing Plan." In it she wrote, "At a time when the average American is deluged with upwards of 16,000 advertisements a day, studies show that corporate credits on public TV stand out. Your message breaks through the clutter. ...When Toyota launched its new Lexus luxury car, it knew its principal market would be people who are affluent, sophisticated, and active. That's why Lexus decided to underwrite the WNET-produced series, *Travels*."[48]

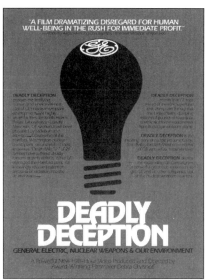

"A FILM DRAMATIZING DISREGARD FOR HUMAN WELL-BEING IN THE RUSH FOR IMMEDIATE PROFIT."

DEADLY DECEPTION

GENERAL ELECTRIC, NUCLEAR WEAPONS & OUR ENVIRONMENT

PBS, often accused of avoiding controversial programs, refused to air *Deadly Deception*, an Academy Award–winning documentary on General Electric's nuclear weapons plants. Critics charge that General Electric's sponsorship of public broadcasting influenced the decision.

THIS MODERN WORLD by TOM TOMORROW

Corporations Influence Programming

Corporate dollars buy more than advertising on public broadcast stations; they also influence the content of programming. Public television as a whole receives 37 percent of its support from taxpayers, 21 percent from viewer donations, and 17 percent from corporations. However, as noted above, corporations supply 30 percent of PBS's national programming budget.[49] Viewer and taxpayer dollars are used to defray day-to-day operational costs; corporate money is often earmarked for specific projects. According to Pat Aufderheide, a professor of communications at American University, "That makes big business the most influential agenda-setter in public television programming."[50]

Public radio is also indebted to corporate America, which provided an average of 32 percent of its budget between 1988

and 1992.[51] To protest sponsors' influence on public radio, the late Richard Salant resigned from NPR's board of directors in 1990. Salant wanted NPR to stop accepting grants that were earmarked for coverage of particular issues or regions. "My concern," he said, "is that when you accept funds for specific purposes in news, that permits the funder to participate in news judgments, which I think should be strictly made by the news organization."[52] Unfortunately, Salant's protest went unheeded. In 1994, NPR's new president, Delano Lewis, said he eagerly encouraged businesses to support programs related to their industry. In fact, he suggested approaching companies with the pitch, "I think it would be worth your while to be associated with [a specific program] because it has got such and such a listenership and your marketing people may be interested." For instance, Lewis envisioned a car company sponsoring the spunky *Car Talk* show. He admitted that there might be potential conflicts of interest, but said "We'll have to work out each situation."[53]

When corporate sponsors set the programming agenda, they often steer clear of challenging subject matter. In 1991, for example, the Ford Motor Company backed out of sponsoring an Audubon Society documentary called *The New Range Wars.* The Audubon film charged that cattle ranchers overgraze fragile grasslands and threaten endangered species—all with a hefty public subsidy. A Ford spokesman explained the company's withdrawal by saying, "We felt simply the program was just too controversial."[54] The Audubon film was aired anyway, but the lesson for public broadcasters was clear: If you want to attract corporate bucks, stick to films about cute animals.

Perhaps not surprisingly, the critically acclaimed but controversial documentary series *P.O.V.* (for point of view), which explored issues and themes related to gay life, failed to attract corporate donors. Marc Weiss, the executive producer of *P.O.V.*, recalls, "We knocked on a hundred corporate doors and they said, 'We'll pass, thank you.'"[55]

Some corporate underwriters have a vested interest in the material covered on public TV, a situation that invites blackmail. For instance, when PBS's *Frontline* aired a documentary critical of General Motors, the car company threatened to withdraw its support of public television. GM issued a written statement that said, "We will be re-evaluating our corporate involvement and financial underwriting of Public Broadcasting Service shows, if programs such as *Frontline* reflect a value shift on the part of PBS." A GM spokesperson told the *Detroit Free Press* that it would "think twice" about contributing to a "hostile environment."[56]

As public broadcasters become more dependent on corporate funds, they may practice self-censorship by avoiding

potentially controversial subjects. According to Don Boswell, vice president of marketing for PBS affiliate KERA/KDTN in Dallas, "We now work more closely with the creative department at the station to try to keep them from producing 'unfundable' projects."[57] Perhaps fearing the wrath of sponsors, eighteen PBS stations refused to air the *P.O.V.* program "Tongues Untied," about the black gay subculture. And PBS canceled its showing of another *P.O.V.*, "Stop the Church," which chronicled AIDS activists' disruption of a mass led by Cardinal John O'Connor.

PBS also declined to air *Deadly Deception: General Electric, Nuclear Weapons, and Our Environment,* which won an Oscar for

best short documentary in 1992. The reason? Supposedly, PBS does not air films in which the producer is also the subject. *Deadly Deception* was partly funded by INFACT, the group that coordinates the GE boycott, and INFACT was featured in the film. This argument might have more weight if the PBS lineup did not include other shows that highlight their sponsors' products. For example, Unisys Corporation funded a PBS documentary called *The Machine That Changed the World,* a video paean to computers that profiles the evolution and achievements of Unisys.[58]

Some observers believe that corporate sponsors exert a subtle influence on the

Critics charge that Chicago's WTTW violated the noncommercial charter of public broadcasting by running a two-week home-shopping program.

daily news programming at PBS as well. The liberal media watchdog group Fairness and Accuracy in Reporting (FAIR) notes that several conservative news programs are underwritten by corporate giants, but programs that are critical of government and corporate policies, such as *The Kwitney Report,* have expired for lack of funding.[59] FAIR also published a 1993 study that detected a distinct right-wing corporate bias in PBS programming.

Put the Public Back in Public Broadcasting

Certainly not all corporate sponsorship of public broadcasting is harmful. Indeed, some argue that public broadcasting wouldn't exist without *some* corporate underwriting. But it's a matter of balance; when underwriters gain a controlling interest, the public airwaves become jammed with advertisements, "commercial values," and bland, noncontroversial fare.

If public broadcasting is beholden to the same commercial interests as network television, some critics wonder if it has outlived its purpose. "Everybody must know that the conditions of public television's existence...require its strict conformity to the norms of expression deemed proper by the corporations that sustain its pretensions to intellectual freedom," wrote *Harper's* editor Lapham in an essay. "At the bidding of the corporations that gaze upon the images of their own magnificence, PBS resigns its task of look-ing outward into the world and turns inward upon the reflections in a courtesan's mirror."[60]

Though in 1992 Congress increased funding for PBS by 50 percent, in 1995 the new Republican majority was proposing to cut government support for public broadcasting completely. While many legislators saw the funding cuts as a way to reduce government spending, America's investment in public broadcasting is relatively small—just over $1 per person per year, compared to $18 and more invested by the Japanese, Canadians, and British.[61] NPR still only receives 12 percent of its funding from government sources.[62]

Increased funding for public broadcasting need not mean higher income taxes. Innovative funding proposals include reviving President Johnson's TV surcharge idea, taxing ads on commercial television, or charging spectrum-use fees for commercial broadcasters. The Twentieth Century Fund, a nonprofit think tank on media policy, recommended in 1993 that the federal government raise revenues for public TV by *auctioning* unused commercial broadcast frequencies rather than giving them away by lottery. In 1987, a proposal to fund public broadcasting through new sources of revenues advanced to the final stages in Congress but was killed at the last minute. Senator Ernest Hollings (D-S.C.), the chair of the committee that proposed the bill, lamented, "We had unanimity, but the broadcasters are way more powerful."[63]

WHAT YOU CAN DO

- *Support your local public radio and TV station.*

- *Tell your senators and representative that you support increased funding for public broadcasting.*

- *Complain to PBS, NPR, and your local affiliate stations about "enhanced identification credits," and tell them that you support innovative programming. Contact them at*

PUBLIC BROADCASTING SERVICE
1320 BRADDOCK PL.
ALEXANDRIA, VA 22314
703-739-5000

NATIONAL PUBLIC RADIO
635 MASSACHUSETTS AVE., NW
WASHINGTON, DC 20001
202-822-2000

As we become more skeptical about advertising claims, marketers seek ways to pierce our defensive layer by using hidden advertising and other forms of commercial trickery. ❋ One form of such trickery is the fusion of commercials and programs on TV. Producers and advertisers join forces to produce program-length commercials that look like regular news or entertainment shows. This chapter illustrates how both broadcasters and publishers are blurring the distinction between commercial and noncommercial media. ❋ Another form of hidden advertising is product placement in movies. As described in the second section of this chapter, movie studios enter lucrative deals with product manufacturers to weave brands into scripts and movie sets. Emboldened by their success in Hollywood, marketers are also inserting their products into TV shows, books, and Broadway plays.

Blurring the Distinctions

Infomercials, Advertorials, and More

Late-breaking news bulletin: To announce the introduction of its new Almond Kiss, Hershey Foods drops a 500-pound replica of the candy from a building in Times Square. Cut to commercial. Good Morning America *host Joan Lunden sits behind an anchor desk, reporting authoritatively on a breakthrough in "skin science"—the discovery that Vaseline Intensive Care lotion helps dry skin.*

FREQUENTLY, NEWS ITEMS BEAR AN UNCANNY resemblance to commercials, and commercials masquerade as news. Who can tell the difference? Often we can't, and that's the point. Knowing that consumers view ads with skepticism, marketers sneak through our defenses by blurring the lines between advertising, news, and entertainment.

Newsfakers: The Video News Release

One of the most sinister line-blurring innovations is the video news release (VNR). Descendants of the printed press release, VNRs are supplied to news broadcasters on tape or by satellite. VNR providers include corporations, public relations firms, government, advocacy groups—virtually anyone with a product to plug or a spin to doctor. A VNR may contain background footage on a particular issue or a complete, ready-to-roll canned news story. It usually offers a news "hook," however manufactured or self-serving, and features compelling visuals. "A good VNR should be indistinguishable from a news story," says producer Larry Pintak. "The key is to look like, sound like, and have the elements of a news story."[1]

VNRs blend seamlessly into news programs. In June 1991, for example, 17 million Americans watched a "news" story on the fiftieth anniversary of Cheerios cereal. The feel-good report included a tour of the Cheerios factory and some footage of a giant Cheerio made specially for the occasion. Few viewers suspected—and were not told by newscasters—that the segment was conceived, filmed, and produced by Cheerios manufacturer General Mills, then beamed via satellite to local television stations across the country. Similarly, when *Good Morning America* ran a lighthearted human-interest story about a Maine farmer's cow with spots shaped like Mickey Mouse's head, few guessed that the tape had been supplied by a thoughtful Disney World.

Why, you may ask, do newscasters air these obvious promotional pieces? In a word, desperation. Competition from cable and other factors has forced deep budget and staff cutbacks at many stations. At the same time, programmers have allotted more time for news shows, which are less expensive to produce than entertainment programs.[2] As a result, news departments have lots of airtime to fill, but they must do so cheaply. VNRs, which offer high-quality, prepackaged "news" for free, are an irresistible temptation. According to Nielsen Media Research, 80 percent of the nation's news directors say they use VNR material at least several times every month.[3] A 1993 Nielsen study found that every one of the ninety-two stations surveyed used VNRs,[4] and another study found that less than 50 percent of the VNR segments identified their source.[5] Medialink, a company that distributes VNRs, says that 5,000 VNRs were sent to newscasters in 1991, up from 700 in 1986.[6]

For marketers, VNRs are an inexpensive way to reach a huge audience. It costs between $15,000 and $80,000 to produce and distribute a VNR nationwide; in comparison, a thirty-second commercial can run to $250,000.[7] There is no guarantee that stations will air VNR footage, but many have achieved astonishingly high visibility. McDonald's VNR on the introduction of its

Mademoiselle magazine runs what appears to be a consumer column recommending specific beauty products. Only the word "advertisement," printed in minuscule type, warns readers that the product plugs were paid for.

McLean Deluxe hamburger was seen by approximately 22 million Americans, and Coors reached 27 million with news of a court victory in a battle over its ads.

Disturbingly, some corporations use VNRs to circumvent restrictions—or bans—on advertising their products. For instance, in 1987 the James B. Beam Distilling Company issued a VNR congratulating itself for using only American grains in the manufacture of Jim Beam bourbon. The video was seen by TV viewers in forty cities, although network and industry guidelines expressly forbid television advertising of distilled spirits.[8]

Drug companies have also used this ruse. Advertising claims about pharmaceutical products are strictly regulated by the Food and Drug Administration (FDA), but for many years the FDA did not screen VNRs sent out by drug companies. Not surprisingly, drug-company VNRs touted new products as miracle cures and neglected to mention side effects or contraindications. In one case, a VNR was used to hype a drug that proved deadly. In 1982, Eli Lilly and Company sent out a video extolling the virtues of Oraflex, its new arthritis drug. Within a few months, Oraflex had been blamed for twenty-six deaths in the United States, and the drug was discontinued. Lilly was later found guilty of suppressing information about severe adverse reactions, including deaths, during Oraflex trials overseas.[9] Newscasters contributed to this tragedy by uncritically airing Lilly's video as though it were an unbiased source of news. In response to criticism, the FDA has begun to review pharmaceutical VNRs before they are sent to stations.

But drug companies plant news stories in other media as well. *Consumer Reports* magazine raised the issue, stating, "So much of what we are told about health and disease now comes in some way from the people in business to sell drugs."[10] *Consumer Reports* interviewed several freelance health writers, who reported that drug companies had offered them money to write stories about their products and pitch them to national magazines without revealing the financial arrangement to the editors of those magazines.[11]

VNR producers say they offer a valuable public service. The videos, they say, provide broadcasters with free footage that might otherwise be costly or impossible to obtain. Moreover, they argue, a VNR is just a high-tech version of the press release, which has long been considered a legitimate news source for reporters. But VNRs and other planted news stories give corporations an unparalleled opportunity to define and interpret current events. Would a news organization run a story about the anniversary of a breakfast cereal—*unless* it were ready-made with a catchy visual? Corporate propaganda also fills airtime that might otherwise be devoted to real news. Faced with a choice between running a prepackaged bit of commercial fluff or sending out a news crew to do some investigative reporting, many news direc-

Pop Life: The Magazine for Teens was distributed in Canada. Adolescents are baited with a cover photo of model Cindy Crawford, but the publication is created by Pepsi, and eight of the thirty-two pages are ads for Pepsi or other products.

tors choose the former. Furthermore, when corporate videos are the *only* source of information on a given topic—as is often the case in stories on medical or technical subjects—how can we know the information they provide is objective?

Press releases, too, have been subject to abuse; reporters have been known to write entire articles straight from releases. But good reporters always attribute information drawn from press releases; most VNR broadcasts go unacknowledged. Eugene Secunda, a professor of marketing at Baruch College, believes that news directors fear disclosure would hurt their image of objectivity. "If you are a news director," he says, "why would you do anything that might in any way compromise the believability of your program?"[12]

Clearly, the biggest problem with VNRs is that viewers usually don't know they're watching them. For marketers, this is the whole point. A commercial is immediately identifiable as corporate propaganda, but a VNR masks propaganda as fact, borrowing the objective aura of the newsroom. "That's the great thing about VNRs," said Susan Fleming, an account executive at a company that produces VNRs. "Everybody sees them, but nobody realizes it. You have a corporate message to get across, and there's a television news anchor saying it to millions of people. It's one of the most legitimate ways to get your message to the public."[13]

Many marketers conduct slick publicity campaigns to promote "new" or "improved" products, and the media obligingly present them as news. For

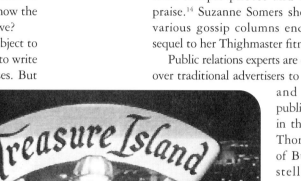

NBC disguised an hour-long advertisement for Mirage Resorts' casino "Treasure Island" as an adventure program. Bryant Gumbel of NBC's *Today* show interrupted the program for a "live report" to interview Mirage CEO Steve Wynn in front of his Las Vegas casino.

instance, when Polaroid introduced its new min-instant camera, *USA Today* ran a half-page editorial spread, complete with sample photos and customers' praise.[14] Suzanne Somers showed up in various gossip columns endorsing the sequel to her Thighmaster fitness gadget.

Public relations experts are eager to win over traditional advertisers to such free—and quality—publicity. Writing in the *Advertiser*, Thomas Mosser of Burson-Marsteller Public Relations urged companies to work the news media into their ad campaigns. "The implied editorial endorsement created by national publicity efforts can give a brand promotion added impact," said Mosser. "Just think how much more credible the advertising for McDonald's McLean sandwich was after the *New York Times* ran a Sunday front-page story about how good the sandwich tasted."[15]

It's a Program…It's an Ad …It's an Infomercial!

When they're not sneaking into the evening news, commercials are posing as regular TV shows. "Infomercials" or "program-length commercials," as these impostors are known, mimic the format of talk shows, newscasts, sitcoms, or investigative news programs. These half-hour-long superblurbs have many of the trappings of regular programs: theme music, production credits, listings in the television-guide sections of newspapers, and a "studio audience" of regular-looking folks who have been paid $50 to $75 apiece to feign enthusiasm.[16] They even have "commercial breaks"—for the same

Number of people who think Central Park is actually shaped like an Absolut Vodka bottle: 19,042. ❑ Chances an Absolut Vodka drinker has been to college: 5 in 6. Chances that an Absolut drinker would notice the misspelling in the previous sentence: 1 in 10. ❑ Number of jelly beans needed to fill an Absolut bottle: 122. Number of ex-presidents who have tried this: 1. ❑ Number of times Absolut was given as a gift to a host in 1992: 396,229. Number of promotions to visit president, 1992: 396,229. ❑ Rank of Absolut among imported vodkas: 1. Percentage of drinkers who drink Absolut for this reason only: .0000002. ❑ Number of bars and restaurants in New York City that feature Absolut: 11,000. Number that serve water: 11,000. ❑ Average number of Absolut bottles needed to fill an Olympic-size swimming pool: 315,418. Number of times this has been done: 0. Are you kidding? Waste fine vodka? ❑ Number of people who have been inside the Absolut Miami building: 0. Number of people who have been swimming in the Absolut LA pool: 0. Percentage of Americans who know the reason why: 2. ❑ Percentage of alcohol advertising that features bikini-clad women: 27. Percentage of Absolut advertising that features bikini-clad anything: 0. ❑ Longest solo flight (miles) in the Absolut hot air balloon: 2,345. ❑ Amount of money raised by Absolut Artists Against AIDS: $150,000. ❑ Number of homes in Sweden heated with energy generated from the Absolut purification process: 10,000. ❑ Distance (km) reached by lining up world supply of Absolut bottles around the equator: 27,300, or once around the United States, or 14 times around Sweden. ❑ Average times size used in Absolut fashion show: 6. ❑ Ratio of calories in 1 oz. cheesecake to 1 oz. Absolut: 9 to 1. ❑ Number of people who can identify the man on the Absolut bottle: 47. Number who aren't Absolut employees: 3. ❑ Average number of words in an Absolut ad: 2. Number of words in Absolut limits: 191. ❑ Percentage of people who read all the words in an Absolut ad: 99.7. Number of people who have read all of this ad: You're the first.

Even a high-brow magazine like *Harper's* sells off its editorial uniqueness to advertisers. Above, *Harper's* allowed Absolut vodka to borrow its trademark Index format for use in an ad placed in *Harper's*.

product that has been advertised throughout the "show," of course.

Typical of the genre is "Morgan Brittany on Beauty," an infomercial that appeared to be a late-night talk show hosted by the former *Dallas* star. Brittany first introduced the actor George Hamilton, promising, "Today, for the first time ever, he's going to reveal his very own personal method for looking so good." His secret turned out to be the George Hamilton Skin Care System, which viewers were urged to purchase for $39.95 by calling a toll free number. Alert viewers may have noticed a few departures from talk-show convention. For example, Hamilton was the only guest, and the conversation did seem peculiarly limited to the subject of skin care. But the talk-show illusion was carefully maintained: Brittany welcomed "my guest today" as though she were hosting an ongoing program that had other days, other guests. And at another point, Brittany said to Hamilton, "When I heard you were going to be on the show…" as if he were not the show's sole reason for being.

The infomercial concept is not new; for decades marketers have tried to get their commercials to blend in with the shows

Several news programs used a video news release announcing Starkist's new "dolphin-safe" tuna without disclosing that Starkist provided the footage.

they interrupt. In the 1970s, "Great Moments in Music" and "100 Paintings" were mail-order ads in the guise of cultural programs. But these early infomercials were forced off the air by limits on commercial length and other regulations. It was not until 1984, when Reagan's FCC lifted restrictions on broadcast ads, that infomercials truly began to flourish.[17] (Appropriately enough, Reagan's deregulation paved the way for his son, Michael, to appear in a 1990 infomercial for the EuroTrym Diet Patch, a bogus weight-loss aid. EuroTrym's manufacturer was nabbed by the FTC and forced to refund money to its many disgruntled customers.)

Deregulation, along with the availability of cheap airtime that accompanied the soaring popularity of cable TV, brought forth a deluge of infomercials. By 1993, some 175 products vied for infomercial spots,[18] and according to *Advertising Age*, 90 percent of all U.S. television stations broadcast infomercials.[19] Cable was the first to exploit the infomercial genre and continues to support it heavily: Lifetime airs about forty-three hours of infomercials per week and the Family Channel averages twenty-eight hours a week.[20] Regular broadcasters are also waking up to the $400 million spent on infomercial airtime per year; noncable stations now make 60 percent of infomercial sales.[21]

Initially confined to off-peak time slots, infomercials can now be seen at all hours of the day and night, with nearly 15 percent shown during prime time, according to a 1993 industry survey.[22] Cable executives are developing many infomercial-based channels as part of their interactive TV ventures.[23] In 1994, CBS announced plans to run on the stations it owns prime-time promotions of late-night infomercials, urging early-to-bed audiences to *videotape* the infomercials for later viewing.[24]

In addition to the usual dice-o-matics and costume jewelry, infomercials increasingly feature main-stream companies such as General Motors' Saturn division, McDonald's, Volvo, and Philips Electronics. In fact, one ABC affiliate in Miami preempted the popular *Wheel of Fortune* to air the Philips CD video player infomercial in prime time. Mean-while, *Wheel*'s host-ess, Vanna White, stars in her own infomercial for Perfect Smile tooth whitener.[25]

Although most infomercials feature bouncy, entertaining formats, some companies are going after the skeptical, upscale audience with a softer sell. For instance, McDonald's produces "The Mac Report," which masquerades as a sophisticated business newsmagazine—but only about McDonald's.[26] As infomercials earn broader acceptance, they are also attracting a higher order of celebrity hosts: Ted Danson, Cher, and Jane Fonda have appeared in recent infomercials.

Infomercials are likely to continue thriving with the expected boom in new cable channels. Tele-Communications Inc. (TCI) is creating as many as twenty-five single-subject channels, primarily to showcase the products of sponsors. William Airy, a TCI executive overseeing the marketing of new cable ventures, prophesized, "The future…includes special-interest channels that will provide opportunities for infomercial advertisers that are able to target by lifestyle, target demographically, psychographically." The only channels to survive, according to Craig Evans, author of *Marketing Channels: Infomercials and the Future of Televised Marketing,* "will be the advertiser-supported channels that in some way, shape, or form promote product brands or images."[27]

The success of infomercials leads inescapably to the conclusion that *people must be watching them.* Infomercials sold between $750 million and $900 million worth of products in 1993 alone.[28] "What people seem to want from the infomercial is an experience that is wholly and brainlessly affirmative," said Mark Crispin Miller, professor of media studies at Johns Hopkins University.[29] And as Rick Marin concludes in a *New York Times* article, "In a decade with much talk about dysfunction, the world of the infomercial is mesmerizingly functional, even multifunctional. Everything works, or seems to. And if it doesn't? There's always the money-back guarantee."[30]

So what's wrong with infomercials? First, despite the proliferation of infomercials for better-quality products, many of the goods sold this way are ripoffs: weight-loss plans, get-rich-quick schemes, "cures" for baldness, aging, and impotence. And like the home-shopping channels, infomercials owe their success to impulse buying based on limited, biased information. Moreover, infomercials further convert the news and infor-

Joan Lunden exploits her credibility as co-host of ABC-TV's *Good Morning America* to flak for Vaseline Intensive Care in a documentary-style advertisement.

mation medium of television into a sales device and add to the chorus of voices urging us to *consume*.

Proliferating infomercials are also forcing conventional shows off the programming schedule. That arrangement suits both advertisers and broadcasters: Infomercial time is cheaper for advertisers than the equivalent in traditional advertising, and television stations can make more money on one thirty-minute block than on a series of thirty-second ads within a regular broadcast. "It's schlock TV," admitted one broadcasting executive at a major station. "But it's a lot of money. If your competitors do that business and you don't, then you lose."[31] Jayne Adair, program director at Pittsburgh's KDKA-TV, is equally positive. "[Infomercials] are the fastest-growing program segment in terms of production values and the quantity of programs being produced," she said. "They are a legitimate form of programming."[32]

USA Today features ads at the top of each inside section; their format, color, and placement often mimic news headings.

MCI uses *Star Trek* characters (Mr. Spock, Captain Kirk, and Scotty) to advertise its phone services.

But perhaps the biggest problem with infomercials is the element of deception. Infomercials invariably seek to make viewers forget that they are watching a commercial and believe that the advertised product is really the subject of a talk show or news report. Most infomercials provide only cursory notice of their true commercial nature at the beginning or end and at the "commercial" breaks. In an age of remote-controlled electronic

"grazing" among channels, many viewers are likely to miss these disclaimers entirely. According to Rader Hayes, a professor of consumer science at Marquette University, there has been no research to determine whether a "reasonable consumer" could distinguish infomercials from regular programming. Hayes, who has studied infomercials since 1985, says they can escape detection even by a trained eye. "Even after all my years of watching," she says, "I was fooled by one this spring."[33] More troubling still are infomercials aimed at kids, who have even fewer skills to make the call (see Chapter 1, "The Littlest Consumers").

In their defense, marketers argue that infomercials offer an opportunity to provide in-depth product information. "What better mass vehicle to inform, educate, convince, motivate and sell is there than thirty minutes of TV time?" asked Gene Silverman, vice president of marketing at Hawthorne Communications, in a letter to *Advertising Age*.[34] That is a defensible proposition as long as viewers *know* they are watching a commercial. Broadcasters could, for example, superimpose an easily recognized icon—say, the word "AD" in a circle—in a corner of the TV screen during infomercials. (A similar icon could be used to identify VNR tapes on newscasts.) This simple remedy has been suggested by media critics and consumer advocates but has been rejected by marketers and broadcasters.

The New Hybrid Breed

Marketers continue to experiment with new hybrid formats that merge news, entertainment, and advertising. Bell Atlantic, for example, has produced a "sitcommercial" ad that poses as a situation comedy. "The Ringers," as the show is called, follows the adventures of a suburban family that gets out of typical sitcom dilemmas with the help of call waiting, speed dialing, and other telephone services. The *Wall Street Journal* observes that the sitcommercial's "jokes aren't any worse than any network sitcom"[35] (a depressing commentary on current network fare). The ads' creators believe that by drawing in viewers with a story line, they'll improve sales. "If people actually enjoy watching it and get interested in the characters, they will respond more positively," says Richard Alston, vice president of marketing at Bell Atlantic.[36] In the same spirit, Sominex sleeping pills were the focus of "The Good Night Show," a skit-filled infomercial from the fictional Cable Snooze Network. To its credit, the Sominex infomercial did contain many on-screen disclaimers.[37]

Ads also impersonate documentary films. For example, SmithKline Beecham USA produced a half-hour "documercial" on the importance of calcium in women's diets. SmithKline Beecham makes TUMS antacid, which has been promoted as a source of calcium. Here, the company is trying to fool not only viewers but television stations as well. "When we go to stations and try to get them to run this, we don't want them to think this is a commercial," said Pat McGrath, president of the ad agency Jordan, McGrath, Case and Taylor, which is credited for developing both the sitcommercial and the documercial.[38]

Ads have even been disguised as TV movies. In 1994, NBC sold Mirage Resorts an hour of prime

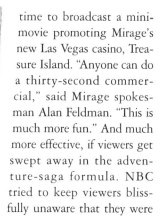

Ad or news? *USA Today* ran an "article" on celebrities who tested wrinkle-free pants—above a J.C. Penney ad promoting the same product.

New Yorker cartoonist Robert Weber used his recognizable drawing and humor style in a Diet Coke "advertoon." Both the ad and a regular cartoon by Weber (below) appeared in the same issue of the magazine.

time to broadcast a mini-movie promoting Mirage's new Las Vegas casino, Treasure Island. "Anyone can do a thirty-second commercial," said Mirage spokesman Alan Feldman. "This is much more fun." And much more effective, if viewers get swept away in the adventure-saga formula. NBC tried to keep viewers blissfully unaware that they were viewing a commercial; NBC spokeswoman Mary Neagoy said they were calling it "an entertainment show, an extravaganza."[39] Neither the TV listings nor the network promotions made reference to the show's sponsor.

Another recent innovation that blurs the line between advertising and entertainment is the use of celebrity endorsers who play their TV-character roles in television commercials. Advertisers have always used celebrities to pitch their products; the new wrinkle is that the celebrities appear not as themselves but as the characters they play on TV. For example, Tim Allen, star of *Home Improvement*, played the quirky do-it-yourselfer in a commercial for Kmart's Builders Square. Craig T. Nelson and Shelley Fabares star in a commercial for Kraft Healthy Favorites that could pass for a scene from their popular serial *Coach*. Jerry Seinfeld jokes his way through a commercial for American Express, Sinbad performs his characteristic antics in a Polaroid commercial, and Bart Simpson and family advertise Butterfingers in their trademark dysfunctional style.[40]

Similarly, talk shows have revived the practice of live endorsements, whereby the show's host personally plugs a sponsor's product. When Jay Leno announced that he would endorse products on the *Tonight Show*, the *Wall Street Journal* reported

Vaseline Skin Care sponsored a promotional climb up Mount Everest, calling it the Vaseline Research Everest '94 Expedition. In a publicity shot, climber Sandy Pittman appears with a Vaseline logo on her jacket and the company's lip balm hanging around her neck. *USA Today* published installments of Pittman's diary as "news."

that advertisers "applauded Mr. Leno's move, since they believe viewers are less likely to zap a commercial if it's performed as part of the show."[41] In one episode, Leno held up a giant Intel Inside logo and welcomed the chip manufacturer as a new sponsor on the air. (Late-night rival David Letterman refuses to endorse sponsors on his show.)

Particularly disturbing is the use of former or current newscasters in ads to create an impression of objectivity. For instance, former *CBS This Morning* cohost Kathleen Sullivan appeared in an ad for the Collagen Corporation. In what looked like a scientific news show, Sullivan presented collagen injection as a safe, effective treatment of skin problems—despite intense debate within the medical community over its safety.[42] Mary Alice Williams also used her credibility as an Emmy Award–winning newsanchor to flack for NYNEX, a telecommunications company. "My job is to stay on top of what they're doing and keep you posted," she said in a TV ad.[43]

One of marketers' newest gambits appeared in September 1994 in the form of a hybrid TV show called *Main Floor*. The half-hour show includes brief features about fashion and beauty. The catch is that some of the features are paid commercials, while others are not; viewers may not be told which are which until the credits at the end. For a fee of about $25,000 (much cheaper than a typical thirty-second commercial),

Lee jeans, Chanel cosmetics, and other sponsors can buy two-to three-minute spots to feature their products in the show.[44]

Walt Disney Co. has sponsored what is perhaps the most egregious example of hidden advertising. The company bought time in local newscasts for its "Movie News" spots. The ads, which include an anchorman who sits behind a desk and clips from *The Lion King* and other new movies, are designed to look exactly like the entertainment segment of a newscast, but they are pure hype for the movies. Only an easy-to-miss notice at the end of the minute-long spots indicates they are "Paid for by Buena Vista," Disney's distribution company.[45]

Blurring the Lines on Radio

Radio, too, is breaking down the barriers between ads and programming. In Washington, D.C., WPGC-AM runs several talk shows on financial topics that are actually program-length ads for their sponsors' products. Ron Petersen hosts a show about investments, which serves to drum up business for his brokerage firm; Jerome Wenger's talk show is really an ad for his financial newsletter. A single sentence at the beginning of each program informs viewers that the show is "furnished," "sponsored," or "brought to you" by its hosts. However, most listeners miss the implications of the disclaimer. The shows are effective marketing tools precisely because most people do not identify them as ads. According to Arnold Sanow, a small-business marketing consultant who once hosted a weekly business show on WPGC, "Having *you* on the radio, nobody realizes that you've paid to be the host of that show. They don't think of that."[46]

Moreover, having one's own radio show provides instant respectability. Carolann Brown, who uses her WPGC program *The Money Manager* to promote her book of the same name, says, "It does give you a lot of credibility....Somehow [people] think that if you're on TV or on the radio that you're already credible."[47] Such deceptions are particularly disturbing when used to sell financial services, where life savings are invested on the strength of perceived reputation and objectivity.

Imitation Editorial

In 1988, Ann Landers received a letter from a reader wanting more information on a miraculous diet pill that dissolves fat while you sleep, based on what appeared to be a legitimate news story. Landers replied, horrified, "What you read wasn't a news story but an advertisement....How these charlatans get away with this stuff is beyond me."[48]

Landers and her reader had stumbled upon the print media's version of the infomercial—the "advertorial," or advertising disguised as editorial copy. Advertorials—and consumer complaints about their deceptive nature—have been around for decades. They evolved from "reading notices" of the late 1800s, in which advertisers paid newspapers—or promised them future business—to publish news stories lauding their product or service. Although a 1912 provision to the Newspaper Publicity Act banned advertising disguised as news copy, advertisers and publishers today continue to push the legal limits.[49]

In 1967 the FTC ruled

that advertorials must carry the word "advertisement" at the top of the page. Still, it's easy to get fooled. An advertorial spread in the August 1993 issue of *Mademoiselle* titled "What's Next" plugs a variety of products: clothes, makeup, shampoo. The ad's copy style, layout, and photos all mimic the magazine's regular features. A quiz prepared by Centrum titled "How healthy is your diet?" is placed next to an ad for Centrum vitamins. An advertorial in *Travel and Leisure* for Stouffer's Vinoy Resort includes an engaging essay by George Plimpton about a friend with writer's block who checks into the hotel to finish a novel. Again, the ad's title, byline, and typography closely match the magazine's editorial articles.

Advertorials are proliferating madly. According to *Advertising Age,* the recession of the early 1990s gave advertisers more power, which they are using to demand advertorials as part of their contract deals with publishers. In 1992, advertorials filled 6,998 pages in the magazines

Crisco sponsored a Hispanic cooking program to promote its brand of oil—bottles of which appear frequently during the show.

Sominex, maker of sleeping pills, produced a humorous infomercial from the fictional Cable Snooze Network; a series of skits all related to falling asleep.

American Greetings, the card company, is featured prominently in a segment of ABC's *Entertainment Tonight* in which entertainers are wished Happy Birthday.

tracked by the Publisher's Information Bureau. This number was down slightly from the previous year, but up 51 percent from 1986.[50] Even industry organ *Advertising Age* worries about the ethical implications of advertorials. Reporter Scott Donaton writes that "there's a danger that it becomes more difficult for readers to make the distinction between regular editorial matter and special advertising sections."[51]

But fooling the reader is what advertorials are all about. As Ruth Whitney, editor in chief of *Glamour,* told Donaton, "The only thing that's bad about [advertorials] is the effort to deceive the reader, which was really their purpose in the beginning, to convince the reader that this was editorial material. It's imitation editorial."[52]

Now, marketers are taking the advertorial one step further by producing entire magazines to flaunt their products and advertising. Called magalogs, these custom publications sell at newsstands, contain articles and regular ads—but, unlike real magazines, they are published expressly to promote the sponsor's products.[53] For instance, Mary Kay cosmetics publishes *Beauty* magazine, which could be easily mistaken for any other women's magazine. General Motors puts out *Know How*, which covers car matters for women. (*Know How's*

premiere issue was even reviewed in *USA Today.*[54]) Pepsi publishes *Pop Life,* which claims to be a "magazine for today's teens." The publication—full of Pepsi ads—includes interviews with Cindy Crawford and Pepsi's other celebrity spokespeople. Although magalog publishers claim to offer a legitimate information source, the contents are biased by definition; single-sponsor magazines will not include any information that could threaten the profits of their backers.

What People Have Done

VNRs, infomercials, and advertorials all disguise their advertising content in order to fly beneath consumers' commercial-detecting radar. The only way to make these "stealth ads" less deceptive is to require a clear indication of their commercial nature. For example, radio infomercials would be punctuated with clear announcements every several minutes, and TV infomercials would include a constant on-screen notice identifying the broadcast as an advertisement. In 1991, the Center for the Study of Commercialism (CSC), together with other consumer-advocacy groups, petitioned the Federal Communications Commission (FCC) to require better identification of infomercials (the FCC had not acted by October 1994). In 1993 the FCC also invited comments on whether to impose commercial time limits

on broadcasters; CSC recommended a daily or weekly maximum of commercial content, which would restrict the amount of commercially blurred material allowed on the public airwaves.

WHAT YOU CAN DO

- *Write to the FCC and urge it to require better disclosure of infomercials, VNRs, and other deceptive formats. Also press for a limit on the amount of commercial time allowed on the airwaves.*

- *Write to companies (or call their 1-800 consumer hotlines) that use hidden ads and tell them you will not buy their products until they stop.*

- *Call or write your local TV station's news bureau to protest the use of corporate VNRs on newscasts.*

Product Placement

There you are, settling into your seat in a darkened movie theater, anticipating two hours of commercial-free entertainment. But first, a few words from our sponsors: five minutes of onscreen plugs for banks, dog food, airlines. Next, another ten minutes of ads for upcoming attractions. ✳ *At last, the film. Tonight's feature is* Other People's Money, *starring Danny DeVito. Although it is ostensibly a comic fable about corporate greed, the film's subtext emerges in the second scene. Seated before a plate of sugar-coated, deep-fried doughnuts, DeVito looks into the camera and exclaims, apropos of nothing, "If I can't count on Dunkin' Donuts, who can I count on?" Dunkin' Donuts' doughnuts are discussed, presented, or consumed in at least nine more scenes in the movie.* ✳ *So much for commercial-free entertainment.*

IT TURNS OUT THAT A PUBLIC-relations firm named Baldwin, Varela and Company brokered a deal between Dunkin' Donuts and Columbia Pictures (which released *Other People's Money*) to work the sugary treat into the movie's script. "Product placement"—advertising brand-name goods by showing them in films or TV shows—is increasingly common, but few viewers are aware that it exists.

***Total Recall* plugs Miller Lite beer in a barroom scene. The movie showed at least 28 brand-name products a total of 55 times.**

Product placement works precisely because it doesn't seem like advertising. Surveys indicate most people think ads are deceptive and misleading. So when a celebrity endorses a product in a television commercial, viewers correctly assume that he or she has been "bought." But when the same celebrity uses a product in a movie, viewers are more likely to accept the endorsement, at least at an unconscious level. Moreover, because corporations take great pains to ensure that their products are shown in a favorable context, they encourage the viewer to associate their product with pleasant scenes, likable characters, romance, glamor, and fun. This practice is inherently deceptive—another kind of stealth advertising. As one product-placement agency describes the "subliminal" benefits of advertising in films, "Imagine the impact of *your* customers seeing *their* favorite star using *your* product in a feature film.…Both YOUR COMPANY'S NAME AND PRODUCT thereby become an integral part of the show, conveying both subliminal messages and implied endorsements."[55]

Brand-name products have appeared in movies for decades. However, until recently, product plugs were the result of an informal barter system between advertisers and movie producers or set designers. In return for featuring its brand of soda in a film, for example, a beverage manufacturer would provide a year's worth of free soda to the studio. From an advertiser's perspective, that system was flawed because it offered no guarantees that the product would appear at all, much less in a flattering light.

Paid product placements—like many other forms of marketing excess—were pioneered in the 1980s. Steven Spielberg's 1982 film *E.T.* is credited with starting the trend. When the lovable alien E.T. gobbled Reese's Pieces onscreen, national sales of the candy soared by 66 percent. Although Reese's

Lowenbräu beer appeared on the TV show *Miami Vice* as this racecar driver's shirt logo.

The Dodge Viper car has its own show on NBC.

Ford Explorer got a high-profile plug as the official vehicle in *Jurassic Park*, which Ford advertised in this newspaper ad.

did not pay for the placement until the movie came out, both Hollywood and Madison Avenue learned an important lesson. Hoping to duplicate Reese's results for their clients, a host of marketers rushed in and a minor industry was born.

Today, some thirty-five agencies arrange cash deals between filmmakers and corporate sponsors. Typically, a corporation will retain a product-placement agency for an annual fee, then pay extra for each placement in a film. Placement fees vary according to the prominence of the plug. In 1989, one agency charged $2,500 for a mere appearance in the background and $18,000 for "hands-on use" combined with "verbal mention."[56] Placements can command staggering sums. Huggies paid $100,000 to outfit the infant in *Baby Boom*,[57] and Philip Morris reportedly paid $350,000 to make sure James Bond smoked Lark cigarettes in *License to Kill*.[58] That move generated so much uproar that the tobacco industry has publicly renounced product placement.

Disney solicited product placements for a film called *Mr. Destiny* according to a hierarchy of prominence: $20,000 to appear on screen, $40,000 for a verbal mention, and $60,000 if the product was actually used by an actor or actress.[59] Ironically, Disney has gotten kudos for prohibiting commercials before its movies. Perhaps Disney simply doesn't want to detract attention from the commercials *in* its movies. And because Disney owns no theaters, it does not stand to profit from prefilm commercials, as do some of its rivals.

Some companies have made product placement deals directly with actors. According to 1983 internal memos, Brown and Williamson tobacco corpora-

tion—maker of Kool cigarettes—gave Sylvester Stallone hundreds of thousands of dollars worth of gifts for promoting their cigarettes in five movies. Stallone's reported take included a $97,000 car, $80,000 horse, and $24,000 worth of jewelry.[60]

The high stakes of product placement often lead to touchy negotiations and legal wrangling. Cato Johnson Entertainment, hired by Twentieth Century Fox to broker product placements, offered Black and Decker a cameo role in *Die Hard 2*. For $20,000, Black and Decker demanded strong exposure, a line of dialogue, and incorporation of its advertising slogan into the script.[61] In the end, the filmmakers decided to cut Black and Decker's scene, but they paid for their artistic independence. The tool company sued Fox for $150,000 in damages; the case was settled out of court.[62]

Competition for placement in movies can be intense. In *The Firm*, Mercedes outbid BMW (which was featured in the book) for a role as Tom Cruise's fancy wheels.[63] In the 1987 movie *Wall Street*, Michael Douglas holds aloft a copy of *Fortune* magazine, calling it "the Bible." Douglas neglects to mention that *Fortune* was the victor of a bidding war with *Forbes* for the honor of appearing in the film.[64]

Product placements are proliferating rapidly. *Home Alone*, the top-grossing film of 1991, contained no less than forty-two mentions of thirty-one brand-name products. *Bull Durham* contained fifty brand-name references, an average of one every two minutes.[65] Displaying a characteristic inability to restrain themselves, marketers are monopolizing more and more of the movies we watch. Adidas managed to shoehorn an entire commercial for its sneakers into Orion's *Johnny Be Good*. "It tied in visually so well," smirks Orion executive Jan Kean, "you didn't even know you were seeing a commercial."[66]

In the megahyped *Jurassic Park*, Ford Explorer won a starring role as dinosaur snack food, and in another scene, the camera slowly pans a gift shop that showcases the entire line of Jurassic Park accessories. The movie spawned a thousand licensed products, including Jurassic Park Flavored Lip Balm with Dinosaur Topper and a Jurassic Park 3-D Stand-Up Puzzle.

Despite the clutter, as advertisers have discovered, audiences *do* notice on-screen products. Industry research has shown that audience recall of product placements is two and a half times greater than that of TV commercials.[67] Sales confirm those results; after Tom Cruise wore Ray-Ban's Wayfarer sunglasses in the 1983 hit *Risky Business*, Ray-Ban reportedly sold 18,000 pairs of that style in one month—more than the total sales of the previous three years. Following that lucrative precedent, Ray-Ban now places its products in about 160 movies a year.[68] Red Stripe beer also made out well on its investment of $5,000 (mostly in free brew) to the producers of *The Firm*.[69] Red Stripe sales increased by 50 percent after the movie's release in 1993.[70] (The original script left out the beer, which appeared in the book, but Red Stripe convinced the producers to reinsert it.)

Some corporations have even used product placements to sabotage their competitors' brands. In 1982, Coca-Cola

purchased 49 percent of Columbia Pictures and immediately began using the studio's movies to plug Coke and cast subliminal aspersions on Pepsi. In *Murphy's Romance*, for example, Coca-Cola logos fill the hero's cozy general store, and Coke is the beverage of choice of the film's sympathetic characters. When Sally Field's teenage son applies for a job, two Pepsi signs stare down from the wall of a supermarket where he is told curtly that he is not needed.[71]

Certainly, not every brand-name product in a film represents a paid placement. Directors sometimes employ products to indicate something about a scene or char-

After Miller Brewing Company and CBS announced a joint promotion for *Northern Exposure*, Miller beer was mentioned in a scene on the show.

Although the character Wayne in *Wayne's World* made fun of product placement by exaggerating plugs for Pizza Hut, Dorito's, and Pepsi, those products nevertheless received major exposure in the movie.

acter. In fact, when executives for Yoo-Hoo chocolate drink refused to pay for a prominent plug in the 1992 film *A Few Good Men*, the director used the product anyway because it "provid-

Travel scenes in *Home Alone*, above and below, presented perfect placement opportunities for rental cars and airplanes.

ed texture."[72]

There is, however, a critical distinction between a *director* using a product in a film for artistic reasons and an *advertiser* placing it there with the sole intent of selling more goods. Advertisers and filmmakers like to blur this distinction, arguing that the use of brand-name products makes films more naturalistic. One placement broker asserts that "product placement comes out of a creative need—filmmakers are only trying to reflect life." Moreover, defenders argue, product placement has no effect on a film's

artistic content. According to Jack Valenti, president of the Motion Picture Association of America, "[Filmmakers] are the captains of their creative ship. They would resent outsiders telling them how to shape their creative design."[73]

But who is really at the helm of this creative ship? When promoting their services, product-placement agencies tout their ability to manipulate movie scripts to the product's best advantage. As one agency boasts, "[Associated Film Productions] carefully controls the appearance of the client's product in films....It is the stars who will use the product, always in a positive and memorable manner....Producers and directors frequently ask AFP to recommend ways in which brand-name products can be creatively used to enhance a scene. This has led to many beneficial exposures of products in *specially devised scenes* that have great brand-name impact" (emphasis added).[74]

These "specially devised scenes" rarely "reflect life." Consider, for example, the scene in *Rocky III* that was amended to include a prominent box of Wheaties, with Rocky advising his young son to eat the "breakfast of champions" if he wants to grow up big and strong.[75] Or the following stilted dialogue, from the 1989 film *Who's Harry Crumb?* starring John Candy and Jim Belushi:

CANDY (offers Belushi a cherry): Cherry?

BELUSHI: No fruit, thank you.

(Candy pulls a can of Diet Coke from his valise)

CANDY: Coke?

BELUSHI: No, thank you.

CANDY: Mix 'em together, ya got a cherry Coke. Ah ha ha ha ha ha! A cherry Coke, ha ha ha ha!

Many filmmakers are now willing to take artistic advice from manufacturers. Andrew Varela of Baldwin, Varela and Co. admitted to tinkering with the script of *Home Alone* on behalf of his client, Kraft General Foods. "We thought it made sense for Macauley Culkin to fix macaroni and cheese for his solo Christmas dinner. The script originally called for him to heat a turkey dinner, but we believed that this kid—left on his own and scared—would reach for something familiar…a comfort food."[76]

Other filmmakers have allowed their creative ship to be pirated by marketers. A 1988 flop called *Mac and Me* functioned as one long "specially devised

scene." *Mac* features an E.T.-like alien who lives on Coca-Cola, and a birthday party at McDonald's where everybody drinks Coke while Ronald McDonald sings the company's theme song. Not exactly cinema verité.

Product Placements Everywhere

Evidently, movies are not exactly commercial free. So you turn on the tube, thinking that on TV, at least, commercials *look* like commercials. Don't bet on it. Although the federal communications code requires broadcasters to acknowledge any paid promotions, advertisers have identified ways to get around the rules. Brand-name products can appear in TV shows if the manufacturer has not paid for airtime and if the products are "reasonably related" to the content of the show. That means that advertisers now lobby producers for the right to "donate" their products

as props, often stretching the legal limits. Dodge, for example, managed to ensure that its product related to the content of a show because it *is* the show; NBC named its 1994 TV series *Viper* after the Viper sports car.

By adhering to the letter, if not the spirit, of the FCC's rules, advertisers have found yet another way to bombard us with product plugs. According to *TV Guide,* a new industry has emerged to facilitate donations to

In *Back to the Future,* Texaco endures as the town's trusty gas station from the 1950s to the 1980s. In another scene from the movie, (below left), J.C. Penney is prominent.

television: "At least half a dozen 'place-ment' companies are in the business of providing products for TV shows. . . .The companies supply the merchandise requested, free of charge, making their money from fees paid by manufacturers." The result? Prime-time product place-ments *doubled* between 1986 and 1988.[77]

And we can expect even more in the future. New VCRs will be capable of automatically editing out commercials when playing taped broadcasts, so adver-tisers are seeking new ways to embed their pitches in the programs themselves. A study of the threat posed by the new VCRs, conducted by a New York adver-tising firm, recommended that "ads may have to be situated within the confines of a program and may have to become more subliminal in nature."[78]

And don't think you can avoid product place-ment by going to see a play. Enterprising mar-keters have even managed to insinuate brand-name products into Broadway plays. For example, Topps (baseball) trading cards paid for a plug in the 1994 revival of *Damn Yan-kees.* Booze importer Schiefflin and Som-erset helps sponsor the musical *City of Angels,* in return for which a bottle of its Johnnie Walker Black appears onstage. Product placement is an excellent way to attract corporate benefactors, says *Angels* producer Barry Weissler. "You've got to offer [sponsors] something that's attrac-tive to them, and you've got to expose them to a market."[79]

Disgusted with the crass commercial-ism of the entertainment industry, per-haps you seek the solace of a good book. Here, too, you'll find the tentacles of marketing. Occasionally, advertisements are inserted into books or, more insidi-ously, woven into the text. In 1989, Maserati commissioned an author to incorporate plugs for its sports cars into *Power City*, a novel about life in Holly-wood, and picked up the $15,000 tab for the author's promotional book tour.[80] Music videos work product plugs into the performance, such as Miller beer in a Madonna video.[81] Even board games have succumbed to the temptations of hucksterism. It's Only Money, for exam-ple, includes a board riddled with real brand names. To appear in the game, each sponsor paid $30,000.[82] Although It's Only Money is targeted at children "age eight and up," it features two casi-nos and three brands of liquor.

What People Have Done

What's the solution? Ban product placements in children's media and require disclosure in all other media, argues the Center for the Study of Commercialism. When newspapers or magazines run ads that look like editorial copy, they are required to print "advertisement" at the top of the page. Why not apply the same rule to analogous kinds of ads in movies and television shows? CSC is pressing for reforms that would require filmmak-ers and others to prominently disclose all paid product placements. (The FTC denied CSC's petition to require an on-screen notice before a film begins of all paid product plugs.) On occasion, some films do mention placement deals in tiny print in the closing credits, but few moviegoers stick around to see them. Perhaps to forestall punitive legislation, product-placement executives in Holly-wood have established a new trade associ-ation, Entertainment Resource Market-ing Association (ERMA), to self-regulate their industry. ERMA distributes a vague code of standards and ethics that ad-dresses client-agent relations, but offers no guidelines on fair practices vis-à-vis movie-goers.[83]

WHAT YOU CAN DO

- *When ads run before films, don't just sit there and take it. BOO loudly and complain to the theater manager.*

- *Write to your representatives in Congress, the Federal Trade Commission, or your state attorney general and demand that ads in movies be identified as such by a disclaimer at the beginning of the film.*

CHAPTER FOUR

Sexism and Sexuality in Advertising

*Women's bodies have been used whole, or in
parts, to market everything from brassieres to monkey
wrenches. One effect of such ads is to give women unrealistic
notions of what they should look like. After instilling anxiety and
insecurity in women, the ads imply that buying consumer products
can correct practically any defect, real or imagined. Moreover,
the women's magazines that could be telling the truth
about such marketplace fraud are largely co-opted
by their advertisers. Nor are men immune from
exploitation. As more idealized male bodies
appear in ads, men may, at last, really understand
what upsets women about the way they are depicted in ads.
✻ In addition to reinforcing sexist notions about ideal woman-
and manhood, ads exploit sexuality. Many products are pitched
with explicit sexual imagery that borders on pornography. Not only
do these ubiquitous images encourage us to think of sex as a commodity, but they often reinforce stereotypes of women as sex
objects and may contribute to violence against women.*

The Iron Maiden

How Advertising Portrays Women

Fourteen year-old Lisa arranges herself in the mirror—tightening her stomach, sucking in her cheeks, puffing her lips into an approximation of a seductive pout. It's no use, she thinks, as she glances down at the open magazine on her dresser table. I'll never look like the women in the ads. She flips through the pages, studying the beautiful women with their slender hips, flawless skin, and silky hair. Well, maybe if I lost twenty pounds, she thinks, pinching her baby-fat tummy with an acid feeling of despair. Or if I had the right clothes and makeup…

EVERYWHERE WE TURN, ADVERTISEMENTS tell us what it means to be a desirable man or woman. For a man, the message is manifold: he must be powerful, rich, confident, athletic. For a woman, the messages all share a common theme: She must be "beautiful." Advertising, of course, did not invent the notion that women should be valued as ornaments; women have always been measured against cultural ideals of beauty. But advertising has joined forces with sexism to make images of the beauty ideal more pervasive, and more unattainable, than ever before.

In her 1991 book *The Beauty Myth,* Naomi Wolf compares the contemporary ideal of beauty to the Iron Maiden, a medieval torture device that enclosed its victims in a spike-lined box painted with a woman's image. Like the Iron Maiden, the beauty ideal enforces conformity to a single, rigid shape. And both cause suffering—even death—in their victims.

The current Iron Maiden smiles at us from the pages of *Vogue* magazine. She's a seventeen-year-old professional model, weighing just 120 pounds on a willowy 5'10" frame. Her eyes are a deep violet-blue, her teeth pearly white. She has no wrinkles, blemishes—or even pores, for that matter. As media critic Jean Kilbourne observes in *Still Killing Us Softly,* her groundbreaking film about images of women in advertising, "The ideal cannot be achieved; it is inhuman in its flawlessness. And it is the only standard of beauty—and worth—for women in this culture."[1]

The flawlessness of the Iron Maiden is, in fact, an illusion created by makeup artists, photographers, and photo retouchers. Each image is painstakingly worked over: Teeth and eyeballs are bleached white; blemishes, wrinkles, and stray hairs are airbrushed away. According to Louis Grubb, a leading New York retoucher, "Almost every photograph you see for a national advertiser these days has been worked on by a retoucher to some degree….Fundamentally, our job is to correct the basic deficiencies in the original photograph or, in effect, to improve upon the appearance of reality."[2] In some cases, a picture is actually an amalgam of body parts of several different models—a mouth from this one, arms from that one, and legs from a third.[3] By inviting women to compare their *unimproved* reality with the Iron Maiden's airbrushed perfection, advertising erodes self-esteem, then offers to sell it back—for a price.

The price is high. It includes the staggering sums we spend each year to change our appearance: $33 billion on weight loss;[4] $7 billion on cosmetics; $300 million on cosmetic surgery.[5] It includes women's lives and health, which are lost to self-imposed starvation and complications from silicone breast implants. And it includes the impossible-to-measure cost of lost self-regard and limited personal horizons.

The Beauty Contest of Life

Ads instruct us to assume a self-conscious perspective; to view our physical selves through the censorious eyes of others. To those of us who grew up in the consumer culture, intense self-scrutiny has become an automatic reflex. But this reflex is not God-given; it is the product of decades of deliberate marketing effort. Since the birth of the modern advertising industry in the 1920s, marketers have sought to foster insecurity in consumers. One advertiser, writing in the trade journal *Printer's Ink* in 1926, noted that effective ads must "make [the viewer] self-conscious about matter of course things such as enlarged nose pores, bad breath." Another commented that "advertising helps to keep the masses dissatisfied with their mode of life, discontented with the *ugly things* around them. Satisfied customers are not as profitable as discontented ones."[6]

We'll make a non-competitive suit when they make a non-competitive beach.

The Beauty Contest of Life: Advertising encourages women to compare themselves to one another, fostering feelings of competition and inadequacy.

Advertisers in the 1920s did everything they could to create profitably discontented customers. Their ads depicted a hostile world peopled with critical strangers who would fasten on some part of one's anatomy and deliver a negative judgment. "The Eyes of Men...The Eyes of Women Judge Your Loveliness Every Day," warned an ad for Camay soap. "You can hardly glance out the window, much less walk in town but that some inquiring eye searches you and your skin. This is the Beauty Contest of Life." For women, of course, participation in this contest was compulsory.

In the 1920s, before Americans had learned to dread ring-around-the-collar and halitosis, blunt instruments were needed to instill the self-consciousness that would eventually fuel the consumer culture. Perhaps because today's audiences are more predisposed to self-examination, contemporary ads can afford to be more subtle. Nonetheless, the Beauty Contest of Life continues. "We'll make a non-competitive suit when they make a non-competitive beach," reads the copy of an ad for Speedo bathing suits.

Countless ads reinforce insecurity by asking women to view their faces and bodies as an ensemble of discrete parts, each in need of a major overhaul. An ad for foundation garments depicts two disembodied backsides and promises "New improved fannies." "If your hair isn't beautiful," warns a shampoo ad, "the rest hardly matters." Another demands to know: "Why aren't your feet as sexy as the rest of you?" And an ad for Dep styling products suggests that we beautify our hair in order to counteract our other glaring flaws: "Your breasts may be too big, too saggy, too pert, too flat, too full, too far apart," the copy reads, "but...at least you can have your hair the way you want it."

The psychological costs of advertising-induced self-consciousness are difficult to quantify. For most women, they include an endless self-scrutiny that is tiresome at best and paralyzing at worst. As Susan Brownmiller writes in *Femininity,* her classic treatise on the feminine ideal, "Because she is forced to concentrate on the minutiae of her bodily parts, a woman is never free of self-consciousness. She is never quite satisfied, and never secure, for desperate, unending absorption in the drive for perfect appearance— call it feminine vanity—is the ultimate restriction on freedom of mind."[7]

Men also lose out in a culture dominated by Iron Maiden imagery; advertising encourages men to measure their girlfriends and wives against a virtually unattainable ideal, perpetuating frustration among both genders. Wolf says that ads don't sell sex, they sell sexual discontent.

Sexual discontent fuels the engines of the consumer culture. The ideal bodies presented in the ads invite comparison to ourselves and our mates, and in the likely event that the comparison is unfavorable to us, the ads suggest we attain the ideal by buying another product. According to Wolf, "Consumer culture is best supported by markets made up of sexual clones, men who want objects and women who want to be objects, and the object desired ever-changing, disposable, and dictated by the market."[8]

The Thinning of the Iron Maiden

Women come in an endless array of shapes and sizes, but you'd never know it from looking at ads. In every generation, advertisers issue a new paradigm of female perfection. The very rigidity of the ideal guarantees that most women will fall outside of it, creating a gap between what women are and what they learn they should be. This gap is very lucrative for the purveyors of commercialized beauty.

In the portrayal of women's bodies, the gap has never been wider. The slender reigning ideal provides a stark contrast to the rounder curves of most women's bodies. As an adaptation to the physical demands of childbearing, women's bodies typically have a fat content of around 25 percent, as opposed to 15 percent in men. For much of human history, this characteristic was admired, sought after, and celebrated in the arts. But the twentieth century has seen a steady chipping away at the ideal female figure. A generation ago, according to Naomi Wolf, a typical model weighed 8 percent less than the average woman; more recently she weighs 23 percent less. Most models are now thinner than 95 percent of the female population.[9]

In the early 1990s, the fashion industry promoted the "waif look," epitomized

Many charge that superthin models provoke eating disorders in women. The Diet Sprite ad (top left), which says that its model's nickname is "Skeleton," was the target of a boycott by Boston-based BAM (Boycott Anorexic Marketing). Top right, gaunt models pose for *Elle* magazine, wrapped in cords suggestive of bondage. Below, supermodel Kate Moss embodies the fashion industry's "waif" look.

by Calvin Klein's young supermodel Kate Moss. At 5'7" and an estimated 100 pounds, "Moss looks as if a strong blast from a blow dryer would waft her away," according to *People* magazine.[10] Marcelle d'Argy, editor of *British Cosmopolitan*, called fashion photos of Moss "hideous and tragic. If I had a daughter who looked like that, I would take her to see a doctor."[11]

As the gap between ideal and reality has widened, women's self-esteem has fallen into the void. A 1984 *Glamour* magazine survey of 33,000 women found that 75 percent of respondents aged eighteen to thirty-five thought they were fat, although only 25 percent were medically overweight. Even 45 percent of the *underweight* women believed they were fat. Weight was virtually an obsession for many of the *Glamour* respondents, who chose "losing 10–15 pounds" as their most cherished goal in life.[12] Another study in Boston found that fifth-, sixth-, and ninth-graders were much more critical of their body shape after looking at fashion advertising.[13]

Although the glorification of slenderness is sometimes defended in the interests of health, for most women it is anything but healthy. Almost 40 percent of women who smoke say they do so to maintain their weight; one-quarter of those will die of a disease caused by smoking.[14] In one scientific study, researchers found that women's magazines contained ten times as many advertisements and articles promoting weight loss as men's magazines–corresponding exactly to the ratio of eating disorders in women versus men.[15] And recent studies have suggested that it may sometimes be healthier to be overweight than to repeatedly gain and lose weight through "yo-yo dieting."

Surrounded by ads that depict the Iron Maiden as a stick figure, few women can eat in peace. On any given day, 25 percent of American women are dieting, and another 50 percent are finishing, breaking, or starting diets.[16] The *Glamour* survey found that 50 percent of respondents used diet pills, 27 percent used liquid formula diets, 18 percent used diuretics, 45 percent fasted, 18 percent used laxatives, and 15 percent engaged in self-induced vomiting.[17] While women have purged and starved themselves, the diet industry has grown fat.

The cycle of self-loathing and dieting begins early. In a survey of 494 middle-class San Francisco schoolgirls, more than half thought they were fat, yet only 15 percent were medically overweight. And preadolescent dieting has increased "exponentially" in recent years, according to Vivian Meehan, president of the National Association of Anorexia Nervosa and Associated Disorders.[18]

The Iron Maiden may be a stick figure, but she is often endowed with a pair of gravity-defying breasts. The laws of physics dictate that large breasts eventually droop downward, but the breasts depicted in ads are typically high, firm, and round—a shape that is only attainable by very young or surgically altered women. This, too, takes its toll on women's self-esteem. In 1973, *Psychology Today* reported that one quarter of American women were unhappy with the size or shape of their breasts. By 1986, a simi-

"Slim" cigarettes trade on tobacco's reputation as an appetite suppressant. Almost 40 percent of women who smoke say they do so to maintain their weight; one-quarter of those will die of disease caused by smoking.

lar study found that number had risen to one-third.[19] Tragically, millions of women sacrifice their health—and even their lives—to conform to the shape of the Iron Maiden. Roughly 80 percent of the 150,000 women who have breast-implant surgery each year do so for cosmetic reasons, most often to enlarge their breasts.[20] Recent revelations, which came to light despite suppression by implant-maker Dow Corning, suggest that silicone implants may cause immune-system disorders and death. In response, the Food and Drug Administration has sharply limited implants.

"You've Got to Be Young and Beautiful if You Want to Be Loved"

The Iron Maiden is not shaped like most women. Moreover, she never ages; she is merely replaced with a newer, younger model. Why? A recent TV commercial for Nike and Foot Locker puts it succinctly: "You've got to be young and beautiful if you want to be loved."

Although *Adweek's Marketing Week* reports an increased demand for "older" models (defined by the advertising industry as women in their late twenties), most professional models are considered over the hill by the time they're twenty-four.[21]

If older women manage to make it

into ads at all, visible signs of age are retouched out of their photographs. Naomi Wolf invites us to imagine a parallel—say, if all photographs of blacks in advertising were routinely lightened. "That would be making the same value judgment about blackness that this tampering makes about the value of female life: that less is more," she writes.[22]

Innumerable ads reinforce—and prey on—women's fear of aging. For example, Jean Kilbourne cites an ad headlined "My husband is seeing a younger woman these days…Me!" Kilbourne notes that "the ad wouldn't work if there wasn't the fear that, if she didn't use the product, he would in fact replace her with a younger woman."[23]

Seeking to forestall the inevitable, women spend an estimated $20 billion worldwide each year on skin-care products that promise to eliminate wrinkles and retard aging. Yet even some marketers of these products privately admit that they are worthless. Buddy Wedderburn, a biochemist for Unilever, confessed that "the effect of rubbing collagen onto the skin is negligible.…I don't know of anything that gets into these areas—certainly nothing that will stop wrinkles."[24] In his exposé, *The Skin Game: The International Beauty Business Brutally Exposed,* Gerald McKnight called the skin-care industry "a massive con…a sweetly disguised form of commercial robbery."[25]

Fear of aging also fuels the booming cosmetic-surgery business. Despite the expense and danger, thousands of women submit to the knife in order to preserve the appearance of youth. Although it may be derided as narcissistic, the choice to undergo surgery may seem to be a rational one in a culture where advertisers and media "disappear" older women—with a retoucher's brush or simple exclusion.

Little Miss Makeup

Girls and teenagers are perhaps most vulnerable to beauty-industry propaganda. For them, advertising is a window into adult life, a lesson in what it means to be a woman. And lacking the sophistication of their older sisters and mothers, girls are less likely to distinguish between fact and advertising fiction.

Marketers increasingly target the lucrative teen and preadolescent market with ads for beauty products. And they are having an effect: Female teens spend an average of $506 per year on cosmetics and beauty salon visits. Most wear makeup by the time they are thirteen, and 26 percent wear perfume every day.[26] Ever-younger girls are being fitted for miniature Iron Maidens: Christian Dior makes bras and panties with lace and ruffles for *preschoolers.*[27] One toymaker produces a Little Miss Makeup doll, which looks like a five- or six-year-old girl. When water is applied, the doll sprouts eyebrows, colored eyelids, fingernails, tinted lips, and a heart-shaped beauty mark.[28]

Sexualized images of little girls may have dangerous implications in a world where 450,000 American children were reported as victims of sexual abuse in 1993.[29] It also robs girls of their brief freedom from the constraints of the beauty imperative; they have little chance to develop a sense of bodily self-worth and integrity before beginning to compare themselves to the airbrushed young beauties in *Seventeen.*

If little girls are presented as sex objects, grown women are depicted as children. A classic example is an ad that ran in the 1970s for Love's Baby Soft cosmetics. The ad featured a grown woman in a little-

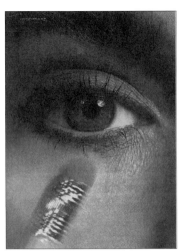

Avon promises to erase the signs of aging from women's faces.

Implying that success is proportional to breast size, a cosmetic surgeon beseeches women to "Reshape Your Future Through Breast Enhancement Surgery."

RESHAPE YOUR FUTURE
Through Breast Enhancement Surgery

*B*reast augmentation surgery can give you larger, more firm, uplifted breasts, reshaping you for a more pleasing appearance. To arrange a free confidential consultation with a board certified surgeon call;

Roger W. Anderson, M.D.
COSMETIC SURGERY

Washington (202) 775-5873 • Rockville (301) 770-6627 or
1 800 THE NEW U.
(1 800 843 6398)

THE STRONG SILENT TYPE: MEN IN ADS

We have focused here on the portrayal of women in advertising because the barrage of demeaning, sexist images of women causes so much harm. But men, too, are hurt by sexist ads. **C**learly, advertisers have learned from women that fomenting insecurity through unattainable media images is good for business. The masculine ideal, as perpetrated by advertising, is not quite as rigid as the Iron Maiden, but it calls on men to exude an aura of physical strength, power, dominance, and detachment. Such men never crack a smile, indeed they practically scowl at us from the magazine page or television screen. In an ad for Brut cologne, for example, an angry-looking muscular boxer wraps his hand with gauze; "Men Are Back" reads the headline. Men in such ads have no need to ingratiate themselves with a hint of sensitivity—or even a pleasant expression; they are perfectly self-sufficient. Many exist in a female-free masculine paradise, like the Marlboro Man. If a man is shown with a woman, he appears to be merely tolerating her presence while she clings desperately or prostrates herself before him. **O**f course, men do deviate from this ideal in ads, but the deviants are often presented for purposes of mockery. Husbands are the butt of much ribbing in ads; the surest way to be demoted from macho sex god to buffoon is to get married. Media critic Jean Kilbourne notes that although "single men are generally presented as independent and powerful, married men are often presented as idiots."[1] **T**he one-dimensional portrayal of masculinity in ads exacts a personal cost. Kilbourne observes that it is as though the full range of human characteristics had been divided arbitrarily into "masculine" and "feminine"—and the feminine half substantially devalued. Women are taught to repress their "masculine" traits (such as self-determination and aggression) and men are taught to repress, and loathe, their "feminine" traits (such as vulnerability and compassion). In this way, ads help prevent both men and women from realizing their potential as full, complex human beings capable of independence *and* vulnerability, aggression *and* compassion. **A**dvertisers also impose a physical ideal on men. Though much less prominent than Iron Maiden imagery, ads for cologne, deodorant, beer, and other masculine products feature muscular models with flawlessly sculpted bodies, square jaws, and full heads of hair. Just as media-induced self-consciousness among women leads to serious health problems, men are suffering from eating disorders (about 10 percent of the number of women)[2] and resorting to cosmetic surgery to build up pectoral, buttock, and calf muscles; reduce nipple size; and reshape their ears.[3] The use of muscle-building steroids is also on the rise among young men.[4]

Men Are Back—and boy are they mad! The male ideal, according to advertising, is brawn and brutishness.

girl dress, licking a lollipop and hiking up her short skirt next to phallic-shaped bottles of Love's Baby Soft. The tag line read, "Because innocence is sexier than you think." And an ad for Cutex lipstick shows a cartoon of a woman's bright red lips with a pacifier stuck in them, and the caption "lipstick that makes your lips baby soft." Such ads, says Kilbourne, "send out a powerful sexual message at the same time they deny it, which is exactly what the ads are telling women to do. The real message is 'don't be a mature sexual being, stay like a little girl'—passive, powerless, and dependent."[30]

Women's Magazines and the Iron Maiden

Advertising's images of the Iron Maiden are everywhere, but women's magazines deserve a special mention for promoting their commercialized beauty ideal. These magazines, so widely read that they are nicknamed "cash cows" in the publishing trade, have a nearly symbiotic relationship with advertisers. Gloria Steinem, describing *Ms.* magazine's largely unsuccessful attempts to attract ad revenue (before that magazine went ad-free), explains that advertisers for women's products demand "supportive editorial atmosphere," that is, "clothing advertisers expect to be surrounded by fashion spreads (especially ones that credit their designers); and shampoo, fragrance, and beauty products in general usually insist on positive editorial coverage of beauty subjects."

Advertisers influence the content of virtually all media, but their stranglehold over women's magazines is especially unyielding. Steinem notes, "If *Time* and *Newsweek* had to lavish praise on cars in

Above: a toddler strikes a seductive pose. Below: Cutex encourages women to remain childlike.

general and credit GM in particular to get GM ads, there would be a scandal—maybe even a criminal investigation. When women's magazines from *Seventeen* to *Lear's* praise beauty products in general and credit Revlon in particular to get ads, it's just business as usual."[31]

Women's magazines are the manifestos of Iron Maidenhood, typically running "objective" editorial copy that touts the products advertised in their pages. These ads too narrowly define the acceptable contours of female shape and appearance. And although women's magazines increasingly publish articles on explicitly feminist themes, their ties to advertisers prevent them from challenging the sacred Iron Maiden. For example, Steinem tells of the time *Ms.* published an exclusive cover story about Soviet women exiled for publishing underground feminist books. This journalistic coup won *Ms.* a Front Page Award but lost it an advertising account with Revlon. "Why?" asks Steinem, "Because the Soviet women on our cover [were] *not wearing makeup*."[32]

The Kitchen and the Bedroom: Limited Views of Women

Clearly, ads present unrealistic images of women's faces and bodies. Just as insidiously, they present highly circumscribed views of women's lives. One study of magazine ads from 1960 to 1979—a time when women entered the workforce in unprecedented numbers—found that ads failed to depict a significant increase in women's employment outside the home. The study also noted that women in ads were apt to be portrayed in traditional female roles: cooking, cleaning, caring for children.[33] And a more recent survey of

Canadian broadcast ads concluded that men were far more likely than women to be presented as experts or authorities.[34]

A quarter-century after the rebirth of the women's movement, women in ads are still depicted as housewives obsessed with ring-around-the-collar and spots on the dishes. If they do work outside the home, they are presented as supermoms who cook, clean, take care of the kids, then slip into something sexy—all with the help of Brand X. (Some ads parrot the slogans of the women's movement while their content explicitly refutes them. As we explain in Chapter 5, "Co-opting Civic Groups, Culture, Sports," advertising has appropriated the jargon, if not the values, of feminism.)

Some advertisers characterize women as crazed shopping junkies. Below, a woman who owns 82 pairs of shoes confesses "I used to tell my father I needed the money for piano lessons."

WHAT YOU CAN DO

- *Complain about sexist ads and boycott products advertised in an offensive manner. The current rash of sexist ads may stem from a perception that women won't object; according to a senior editor at* Adweek *magazine, "Advertisers were more afraid of offending women… when feminists were more unified and quicker to protest."*[36]

- *Show* Still Killing us Softly *to your friends, family, classmates, or community group. Jean Kilbourne's insightful film about advertising images of women is available on video from Cambridge Documentary Films (a nonprofit group): P.O. Box 385, Cambridge, MA 02139, 617-354-3677.*

- *If you have kids, make sure they are exposed to positive, nonstereotypical images of women and men. Talk with them about the content of ads.*

- *Don't give in to the Iron Maiden. Don't buy rip-off cosmetics or fall for hyped-up diet products. And, tough as it may be in this culture, cultivate an appreciation for your own, absolutely unique, beauty.*

Ads that show working women usually focus on their appearance and sexual availability. An ad for Hennessy cognac depicts an after-hours office scene: While a man talks on the phone, a female co-worker in a low-cut blouse seductively hands him a drink. The Maidenform woman disembarks from an airplane, briefcase in hand; her businesslike raincoat blows open to reveal lingerie. Women's work is trivialized, as in an ad declaring that "Phoebe chose to work, not because she had to, but because it gave her a place to wear her Braeburn sweaters."

To be fair, there have been modest improvements in advertising's portrayal of women since the 1970s. And recently, women have been appointed to high-level positions at some of the nation's leading ad agencies. Although the industry is still heavily dominated by men, the ascension of women to top jobs is prompting some agencies to reevaluate their messages to women.[35]

But ads have a long way to go. Until ads depict women in a realistic way, women will continue to measure themselves against an inhuman ideal. And until they are released from the rigid confines of the Iron Maiden, women will continue to seek commercial remedies for imaginary flaws.

Sex as a Commodity

The naked, apparently lifeless body of a woman is draped over the shoulder of a brawny, muscled man. Two men lie next to each other on a bed, one with his hand inside his pants. A woman kneels on the beach, her breasts bursting out of a loose white shirt, which is all she has on.

PENTHOUSE? *PLAYGIRL? HUSTLER?* Nope, guess again. These images are from ads for Obsession perfume, Calvin Klein sportswear, and Express jeans, respectively. And they all appeared in mainstream, mass-circulation magazines and family newspapers.

Sexual images have been a staple of advertising since the very birth of the industry. Women's faces and bodies adorned Coca-Cola calendars back in the 1890s and have been employed to sell virtually everything since. But in recent decades, sexual imagery in advertising has become more common, more explicit, more exploitative, and more violent. According to the *New York Times,* "Sexual themes... are being used as never before to cut through the commercial clutter and grab the consumer's attention."[37] A publicist for Bugle Boy clothes puts it less prosaically. Blaming the recession for his company's use of scantily clad female models, he confesses that "in an extremely competitive environment, you kind of go back to T & A."[38]

Many ads tread close to the pornographic border. For instance, an ad for Calvin Klein's Obsession shows a naked man and woman on a swing, pressed against each other. An ad for Candies shoes features a naked man in a chair with a naked woman sitting astride him (some tamer versions of the same ad had shorts painted on him, but the woman is always presumed unclothed). A Wilke-Rodriguez clothing ad features an obvious simulation of intercourse—on a city rooftop, a woman in nothing but high heels straddles a man in jeans.

Of course, sexually explicit imagery is proliferating elsewhere in popular culture as well. Television, movies, and music videos now routinely air images that would

This Express Jeans ad, which once would have been relegated to the pages of *Penthouse,* was a *New York Times Magazine* fold-out front cover.

have been taboo just ten years ago. Advertisers take advantage of, and contribute to, that trend and push the envelope of titillation to attract the attention of potential customers.

Pornography itself has grown to be a $7 billion industry worldwide.[39] As porn has become more pervasive, mainstream culture and advertising have increasingly adopted its visual conventions and messages. Many of the sexual tableaux we are bombarded with daily are not of intimate, consensual sex, which one might term erotica. Rather, they present bodies, or body parts, with the cool estrangement of commodities. Or they depict sex that is brutal and violent. Both of these qualities—objectification and violence—are common in pornography. The issue, then, is not just that we are inundated with sexual images but the *kind* of sexual images we are inundated with.

Objects of Desire

Perhaps the most commonplace sexually exploitative ads are those that display women's (and, increasingly, men's) bodies to sell products. These ads are *everywhere.* The corner store is plastered with posters of busty models in wet t-shirts, hawking Budweiser. On a billboard that hovers over a busy intersection, a young woman in a clingy bathing suit arches her back in apparent sexual ecstasy beside an enlarged bottle of Wild Irish Rose. In an ad for Bugle Boy clothes, the camera moves in on the pelvis of a model in panties, pans out to show barely clothed beauties at the beach, and so on, ad nauseam.

The use of women's bodies in ads is essentially a cheap trick that marketers use instead of making more thoughtful arguments on behalf of their products.

Gratuitous sexual imagery is increasingly common in ads. These ads for Calvin Klein's Obsession perfume (right) and Wilke-Rodriguez (below) are essentially soft-core pornography.

blonds in string bikinis. At the Stroh's plant in St. Paul, Minnesota, where Bikini Team posters and porno-graphic materials lined the walls, women employees claimed to be sub-jected to obscene and sexist comments, slaps on the buttocks, and male coworkers fol-lowing them home.[40]

Many ads of this genre take the dehu-manization of women a step farther by focusing on body *parts*—another convention of pornography. A pair of shape-ly female legs emerges from a box of ce-real. A woman's torso is juxtaposed against a photo of a sportscar; we are invited to admire the curves of both. Three women walk along a sunny beach, umbrellas ob-scuring all but their bikini-clad backsides. Women in these ads are not even whole objects; they have been reduced to an as-semblage of dismembered parts.

The mechanism used in these ads is quite simple: Attractive bodies are employed to grab attention and stimulate desire, which advertisers hope will then be transferred to the product. Buy the beer, get the girl. In this way, women's bodies are equated with commodities, pre-sented as the rewards of consumption.

By instructing men to regard women's bodies as objects, ads help create an at-mosphere that devalues women as people, encourages sexual harassment, and worse.

Below: Ads that separate a woman's limbs from her body reinforce the notion that she is not a whole person, but an ensemble of erotic parts.

For example, in 1991, four women employees of Stroh's Brewery sued their employer, charg-ing that the company's sexist ads gave the com-pany's imprimatur to sexist attitudes and sex-ual harassment in the workplace. Especially targeted in the lawsuit was an ad campaign for Old Milwaukee beer (made by Stroh's) that featured the Swedish Bikini Team, a bunch of buxom, bewigged

Such ads degrade women, and men are diminished by them as well. For one thing, exploitative ads insult men's intel-ligence. One Canadian advertiser, defending a campaign for Molson beer that featured women's body parts, reveals this contempt: "I am playing upon the less positive attributes of females," he said, "but I have to put my personal feelings aside when I'm address-ing the great unwashed. To them, the most attractive qualities about a woman are her measurements."[41]

Men's bodies, too, are no longer immune from exploitation in advertising. Recent years have seen a veritable deluge of beefcake photos in ads glorifying men's muscled torsos, backs, and thighs. Often aimed at women, who make the majority of consumer purchases, these ads are the

mirror image of "t & a." Typical of the genre is an ad for Cool Water cologne, which features the torso of a water-sprayed nude male basking in the sun. A Calvin Klein ad supplement to *Vanity Fair* contained no less than twenty-seven bare-chested and two bare-bottomed men, two bare-bottomed and four topless women. In a 1994 Hyundai television commercial, two women coyly estimate men's physical endowment, based on the car they drive. While assuming that men in fancy cars are lacking elsewhere, the women are clearly impressed by the Hyundai driver: "Wonder what he's got under the hood."

"Women are recognizing that they like men's bodies," Judith Langer, head of a market research firm, told the *New York Times.* "It used to be that men offered power and women offered beauty. Now men have to be on their toes and in shape. They can't allow themselves to go to pot."[42] Not surprisingly, many men feel uneasy about being held to the standard presented in the ads—as women

Women's bodies are used to sell everything. These ads depict women in apparent sexual ecstasy over a beeper (top); an exhaust system (right); and book club membership (above).

have been for generations. Women's unclothed bodies have proliferated in ads and other media, but male nudity has historically remained off-limits. Interestingly, much outcry about sex in advertising has accompanied the crossing of this sacred line. For example, a *New*

York Times article entitled "Has Madison Avenue Gone Too Far?" cites ten examples of sexually suggestive ads, *all* of which featured male models.[43] Exhibiting a similar double standard, *Sports Illustrated* editors refused to run a 1993 Adidas ad that featured a Canadian soccer team of naked men squatting and covering their genitalia with soccer balls, trophies, and their hands.[44] *Sports Illustrated* is far less prudish when it comes to the annual swimsuit issue, which flaunts nubile women in tiny bikinis. Ubiquitous images of women's bodies seem somehow natural in a culture that sanctions the objectification of women; subjecting male anatomy to the same cold, critical gaze is going "too far."

Advertising Violence Against Women

In 1977, when *Vogue* published Chris Von Wangenheim's now infamous fashion spread of Doberman pinschers attacking a model, many viewers were appalled. Today, Von Wangenheim's imagery seems almost restrained. In an ad for Newport cigarettes, a pair of men tackle two screaming women, pulling one by the hair. Another Newport ad shows a man forcing a woman's head

Ads frequently make light of, if not actually celebrate, violence against women. Top left: Georges Marciano Jeans by Guess recreates the aftermath of rape. Top right: Parfum d'Hermes shows a bound woman who is clearly enjoying her strangulation. Right: Three fraternity boys point mock guns at an apparently dead woman in an ad for Gotcha clothing.

down to get her mouth around a spurting garden hose. In an ad for Gotcha sportswear, an attractive young murder victim dangles from a couch. The red design on her shirt resembles a stylized gunshot wound; her legs are splayed apart. A young model in an ad for Georges Marciano clothes cradles her head and cries; her tousled hair and disheveled clothes suggest sexual struggle. A man sitting next to her looks away impassively. An Old Spice cologne ad shows a man leaning over a woman who is playfully pushing him away; the huge headline says "No," but she is smiling. The message: Don't take No for an answer; she probably doesn't mean it.

Violence against women in ads raises

sweat. Go all out. We'll keep up. New Old Spice Anti-Perspirant helps stop the sweat that causes odor. The proof? You're looking at her. For great odor protection, now you've got **proof** not promises

"No" clearly means "Yes" in an ad for Old Spice deodorant.

most among them—argue that sexually violent images are *in themselves* harmful to women, regardless of whether they incite "real" violence.

Again, we are stuck with the chicken-and-egg question of whether ads cause harmful social effects or simply mirror them. In either case, advertising fuels the perception that women are *things,* to be used or abused as men see fit. "Turning a human being into a thing is almost always the first step in justifying violence against that person," says Jean Kilbourne.[45]

In complaining about sex in ads, one risks being accused of puritanism. Can we object to the use of sex in ads without sounding like Jesse Helms or Anita Bryant? Doesn't the proliferation of sexual imagery simply reflect the loosening of repressive sexual mores that were rooted—let's not forget—in sexist, patriarchal ideology?

The problem is that repression has been replaced by exploitation. Sex in ads is inherently exploitative; it seeks to arouse us in order to sell us things, to press our sexuality into the service of the consumer culture. The rigid gender roles of the 1950s denied men and women their full range of sexual and human possibilities, but so does the commodified sex depicted in advertising. Ads that depict women and men as sexual objects to be bought, admired, and consumed (or brutalized) offer a bleak, limited view of sexuality

many of the same questions—and sparks the same debate—as violent pornography. Some analysts discern a link between eroticized images of violence against women and the escalating incidence of real-life rape and abuse. Others claim that such images actually defuse men's aggression toward women or that these images *reflect* the broader oppression of women but don't *cause* it. Still others— legal scholar Catherine MacKinnon fore-

WHAT YOU CAN DO

- *Complaints to offending advertisers—especially when backed up with boycotts—can be a powerful weapon against exploitative ads.*

- *Write letters to publications or TV stations that print or broadcast offensive ads.*

- *Contact groups fighting ads offensive to women:*

  MEDIA WATCH
  P.O. BOX 618
  SANTA CRUZ, CA 95061
  408-423-6355

  CHALLENGING
  MEDIA IMAGES OF WOMEN
  P.O. BOX 902
  FRAMINGHAM, MA 01701
  508-879-8504
  OR 617-327-1093

CHAPTER FIVE

Co-opting Civic Groups, Culture, Sports

The mass media are saturated with advertising, so businesses seek out new ways to deliver their messages to consumers. Some burnish their corporate images by donating small percentages of their sales or profits to nonprofit partners. Businesses portray that as a win–win situation, but, in fact, the consumer often loses, especially if the marketer pushes a product (such as tobacco or dangerous chemicals) that endangers consumers' health or the environment. In this chapter we explore the benefits and risks of this novel means of marketing. ✱ Other companies shift money from media advertising to public relations and sponsorship of art exhibits, dinners at civil-rights organizations' conferences, or rock concerts. The sponsorship money is always a welcome benefit to the recipient, but problems arise when marketers improve the image of dangerous products, influence the content of exhibits, or dictate the agendas of civic organizations. ✱Sports are perhaps the most thoroughly commercialized sector of our culture. Companies pour billions of dollars into sponsorship of sports events, basking in the glamor and power of athletics. Broadcasts, stadiums, race cars, even athletes' bodies are decorated with corporate logos. Even nonprofessional sports, from high school leagues to the Olympics, are now being turned into advertising vehicles.

Selling with Social Issues

Environmentalism is used to sell cars and nuclear power plants. Feminist slogans are employed to hawk cigarettes and jogging shoes. Bleak images of war, disaster, and human suffering appear in magazine ads for sportswear. Even the counter-cultural rejection of consumerism is invoked as a sales pitch. What gives?

MARKETERS HAVE DISCOV-ered that social issues sell. So in recent years, many have sought to do well by doing good—or at least by *appearing* to do good. Some companies, notably Ben & Jerry's, the Body Shop, and Patagonia, have built their corporate identities on earnest attempts to be socially responsible. "Cause-related marketing," whereby companies donate a portion of their income to nonprofit groups and publicize the gesture, is an increasingly popular way to boost profits while generating funds for worthwhile causes. However, some companies compensate for bad behavior—such as selling unhealthful products or wreaking environmental havoc—with conspicuous good works. Or they may simply appropriate the language or imagery of social-change movements such as environmentalism or feminism. As we'll see, many marketers who sell with social issues are more concerned about public relations than about the public interest.

Absolut Vodka commissioned a series of works by artists from every state for its "Absolut Artists Against AIDS" campaign. Each work, featured in weekly full-page ads in *USA Today*, included a plug for Absolut Vodka. Absolut then sold copies of the self-promotional lithographs and gave the proceeds to an anti-AIDS organization.

Green Marketing

The photo shows a pristine mountain lake surrounded by snow-covered peaks. "Earth Day 1990," reads the caption, "General Motors Marks 20 Years of Environmental Progress."

General Motors? Environmental progress? You may wonder if this is the *same* General Motors that spent decades lobbying vigorously against clean-air laws and fuel-economy standards. Indeed it is. These days, even the most wolfish polluters are donning the sheep's clothing of environmentalism, seeking to cash in on public concern about the fate of the planet. But GM's Earth Day ad was so hypocritical it even drew the wrath of an advertising-industry publication. "Talk about nerve. Talk about shamelessness. Talk about chutzpah," wrote Bob Garfield in *Advertising Age,* "This is like [Texas child-killer] John Wayne Gacy celebrating the International Year of the Child."[1]

GM is one of dozens of corporations to adopt "green" marketing themes in recent years. In the late 1980s, after scientists found alarming evidence of global climate change and holes in the ozone layer, pollsters measured a sharp increase in public concern about the environment. One study showed that consumers were willing to spend as much as ten cents more on the dollar for environmentally benign products.[2] Marketers, seeking to increase profits or score public relations victories, quickly jumped into the fray. In the first half of 1991, nearly 13 percent of all new products made some sort of environmental claim.[3] *Advertising Age* heralded green marketing as "the marketing tool of the '90s—at least until the next hot button starts glowing."[4]

TODAY'S SCHOLARS. TOMORROW'S LEADERS.

These students represent the first graduating class of the Thurgood Marshall Scholarship Fund. Dedicated young men and women who earned their scholarships through outstanding academic achievement and commitment to excellence.

The Thurgood Marshall Scholarship Fund was created to help young scholars earn a college degree and fulfill their highest potential. A national *merit*-based program, it is the only one that awards four-year scholarships to students attending historically black public colleges and universities.

The results have been exceptional. These scholars have an outstanding four-year academic average of 3.3 or better. In fact, more than 65% of them plan to go on to graduate school.

The Miller Brewing Company is proud to congratulate these very distinguished graduates. Supporting the best and the brightest students today means supporting the leaders of tomorrow.

Give to the Thurgood Marshall Scholarship Fund.

THE THURGOOD MARSHALL SCHOLARSHIP FUND.
PUT A YOUTH IN A SEAT OF POWER.

For fundraising program information, call 612-855-7838. Write or send donations to: Thurgood Marshall Scholarship Fund, Processing Center, P.O. Box 59982, Washington, D.C. 20036

Miller Brewing Company reportedly spent twice as much publicizing its support of the Thurgood Marshall Scholarship Fund as it spent on the original donation.

The new eco-consciousness could spur a genuine greening of corporate America if companies honestly addressed concerns about excess packaging, harmful chemicals, and threats to wildlife. There have been measurable improvements: dolphin-safe tuna, for example, and recycled paper packaging. A few pioneering companies are turning conscionable profits by selling energy-efficient light bulbs or nontoxic household cleaners. But far more often, corporations make exaggerated claims about the environmental benefits of their products or simply co-opt the rhetoric and images of the conservation movement.

For example, in 1989 Mobil Chemical Company began marketing "degradable" Hefty garbage bags.

Advertisements and packaging claimed that when exposed to sunlight, the bags would break down into harmless substances. Mobil's lie was one of omission: The ads neglected to mention that garbage in a typical landfill receives almost no light, so the bags never decompose. This disingenuous ad campaign was retracted after it drew lawsuits in seven states.

Similarly, Procter and Gamble ran an ad showing a pile of rich soil under the headline "Ninety days ago, this was a disposable diaper." Then New York City consumer affairs commissioner Mark Green attacked the ad, pointing out that only 80 percent of a disposable diaper could be composted. The remainder is made of plastic, which persists in the environment for all eternity. And because so few municipal composting facilities exist, virtually all disposable diapers get dumped in landfills, where they contribute to the solid waste problem. P&G relented and withdrew the ads.

Even proponents of nuclear power are masquerading as environmentalists. The U.S. Council for Energy Awareness—a nuclear-industry front group—has taken out a series of magazine ads boasting that nuclear power plants "are good for the atmosphere" because they emit few airborne pollutants. "More plants are needed," one ad concludes, "to help satisfy the nation's growing need for electricity without sacrificing the quality of our environment." Of course, nuclear plants *do* produce tons of deadly radioactive waste, but the industry apparently does not think that constitutes a threat to the environment.

A commercial for DuPont Chemical features sea lions clapping, ducks flapping, and dolphins jumping—all in apparent celebration of

Stop squeaks, prevent rust, and preserve National Parks.

DuPont's investment in double-hulled oil tankers. The use of such tankers is certainly a worthwhile step, but the aquatic creatures pictured in the ad might hold their applause if they knew the facts. The environmental group Greenpeace points out that DuPont's new tankers were not yet in the water when the commercial ran and that its entire fleet will not be double-hulled until the year 2000.[5] Moreover, the feel-good commercial masks a grim environmental record. DuPont invented ozone-destroying CFCs (chlorofluorocarbons), and some contend that the company dragged its feet about dis-

National Parks." The connection between a household lubricant and the wilderness is tenuous, at best. And the amount of WD-40's contribution to the park system—$50,000—is probably less than the cost of the magazine ad.

The profusion of green ads has produced a backlash of scrutiny and mistrust. One recent study, cited in *Advertising Age,* showed that only 7 percent of Americans believe corporations are taking appropriate steps to save the environment. Another suggests that 47 percent of consumers dismiss environmental claims as gimmickry.[7]

Philip Morris advertises its support of the STRIVE job-placement program for the disadvantaged, many of whom are harmed by the beer and cigarettes that Philip Morris promotes in their communities.

continuing CFC production. DuPont is also one of the world's largest producers of hazardous waste and aggressively promoted the use of leaded gasoline.[6]

If a corporation can't think of anything to say in its own defense, it may simply sidle up to environmental groups with gifts of cash. But those acts of corporate benevolence are usually transparent public-relations ploys. For example, WD-40 ran an ad urging consumers to "stop squeaks, prevent rust, and preserve

In the early 1990s, consumer groups and state attorneys general joined forces to seek regulation of green claims. Some states, notably California, set stringent rules on the use of environmental terms in advertising and labeling. Hoping to head off the passage of numerous tough and possibly contradictory state laws, corporations and trade associations pressed the Federal Trade Commission to develop a set of national guidelines. In 1992, the FTC released its guidelines, which pro-

Appropriately, NutraSweet's "Equal" sugar substitute sponsors the American Diabetes Association's Walktoberfest—a fundraising event for those who must watch their sugar intake.

Green ads by car companies obscure the true environmental costs of automobiles—and the companies' efforts to fight increased fuel efficiency and emissions standards.

hibit unsubstantiated claims and establish rules for the use of terms like "recyclable" and "biodegradable."

Perhaps as a result of state and federal regulations, many marketers are backing away from overt environmental claims. Ron Smithies, director of the National Advertising Division of the Council of Better Business Bureaus, told *Advertising Age* that green claims are an "endangered species" because advertisers are unwilling to take the heat from consumer groups and government. But don't assume they're gone for good: "What I'm hearing [from advertisers]," says Smithies, "is 'We'll come back to it when things have cooled down a bit.'" [8]

Marketers may be temporarily refraining from making explicit environmental claims about their products, but they still conjure up the green spirit to sell goods. By borrowing the language and imagery of environmentalism, they trivialize and subvert its messages. Take, for example, this 1991 TV ad for the Toyota Tercel: A smiling, earnest-looking young woman separates her cans and bottles, then ties her newspapers in bunches. "Everything's changing," she says as she piles the recyclables into the trunk of her car. "Wasting is out. Saving, conserving, all that stuff is in. . . . It's simple. New values, new car."

The Toyota ad deftly translates environmental messages into the language of commodities, but their meaning gets lost in the translation. "Wasting is

out," we are told, gone to the great landfill of defunct fads. In its place, saving and conserving are in. But to be in, we must buy a new Toyota. The Toyota ad, like virtually every other advertisement, implicitly encourages waste by promoting premature obsolescence (your old car is out-of-date because it doesn't represent the "new values") and imploring us to consume more.

To use the rhetoric of the environmental movement to sell consumer goods is ironic enough, but to employ it to sell automobiles is a monumental act of bad faith. Auto emissions cause tree-killing acid rain and lung-damaging ozone smog. Cars also produce 20 percent of atmospheric carbon dioxide, which has been implicated in global climate change.[9] But in the world according to Toyota, driving a car has become an act of environmental heroism.

Some companies transmit environmentally responsible messages, but their very nature of business tends to counter their own advertisements. For instance, in a simple, earthy-looking 1990 ad for Esprit clothing, the text declares: "By changing the things that make us happy and buying less stuff, we can reduce the horrendous impact we have been placing on the environment. We can buy for vital needs, not frivolous, ego-gratifying needs. We do need clothes, yes, but *so many?*"

The company's retail outlets, however, are filled with an endlessly changing array of clothing that is, for many, in the "frivolous, ego-gratifying" department. The fashion industry, of which Esprit is undeniably a part, changes styles frequently in order to render our wardrobes passé and stimulate more sales. If we truly bought clothing that met only our vital needs, Esprit and a lot of other clothiers would go out of business. There is an obvious contradiction here. On one hand, Esprit delivers a stern lecture about overconsumption; on the other, it shows us beautiful goods designed to arouse our material desires. In effect, by aligning itself with "responsible consumption" Esprit assuages our eco-guilt and gives us *permission* to consume—but only if we buy its products.

One Percent for Peace, 99 Percent for Profit

For the consumer, cause-related marketing is a simple, painless way to ease the conscience.
—Mava Heffler, former director of sales promotion, Johnson and Johnson[10]

Is Sprint doing this to get your business? What difference does it make? We're doing it.
—Candace Bergen, Sprint spokesperson, on a TV commercial for the company's campaign to donate profits to environmental groups[11]

Many companies find that donating a portion of their sales to charity more than pays for itself in publicity, goodwill, and, ultimately, profits. This marketing strategy is particularly effective in reaching the grown-up children of the 1960s. "Research shows that as baby boomers move into affluence, you can appeal to them much more through their sense of social responsibility," explains Craig Smith, editor of *Corporate Philanthropy Report.*[12]

"Cause-related marketing," as the strategy is called, was pioneered over a decade ago by American Express. In a high-profile 1983 ad campaign, the charge-card company offered to give a percentage of its profits for three months to the Statue of Liberty Restoration Fund. In response, AmEx cardholders increased card use by 28 percent while new card applications rose by 17 percent. Although the campaign raised $1.7 mil-

Stolichnaya Vodka bought a full-page ad in the *New York Times* to announce that the following week it would donate the cost of an ad to an organization fighting AIDS.

lion for statue restoration, American Express spent *$6 million* to advertise it.[13]

Since then, corporations have clamored to exploit the public's concern for social issues. Although some corporate philanthropy (especially that dispensed by foundations) is motivated by genuine goodwill, charitable giving is increasingly driven by marketing considerations. For instance, when Revlon wanted to push its Creme of Nature hair-care products among African Americans, the company promised to make a contribution to the United Negro College Fund for every item sold.[14]

Often, companies use their marketing-based philanthropy as a diversionary tactic. During the 1990 Persian Gulf crisis, Amoco was worried about consumer backlash to rising oil prices, so it recruited thousands of local dealers to participate in the "Pump-a-Penny" promotion with Children's Miracle Network. For every gallon of gas pumped, Amoco would donate a penny to a local children's hospital.[15]

Sure, some people know perfectly well that high-profile charity is merely a cynical sales ploy, but they would rather that a portion of their money go to a good cause than none at all. However, consumers may win a false sense of having done good, when in fact a direct donation to a charity or nonprofit would have done much more. Moreover, companies are cutting back on no-strings-attached charitable contributions because cause-related campaigns can be so much more lucrative. And in some cases, the non-profits that accept corporate contributions are in effect abusing the sympathy their name evokes in order to turn a profit. In the meantime, people buy products they may not need, driven by what newspaper columnist Colman McCarthy calls "commercial correctness." "With causes on sale," McCarthy writes, "people who once felt guilty for buying too much now risk a bad conscience for buying too little."[16]

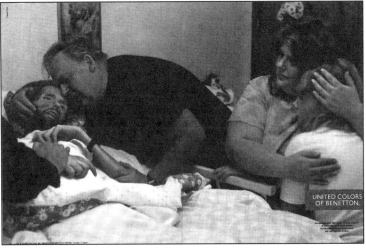

Benetton clothing uses shocking real-life photos to draw attention to its new fashion lines. These ads show a dead Bosnian soldier's bloodied uniform (opposite page) and a family grieving over their son's death from AIDS.

Liberation Through Consumption

Advertising has a long history of appropriating and defusing images of social discontent. Frequently, ads speak directly to our innermost, unarticulated needs, proffering ineffective (or even dangerous) palliatives for real social and personal problems.

Many of these ads are addressed to women, promising liberation with rhetoric borrowed from feminism. Indeed, it seems that each wave of feminist activism is followed by a backwash of feminist-theme ads. Consider this ad, which appeared in the *Chicago Tribune* in 1930, ten years after women won the right to vote: "Today's woman gets what she wants. The vote. Slim sheaths of silk to replace voluminous petticoats. Glass-

ware in sapphire blue or glowing amber. The right to a career. Soap to match her bathroom's color scheme."[17]

Obviously, by equating suffrage and a career with glassware and soap, this ad demeans the goals of the women's movement. The "second wave" of feminism unleashed a host of similar ads, the most notorious of which is Philip Morris's "You've Come a Long Way, Baby" ad campaign for Virginia Slims cigarettes. That ad campaign, which was launched in 1969, celebrates women's "freedom" to smoke (and die from lung cancer) just like men. (See Chapter 7, "Ads That Kill I: Tobacco," for more on the Virginia Slims campaign.) In the same vein, a 1970s TV commercial featured a newly liberated woman brandishing a red box of Stouffer's frozen beef stroganoff, declaring: "To me, freedom comes in a bright red package." Around the same time, Hanes introduced its "latest liberating product"—a new kind of pantyhose, which the company promoted at a fashion show called "From Revolution to Revolution: The Undercover Story."

A 1993 ad spread for Donna Karan clothing, titled "In Women We Trust," exploits feminist hopes by portraying a woman as president of the United States. But instead of emanating power and authority, the woman (who is probably younger than the legal age for the presidency) is provocatively dressed and gazes dreamily into the air. In one scene, the model has her shirt unbuttoned and her brassiere showing as she rides in a presidential motorcade. Her male "aides," on the other hand, are older, graying, and conspicuously busy.

Many ads recount the history of feminism, but again, much is lost in the retelling. For example, a 1988 ad for Reebok shoes presents an antique-looking photograph of women in nineteenth-cen-

tury footwear. "They weren't called suf-
fragettes for nothing," the copy proclaims.
"Look at the shoes they wore. Now your
feet have equal rights. After years of campaigning for shoes that have style *and*
comfort, women have won." It's a joke,
of course. But what is the cumulative effect of many such "jokes"? We learn that
feminism and feminists are a laughing
matter. As Susan Faludi writes in *Backlash:
The Undeclared
War Against Amer-
ican Women,* it
is "as if women's
secondary status
has become no
more than a long-
running inside
joke."[18]

Of course, ads
that poke fun at
feminism reflect
the pervasiveness
of sexism in our
culture. Imagine,
if you will, the
liberation strug-
gles of any other
group being
treated as lightly.
"Today's African-
American gets
what he wants.
Civil rights. Soap
to match his bathroom color scheme." Or
how about a cigarette ad depicting enslaved
blacks comically sneaking a smoke behind
the overseer's back? Unthinkable, right?

This is not to say that the liberation
struggles of African Americans are *not* exploited by advertisers. Far from it. They may
be treated more respectfully, but they are
exploited nonetheless—often to sell products that are downright deadly. For example, R. J. Reynolds Tobacco Company ran
a full-page ad with a montage of images
from black history and a poem by James
Weldon Johnson. Coors Brewing Company sponsors literacy programs in the black
community and takes out ads touting

Coors's commitment to promoting "greater
self-esteem, self-confidence and motiva-
tion" among African Americans. Publications catering to African Americans are
saturated with ads for alcohol and tobacco products. The December 1993 issue of
Ebony, for example, contains fourteen pages
of ads for booze and cigarettes. (For comparison, *Esquire* has more pages but only
ten such ads.) Perhaps due to their depen-
dency on those ad
revenues, many
major black pub-
lications have
been noticeably
quiet about the
health risks posed
by drinking and
smoking.

By aligning
themselves with
African-Ameri-
cans' ongoing
struggle for equal-
ity, alcohol and
tobacco mer-
chants mask the
destruction they
wreak in the
black commun-
ity. According to
the National In-
stitute on Alco-
hol Abuse and
Alcoholism, alcohol abuse is the leading
health and safety problem in black America. Although African Americans consume less alcohol per capita than whites,
poverty and poor health care in the black
community result in disproportionately
high rates of cirrhosis of the liver,
esophageal cancer, and alcohol-related
crime and accidents.[19] Blacks are also one
and a half times more likely to contract
lung cancer than whites.[20]

Alcoholic-beverage and cigarette
companies are also big donors to
African-American (and Latino) organizations. Those companies buy invaluable
goodwill when they donate to black

Ben and Jerry's, known for its support of social causes, seeks to reach Baby Boomers by depicting activist-entertainers eating its new ice cream flavors. The unidentified spokes-activists include Pete Seeger, Michelle Shocked, and Buffy Saint-Marie.

organizations. Often, the amount of support is meager compared to what is spent on the public-relations campaigns that follow the donations. For example, Miller Brewing Company donated $150,000 to the Thurgood Marshall Scholarship Fund, but spent $300,000 advertising its gift.[21] In some cases, companies also buy the silence of minority leaders about the grave health problems associated with their products. (See Chapter 7, "Ads That Kill II: Alcohol.")

Death Is a Salesman

Pollution, injustice, the oppression of women—are there any social problems marketers *won't* exploit?

Apparently not: In the 1990s, the upscale clothier Benetton has run a series of ads using vivid news photos of war, disaster, and even death. Each image is softened by hand coloring, providing a thematic link to the United Colors of Benetton slogan. The ads depict a

bombed car ablaze on a dingy street; refugees clambering aboard a packed ship; an Indian couple wading through waist-deep floodwaters; and a man with a rifle slung over his shoulder, clutching what appears to be a human bone. One particularly controversial ad features a photograph of a young man who had just died of AIDS, cradled by his sobbing father and surrounded by other family members in an evident state of extreme grief. Another shows the bloodied uniform of a Bosnian soldier killed in combat. Both ads triggered a public furor, and the Bosnian ad was attacked by the soldier's father, who said he had not authorized the use of his son's clothes in a commercial advertisement.[22]

Why would any right-thinking sportswear manufacturer associate itself with horrifying images of death and disaster? During the hailstorm of publicity that followed the ads, Benetton's communications director, Peter Fressola, offered an explanation: The ads, he said, were intended to "raise social consciousness."[23] But the company's true motives may be better expressed by Fressola's admission that the ads will promote "brand awareness, name recognition, that sort of thing."[24] The Benetton ads are yet another response to advertising "clutter"—the mind-numbing barrage of ads Americans are bombarded with each day. To break through the clutter, advertisers resort to ever more arresting images. But what images retain the capacity to shock an audience grown inured to sex, immune to violence? Real-life suffering, answers Benetton.

The Benetton ad campaign is, unquestionably, an attention-getter. It garnered plenty of media coverage; the company estimated that between 500 million and 1 billion people saw the AIDS ad—many through news stories about the campaign in newspapers, magazines, and on TV.[25] But the campaign is less successful at raising "social consciousness." Devoid of context, the images are divested of any power besides shock value. Unlike a genuine public service message, the AIDS ad offers no information on how to avoid contracting or transmitting the deadly disease or how to help people with AIDS. The soldier's-uniform ad included no explanation of the complexities involved in the Bosnian war. The refugees, conflicts, and disaster victims are not identified, so our sympathy is aroused but left hanging. We cannot help. We can, however, go shopping. In many of the ads, the only copy is the company slogan, a reminder that "Our spring/summer 1992 edition of Colors magazine is now available at Benetton stores," and a number to call for the store nearest you. Like many other advertisements, the Benetton ads imply that all problems can be solved by buying more *stuff.* Benetton raises disturbing social issues not to stir us into action but to get our attention and align itself with high-minded causes.

Befriending Health and Medical Associations

Corporations are increasingly giving financial contributions to professional associations and fund-raising charities that relate to their area of interest. The organizations receive valuable funding, and the companies hope that the credibility of the groups will rub off on them and their products. While some portray such partnerships as "win-win" situations, the integrity of the professional group may be eroded and the public interest may get lost in the shuffle.

The American Medical Association, for instance, long invested some of its cash reserves in tobacco stocks. Also, the AMA has recieved funding from the liquor industry and Monsanto to produce programs for its weekly cable television show.[26] Monsanto makes chemicals

including rBST, the controversial genetically engineered hormone that increases the production of cow's milk.

The American Dietetic Association (ADA), the professional organization for dietitians, frequently makes public statements on current nutrition policies and controversies. However, by accepting major funding from food companies, the ADA limits its ability to criticize those

companies or their products. Its "industry partners" contributed approximately $2 million in a recent year, including $86,000 from Campbell Soup, $66,000 from Kraft General Foods, and $444,000 from Nestle USA, Inc.[27]

In a particularly questionable example, Genentech, a giant biotechnology firm, provided the nonprofit Human Growth Foundation with more than half its budget. The foundation encourages parents to have their children screened for growth disorders; Genentech markets a drug that stimulates growth. In effect, the foundation was serving as a secret marketing arm of the corporation.[28]

The Damage Done

Is it really so bad for advertisers to make reference to social problems and movements? Doesn't that just reflect the degree to which those ideas have permeated our

American Express gave $5 million to the anti-hunger group "Save Our Strength" but spent more than that advertising its good deed in a series of TV commercials.

national consciousness? And what's wrong with companies sponsoring organizations that are working for social change?

First, as we have seen, advertisers garble the real meaning of social-change messages. When environmentalism is used to sell pollution-spewing cars, feminism is used to sell a life-threatening addiction, and booze is linked to civil rights, reason flies out the window. Public discourse—of which advertising is a part—becomes rife with dangerous nonsense. War is peace, freedom is slavery, ignorance is strength.

When corporations, particularly makers of dangerous products, sponsor social-change groups, they rarely do so out of the goodness of their hearts. At best, they seek to associate their products with positive values such as environmental quality, feminism, or civil rights—hoping to achieve "innocence by association." Often, the association is absurd. At worst, marketers effectively purchase the silence of opinion leaders about the threats posed by their products.

And high-profile displays of benevolence mask the fact that total corporate philanthropy (adjusted for inflation) actually declined by 13 percent between 1987 and 1992. As a percentage of pretax profits, charitable giving hit a ten-year low in 1992—one-third less than

the 2.4 percent of profits in 1986.[29]

Moreover, ads that borrow from the history of social-change movements sever our links with traditions of activism. Earlier activists are often portrayed as unfortunate, unliberated souls defined by the primitive consumer goods they used and wore. Other versions of history are certainly available, but young people are far more likely to see an ad for Virginia Slims than to read a thoughtful history of the suffrage movement. So for most, the Philip Morris version of history prevails. Thus we are robbed of our identification with men and women who fought for various kinds of freedom, and their messages to us are lost.

Finally, advertising subverts real solutions to social problems. Why bother to go to that demonstration for women's rights in Washington when you can achieve liberation simply by smoking or wearing Reeboks? Why write letters to your state legislator about getting a recycling program in your area if you're doing your part for the environment by driving a Toyota? Advertising teaches us that all of life's problems can be solved with a trip to the mall. As long as freedom is perceived as a commodity, we will continue to confuse real personal and political choice with the endless diversions of the consumer culture.

WHAT YOU CAN DO

- *Scrutinize "social issue" ads carefully. Are environmental claims credible? (You might want to check with your state attorney general or an environmental group.) If a portion of sales profits is donated to a nonprofit group, does the ad say what portion? Don't buy something you wouldn't otherwise buy just to donate money to a nonprofit group—it's simpler to give to the group directly. Is the advertiser really a good corporate citizen? Does the ad merely manipulate your social conscience in order to sell you a bill of goods?*

- *If an ad campaign offends you, contact the manufacturer and boycott the product.*

- *If you belong to a community group or social-change organization, beware of corporations bearing gifts. Don't accept gifts from companies whose products are harmful; you will boost their credibility at the cost of your organization's integrity.*

- *Urge civil rights, environmental, and women's groups to become more active in fighting ads that rip off their movements.*

Corporate Culture

From the rarefied realm of the Smithsonian Museum to the dusty hog pens of the Ohio State Fair, marketers are infiltrating every corner of our culture. By underwriting a broad range of activities and events, companies whitewash their images, turn cultural heroes into hucksters, and even dictate the content of artistic expression.

IN THE ARTS, OF COURSE, sponsorship is not a new phenomenon. For millennia, those seeking to win people's hearts and minds have attempted to steer the mythmaking machinery of culture. And patrons have *always* influenced the content of artists' work: Painters under contract to the Medicis did not depict the violent overthrow of the moneyed class, nor did those employed by the Catholic Church glamorize devil worship.

In recent years, however, corporations have taken a giant step beyond patronage. No longer content with the public relations benefits of arts sponsorship, corporations are now using art and artists as overt marketing tools. The result? Ever more of our shared cultural space is devoted to commercial messages.

Corporate sponsorship is hastening the intrusion of marketers into institutions and endeavors that were once ad-free. Fleeing their own numbing cacophony of commercial messages, advertisers seek new ways to be seen and heard in an environment uncluttered by other ads. Corporate sponsorship increasingly provides the answer; a relatively low-cost, high-visibility means of reaching consumers in their most unguarded moments.

Although each instance of sponsorship, taken by itself, may not seem particularly alarming, the

SALVATORE FERRAGAMO

SALVATORE FERRAGAMO

Los Angeles County Museum of Art

Ferragamo sponsored an exhibit of its own shoes at the Los Angeles County Museum of Art.

cumulative effect is nothing less than the corporate takeover of culture. There are fewer places we can go to escape ads, and fewer venues of creative expression that are not beholden to commercial interests. When corporations control the means of expression, there is no refuge from commercialism. Without that refuge, we may well lose the perspective and capacity to distinguish *corporate* interest from the *public* interest and to balance bottom-line concerns against the greater social good.

Art or Advertising?

Nowhere is the corporate co-optation of culture more evident than in the museum world. It must be noted, however, that museums were never grassroots institutions; most were founded by wealthy patrons or private endowments. As Herbert Schiller, professor of communications at the University of California at San Diego has pointed out, "The museum building itself was customarily a tribute to older fortunes, whose owners' names often prominently adorned the masonry." However, he notes, "such tributes were not advertisements for current enterprises."[30]

In the mid-1960s, that began to change. Around that time, the Metropolitan Museum of Art in New York began to seek corporate funding for big, crowd-pleasing temporary exhibits. Those exhibits were advertised on huge banners draped outside the museum, often crediting their corporate benefactors. The idea caught on: From 1967 to 1987, corporate funding for the arts jumped from $22 million to nearly $1 billion.[31] Soon, museums came to depend on corporate largess. At first, corporate donors were satisfied to bask in the reflected glow from their good works, but eventually they began to seek more tangible returns on their investment. As the *New York Times* reported in 1990, "Art museums are increasingly promoting the commercial interests of companies giving them money—not just indirectly, by enhancing a sponsor's public image, but directly, by helping to hawk wares ranging from perfume to vodka to credit cards. . . . We are now seeing shows whose content is directly influenced by corporate sponsors, and, in some cases, shows that were initiated by the sponsor and brought to the museum, instead of the other way around."[32]

Appalling illustrations abound.

For example,

The Smithsonian allowed Lego to plaster its logo throughout an exhibit featuring large animals made of Lego building blocks.

- *Tiffany and Company initiated and paid for two shows in major museums—"150 Years of Gems and Jewelry" and "The Silver of Tiffany & Co.," which featured its own products.*[33]
- *Daimler-Benz A.G., makers of Mercedes-Benz automobiles, sponsored an Andy Warhol exhibit called "Cars" at the Guggenheim Museum. On display were thirty-five paintings and twelve drawings of Mercedes-Benz cars, commissioned by the manufacturer.*[34]
- *Shiseido cosmetics introduced a new perfume, Enchanting Dance, to commemorate its sponsorship of the "Dance" exhibit at the Metropolitan Museum of Art. Just like in department stores, the perfume was spritzed on unwitting museumgoers throughout the exhibit's nine-month run.*[35]
- *The Formica Corporation organized and paid for exhibits that toured museums across the country, featuring objets d'art made*

from Formica. Susan Grant Lewin, the company's creative director, referred to this as "using the museum as a vehicle for our corporation."[36]

- *Coca-Cola suggested and sponsored an exhibit at Toronto's Royal Ontario Museum entitled "Santa—The Real Thing." The show featured a commercial artist's renderings of Santa guzzling Coke in the company's past Christmas ad campaigns.*[37]
- *The Los Angeles County Museum of Art held an exhibit called "Salvatore Ferragamo: The Art of the Shoe, 1896–1960," paid for by—you guessed it—Ferragamo, a high-priced Italian shoe company. After the gala opening preview, a reception was held at a Ferragamo store, and a Ferragamo boutique was installed in the museum's lobby. Although the artistic merits of the show are open for debate, it was unquestionably a commercial success: Sales of the pricey footwear at one nearby store jumped by nearly 20 percent after the show began.*[38]

Clearly, in those and many other instances, marketers are directly controlling what museums exhibit. After all, few curators would have independently thought up a show featuring Formica knickknacks or Ferragamo shoes. And few would host such exhibits without a generous corporate donation.

But sponsors can exert influence in more subtle ways as well. As museums become more dependent on corporate funds, curators naturally choose exhibits that will attract sponsors. According to the *Corporate Philanthropy Report,* most arts groups deny altering their programming to suit the tastes of marketers. But, tellingly, many blame their peers for doing so, and 30 percent fear that they, too, would soon be forced to accede to marketers' demands.[39]

Some corporate sponsors do fund artwork that is stylistically avant-garde. For example, tobacco giant Philip Morris funds a broad range of cutting-edge work, such as the Alvin Ailey Dance Theatre. But what does Philip Morris *buy* with this seeming benevolence? For one thing, it burnishes its image as a good corporate citizen, drawing attention away from the fact that it aggressively markets a product that kills hundreds of thousands of Americans each year. In 1994 the "good citizen" became a bit of a bully when it called on its New York City grant recipients to help stop the city council from adopting a tough new anti-smoking ordinance. Also, by supporting free expression in the arts, Philip Morris bolsters its self-serving support for the First Amendment—a defensive maneuver against restrictions on tobacco advertising. Ironically, between 1987 and 1992 Philip Morris and other tobacco companies gave more than $44,500 to the most vocal proponent of arts censorship, Senator Jesse Helms. Helms represents the tobacco-producing state of North Carolina.[40]

Marketing Other Museums

It is not just art museums that have sold out to sponsors; science and children's museums are also beholden to corporate America. Although some of these institutions receive substantial taxpayer support, their exhibits often reflect the views and interests of their corporate sponsors.

Philip Morris was credited on prominent outdoor banners for sponsoring the Los Angeles County Museum of Art's exhibit on Korean art.

In 1993, the National Museum of Natural History opened the O. Orkin Insect Zoo to swarming crowds. Visitors were welcomed to the exhibit by the diamond logo for the Orkin pest control company, which contributed $500,000 to renovate the zoo.[41] The Smithsonian apparently saw no contradiction in naming an exhibit that celebrates the diversity and beauty of insects after the country's biggest bug killer. Although the company's services are not overtly pitched, there is one display of annoying household pests in a cutout house. The implication is clear: Some insects are neat, some need to be exterminated. There is no mention of the environmental or health-related harms of pesticides.

Orkin was not the first to seek out

An Andy Warhol
rendering of a
Mercedes from
the Guggen-
heim Museum
exhibit spon-
sored by the
carmaker.

museum space to promote its wares. In 1979, the Center for Science in the Public Interest (CSPI), a nonprofit consumer-advocacy organization, conducted a study of twelve major science and technology museums across the country. CSPI found

California and others to replace Los Angeles's clean, efficient public rail network with a polluting system of diesel- and gas-burning buses and cars. (For those activities, GM was convicted on criminal conspiracy charges in 1949.[42]) At New York's Hall of Science, Consolidated Edison trumpeted the virtues of nuclear power at the same time that it was embroiled in regulatory hearings over the safety of its Indian Point nuclear power plant. And Chicago's Museum of Science and Industry offered a veritable bazaar of corporate promotion: a pronuclear energy exhibit by Commonwealth Edison, an Amoco-sponsored ode to petroleum, and a farm exhibit paid for by International Harvester.[43]

that many of the museums' exhibits were underwritten by industries with a financial interest in the subject of the exhibit and that those exhibits served as public-relations tools for their sponsors.

At the California Museum of Science and Industry, for instance, an exhibit sponsored by General Motors lauded all GM had done to clear the air over Los Angeles. The exhibit did not mention the fact that in the 1930s, GM conspired with Standard Oil of

After the release of the CSPI report, officials at the Chicago Museum of Science and Industry acknowledged the biases of some exhibits and pledged to increase its independence from corporate funders. But a follow-up visit by CSPI in 1993 found that the museum had, if anything, become *more* commercialized in the intervening decade. Its National Business Hall of Fame serves as a shrine to commerce, complete with logos of forty major corporations. A lavish exhibit entitled "Food for Life" purports to be about nutrition but instead serves up a hefty helping of propaganda for its food-conglomerate sponsor, ConAgra. A display of eggs offers not a word about cholesterol. Another display showcases an array of Swift-brand processed meats (a division of Con-Agra) but does not mention that such high-fat foods are a major cause of heart disease.[44]

The "Food for Life" exhibit may have little value as an educational tool, but *someone* is learning from it. While studying the exhibit, the CSPI representative was approached by a woman with a clipboard, who asked if he would participate in a survey about sausages. As it turns out, the "Food for Life" exhibit at the publicly supported Chicago museum houses the private Consumer Research Center, which conducts market research for food manufacturers and advertising agencies.[45]

The Chicago museum is not alone in its dependence on corporate funds. In 1991, the venerable Smithsonian Institution began allowing corporate donors to display their logos and trademarks near exhibits. Shortly afterward, an exhibit was installed featuring nineteen large animals constructed of Lego building blocks. The bold Lego logo appeared more than thirty times on the animals and their accompanying information cards.[46] And at the National Aquarium in Washington, D.C., Chevron sponsored an exhibit of artificial coral reefs made of sunken oil rigs. Chevron's logos appeared on lighted panels above and beside the tanks. Also at the aquarium, Coors sponsored a river exhibit that touts its questionable Pure Water 2000 environmental campaign and ties in neatly with the beer company's claim that it uses "Pure Rocky Mountain Spring Waters."

Children's museums have also taken the corporate bait. In 1993, Philips Consumer Electronics Company signed deals with six children's museums to promote its CD-Interactive "edutainment" system, which lets users participate in various activities through a video monitor. Philips paid $5,000 to $15,000 per museum to install promotional kiosks for the exhibit. In return, museums promised to sell Philips software in gift shops and even send out mailings to promote the Philips kiosk.[47] "In addition," said Philips spokesman Jon Kasle, "consumers get to use the product in a setting that is not overtly commercial."[48]

Some children's museums aggressively court marketers. An article in *Marketing News* by David A. Adair, public relations director for the Pittsburgh Children's Museum, notes that sponsorship can cultivate brand loyalty. "Children's museums offer fertile ground to plant seeds and nurture a long-lasting partnership between a product and its consumer," writes Adair, "It is to the advantage of any company in any industry to associate itself with an organization which proves to be a first memory for many children."[49] With funding from ski resorts, the Denver Children's Museum has erected an artificial ski slope. The Denver museum also hosts a Halloween program sponsored by Pizza Hut that has generated a 17 percent increase in sales at local Pizza Hut franchises during the week of the program.[50]

Dancing for Dollars

Performing artists, too, are dancing to marketers' siren song. Cover Girl commissioned the renowned Lars Lubovitch Dance Troupe to choreograph a dance to promote

Visitors are welcomed to the Smithsonian's Orkin Insect Zoo with the diamond logo for Orkin Pest Control.

COLORADO TROUT STREAM

The streams of Colorado are renowned the world over for their beautiful rainbow and cutthroat trout. Anglers travel from around the globe to experience the scenic beauty and great fishing the state has to offer.

Sponsored by Coors Pure Water 2000

The National Aquarium in Washington, D.C., solicits corporate sponsorship for its marine exhibits. Coors, which donates money to water conservation projects, sponsored an exhibit on pure Colorado streams.

At the Chicago Museum of Science and Industry, an Amoco-sponsored exhibit celebrates petroleum.

AN APPETITE FOR COUNTRY.

When Fritos® said wanted crisp news for their FRITOS® corn chips, they dipped deep into country music. And loaded up on a nice tasty country concert tours and TV sponsorships.

Last year a program brought FRITOS a snappy, double-digit increase in sales. And this year's 90-city sponsorship of Reba McEntire's concert tour for new FRITOS SCOOPS!™ promises to serve up even bigger numbers.

From Taco Bell® to AT&T, more marketers are buying into country music, media and artists every day.

To learn more, call for The Country Fact Book at 1-800-492-5984.

Once you get a taste of what country can do, you'll be sold on it, too.

cma

America's sold on country.

Country music, enjoying renewed mainstream popularity, has become a major marketing vehicle. Above, the Country Music Association (CMA) took out a trade ad to offer its musicians as endorsers.

Texaco targets elite consumers by sponsoring New York's Metropolitan Opera.

CONNIVING, PLOTTING & SCHEMING HAVE NEVER BEEN MORE FUN.

THE METROPOLITAN OPERA PRESENTS

Falstaff

Sir John Falstaff — liar, lecher, booster and braggart — didn't know what he was getting himself into when he tangled with the merry wives of Windsor. But his problems are your pleasure thanks to Verdi's charming and witty music.

Paul Plishka
Mirella Freni
Marilyn Horne
Bruno Pola
Barbara Bonney
Frank Lopardo
James Levine

Monday, September 14
and on Eastern Time on PBS
Check local listings.
Stereo simulcast on many radio stations.

TEXACO

a new fragrance. Procter and Gamble paid the Dance Theater of Harlem to appear in a Tide commercial, dropping their dirty socks into a washing machine. And Cirque du Soleil, the avant-garde Canadian circus troupe, now bends over backward to attract corporate sponsors such as AT&T, which contributed $500,000 for a twelve-city tour.[51] "We started out saying we were a cultural enterprise," rationalizes Jean David, the group's head of marketing. "Now we say 'focus on the enterprise.'"[52]

Symphonies, whose upscale audiences are coveted by makers of cars, computers, and other big-ticket items, are favorite targets of sponsorship marketing. According to one advertiser, "Arts festivals and music are now getting more attention, primarily because they are uncluttered areas and you can still go in and make your mark."[53] In return for a hefty donation to the Los Angeles Philharmonic, American Airlines got its company logo lit up in fireworks at a concert in the Hollywood Bowl. And as part of a deal with L.A.'s Music Center Theater Group, Lexus Motors got to display one of its cars in the Music Center Plaza. The New York Philharmonic, in fact, was wooed by so many carmaker sponsors seeking to display their wares that Lincoln Center management had to institute a "one car on display at a time" rule. Otherwise, said the Philharmonic's development director, "this place will turn into a parking lot."[54]

Hollywood, of course, has long been a citadel of commercialism (see Chapter 3, "Product Placement"). Broadway, however, has historically aspired to loftier standards. But in recent years, Broadway plays have been used as marketing vehicles, literally. In 1992, the Chrysler Corporation cemented a sponsorship deal with producers of the hit musical *Will Rogers Follies* to promote its Jeep Grand Cherokee. The resulting cavalcade of plugs, said the *Wall Street Journal,* "makes the Super Bowl look practically commercial-free."[55] At each road-show performance of *Will Rogers*, a Jeep Grand Cherokee was parked outside the theater, surrounded by cardboard cutouts of the show's chorus members. Once inside the lobby, theatergoers were confronted with a huge cardboard Jeep replica (or the car itself, if space allowed) filled with more cutouts of the cast. And the plugs didn't stop once the show began: The script was actually rewritten to include references to the Jeep Grand Cherokee. At the end of the show, star Keith Carradine—while still in character as the folksy comedian Will Rogers—told the audience, "If you want to get home safe, think about considering one of these Grand Cherokees."[56]

Bucks, Plugs, and Rock and Roll

The din of commercialism is even louder in the world of popular music. Of course, popular music is, by nature, a commercial enterprise. But rock and roll originally offered an alternative to slick, mainstream musical fare. Back in the late 1950s, 1960s, and early 1970s, rock was a heady cross-pollination of rhythm and blues, country-western, and traditional folk music infused with the rebellious energy of the times. Rock gave voice to the marginalized, to protests against social injustice and the war in Vietnam. But gradually, many factors, including the growing influence of corporate sponsors, helped to blunt the countercultural force of rock and roll.

In the early days of rock and roll, advertisers were leery of aligning themselves with rock stars, who periodically got arrested for indecent exposure, died of drug overdoses, or otherwise disqualified themselves as corporate spokespersons. Likewise, many musicians scorned corporate sponsorship as "selling out." Ex-Beatle Paul McCartney remembers, "We were offered Disney, Coca-Cola, and the hugest deals in Christendom and beyond. And we never took them, because we thought, 'Nah, kind of cheapens it.' It cheapens it if you go commercial, I think."[57] But then, in the mid-1970s, New York marketer Jay Coleman managed to convince a few companies that rock and roll was a great way to sell things to young people. "For baby-boomers and young kids, music was the universal language," says Coleman. "So I tried showing corporations that, just as they used sports to reach people, they could use rock to do the same."[58]

Soon, all kinds of marketing messages were being translated into the universal language of rock and roll. In 1981, Jovan cologne sponsored a Rolling Stones tour. This was an odd alliance, because the Stones, writes Peter Carlson in the *Washington Post Magazine*, "were more closely identified with drug busts and arrests for public peeing than they were with pleasant fragrances. . . . But under the Jovan banner, rock's bad boys behaved like choirboys, thus consummating the marriage of rock and advertising."[59] Now, some 75 percent of rock tours have corporate sponsors. Marketers sponsor the music industry to the tune of $330 million a year—accounting for 13 percent of the entire $2.5 billion corporate sponsorship pie.[60]

Examples of pop-rock stars shilling for marketers are legion. Lionel Richie, Tina Turner, Ray Charles, David Bowie, and

Even religion is a commodity. After the Pope visited Denver in 1993, the church marketed a variety of Pope-sanctioned accessories, including the Miracle Mug advertised above.

Barbara Mandrell melded music and marketing, naming her album *"No Nonsense"* after the pantyhose she endorsed.

Michael Jackson (until his 1993 child-molestation scandal) have all hawked Pepsi; Robert Plant, Whitney Houston, the Pointer Sisters, and Run-D.M.C. sing the praises of Coke. Eric Clapton is accompanied onstage by a fifty-foot replica of a Diet Coke can, and at M. C. Hammer concerts the stage is draped with a Kentucky Fried Chicken banner. Anthony Kiedes, lead singer of the Red Hot Chili Peppers, promotes Gap Jeans. Lou Reed, famous for ballads about heroin and transvestites, now sells Honda motorcycles on TV. Fans of country singer Reba McEntire, who is sponsored by Frito-Lay snack food, had to sit through a minute-long retrospective of Frito-Lay commercials before a concert.[61] Patti LaBelle touts the virtues of Carefree Curl, which is given out free at her concerts. And MTV's 120 Minutes tour is sponsored by Hyundai, in order to "reach new car buyers in a quality environment."[62]

But the Musical Marketing Madness Award goes to country singer Barbara Mandrell. After pocketing a check for $15.5 million to promote No Nonsense pantyhose, Mandrell named her new album—yes, it's true—*No Nonsense*. Those who purchase the album get a coupon for a free pair of pantyhose, and life-size images of Mandrell adorn sales displays. (The *No Nonsense* album includes the song "I'd Rather Be Used Than Not Needed at All," which may reflect Mandrell's philosophy about corporate sponsorship.) The marketers who thought up the No Nonsense deal worry that consumers don't "think enough" about packaged goods such as pantyhose. Music tie-ins provide "a way

In 1989, the Coors National Hispanic Art Exhibit and Tour raised the company's visibility and won allies in the Hispanic community.

Corporations sponsor musical performers in an effort to win the loyalty of the stars' fans, but controversy can send corporations running. Pepsi broke off its long relationship with Michael Jackson after the pop star was accused of child molestation and admitted an addiction to painkillers.

packaged goods can be a bit more intrusive," says Michael Omansky, head of Worldwide Entertainment Marketing.[63]

Defenders of corporate sponsorship claim that it helps keep ticket prices down and that, with the escalating costs of concert tours, sponsorships keep a lot of deserving musicians on the road. So what's the problem? First, as with the fine arts, sponsors can effectively censor artistic expression. Pepsi dropped Madonna after she produced a controversial video; a performer of lesser means may have thought twice before offending her patron. And it may not be coincidental that many of the most politically outspoken musicians—R.E.M., Pearl Jam, Bruce Springsteen, Bonnie Raitt, U2, Neil Young, Stevie Wonder—eschew corporate sponsorship.

But the most obvious problem with corporate sponsorship of pop music is *what* the sponsors are selling. The vast majority of pop music sponsors are alcohol or tobacco companies. The beer industry alone spends around $50 million a year to subsidize concert venues—more

than it spends on magazine and newspaper ads combined.[64]

Countless musicians have sold out to alcohol and tobacco companies. Phil Collins sang "Tonight, Tonight, Tonight" as a TV ad for Michelob, and banners on the stage at Genesis concerts read "The Night Belongs to Michelob." Ringo Starr, a recovering alcoholic, hawked Sun Country Wine Coolers (he now repents). Gloria Estefan, who was once a spokesperson for the "Stay Smart, Don't Start" antidrinking campaign aimed at teens, accepted $10 million to promote Bacardi Breezers, a rum drink popular among underage drinkers. She has now modified her message to a less-sweeping "Don't Drink and Drive."[65] Camel cigarettes sponsored Eric Clapton's 1983 tour, and Marlboro hosts a country music festival that has featured Alabama, the Judds, Merle Haggard, and Randy Travis.[66]

Because the pop-music audience includes a sizable number of teenagers, sponsorship provides alcohol and tobacco companies with a way to reach youth below the legal drinking age (see Chapter 7). Rock stars lend an ineffable aura of coolness to smoking and drinking, and this message is particularly dangerous to kids. Alcohol abuse is the leading drug problem among adolescents, and, in fact, alcohol is the leading cause of death among young people.[67] Cigarette makers *need* to appeal to the young because their old customers keep dying off. The best way to ensure a lifetime of bondage to this life-threatening addiction is to get people smoking when they're young.

A Few More Words from Our Sponsors

Corporate sponsors don't stop at arts and entertainment. In their never-ending search for uncluttered advertising venues, marketers have sponsored state fairs, theme parks—even an entire American city.

Once upon a time, the Ohio State Fair was a homey rural event featuring lots of prize livestock and baked goods. Now the

Pepsi's "Dangerous" days are over, now that Michael Jackson has cut short his tour to get

THE BRAND OF GOD

Organized religion can serve as a countervailing force against the excesses of commercialism. However, some religious leaders are not above using Madison Avenue marketing tactics to fill church coffers.

In 1992, for example, England's Salisbury Cathedral signed a tie-in deal with fast-food giant McDonald's. For two months, all visitors to the cathedral received scrolls describing the history of the building. The tape holding the scrolls together doubled as a buy-one-get-one-free coupon for a Big Mac or McChicken sandwich, redeemable at a nearby McDonald's. The cathedral received a cut of the profits.[1]

Rather than shill for a corporation, the Catholic Church markets its *own* line of goods and services. Before the Pope's visit to Denver in August 1993, for World Youth Day, the Vatican gave its blessing to a full line of papal merchandise. There were Pope t-shirts, Pope posters, a Pope fanny pack, and a "Popescope" periscope for easier viewing. Official souvenirs included a Miracle Mug—just add hot liquid and an oversized Pope appears to hover above the Denver skyline.[2]

The Pope also has his own 900 number. For $1.95 per minute, Catholics seeking spiritual solace may call Dial-a-Pope and hear a recorded papal message, followed by a reminder to "Please call again tomorrow."[3]

For those whose religious inclinations run toward the East, there is a 900 number called Dial-a-Chant, a recorded assortment of Tibetan, East Indian, and other chants "geared to reducing stress." (Callers will *need* to achieve tele-nirvana before they get their phone bill; Dial-a-Chant costs $99.99 per call.[4])

fair rakes in about $650 million a year in corporate contributions and resembles a corporate theme park. Fairgoers can attend the Clorets Chili Cook-Off, watch the Wendy's Parade, thrill to the Bulls-Eye Barbecue Sauce Fireworks Show, or take the kids on a NutraSweet Sky Ride. Events are held in the Arby's Arena and the Taco Bell Coliseum. An entire day is devoted to the adulation of McDonald's; visitors on that day get their hands stamped with the familiar golden arches.[68]

Perhaps the ideal way to spotlight a company's product is to sponsor a park in its honor. Lego operates such a park in Denmark and plans to open an American counterpart. Visitors to the park, which features models constructed entirely from Lego building blocks, pay roughly $26 each to enter what is essentially a walk-in advertisement.[69]

An even more ambitious sponsorship scheme is the partnership between Visa and the city of Atlanta. In January 1993, Visa announced that it would pay $3 million to become the "official credit card of Atlanta" for a period of five years,[70] which will last through the high-profile 1996 Olympics in Atlanta. This novel marketing strategy was dreamed up by Joel Babbit, a former advertising executive hired to help Atlanta sell itself. Babbit's plan also involved auctioning off pieces of the city to the highest corporate bidder: He advocated renaming streets and parks for corporate sponsors, implanting advertisements in city sidewalks, and plastering company logos on the sides of garbage trucks. Babbit assured Atlantans that not just *any* sponsor would be welcome—he would draw the line at firearms and sexual products (to the relief of those who envisioned "the official assault rifle of Atlanta," or condoms imprinted with the city seal).[71] Not all of Bab-

Companies back soulful music events to win approval among African Americans. Burger King sponsors the annual television tribute, "Celebrate the Soul of American Music"; McDonald's holds its Gospelfest at the Lincoln Center in New York.

bit's ideas were warmly received. As one councilmember groused, "Maybe we should just let private companies privatize government entirely. In the case of Atlanta, we'll just become Coca-Colaville."[72] Babbit has since left the Atlanta post.

Speaking of privatizing government, corporations have even sponsored official occasions of state. When President Clinton and Russian president Boris Yeltsin met in Vancouver for the 1993 Russian-American summit, Benson & Hedges (a Philip Morris subsidiary) sponsored a $100,000 fireworks display. (Ironically, the Clintons won't even allow cigarettes in their own house.) Seventy other businesses contributed more than $200,000 in goods and services to defray the summit's cost, including $50,000 from McDonald's.[73]

In the end, taxpayers foot a portion of the bill for corporate sponsorship. Corporations can write off the money they spend on sponsorship—whether they call it charity or marketing—and the nonprofit recipients are exempt from paying taxes on their advertising income. In 1992, the Internal Revenue Service (IRS) proposed taxing nonprofits such as universities, symphonies, and museums for money received through some sponsorship deals, such as the Mobil Cotton Bowl, Orkin Insect Zoo, or local companies sponsoring community organizations. The IRS argued that high-profile sponsorship amounts to advertising and therefore does not relate to the organization's charitable purpose.[74] However, massive pressure from universities, nonprofits, and the business community led the IRS to reverse its position.

What People Have Done

Not *everyone* has sold out to the corporate culture; there are a number of con-

scientious objectors. In 1986, when rock band R.E.M. found "Miller Music" banners plastered all over the Milwaukee concert hall where they were to perform, lead singer Michael Stipe had the roadies tear down the signs. During the concert, Stipe unfurled the banners and said, "I don't know who put those banners up, but I'd like to verify that we don't believe in 'Miller Music' or corporate sponsorship. I wouldn't drink Miller if they paid me."[75]

Neil Young wrote a song called "This Note's for You," an angry indictment of the commercialization of rock and roll by Anheuser–"This Bud's for You"–Busch and other companies. (Not surprisingly, MTV initially declined to air the video for fear of offending sponsors.) Bruce Springsteen and Bob Seger have turned down lucrative sponsorship deals. Kool & The Gang decided to stop endorsing Schlitz malt liquor because of its ads' effect on kids.[76] The Black Crowes were booted out of the Miller Lite–sponsored Z.Z. Top tour for mocking corporate sponsorship during their opening act.[77] New York performance artists Karen Finley and Danitra Vance withdrew from the New York Dance and Performance Awards to protest sponsorship by Philip Morris.

Some museums—including the National Gallery of Art and the Hirschhorn—accept corporate funds but do not permit companies to display logos or hawk their products in the museum or in exhibit advertisements. Others resist corporate-sponsored shows. John Ross, manager of public information at the New York Metropolitan Museum of Art, when asked about the Ferragamo shoe exhibit, said, "We would not show an exhibition from a manufacturer."[78]

WHAT YOU CAN DO

- *Support increased public funding for the arts and other cultural activities.*

- *Write to the editor of your newspaper about corporate-sponsored exhibits in local museums.*

- *Don't buy albums or attend concerts of musicians whose endorsements offend you.*

Sports

Marketers Go for the Green

When basketball star Michael Jordan retired from professional sports in 1993, his fans lamented the loss of a great athlete. But their sorrow was eclipsed by that of companies such as Nike, McDonald's, and Quaker Oats, who lost a major product endorser. Jordan, who was earning approximately $30 million in endorsements a year,[79] epitomized the close relationship between sports and commerce.

INDEED, SPORTS MAY BE THE MOST commercialized sector of popular culture. From Little League jerseys to Bo Jackson's sneakers, advertisers have plastered their names and logos in nearly every corner of every sport. In 1992, marketers spent more than $2 billion on sports sponsorship.[80]

Professional sports has always been, at bottom, a business, but it has become increasingly dominated by pecuniary concerns. Players' salaries, the profitability of franchises, receipts from network television contracts, and union negotiations are featured as prominently on sports pages as the scores of games. As Barry Schwartz, in his book *The Costs of Living*, argued, "The commercial side of sports moved from the periphery of its conduct and of public awareness to the very center...We have allowed sports more and more to become *just* a business"[81] (emphasis added).

It is easy to understand why marketers are drawn to sports sponsorship. Sports are associated with youth, athletic prowess, and good times. Compared to artists and musicians, athletes are less likely to promulgate controversial ideas that might reflect badly on a sponsor (although there is the ever-present danger that an athlete endorser will test positive for drugs or get caught driving drunk). Moreover, fans tend to develop deep attachments to their home teams. Advertisers hope that by grafting their product onto a team's

Baseball stadiums are plastered with prominent corporate logos, seen over and over again by fans at the games and during telecasts.

image, consumers will make the synaptic leap from team to product loyalty.

At professional sporting events, advertisements are more intrusive than ever. At Chicago's new Comiskey Park, for example, ads stare down at fans from left- and right-field walls, from behind the foul line, from the scoreboard, from stadium hallways—and huge video screens periodically assault the audience with commercials. Comiskey Park has 300 "stadium sponsors," each of which gets at least one mention per game for a price of $30,000–$75,000 for the year. Laboring to meet their product-plug quotas, announcers celebrate "another Dove Bar double play!" and introduce the "Milk Duds/Jolly Rancher batboy and batgirl."[82] At Baltimore's Camden Yards, a total of sixty-five huge billboards and other advertisements loom over the field and stands.[83] Although ads have adorned stadium walls for decades, they have become much more numerous in recent years. A survey of twenty-eight major ballparks, conducted by the accounting firm of Ernst and Young, found that the number of commercial signs in stadiums increased by 47 percent between 1992 and 1993 alone.[84]

Stadium ads can be quite distracting: Detroit's Tiger Stadium and the Milwaukee County Stadium have both installed revolving signs directly behind home plate. The National Hockey League now permits commercial logos to be embedded in the ice, as well as on billboards around rinks. Broadcasters have even invented "virtual billboards"—computer-generated ads that appear in central locations on the baseball field, but only to TV viewers. By electronically inserting ads into moving TV pictures marketers will be able to target geographically and change signs during games,[85] making sure that no play goes unexploited.

Mobil inserts its name at the finish line of a high-profile track meet.

Some stadiums themselves have mutated into giant advertisements. For instance, the Utah Jazz play at the Delta Center (after the airline), the L.A. Lakers call their facility the Great Western Forum (after Great Western Bank), and in 1993, Washington, D.C.'s twenty-year-old sports and entertainment arena, the Capital Centre, sold its name to USAir for $10 million—spawning the USAir Arena.[86]

Reebok contributed to the approximately $10 million in endorsement contracts to Olympic skater Nancy Kerrigan–and Reebok doesn't even sell skates.

Some would take the commercialization of sports even further: Plans are under way to create a new football league owned and run solely by corporate sponsors. Tentatively called the "A" league (for advertiser), it could rival the National Football League in TV exposure and quality of players. Not only would companies be able to plaster logos on team uniforms and around stadiums, but the loyalty afforded hometown teams would be transferred onto companies.[87]

Even less-commercialized sports are

now competing for corporate dollars. Competitive runners offer their bodies up as billboards, wearing five or six sponsors' logos on their clothes during races. At the 1993 New York Marathon, Mercedes provided cars to the winners, who were required to thank the company on TV. And mountain biking, still relatively virgin territory for corporate sponsors, is attracting eager newcomers. "Miller, Bud, and Coors already have bought everything big," said Joe Herget, marketing executive for Dos Equis beer. "Mountain biking reaches our target and lets us make a splash because all the big guys aren't there."[88]

Higher, Faster, Stronger, Richer

Professional sports has always been an unapologetically commercial enterprise. Amateur athletics, however, have traditionally embraced a different, and higher, standard. But in recent years, the tentacles of commercialism have reached deeply into amateur athletics as well. Nowhere is this more apparent than in the transformation of the Olympic Games.

Once upon a time, the Olympics was the ultimate amateur athletic event. Cloaked in reverential Hellenic hype, the games aspired to be pure contests of skill, untainted by the corrupting influence of money. Judges piously policed the amateur status of Olympic athletes: In 1912, superathlete Jim Thorpe was stripped of his two gold medals when judges learned that he had once played semiprofessional baseball for a small salary.

Times have changed. Since the 1950s, the Olympics have degenerated into a corporate sponsorship free-for-all where organizers and athletes compete to sell endorsements to the highest bidders. By the summer of 1992, advertising tie-ins to the Olympic Games were a $2.65 billion business worldwide. Advertisers spent $665 million in official sponsorship fees, $790 million on advertising during broadcasts, and another $1.19 billion on Olympics-related commercials.[89] The fees paid to today's Olympians would astound Jim Thorpe. Dream Team member Michael Jordan commanded $20 million a year to endorse Nike; Shaquille O'Neal, relatively unknown at the time of the 1992 Olympics, got $3 million to wear Reeboks.[90]

Olympics rules prohibit ads in the stadiums, so advertisers compensate by donating products and outfitting athletes head-to-toe in logo-emblazoned gear. Ray-Ban, for example, was reported to pay athletes every time they appeared on TV wearing its brand of sunglasses. And Evian donated thousands of bottles of its spring water—dispatching representatives to hand bottles to athletes just before TV interviews.[91]

Those watching the Olympics on TV must endure not only incessant product plugs but a barrage of commercials as well. During the 1992 winter games, CBS punctuated three hours of Olympics coverage with forty-four minutes of commercials.[92] In a study of the 1992 summer games, the Center for the Study of Commercialism logged an average of almost seventeen minutes of traditional ads per hour of coverage, in addition to "covert advertising" such as close-ups of the Virgin Atlantic Blimp, Seiko clocks at the end of swimming lanes, and sportscasters' announcements of brand names on the air.[93] During the 1994 winter games, a man who recorded sixty-one minutes of televised coverage noted fifty-one commercials (including network promotions) totaling twenty-six minutes of airtime.[94]

Sponsors pay huge sums for the right to advertise their "official" Olympics products. The

Marking the take-over of college sports, Coca-Cola's Powerade sports drink bought rights to be the "official sports drink of Florida State Football."

Stock car racing is heavily sponsored. Tide's racecar driver Ricky Rudd, decked out in Tide apparel, paints his car with the Tide logo and sells a line of Tide/Ricky Rudd merchandise.

Philip Morris publicizes its racecar sponsorship in *Sports Illustrated*. Tobacco companies spend over $108 million annually on sports promotions.

investment pays off: According to David D'Alessandro, senior executive at John Hancock Financial Services (which sponsors the Boston and New York Marathons and the John Hancock Bowl), 94 percent of Olympics viewers see sponsors as successful companies; 81 percent consider the companies vital, energetic, and dedicated to excellence. In the early days of the Olympics, sponsors' products had some thematic link with athletics, such as timers and warm-up suits. Now they may have little or no connection to the matter at hand; there are "official" Olympics credit cards, cosmetics, candy bars, and even dog food.[95]

Not only do the frequent ads often distract from the games, the drama of dueling sponsorships at times upstages the competition between Olympians. Take the defeat suffered by Reebok in 1992 when one of its star endorsers, Dan O'Brien of the company's "Dan and Dave" ad campaign fame, failed to make the U.S. team. Or the sniping between American Express and Visa (the "official" Olympics credit card) when AmEx ran a series of ads that coyly suggested, "To visit Spain, you don't need a visa."[96] The rivalry between Coke and Pepsi achieved the intensity of a spy thriller when Coke, having paid $40 million to be the official soft drink of the Olympics, ordered representatives to search all pizza deliveries to the pressroom, fearing infiltration by the Pepsi empire.[97]

In the high-stakes Olympics competition for corporate sponsorship, brand loyalty often transcends mere national affiliation. Dream Team players Michael Jordan and Charles Barkley, Nike's extravagantly paid endorsers, flatly refused to wear the U.S. team's award-acceptance suit, which bore

Popular sports heros are much-coveted—and highly-paid—product endorsers. Basketball star Shaquille O'Neal, considered heir to Michael Jordan's endorsement empire, does Pepsi ads.

Even the official ballot for baseball's All Star players belongs to a corporate sponsor.

the logo of rival Reebok. "Us Nike guys are loyal to Nike because they pay us a lot of money," explained Barkley. "I have 2 million reasons not to wear Reebok."[98] The athletes were finally coaxed into the suits when the U.S. Olympic Committee allowed them to unzip the jacket to hide the offending logo.

If you think the Olympics could not possibly get any more commercialized, just wait until the Atlanta Summer Games in 1996. The 1996 Summer Games will be held in the United States for the first time since 1984—a year that was considered the previous high-water mark of Olympic sponsorship. In 1993, Coca-Cola, NationsBank, and Sara Lee Corporation had each already committed $40 million for exclusive rights to their product categories' sponsorships of the games.[99] By early 1994—more than two years before the Games—Olympics-related merchandise sales had exceeded $75 million.[100]

The Selling of School Sports

As professional sports and the Olympics approach commercial saturation, marketers are turning their attention to the last bastions of amateur athletics: college and high school sports. School sports offer many advantages to marketers, most notably inexpensive access to the coveted young adult market. "You're talking about young men and women between eighteen and twenty-

four years of age," says Brian J. Murphy, publisher of *Sports Marketing Letter,* "and they're going out for the first time to make important consumer decisions . . . which is why sponsors want to be there."[101]

And they *are* there. Most of the college bowl games have taken the names of their corporate benefactors: Fans now attend the Federal Express Orange Bowl Classic, the Mobil Cotton Bowl, the John Hancock Bowl (formerly the Sun Bowl) and the U.S.F.&G. Sugar Bowl. Blockbuster Video spent $2.5 million to create its own col-

Coca-Cola plastered major cities with thousands of posters and banners advertising its sponsorship of the 1994 World Cup.

lege football event, the Blockbuster Bowl,[102] which became the Carquest Auto Parts Bowl in 1994. Lest fans think sponsors are motivated by the love of the game, Jack Mahoney, director of sports marketing for John Hancock Financial Services, said, "We're in this for one thing: visibility."[103]

At high school level, sponsorship has historically been limited to jerseys and scoreboards supplied

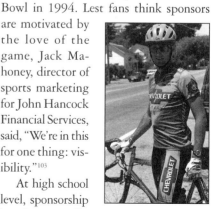

This professional cyclist, whose racing team is sponsored by Chevrolet, trains in corporate uniform.

by the local dairy or pharmacy. Sponsorship of high school sports by national corporations was, until quite recently, unheard of. But today forty of fifty-one state high school athletics associations accept some form of corporate backing.[104]

A company named School Properties USA, Inc. is at the forefront of the high school sponsorship craze. In 1988, School Properties brokered a deal between Reebok and the California Interscholastic Federation (CIF). CIF got $1.25 million; Reebok got to plaster its name on athletic events all over the state and to rename the state championships. The state track meet, for example, is now called the CIF-Reebok Track and Field Championship.[105] Other states have followed suit. High school athletes in North Carolina now compete in the McDonald's Basketball Tournament and the Champion Spark Plug Football Tournament; young Nevadans aspire to the Nevada Interschool Activity Association–Pizza Hut State Championships. In Utah, the High School Activities Association has modified its logotype to include the symbol of its corporate sponsor, the First Securities Corporation of Salt Lake City.

Don Baird, the president of School Properties, effuses about the benefits of high school sponsorship. He notes that a thirty-second commercial during the Super Bowl costs $700,000 and points out that, by sponsoring school sports, an advertiser "could have the whole state of New York for three years for $750,000!" Moreover, high school sponsorship enables advertisers to penetrate a community in a way that is not possible with a TV spot.

Sponsorship of high school athletic events raises many of the ethical issues discussed in "Schools Go Commercial," Chapter 1. Notably, is it right to auction off the right to sell to kids in public schools? Although sponsorship of sports is certainly less insidious than advertising to kids in classrooms, sports underwriting may give marketers a foot in the door

that will lead to further commercial incursions into schools.

Another problem with corporate sponsorship of sports in general is that sports advertisers often sell products that are manifestly unhealthy. According to the publisher of the *Sports Marketing Letter,* the leading U.S. sports sponsors include Anheuser-Busch (Budweiser beer), Philip Morris (Marlboro cigarettes and Miller beer), RJR Nabisco (Camel cigarettes), Coca-Cola, McDonald's, Pepsi-Co, and Coors. Of the $80 million tobacco companies spend on event sponsorships, $75 million goes for sports.[106] Clearly, those marketers hope their products will bask in the healthy glow of the athletes they endorse—and take our minds off the cirrhosis, cancer, clogged arteries, and tooth decay their products promote.

The commercialization of sports is yet another illustration of the way practically every activity, diversion, and form of expression is pressed into corporate service. As any fan will tell you, something intangible gets lost when a sport goes commercial. If one could distill a "pure" essence of sport, it might be a spirit of serious play—an absorbing, ritualized concentration of effort on a goal that is, in itself, worthless. Because that sort of play is common in most cultures,

Companies clamor to be seen during the Super Bowl—traditionally the most expensive ad time on television. Playing off the Super Bowl theme during breaks in the game, Anheuser-Busch sponsors the annual "Bud Bowl," a pseudo-competition between two of its beers.

Coca-Cola and Budweiser dominate he commanding scoreboard/video screen at Baltimore's Camden Yard's stadium.

Budweiser gets a choice site on a boxing mat during a televised match.

The Miller Lite Volleyball Open features on-screen plugs for Lite beer and other products.

anthropologists have theorized that it might satisfy a universal human need. As author Michael Novak notes in his study of sports, "The preservation of parts of life not drawn up into politics and work is essential for the human spirit."[107]

Commercialized sports lose that spirit of play—and become indistinguishable from any other business or industry. In *Culture of Narcissism*, social critic Christopher Lasch blamed the degradation of sports on the creeping influence of business and "industrial values." "Prudence, caution, and calculation, so prominent in everyday life but so inimical to the spirit of games, come to shape sports as they shape everything else,"[108] he wrote. Or perhaps Kevin McHale, former star of the Boston Celtics basketball team, put it

best, when he lamented his league's new commercial success: "You don't need the games. With the merchandising and everything, why even play? We should have guys go around and just have card-signings and stuff

Since soccer is played without interruption for forty-five minutes per half, the logos of 1994 World Cup sponsors were superimposed almost constantly on the TV screen. Viewers also saw the 21-foot-long billboards around the playing field for an average of one hour per game.

like that. It's an event now. Before, it was a game. You just go out and sell your soul and maybe get on a Wheaties box or something. . . . I liked it better when everybody hated each other—when we hated Philly and hated L.A. and played blood and guts. Now, everybody has the same agent and they all hug and kiss after the game."[109]

WHAT YOU CAN DO

- *Oppose tobacco and alcohol sponsorship of sports. Fight to remove tobacco and alcohol ads from stadiums and to prohibit beer ads during broadcasts of sporting events. You may want to write letters to the editor of your local paper and television station, as well as to the teams themselves. Contact local advocacy groups working on tobacco and alcohol issues—these groups are listed at the end of the "Ads That Kill" sections in Chapter 7.*

- *If you are a college student, protest the commercialization of school sports by voicing your concerns to the administration and student government.*

- *Find out if marketers sponsor sports at your local high school; if they do, complain to your school board.*

- *Reject the whole sports-marketing complex by getting involved with nonsponsored amateur sports. Lots of*

informal leagues still operate beyond the reach of marketing madness.

- *Contact the nonprofit Sports Fans United, which is an advocate for the rights of sports fans. It addresses problems related to the commercialization of sports.*

SPORTS FANS UNITED
23 WARREN ST.
NEW YORK, NY 10007
212-571-FANS

Once confined to the airwaves and the printed page, advertising now invades our lives in ever more intrusive ways. Leading the charge is the direct-marketing industry—notably, direct mail and telemarketing. These are the people who stuff your mailbox with junk mail and call you at dinnertime to sell you aluminum siding. Direct mail has been blamed for contributing to the solid-waste crisis, but it has also been defended as a lifeline for nonprofit groups. And telemarketing can be disruptive, annoying, and even dangerous. But the most ominous aspect of the direct-marketing industry is

Intrusive Marketing

its collection and use of personal data. Indeed, direct marketers may know more about your financial status and personal tastes than even your closest friends. ✳ *The billboard industry offers a different dimension of intrusiveness. Billboards hover over our homes and communities, blot out the scenery, and hawk their wares day and night. Billboards are at their worst when they push liquor or cigarettes, leaving no way to protect young children from their messages. In this chapter, we explain how the outdoor-advertising industry uses public space for private gain and show you how to rid your community of these eyesores.* ✳ *Finally, we look at the cutting edge of intrusive marketing: video ads in waiting rooms and other public spaces.*

Big Brother and You

The Growth of Direct Marketing

They know who you are. They know where you live, how much you earn, and what kind of work you do. They know your religion, political party affiliation, and marital status. They may even know about your weight problems, your taste in lingerie, and your sexual orientation.

THE "THEY" IS THE DIRECT-marketing industry, and they're busy compiling detailed computer profiles of American consumers. If you have a driver's license, use a credit card, subscribe to magazines or order merchandise by mail, chances are they know a lot about you. "You go through life dropping little bits of data about yourself everywhere," says Evan Hendricks, author of *Your Right to Privacy* and editor of *Privacy Times*. "Most people don't know that there are big vacuum cleaners sucking it up."[1]

Direct marketing is not a new concept. Benjamin Franklin is credited with launching the mail-order industry in 1744 with a catalog selling scientific and scholarly books.[2] Another early proponent was Montgomery Ward, which published its first catalog in 1873. Ward's concept was simple: Sell directly to the consumer and save them the profit of the middleperson. Then, in 1886, Richard Sears got stuck with an unclaimed shipment of $12 gold watches. As the story goes, he sold them by mail to railroad employees for $14 each. Emboldened by this small success, Sears teamed up with A. C. Roebuck and launched a massive mail-order enterprise. By 1927, Sears, Roebuck and Co. was mailing 75 million catalogs a year, selling everything from farm implements to prefabricated houses.[3]

As Americans moved away from rural communities, mail order was mostly eclipsed by retail chains and mass-media advertising. Television emerged as the dominant advertising medium; by the late 1960s, the big three TV networks were beaming commercial-sponsored entertainment into 98 percent of all American households. This was the golden era of mass marketing, when commercials were designed to appeal to the widest possible audience and broadcast coast to coast. But in the 1980s, cable TV and VCRs splintered the viewing audience, forcing advertisers to rethink their strategy. No longer assured of reaching a majority of Americans with a single nationally televised commercial, many advertisers have returned to direct marketing.

Unlike mass marketing, which casts a wide net for potential customers, direct marketing zeroes in on the groups and individuals deemed most likely to buy the product. Of course, mass marketers have always tried to target their ads to some degree; toy commercials air during kids' shows, and ads for disposable diapers and cleaning products are often consigned to daytime TV, when homemakers are presumed to be watching. But direct marketing aims for much greater precision. To sell disposable diapers, for example, a direct marketer might provide free samples in maternity wards or mail coupons to new parents. Direct marketers eschew the mass media, preferring the intimacy of a personalized letter or telephone call. Some companies, such as

The U.S. Postal Service, which receives substantial revenues from direct marketing, promotes advertising by mail. Above, a pamphlet on direct-mail seminars by the Post Office and an open letter from Postmaster Marvin Runyon thanking direct marketers for their "partnership."

Market-research companies offer sophisticated statistical software so that advertisers can target people by habits, income level, and lifestyle.

banks and software manufacturers, use direct marketing as a component of a larger advertising plan. Others, including the fast-proliferating catalog industry, rely solely on direct marketing to advertise and sell their wares. All forms of direct marketing have grown dramatically since the early 1980s: By 1993, direct-mail expenditures totaled $27.3 billion—outstripping all advertising on radio, and cable television, in magazines, and on billboards, combined.[4]

The Data Game

Information is the coin of the direct-marketing realm. The more marketers know about our habits, needs, fears, and desires, the more effective will be their inducements to buy. Technological advances have made it easier (and cheaper) to collect surprisingly detailed data on individual consumers.

Direct marketers compile information from a wide array of sources, then collect and trade the data like baseball cards. Much of the information they gather is in the public domain: marriage and birth records, voter registration, drivers' licenses, and postal change-of-address forms. These skeletal facts are then "enhanced" with information purchased from a variety of sources such as organizational mailing lists, magazine subscriptions, and credit bureaus. The data portrait becomes clearer with the addition of information culled from consumer surveys—like the ones attached to warranty cards, which give consumers the misleading impression that their warranty will not be valid unless they answer the survey questions.

Most consumers remain unaware of the extent to which their activities are tracked. Signing divorce papers, having a baby, endorsing political petitions, answering surveys, getting sued, even dying—all immortalize your most personal information for marketers' open use. Just ordering from Ticketmaster can get you on a list of rock and roll fans or baseball buffs.[5]

By compiling and cross-indexing lists, marketers can target different kinds of consumers with uncanny accuracy. Lists can be sorted by gender, census tracts (areas smaller than zip codes), foreign-car ownership, or membership in a health club. One company, Consumers Marketing Research Inc. (CMR), sells lists sorted by any of seventy-eight ethnic and religious groups. It produced a list of Italian voters for Mario Cuomo's gubernatorial campaign, black households for the United Negro College Fund, and Japanese men for a Brooks Brothers promotion of suits in smaller sizes. For a maker of lederhosen, CMR compiled a list of German names, deleting those thought to be Jewish.[6] One company sells its list of gay men to selected advertisers, which insurance companies actually use to *avoid* targeting what they consider a high-risk population for AIDS.[7] Response Unlimited sells lists of "check-writing Evangelical activists," while The Rich List Co. specializes in "cream of the crop Jewish contributors."[8] Yet another company sells the names of 91,000 men who ordered a "natural nutrient…geared to increase the male sexual appetite in impotent men." Marketers can also purchase lists of overweight women, short men, people with chronic health conditions, multimillionaires, and subscribers to pornographic newsletters.[9] By 1993, some 15,000 consumer lists were on the market, providing information on more than two billion people.[10]

Particularly valuable to the sleaziest marketers are lists of "opportunity seekers"—direct-marketing jargon for "suckers." Those who enter sweepstakes, order cheap cameras or fake diamonds through the mail, or buy merchandise through 900-number hotlines are likely to be branded as opportunity seekers and bombarded with promotions for all sorts of ripoffs. People in desperate financial trouble are another sought-after group. A company called LBMI Direct Marketing Services sells a list that it says was generated "from a postcard offer that targets the lowest end of the socioeconomic spectrum." Each of those hapless opportunity seekers earned their place on the LBMI list by spending $44 on a 900-number call to apply for the Cash Galore credit card.[11]

Sometimes, information gleaned for one specific reason is used for other, unrelated purposes. For instance, Farrell's ice cream stores ran a promotion in which customers could get free ice cream on their birthdays. Farrell's then sold its collection of names and dates to the U.S. Selective Service, which proceeded to remind the eighteen-year-old birthday boys to register for the draft.[12] Johnson and Johnson sold the names of 5 million elderly women who responded to an ad for bladder control undergarments to marketers seeking elderly customers.[13]

Remember that long application you filled out to get your credit card? Chances are that information was sold to the highest bidder without your consent. The nation's two largest credit-reporting bureaus, TRW and Equifax, maintain up-to-date financial profiles of roughly 90 percent of American adults.[14] In 1985, TRW

and Equifax both acquired new data companies to augment their already bulging computer files, then launched marketing divisions to sell those files to advertisers. In 1990, Equifax joined with Lotus Development to market a compact disc of information on almost every American with a credit history—some 80 million households. But when over 30,000 people protested, the firms canceled their plan.[15] Equifax abandoned its direct marketing division in 1991 but still provides banks and retailers with lists of consumers for use in making preapproved credit offers. TRW weathered a lawsuit challenging its information-handling practices brought by the attorneys general of nineteen states and continues to peddle our electronic portraits to advertisers.

Not content to peruse our credit reports and rifle through our personal data, marketers are constantly devising new forms of consumer surveillance. Scanning technology—those lasers that read the ubiquitous UPC (universal product code) bar codes at the supermarket—enable retailers to track every single purchase a consumer makes. One pilot program offers discounts to consumers who present a bar-coded identification card every time they shop; information

Junk mailers use sneaky tactics just to get people to open the envelope. Above, a Mazda dealer disguised its ad as an official government document appearing to contain a check. The contents actually consisted of a discount coupon for a car and a sale announcement.

The New In-Store Medium That Knows Who Needs Your Product. And When.

Catalina Marketing Network monitors shoppers' buying habits using information gleaned from check-cashing cards. By referring to past purchases, the grocery store can issue a coupon at the cash register for a product Catalina estimates the shopper will soon need.

about purchases is then transmitted to a central database.[16] A program called Scan America, now defunct, briefly enabled marketers to correlate information on purchases with TV-viewing data. Scan America was the brainchild of the Arbitron Company, inventors of the People Meter, which monitors TV-viewing habits. Participating households passed an electronic wand over everything they bought, then transmitted purchase and viewing data to Arbitron through a meter attached to the family's TV. Although Scan America garnered a wealth of intriguing information—such as the fact that *L.A. Law* fans drink 64 percent more coffee than other prime-time viewers—Arbitron discontinued the program in 1992. Some observers thought the program was just too labor-intensive to be used widely.[17]

By monitoring consumer habits, marketers can precisely measure the effectiveness of their ads and zero in on individual tastes and needs. Some contend that direct marketing serves both manufacturers and consumers by cutting down on unwanted solicitations and informing consumers about things they really need. Others argue that commercial probing of the minutiae of our personal lives is a gross violation of privacy. "There's something kind of creepy about companies knowing more about you than your own family, and compiling and trading information about you

Upscale companies that sell via catalog, like Neiman Marcus clothing and Horchow home items, rent lists of their unsuspecting clientele.

behind your back," says Robert Ellis Smith, editor of *Privacy Journal*.[18]

The brisk trade in personal data lends itself to many kinds of abuse. Our electronic portraits, it seems, are available to almost anyone with a little cash and determination. Place a call to Telephonic-INFO in Florida and for $24 you can get a credit report on virtually any American, provided you state that you have a "permissible purpose" for obtaining information. For $99, you can get a full employment history and earnings, and $249 grants you access to personal bank account records.[19] In 1989, *Business Week* reporter Jeffrey Rothfeder embarrassed the credit industry by obtaining Dan Quayle's credit report. Rothfeder easily convinced a credit information broker that he had a "legitimate business need" for the information, as federal law requires. In New York City, the Department of Consumer Affairs reported that 35 percent of the city's credit-reporting agencies break the law by making it easy to get unauthorized copies of someone else's credit file.[20] And until 1994, the Post Office sold individual address changes over the counter for $3 to anyone who had the person's old address. Lists of people who recently moved are valuable to marketers of certain kinds of products and services. Although the Post Office stopped giving out that information on a walk-in basis, writing "address correction required" on an envelope will get anyone with an old address the new one. (Drivers' license data is also easily obtained; actress Rebecca Shaefer was killed by an obsessed fan who tracked her down through California DMV records.[21]) As marketers compile more detailed information about our tastes and habits, the potential for abuse increases exponentially.

Stories of marketers misusing personal data are already plentiful. In 1990, for example, thousands of elderly and overweight Americans received "personal" letters containing newspaper clippings of ads for anti-aging cream or diet pills. Each clipping was accompanied by an apparently handwritten note on a yellow Post-it. A typical note read: "*Kathy—Try it. This works.—R.*" Contrary to appearances, these missives were not sent by friends, but by direct-marketing companies. Predictably, many of the recipients grew depressed, believing that their wrinkles or obesity warranted such unsolicited concern. Others got angry, often breaking off relationships with the people they thought sent the notes. One recently divorced woman, who believed the note had been sent by her ex-husband's new wife, killed them both.[22]

Erik Larson points out in *The Naked Consumer* that personal information is a gateway to intimacy; we regulate and measure our closeness to others by sharing such information. When something significant happens—we get pregnant, say, or buy a new home—we make a point of first telling those we feel closest to. But when marketers learn of the milestones in our lives before our loved ones do, we are no longer the gatekeepers of our private lives. The loss of privacy, as law professor Edward J. Bloustein wrote in an influential 1964 article in the *New York University Law Journal,* diminishes our dignity, even our humanity: "A man whose home may be entered at the will of another, whose conversation may be overheard at the will of another, whose marital and family intimacies may be overseen at the will of

another, is less of a man, has less human dignity, on that account. He who may intrude upon another at will is the master of the other, and, in fact, intrusion is a primary weapon of the tyrant."[23]

Not surprisingly, more people are feeling resentful about marketers' intrusions on their privacy. A 1993 Harris poll found that 83 percent of Americans are "somewhat" or "very" concerned about privacy, up from 64 percent in 1977, and just 34 percent in 1970.[24] More revealing, perhaps, is the fact that direct marketers themselves are wary of their industry's information-handling practices. Forty percent of direct marketers questioned in a similar 1990 Harris poll agreed that "consumers have lost all control over how personal information about them is circulated and used by companies."

So Much Mail, So Little Time

In addition to concerns about privacy, the explosion of direct marketing has raised questions about the deluge of junk mail that now besets most Americans. Every day, our mailboxes are stuffed with ever more desperate entreaties to buy, subscribe, and sign up *now*. "YOU MAY HAVE ALREADY WON" screams the caption on the envelope. "SPECIAL OFFER...OPEN IMMEDIATELY... VALUABLE DOCUMENTS INSIDE." In 1992, the U.S. Postal Service delivered 62 billion pieces of third-class direct mail, accounting for nearly 40 percent of domestic postal volume.[25] That's about forty-one pounds of mail for every adult in the country. Roughly 44 percent of that goes straight to the landfill, unopened. Still, *Time* magazine estimates that over the course of a lifetime, the average American professional will devote eight entire months to sifting through and reading mail solicitations.[26]

Direct mail has its defenders. Mail order saves resources by keeping shoppers out of cars, they contend, and catalogs can offer useful information about product specifications—information that is in short supply in most print and media advertising. Direct mail is also less intrusive than other forms of advertising; it may be a nuisance, but at least it's gone with one flick of the wrist.

But is it really *gone*? That forty-one pounds of direct mail for every American adult adds up to a lot of garbage. A mailing is considered successful if it generates a mere 1 or 2 percent response. There is a staggering amount of waste: Every year, another 3.5 million tons of third-class junk mail gets dumped on landfills. (Nonprofit third-class mail accounts for only about 363,000 tons, or less than a quarter of 1 percent of total landfill content.) Catalogs alone account for the destruction of over 74,000 acres of forest per year.[27] (Some small catalogs are starting to use recycled paper, but large companies, such as L.L. Bean, say the additional cost is prohibitive.[28]) And because it often employs coated stocks and plastic stickers, direct mail is difficult to recycle; only 5 percent is recycled each year.[29]

Moreover, as our mailboxes become more cluttered, the direct mail industry goes to greater lengths to attract our attention with gimmicks and doodads. The San Francisco Music Box Company sent out 50,000 catalogs equipped with a concealed microchip that played "Jingle Bells." And the Hartmarx Corporation, a Chicago-based clothing company, mailed videotaped Christmas catalogs to the homes of about 150,000 customers.[30]

Direct mail is a $210 billion industry, but marketers are not the only ones who profit. Even though 42 percent of Americans say they want less mail, the U.S. Postal Service is one of junk mail's strongest

One person received thirty-one credit-card solicitations in one year, totaling $131,800 of preapproved credit, in addition to several "unlimited" or undisclosed amounts.

Direct marketers shop for mailing lists from enormous books like these.

champions. After all, the 62 billion pieces of bulk mail sent each year yield a tidy sum of revenue.[31] It's not surprising that the Washington, D.C., Post Office, in its September 1993 newsletter, dismissed consumer concerns about junk mail and claimed that "advertising mail fuels economic growth ...making it possible for American business to employ millions of people." In a particularly misleading clause, the letter also warned consumers that removing their name from junk mail lists "could prevent you from receiving those magazines and publications you really want."[32] The Post Office has repeatedly opposed legislation that would make it easier for Americans to keep their addresses private.

Mailbox Democracy

Not all third-class direct mail exhorts you to buy. Lots of it implores you to vote—usually for your incumbent elected official.[33] Thousands of nonprofit groups also depend on the mail to get their messages out. Many such organizations alienate people with their aggressive campaigns for members, subscriptions, and donations. One New York man kept track of his nonprofit mail for one year and discovered to his dismay that he received an average of five appeals each from twenty-four different organizations. Several groups sent him eleven different appeals. He figured that some groups spend more money on those solicitations than he gives them in donations.

One nonprofit that relies on direct mail is Greenpeace USA, which sends out 25 million pieces of literature each year. But Peter Bahouth, former executive director of Greenpeace USA, and André Carothers, editor of *Greenpeace* magazine, vigorously defend their reliance on direct mail: "For Greenpeace and a myriad of other public interest groups small and large, the home mailbox has become both a sanctuary and a lifeline: a sanctuary for delivering those political views that cannot survive the media's censorship, and a lifeline for the growth and preservation of the nation's ailing tradition of citizen involvement in public issues."[34]

Perhaps it is necessary to draw a distinction between commercial and nonprofit direct mail. According to Herb Chao Gunther, director of Public Media Center, which designs direct-mail campaigns for nonprofit organizations, there are significant differences: "The direct-mail-as-destroyer-of-the-planet argument may pertain to commercial direct mail, but not to nonprofit mailers," he writes. "There just isn't a comparable volume.... The failure to see the basic distinctions between political discourse and merchandising-by-mail is yet more evidence of the ideological triumph of commerce."[35]

Clearly, direct mail is a mixed bag. On one hand, it provides a forum for a broad spectrum of political views and may offer a convenient, environmentally defensible alternative to shopping at the mall. On the other hand, the direct marketers who send us our daily deluge of junk mail are amassing databases that violate our privacy and have terrifying potential for abuse. And direct marketing generates a massive—and growing—amount of garbage.

What People Have Done

Most other industrialized countries have national agencies that safeguard privacy by regulating the use of personal data. In Germany, companies are prohibited from compiling detailed portraits of consumers; databases may list only a person's name, address, year of birth, profession, and one additional fact. (Interestingly, Germany has Europe's most suc-cessful direct-marketing industry.[36])

Here in the United States, legislators have been slower to respond to privacy threats. Since the early 1970s, Congress has enacted laws to safeguard certain personal information, but all have loopholes and fail to address the many new data-collection technologies. For instance, the Fair Credit Reporting Act of 1970 limits disclosure of credit files, but not by much. The Privacy Act of 1974 prevents federal agencies from disclosing most personal information, but the law is easy to circumvent with emerging technology. The 1988 Video Privacy Protection Act bans the sale of video rental records—largely in response to video information collected on Supreme Court nominee Robert Bork—but information brokers frequently disregard the law.[37] Most types of corporate databases have yet to be targeted for regulation.

In the early 1990s, Congress began to address concerns about eroding privacy. Representative Edward Markey (D–Mass.) proposed a Privacy Bill of Rights, which guarantees Americans the right to know when personal information is being collected, to be told when information is sold or rented, and to have the power to veto use of one's personal data. Markey hopes to incorporate those principles into more far-reaching privacy legislation.[38]

Charged with contributing to the solid-waste problem, the Direct Marketing Association (DMA) instituted a Mail Preference Service, which enables consumers to remove their names from many national mailing lists. DMA makes this list available to marketers for free, but some marketers simply don't bother to use it. Others use the list, but for purposes the DMA did not intend. According to the *Wall Street Journal,* "One leading data executive says he actually helped a company send a special mailing to everyone on the [DMA] list, reasoning that their mailboxes would be wonderfully uncluttered."[39]

WHAT YOU CAN DO

- *Write to your representatives in Washington and encourage them to support privacy legislation.*

- *Support legislation that would require subscription forms, warranty cards, and so on to include a checkoff box enabling you to forbid the company from renting or trading information about you.*

- *Write to the magazines you subscribe to and tell them not to trade or rent your name. Be sure to contact them at the beginning of your relationship, before your name is released. Many catalogs now contain forms that allow you to choose not to have your name rented or traded.*

- *Write to nonprofit organizations that send appeals and ask them to take you off their mailing list or not to rent your name to other groups. Enclose the mailing label they sent you.*

- *Use your credit card sparingly. Information gleaned from your purchases can be used to create a consumer profile.*

- *Don't fill out consumer surveys, such as the ones attached to warranty cards. (Yes, your warranty will be perfectly valid if you don't fill out the survey.)*

- *Don't let merchants intimidate you into giving any personal information that is not necessary to complete the sale. Ask why they want to know.*

- *Don't give out your Social Security number unless it's absolutely necessary.*

- *Subvert the methods of direct marketers by giving out wrong information to market researchers and lying on consumer surveys; in the long run, their lists will be rendered useless if they can't be used to gauge real buying preferences.*

- *Write to one of the credit-reporting and information agencies listed here, and ask them not to sell or rent your name. (TRW, Trans Union, and Equifax share a "no rental list"—writing to one should serve to notify all three.) You may also request a copy of your credit report; frequently these reports contain inaccuracies.*

TRW, INC.
NAME REMOVAL SERVICE
TARGET MARKETING
600 CITY PARKWAY WEST, #1000
ORANGE, CA 92668
1-800-392-1122

TRANS UNION CORPORATION
NATIONAL SERVICE DIVISION
16TH FLOOR
111 W. JACKSON BLVD.
CHICAGO, IL 60604
1-800-851-2674

EQUIFAX
P.O. BOX 2350
CHATSWORTH, CA 91313-2350
1-800-685-1111

MEDICAL INFORMATION BUREAU
P.O. BOX 105
ESSEX STATION
BOSTON, MA 02112
617-426-3660

- *Sign up for the DMA's Mail Preference Service. This will get your name off of some, but hardly all, national, commercial mailing lists. (Note: Be wary of any outfit that charges for this service. Often, a company will charge a fee and then merely pass your name along to the Mail Preference Service.) All requests must be in writing. Write to*

MAIL PREFERENCE SERVICE
c/o DMA
P.O. BOX 9008
FARMINGDALE, NY 11735-9014
212-768-7277

- *Contact the Privacy Rights Clearinghouse, the* Privacy Journal, *or* Privacy Times, *which monitor the state of American privacy.*

THE PRIVACY RIGHTS CLEARINGHOUSE
CENTER FOR PUBLIC INTEREST LAW
UNIVERSITY OF SAN DIEGO
5998 ALCALA PARK
SAN DIEGO, CA 92110
619-260-4806

THE PRIVACY JOURNAL
($109 PER YEAR; STUDENT DISCOUNTS)
P.O. BOX 28577
PROVIDENCE, RI 02908
401-274-7861

PRIVACY TIMES
($250 PER YEAR)
BOX 21501
WASHINGTON, DC 20009
202-829-3660

Assaulting the Home

Telemarketing

It's seven in the morning and Arthur Jennings is in the shower. The phone rings. Thinking it must be important for someone to call at that hour, Jennings bolts from the bathroom, dripping wet, only to be subjected to a recorded sales spiel. ✳ *A woman has just returned home after undergoing outpatient surgery. Still in pain and woozy from the anesthesia, she climbs into bed. The phone rings; she gets out of bed and picks up the receiver to hear a voice urging her to buy aluminum siding. She hangs up and crawls back to bed only to have her rest interrupted by two more telephone calls offering "a really unbeatable new bank card" and congratulating her on winning a contest she never entered.* ✳ *Dr. Peter Novosel stands at the bedside of a patient who has just died, surrounded by grieving family members. Suddenly, his pocket voice-pager blasts a hearty, recorded voice into the room. The voice urges its listeners to enter a sweepstakes for a free trip to Hawaii, repeatedly insisting that they have "nothing to lose, nothing to lose."*[40]

THE PHONE RINGS; WE ANSWER IT. This simple Pavlovian response is being exploited by marketers as never before. Every day, 18 million Americans are subjected to telephone sales pitches, and the telemarketing industry continues to grow at the astounding rate of 30 percent per year.[41] The growth of telemarketing may be an unqualified boon to marketers, but for most of us it is disruptive, annoying, even dangerous. As the real-life examples above illustrate, telemarketing is laying siege to our last vestiges of peace and privacy—a commercial battering ram forcing its way into the last ad-free spaces in our lives.

The rise of telemarketing parallels the increasing clutter of traditional advertising media. For marketers fleeing the crowded fields of television and print, the telephone offers an opportunity to capture consumers' undivided attention. As one ad for a telephone-marketing system put it, "You can talk with your customers without getting zapped, scanned, or flipped....It'll promote your product in a way that can't be turned off,

tuned out, or passed by."[42]

Because most people view their home phones as instruments for communication with loved ones, telemarketers may hope that calling at home lends ersatz intimacy to their sales pitches. But perhaps the greatest attraction of the telephone, for marketers, is its compelling quality. A ringing telephone is an imperative that few can resist or ignore. This reflex is so strong that, reportedly, a man standing on a building ledge, preparing to jump to his death, actually climbed back inside to answer his phone.[43]

Telemarketing may be gaining favor among advertisers, but it is extraordinarily unpopular with the rest of us. A 1990 Roper poll found telephone solicitations at the top of the list of what annoys Americans most, and 70 percent surveyed said telemarketing is "a major annoyance."[44] When columnist Abigail Van Buren (Dear Abby) suggested that people who were tired of receiving computer-generated calls write to the Federal Communications Commission, the agency received 1,500 complaints in two months.[45] Even many telemarketers privately admit that phone solicitations are a pain in the neck. As one lamented, "How can we hope to change our image in the eyes of the rest of the world when we ourselves resent these calls as well?"[46]

Why are telemarketing calls so widely despised? First, they tie up phone lines. Sophisticated computer autodialers dial phone numbers in sequence and deliver prerecorded sales pitches. These

Services like Telematch provide direct marketers with consumers' addresses to go with their phone numbers, or vice versa.

machines are nondiscriminating, equal-opportunity nuisances. With robotic persistence, they dial number after number, not caring whether they have reached an unlisted number, a police station, or the intensive-care ward of a hospital. Autodialer horror stories are common. One heart-attack victim lay in his hospital bed in unstable condition when an autodialer called to offer a dream vacation for two to Las Vegas.[47] (Autodialed calls to hospitals are now banned under a 1991 law.) Another time, an autodialer targeted nearly all of the 10,000 telephone lines at Emory University in Atlanta. The machine methodically called all of the patients in the university hospital, left messages in hundreds of voice-mail boxes, and rang every phone in the library.[48] Another kind of autodialer, the "predictive dialer," calls numbers from a compiled list rather than at random and then transfers the call to a human salesperson when the phone is answered.

Until recently, autodialers did not disconnect when the recipient of the call hung up; they "seized" the line until they finished imparting their message. This problem was worse than annoying; it jeopardized lives. In 1988, a woman in Amsterdam, New York, could not call 911 when her child collapsed because her phone line was tied up with a computerized sales pitch. She was forced to run to a neighbor's house to make the call.[49] Autodialers also seized the telephone lines of public emergency services, preventing people in need from getting help.[50] Recent legislation requires autodialers to disconnect within five seconds after receiving an "on hook" signal indicating that a phone has been hung up. However, in some parts of the country, older switching equipment can take as long as twenty-seven seconds to transmit an "on hook" signal back to the calling number. That means an autodialer can still tie up the line for thirty-two seconds after the phone has been hung up.[51]

The Right to Be Let Alone

Unlike junk mail, which we may open at our convenience, telemarketing calls insist that we answer them *now*. Even if we hang up immediately, the call has pierced the moment, interrupted whatever task, conversation, or train of thought we were engaged in. "It's wrong not because they talk to us on the phone, but because they call us to the phone," says Robert Bulmash, director of Private Citizen, an organization that fights direct marketers' incursions into privacy. Although he acknowledges that junk mail can also be a problem, Bulmash notes that "a piece of junk mail does not demand that we run to the mailbox."[52]

Autodialer calls and "live" calls are each annoying in their own way. Machine recordings can be easily hung up on, but they are also impersonal and deprive the receiver of any way to respond. Live calls are awkward because many people are not comfortable breaking into another person's monologue or appearing rude; skillful telemarketers exploit that instinct and often manage to coerce people into spending time, if not money.

The intrusiveness of telemarketing violates what Supreme Court Justice Louis Brandeis called, in his landmark 1890 definition of privacy, the "general right of an individual to be let alone."[53] Since then, American courts have refined Brandeis's definition, holding that an individual's right to privacy is greatest when he or she is at home. As the Supreme Court justices wrote in 1980: "Preserving the sanctity of the home, the one retreat to which men and women can repair to escape from the tribulations of their daily pursuits, is surely an important value....The State's interest in protecting the well being, tranquility, and privacy of the home is certainly of the highest order in a free and civilized society."[54] Because they violate the sanctity of the home, unsolicited telemarketing calls may be viewed as a form of commercial trespass. Each individual call may be no more than a momentary annoyance, but the cumulative effect deprives us of an ad-free refuge.

Telemarketers argue that they are merely exercising their constitutionally protected right to free speech. However, advertising and commercial speech does not enjoy the same level of protection as, say, political speech (see Chapter 7). And even fully protected speech is subject to conditions on the time, place, and manner in which they are delivered. You may not, for example, shout your political views from the rooftops at three in the morning. Likewise, advertisers have the right to disseminate their messages, but they may not do so in a way that violates the rights of others.

Of course, telemarketers would not continue to deluge us with calls if it were not profitable to do so. Industry defenders note that telemarketing now rakes in some $500 billion per year,[55] proof positive that many people do buy things over the phone. It's worth noting, however, that 70 percent of telemarketing revenues are generated by calls to 800 and 900 numbers—*consumers,* not salespeople or machines, initiate those calls. And many successful telemarketing sales come from calls to businesses, not private homes. Although it is true that some people welcome telemarketing calls, or are at least tempted by them, this group represents a small minority. Typically, a telemarketer must call fifty households in order to get one positive response.[56] In some cases, the calls-to-sales ratio is even higher. One insurance salesman reported that his autodialer commonly makes 2,000 calls before he can close a single sale.[57] Is it fair, then, to disrupt or annoy *thousands* of people in order to make one sale?

Of course, many nonprofit organizations also rely on telemarketing for donations or sales. Should restrictions on commercial telemarketing calls also be applied to nonprofit calls? Some opponents of telemarketing would carve out an exemption for nonprofit groups, for two reasons. First, the calls of many nonprofit groups are closer to political speech than to commercial speech and therefore deserve greater protection under the First Amendment. Second, nonprofits generally call their own members, who have already demonstrated an interest in the subject of the call. A congressional committee investigating telemarketing found that most unwanted telephone solicitations are commercial and that the vast majority of complaints were generated by sales calls.[58]

Autodialers can generate hundreds of recorded calls daily to private homes. They are now banned for most uses.

A Balancing Act

Clearly, a careful balancing act is required to protect the sanctity of the home without violating the free-speech rights of tele-marketers and nonprofit groups. Courts, agencies, and legislatures have attempt-ed to strike this balance since the late 1980s, but the final rules on telemarketing are still taking shape.

By 1991, twelve states had banned the use of autodialers in telemarketing, and twenty-four others restricted their use. But state legislation proved wholly inadequate to curb what is increasingly an interstate industry; telemarketers flouted the laws by calling from states with lax restrictions. Under pressure from con-sumer groups (including the Center for the Study of Commercialism), Congress passed the Telephone Consumer Protec-tion Act in 1991. That legislation restricts the use of autodialers, allows consumers to stop calls from live operators by plac-ing their names on a "do not call" list, and bans junk faxes. However, the Federal Communications Commission, in inter-preting the law, exempted several types of telemarketing calls, including those to businesses and to people with whom the company has an "existing business rela-tionship"—which can be loosely defined.

One day before the new law was to take effect, an Oregon businesswoman named Kathy Moser filed suit to stop it. Moser, who used an autodialer to pro-mote her chimney-sweeping company, claimed that it was unfair and arbitrary to ban autodialers while allowing live-operator calls. A federal judge ruled in her favor, and the autodialer provision of the Telephone Consumer Protection Act was put on hold in Oregon, pending an appeal by the Justice Department. If the government loses the appeal in the Ninth Circuit Court of Appeals, telemarketers in the nine states of that circuit would be able to use autodialers.

Despite a new law banning unsolicited faxed advertisements, junk faxes like this one continue to bombard office fax machines.

The PreFone filter, shown above, is one entrepreneur's invention to weed out annoying telemarketing calls. Before the phone rings, a recording informs telemarketers not to call back and invites personal calls to go through.

The Telephone Consumer Protection Act originally contained a "do not call" provision on live-operator calls, which could have established one national list of people who do not wish to be called by tele-marketers. (That provision was first offered to the public, for a fee, on a state level in Florida.) Marketers would have been required to check their databases against that "do not call" list. But that option was killed by the telemarketing industry. Instead, the FCC required each company to main-tain its *own* "do not call" list. When a telemarketer calls, you may ask to be put on the company's list; if you are called back, you may seek redress. That's the good news. The bad news is that there are as many as 565,000 companies that do telemarketing in the United States,[59] and each of them is entitled to call you once. Moreover, the law's loopholes may make it hard to prove that a company *intention-ally* called an unwilling consumer.

What People Have Done

A few years ago, Robert Bulmash received one too many telemarketing calls during dinner. Bulmash, a Chicago paralegal, decided to draw the line. Now, when a telemarketer calls, Bulmash is excruciatingly polite: "Well, this certainly is a coincidence," he might say, "I was just about to go out and find a subscrip-tion card for that very magazine." Then, congratulating the unsuspecting telemar-keter on his or her exemplary sales job, Bulmash asks for the name of the firm he or she works for. Armed with this infor-mation, Bulmash sends a warning letter to the firm. "I am unwilling to allow your free use of my time and telephone," the letter begins. "I will accept junk calls for a $100 fee, due within 30 days of such use.…Your junk call will constitute your agreement to the reasonableness of my fee." Believe it or not, Bulmash has

actually collected his fee a few times, and he hardly ever gets junk calls anymore.[60]

Encouraged by this success, Bulmash founded Private Citizen, Inc., a nonprofit group dedicated to fighting unwanted intrusions from direct marketers. Twice a year, Bulmash sends the names of Private Citizen members to about 1,100 telemar-keting companies, fundraisers, and list compilers, along with a letter like the one described. Private Citizen members report that their junk calls drop by 75 percent or more. With characteristic flair, Bulmash has helped tap popular resent-ment against what he calls the "telenui-sance" industry. Bulmash once stood out-

THE 900-NUMBER INDUSTRY: MAKING THE CALLER PAY

The union of advertising and telecommunications has produced a mutant offspring: the 900-number industry. The 900 number is essentially a marketing device, a way to sell or advertise goods and ser-vices over the phone—at the caller's expense.

In the late 1980s, mar-keters gleefully discovered that some consumers would actually pay to be advertised to through 900-number hot-lines. Particularly effective, they discovered, were adver-tisements disguised as ser-vices, contests, or entertain-ment—especially the recorded voices of celebrities. For instance, actress Alyssa Milano of ABC's *Who's the Boss* promoted her teen exer-cise video through a 900 num-ber featuring recorded mes-sages that changed twice a day, which callers paid $2 to hear. Soon, according to one trade publication, marketers were using 900 numbers "to pitch everything from records to laundry detergent, encoun-tering remarkably little resis-tance even though they were actually charging consumers up to $2 for each call."[1]

The 900-number industry mushroomed in the 1980s, raking in $1.2 billion in rev-enues by 1991.[2] An astonish-ing array of products and diversions are now offered over the phone—from kinky sex to papal sermons. Certain-ly, some 900 numbers provide worthwhile services. For

instance, Consumers Union, the group that publishes *Con-sumer Reports,* maintains a helpful used-car price service that costs $1.75 per minute.

But much of the 900-number industry is fraught with problems. For one thing, the industry is a hotbed of fraud. According to Assistant Chief Postal Inspector K. M. Hearst, "900 numbers have been a very effective billing and collecting system for fraudulent promotions. Classic fraud schemes are thriving under this new technology." Like many scams, 900-number ripoffs are often aimed at peo-ple who have fallen on hard times. One 900 number pur-ported to offer tips on getting high-paying jobs in Kuwait, then charged callers up to $100 to hear information that was readily available—for free—from government agen-cies. Other 900 numbers sold work-at-home schemes, which left their (mostly elderly, unemployed, or handicapped) customers with lots of expen-sive equipment and unsalable merchandise. "Advance fee" loans are another popular 900-number scam. In one vari-ation on this theme, a 900 number offered $5,000 loans to the families of soldiers serving in the Gulf War. To obtain the loan, however, the families had to pay a $300 advance fee. Couriers came to collect the fees from the unsuspecting families but never paid the loan.[3]

Even legitimate 900 num-bers can be booby traps. Advertisements for 900 num-bers often downplay or omit information about the cost of the call. Now, however, when people call 900 numbers, they must be told the cost up front. The new regulations frustrate 900-number companies that count on consumer ignorance: After they went into effect in 1992, 900-number revenues fell by almost 50 percent.[4] Still, once a call has been placed, it is easy to lose sight of the fact that the meter is running. In fact, 900-number companies routinely employ tricks to keep callers on the line, such as saving important information for last or speak-ing so quickly the caller must call back to hear what was said.

The 900-number industry also serves as a powerful tool of the data collectors—mar-keting firms that are busy compiling electronic portraits of our tastes and buying habits. With Caller I.D., 900-number operators can view the phone number of anyone who calls in. With the right software, they can then match the phone number to the caller's name and address, as well as to information on his or her credit history and buy-ing habits. In addition to a host of disturbing Orwellian possibilities, this capability raises the specter of generat-ing even more junk phone calls.

side a telemarketing conference serving a "Junk Food Feast" of Twinkies and Ding Dongs. "If the junk callers insist on being referred to as 'telemarketers,'" read his press release, "we'll insist on referring to the Twinkies as 'green leafy vegetables.'"[61]

Some consumer groups are encouraging people to make the best possible use of the Telephone Consumer Protection Act (TCPA). The law allows consumers to sue telemarketers for $500 per illegal call, or $1,500 in triple damages for "willful" violation of the law. Michael Jacobson, an author of this book and the founder of the Center for the Study of Commercialism (CSC), tested the law by suing Citibank, the nation's largest bank, for calling his home three times—twice after being told not to. He won an out-of-court settlement of $750, which inspired a number of other telemarketing victims to successfully sue under the TCPA. CSC developed a Stop the Calls kit that includes tips on how to use the law and sue telemarketers.

Robert Buchan, an annoyed consumer and entrepreneur, devised the Junkbuster, a sophisticated answering machine that screens calls for telemarketers before the phone rings. Buchan's company, the PreFone Filter Company, promises to provide legal assistance if telemarketers continue to call.

WHAT YOU CAN DO

Keep a "telenuisance list" by your phone. If you receive recorded calls (outside Oregon), take down any information on the company and the date and time of the call. You may be able to (1) sue them for $500 in small claims court or (2) file a complaint with your state attorney general or the Federal Communications Commission, either of which may sue the telemarketer on your behalf. For live-operator calls, ask the salesperson not to call you again. Record the date and time of those calls, along with the name and phone number of the callers. If the same company calls again, you can take the same legal steps mentioned above. The more people complain or file suit, the more likely it is that companies will comply with the law. For step-by-step guidance on how to sue under the TCPA, order the Center for the Study of Commercialism's Stop the Calls kit by sending $3 to

CSC—STOP THE CALLS
1875 CONNECTICUT AVE., NW, SUITE 300
WASHINGTON, DC 20009-5728
202-332-9110

Don't be reluctant to tell theaters, civic groups, and other nonprofit callers not to call you again.

Urge your representatives in Congress to strengthen the Telemarketing Consumer Protection Act. Ideally, telephone companies would ask all of their customers whether they want to receive telemarketing calls. If not, the phone company could block such calls or add that person's name to a national "do not call" database.

Many consumer transactions can land your name and number in a telemarketer's database. Here are a few ways to keep the calls to a minimum:

Don't have your phone number printed on your checks. Businesses often copy them into databases.

Be careful about dialing 800 or 900 numbers. Often, these lines are programmed to collect the numbers of callers, which are then compiled into telemarketing lists.

Put your name and number on the Direct Marketing Association's list of people who do not want to be telemarketed. Some, but hardly all, telemarketers check their databases against this list.

TELEPHONE PREFERENCE SERVICE
C/O DMA
P.O. BOX 9014
FARMINGDALE, NY 11735
212-768-7277

Join Private Citizen. For a $20 annual fee, Private Citizen will put 1,100 or so telemarketing firms on notice that you do not want to be called. Contact

PRIVATE CITIZEN
BOX 233
NAPERVILLE, IL 60566
708-393-1555 OR 1-800-CUT-JUNK

Contact the PreFone Filter Company for information on the Junkbuster, which is listed at $89.95 for the basic model. Call 1-800-NO2-JUNK

Litter on a Stick

Billboards and Outdoor Advertising

They are huge, intrusive, and obnoxious. They can't be turned off, and they're impossible to ignore. ✳ *In short, they are a marketer's dream.* ✳ *No form of advertising is more "in your face" than billboards. According to industry promotional literature, it is the "world's biggest medium....Outdoor {advertising's} sheer physical size allows for eye-stopping, bigger-than-life illustrations."*[62] *Billboards hover over our communities, stare down at playgrounds, litter our roadsides, and sidle up to schools, churches, and homes. They blot out the scenery and implore us day and night to smoke, drink, and consume. An annoying television commercial is gone with a flick of the remote control; an offensive magazine ad, with a turn of the page. But there's no escaping the billboards that confront you every day in the street or on your way to work.*

AND BILLBOARDS ARE proliferating madly. No one knows for certain how many are out there, but roughly 425,000 billboards line the federal highways alone.[63] Outdoor advertising grew from a $150 million industry in 1966 to a $1.1 billion behemoth by 1993.[64] The growth of the billboard industry serves as a cautionary tale of corporate maneuvering and marketing madness.

Outdoor advertising has been with us for centuries, mostly in the form of small signs for local businesses and attractions. But the billboard industry as we know it is a by-product of the automobile, owing its existence to the growth of public roads and highways.

"Americans love their billboards," croons Roland McElroy, president of the Outdoor Advertising Association of America (OAAA), adding that billboards "reflect visual vitality." But history tells a different story. For decades, many Americans have tried to remove this "visual vitality" from their communities either for aesthetic reasons or because they

Sadly, an empty, sprawling landscape like Monument Valley is the ideal frame for an effective billboard.

don't like what billboards are trying to sell them. "Pictures on billboards can be attractive, ugly, or just ordinary," says Edward T. McMahon, former president of the antibillboard group Scenic America, "but when they are enlarged to 700 square feet, raised 100 feet into the air, and randomly spread along a street, they become a form of litter—litter on a stick."[65]

The first rumblings of discontent were heard back in 1865, when the New York State legislature was moved to ban painted ads on rocks and trees. By the 1920s, many communities were seeking to regulate billboards as "aesthetic nuisances." Outdoor advertisers argued in court that government regulation violated the constitutional rights of property owners to rent their roadside land to billboard companies. But the courts rejected this argument, reasoning that billboards derive their value not from the private land they stand on but from the *public* roads they stand *next to*. Jurists call this the "parasite principle"—because billboards feed like parasites off the resource of public roads, the community has a right to regulate them. To understand this principle, imagine that every billboard in your community was turned around so that the advertising message could not be seen from the road. The billboard would suddenly be worthless, right? In fact, billboard companies are selling something they do not own: our field of view.

After losing the first round, billboard companies sought to make regulation too expensive for communities to afford. When offending signs were removed, the companies contended, taxpayers should compensate billboard owners for lost income. But the courts came up with a way to repay sign owners at no public expense, through amortization. Billboard owners would receive a grace period before their signs were removed, during which they could recover their investment.

As the federal highway system expanded in the 1950s and 1960s, concern about billboards also grew. Lady Bird Johnson launched a crusade against billboards in the early 1960s, which led to the passage of the 1965 Highway Beautification Act. To the amazement of billboard opponents, the OAAA unexpectedly came out in support of the new law. "I am glad to hear," said Oregon senator Maurine Neuberger, "that after years of opposing control of billboards they have finally and reluctantly been dragged in."[66]

Had the billboard industry decided to become a good corporate citizen? Hardly. Behind the scenes, OAAA lobbyists were busy rewriting the Highway Beautification Act to their own specifications. (Only defense contractors and the tobacco industry, some say, have a more powerful lobbying force than outdoor advertisers.[67]) The final result, a loophole-ridden parody of the law's original intent, has been aptly nicknamed the Billboard Protection Act.

For starters, the new law increased the permissible size of billboards from 300 to 3,000 square feet and removed any upper limits on height. It also allowed construction of up to 104 new billboards per mile, permitted signs on urban highways, and required no setback from schools, churches, historic districts, scenic highways, or parks.[68] And although it was intended to confine billboards to commercially zoned areas, the law's zoning requirements are extremely easy to circumvent. Essentially, it was a Highway Beautification Act for people who think billboards are beautiful.

Not surprisingly, the OAAA describes the Highway Beautification Act as "A Law That Works!" adding, "Taxpayers can only dream that every law that Congress passes works as well."[69] But apparently even a law that works sometimes needs fixing, because the OAAA continually lobbies to make it even more billboard-friendly. In 1977, the OAAA persuaded Congress to let it cut down those pesky trees that sometimes obscure motorists' view—of their billboards. Ironically, many of these trees were planted with taxpayer dollars under the Highway Beautification Act. Now billboard owners can even cut down trees in front of signs deemed *illegal* by the Highway Beautification Act.

In 1978, the OAAA got Congress to outlaw the amortization program, meaning that taxpayers must pay cold cash to get rid of illegal billboards. What's more, even the removal of illegal signs is conducted for the benefit of billboard owners. When a state gets federal money to remove billboards, it must pick the signs to be removed from lists supplied by the companies themselves. Naturally, the companies recommend removal of their least profitable, most dilapidated signs. So taxpayers actually pay to remove billboards their owners often want to get rid of anyway. Indeed, the Highway Beautification Act is "a law that works" for billboard owners. The law got rid of 2,657 billboards alongside federal highways between 1986 and 1988; during the same period, 47,519 new ones went up.[70]

Billboard companies also get a free ride

Images of alcohol and tobacco products frequently tower over residential neighborhoods. A billboard for Christian Brothers Brandy stands right next to a church as young children walk by. Billboards for More cigarettes and Hennessy cognac dominate a residential block of modest houses.

Photos courtesy of Scenic America

on taxes. Because the signs occupy only a few square feet of ground space, their property taxes are negligible. In San Francisco, for example, the average billboard grosses $60,000 for its owner but yields the city only $26 in tax revenue.[71] Charles Floyd, former president of Scenic America, protests this injustice: "Why should a business that depends wholly on the use of the roadways for its income not pay taxes?" he asks. "A trucking line may not pay personal property taxes on its trucks, but it sure pays a lot in road-user fees."[72] And although most cities require registration or permit fees for billboards, companies often simply fail to pay them. One Chicago study found that nearly a third of the signs in that city lacked permits.[73]

Perhaps these special tax breaks account for the astounding profitability of the billboard industry. "A finely tuned [billboard] company can operate at 40% profit margins," boasts Arte Moreno, chief executive of Outdoor Systems, Inc. of Phoenix, one of the industry's top ten companies. "Name me a business that can do better than that."[74]

Twenty-Four-Hour-a-Day Drug Promotions

One of the biggest problems with billboards is what they sell. In the early 1990s, nine out of the top ten spenders on outdoor advertising hawked alcohol and tobacco[75]—legal drugs that exact a greater cost in lives and dollars than all *illicit* drugs combined. In effect, billboards serve as "24-hour-a-day drug promotions," says Detroit Congressman John Conyers, Jr.[76]

Driven from television and radio, purveyors of cigarettes (and hard liquor) rely heavily on billboards to promote their products. But the same reasoning that was used to ban tobacco ads from broadcast media could easily be applied to billboards. Like TV commercials, billboards reach all age groups. So, long before they can legally walk into a bar or buy cigarettes, kids get the message that drinking and smoking are cool and glamorous.

Rural areas are scarred by billboards and their remains.

And the billboard industry rarely self-polices the placement of its ads; huge temptations to smoke and drink loom over playgrounds and schools. Research indicates that these ads legitimize the use of legal drugs. One study, funded by the National Highway Traffic Safety Administration, found widespread use of alcohol among teens and showed a link between alcohol ads and acceptance of drinking.[77]

And, for those who are already addicted, ads serve as a potent reminder to smoke or drink. For recovering alcoholics or ex-smokers, the sight of a bigger-than-life cigarette or frosty glass of gin on a billboard can be a painful test of willpower. Health warnings, which are mandated by law on all cigarette ads, are usually unreadable to drivers whizzing past billboards along the road or sitting in a stadium watching a ballgame.

Even more sinister is the fact that billboard ads for cigarettes and booze are concentrated in low-income, minority neighborhoods. Numerous studies confirm this: for example, a 1991 survey of several New Jersey cities found that 76 percent of all billboards in black and Hispanic neighborhoods hawked cigarettes and booze, in contrast to 42 percent in comparable white neighborhoods.[78] Tobacco companies defend their ad "targeting" by saying that blacks smoke more than their white peers, therefore cigarette ads go where the smokers are. But this is a chicken-and-egg conundrum: Which comes

Turning buses into billboards gives an already intrusive form of advertising stalking ability.

School children are never far from a looming cigarette promotion.

first, the ads or the higher rates of smoking? (See further discussion in Chapter 7.) Father Michael Pfleger, whose parish on the South Side of Chicago had been plastered with ads for cigarettes and booze, would argue that the ads come first. Alcohol and tobacco ads "are telling kids, 'This is where the power is, this is where success is,'" he says.[79] To a much greater degree than their white counterparts, black kids grow up literally surrounded by ads showing beautiful, well-dressed models lighting up or sipping cognac. "When you target a race of people for two of the nation's top killers, that's genocide," says Pfleger.[80] Dr. Benjamin Hooks, the former director of the National Association for the Advancement of Colored People (NAACP) denounced concern about billboard targeting as "paternalism." But it's worth noting that the NAACP accepted a hefty donation of free ad space from the OAAA.[81]

At any rate, African Americans are much harder hit by tobacco and alcohol-related health problems than whites. Blacks suffer disproportionately high rates of heart disease, cancer, and cirrhosis of the liver. For example, black males have a 45 percent higher death rate from lung cancer than white males.[82] Considering the magnitude of human

Motorists of all ages are confronted with offensive 30-foot-tall images like this billboard for a strip club in Richmond, Virginia.

suffering at stake, the chicken-and-egg question becomes a meaningless exercise. In either case, the ads are fostering life-threatening addictions. If the ads are *causing* higher rates of smoking in the black community, then Pfleger's genocide charge is not unjustified. But even if the ads merely reflect existing conditions, they serve to reinforce and exploit a deadly trend and blight inner-city neighborhoods.

Intergalactic Billboards

Just how far will marketers go to make sure their billboard gets noticed? As far as the heavens, apparently. In 1993, a firm called Space Marketing Inc. (SMI) proposed sending a mile-long billboard into space. Coated with a reflective, mylar plastic, the orbiting platform would beam down a corporate logo appearing as large as the moon. "Science fiction fantasy? Hardly," mused Atlanta-based SMI in its press release. "Imagine attending the festivities in Atlanta and in the sky above floats the logo and message of your favorite soft drink…actually orbiting in space, miles above the earth, and visible throughout the world with the naked eye."[83]

Almost everyone who imagined the prospect found it both ridiculous and repulsive. Environmentalists and astronomers denounced the idea as visual pollution and a threat to the beauty of the nocturnal skyline. Scientist Carl Sagan called it "an attack on science, an invasion of privacy for everyone, an aesthetic affront, and a misuse of the engineering talent in the national laboratories."[84] In light of such fierce opposition, Space Marketing agreed to withdraw the proposal, at least temporarily, but not before several companies had inquired about joining the project.[85] To discourage future intergalactic marketing, Senator Jim Jeffords (R–Vt.), Representative Edward Markey (D–Mass.), and other members of Congress in 1993 introduced the Space Advertising Prohibition Act, which, if passed, would prohibit outer-space advertising. That bill died in congress in 1994;

meanwhile Rupert Murdoch's Sky TV network was planning to project a hologram of its logo over European skies for five days in 1995.

What People Have Done

In minority neighborhoods around the country, citizens armed with rollers and paint buckets are fighting back against exploitative billboard ads. The revolt began with "Mandrake," a fifty-five-year-old African-American man who started whitewashing tobacco and alcohol billboards on Chicago's South Side in the 1980s. Since then, billboard-painting campaigns have been launched in San Diego, Dallas, Baltimore, Houston, Detroit, New York, and Jersey City.

Alberta Tinsley-Williams got involved when she noticed billboards for Top rolling papers in her Detroit neighborhood. (No matter what their manufacturers tell you, rolling papers are *not* usually used to roll tobacco cigarettes.) "Why should my child and millions of others be bombarded daily with [ads for] a product that I would never permit in my household?" Tinsley-Williams asked herself. So she spoke up at community meetings and in church, contacted her elected officials, picketed company facilities, and talked to the press. Within one month, every single Top billboard in her county had been removed, and the billboard companies promised never to run the ad again. She then began stalking bigger game: alcohol and tobacco ads. Tinsley-Williams formed the Coalition Against Billboard Advertising of Alcohol and Tobacco in 1988 to combat the targeting of blacks by legal-drug peddlers.

Michael Pfleger, the Chicago priest quoted earlier, resorted to billboard-painting after all else failed. A survey of Pfleger's predominantly black neighborhood turned up 118 billboards selling booze and cigarettes, compared to just three in a white area nearby. For months, Pfleger tried to reason and negotiate with the billboard owners. No dice. So he

picked up a can of red paint and obliterated the offending ads. *That* got their attention. Pfleger suspects billboard companies played a role in dousing his car with paint, slashing his tires, threatening his life and the life of his son, staking out his house, and having him arrested for nine counts of vandalism.[86] Pfleger was acquitted because, as one juror put it, he made a "moral statement" that was "wholly justified by the saturation of billboards in the community."[87]

In a similar effort, Reverend Calvin Butts, a minister at the Abyssinian Baptist Church in New York City, led a whitewashing campaign in Harlem. Subsequently, several companies agreed to remove alcohol and tobacco billboards near schools and churches.

Under fire, billboard companies often respond by ingratiating themselves to elected officials. Donating ad space to officials' favorite charities is a common ploy. As *Signs of the Times,* a billboard industry trade publication, suggests, "It would be difficult for the mayor (or other politicians) to sponsor or support anti-billboard legislation or ordinances if he/she had been actively using outdoor advertising for their own projects."[88] To maximize the impact of such "gifts," billboard trade conference attendees were told to "know the public service or charity interest of the Mayor, Planning Director, Council Members…[their] wives and husbands….Direct your public service efforts toward these causes."[89]

Nonetheless, grassroots opposition to alcohol and tobacco billboards has clearly had an impact. Cigarette and booze companies are beginning to reduce their outdoor advertising; the *New York Times* predicted

City bus shelters frequently feature imposing advertisements.

Many urban streets like Sunset Boulevard in Los Angeles are littered with distracting and sexually explicit billboards.

A giant Marlboro cowboy and tequila bottle welcome people to West Hollywood, California.

in 1991 that the tobacco industry will soon lose its distinction as the top outdoor advertiser. And the OAAA has urged its members to limit the number of boards available to cigarette and alcohol companies.[90] It remains to be seen, however, whether these voluntary curbs will have an appreciable and lasting effect.

Led by advocacy groups such as Scenic America, environmentalists are also banding together against billboards as a form of visual pollution. In 1993, when Representative Bud Shuster (R–Pa.) proposed overturning a 1991 ban on building new billboards along federal-aid portions of state-designated byways, Scenic America organized a coalition of thirty-five environmental and public-interest groups to protest the move. Removing the ban would have opened up 15,000 miles of scenic byways to billboard blight. But the public opposition, supported by several members of Congress, led to the demise of Shuster's proposal.[91]

Four states (Maine, Vermont, Hawaii, and Alaska) and hundreds of communities have banned and removed all billboards. Contrary to dire predictions from the billboard industry, tourist destinations report that the bans have had a beneficial effect on local businesses. "One of our greatest natural resources is our scenic beauty," writes the Vermont Travel Division. "Although there was some initial sensitivity that removing billboards might hurt tourism, it has had the opposite effect. Tourism is up for all businesses large and small."[92] According to Scenic America, more than 3,000 communities have prohibited construction of new billboards. Many others, such as Houston, Texas, have pledged to remove all existing billboards through a variety of means, including amortization.

Amid increasingly vocal protests against billboards, the Bush administration announced in March 1992 that it would resuscitate the Highway Beautification Act, but the outdoor advertising lobby has managed to thwart most attempts to strengthen antibillboard legislation. The Federal Highway Administration directed states to remove some 92,000 illegal billboards by December 1993, but Congress failed to appropriate funds for that purpose.

The courts have concluded that billboard regulation does not violate the constitutional right to free speech. In 1981, the U.S. Supreme Court ruled that a community may, if it desires, ban all commercial billboards. Then–Chief Justice Warren Burger put it this way: "Pollution is not limited to the air we breathe and the water we drink, it can equally offend the eye and ear."[93]

WHAT YOU CAN DO

Fight alcohol and tobacco billboards. The Citizens' Action Handbook on Alcohol and Tobacco Billboard Advertising, *published by Scenic America and the Center for Science in the Public Interest (CSPI), provides a blueprint for launching a successful campaign in your community. To receive a copy, send $6.95 to*

CSPI
1875 CONNECTICUT AVE., NW, SUITE 300
WASHINGTON, DC 20009-5728
202-332-9110

• *Work for a billboard ban in your town, city, or state. Information on how to get started is available from*

SCENIC AMERICA
21 DUPONT CIRCLE
WASHINGTON, DC 20036
202-833-4300

• *Pressure your elected officials to strengthen antibillboard legislation.*

Ambush Advertising

Video Monitors Everywhere

Our privacy is defined not only by personal information but also by personal space.

Direct marketers invade the former; a new breed of "ambush marketers" goes after the

latter. Advertisers are scrambling for ways to catch us in moments when we can't escape.

VIDEO MONITORS ARE popping up everywhere, filling our moments of silence with ad-filled programs. For instance, the Travel Preview System bombards those waiting at travel agencies with ads for airlines and resort destinations;[94] video screens playing closed-circuit "Cafe USA" hang above tables at food courts

Video monitors in airplanes play commercials to travelers with nowhere to go.

in malls, pitching products available at nearby shops;[95] Health Club TeleVision Network taunted sweating souls on the treadmill until club members complained;[96] and Ted Turner's Airport Channel snares the "upscale air traveler" stuck between destinations.[97]

The list goes on. As what the industry calls "place-based media" proliferates, every moment of time and every inch of space is fair game.

For example, the ride to and from work used to allow time to unwind or read. But a company called Metro Vision introduced the Commuter Channel, which traps mass-transit passengers with video screens hanging above subway platforms. The channel provides weather, sports, and transit information, and—its raison d'être—advertising. Metro Vision brags that it is "an effective way to reach the upscale commuter during prime times when they are otherwise unreachable by traditional broadcast media."[98] Some cities use the channel without sound, but in 1993, the company signed a contract with the city of Boston that left open the audio option. In response, several subway riders filed a legal complaint against the Commuter

Channel (still pending in late 1994), charging misuse of public space and invasion of privacy.[99]

Such dissenters are far outnumbered by ambush entrepreneurs. In 1992, Turner Broadcasting launched the Checkout Channel in grocery stores. Video screens peered down on people in the checkout line, imposing audible advertisements for grocery items. Although Turner retired the Checkout Channel in 1993 after poor returns (after all, most people in the checkout line have finished shopping), the experiment inspired other similar ventures. For example, NBC plants TV sets showing "On-Site," an ad-filled channel, *throughout* supermarkets and hopes to expand into fast-food chains, drug stores, and convenience stores.[100]

Christopher Whittle, notorious for pioneering in-school advertising with Channel One (see Chapter 1), developed "Special Report News," a video program delivered to over 30,000 doctors' waiting rooms. Patients already aggravated with a long wait, not to mention physical ailments, had to suffer through ads for toiletries, automobiles, and other items.[101] Luckily for patients, Whittle closed down the network in 1994 after disappointing profits.[102]

American movie houses have also entered a pact with the advertising industry. Once inside the darkened theater, moviegoers are at the mercy of the big, looming screen. "A CLUTTER-FREE ENVIRONMENT...A CAPTIVE AUDIENCE...NO ZIPPING OR ZAPPING," promises Cineplex Odeon in an ad placed in trade magazines. The movie chain

Turner Broadcasting's Airport Channel places its video monitors in airport waiting lounges where upscale travelers are likely to see the advertising.

also boasts high audience recall (after all, there are no distractions) and a "creative paradise....Without fixed time constraints, you have the ability to tell the whole story."[103] Of course, that's not what they tell the public. Terry Laughren, chairman of Screenvision Cinema Network, which distributes on-screen ads, denied the notion of a captive movie audience. Instead, Laughren insisted, "It is a *committed* audience—committed to seeing what is on the screen."[104]

Still, many audiences are outraged that a $7 movie ticket no longer buys commercial-free entertainment. In New York, when on-screen ads first appeared in the early 1990s, audiences booed and hissed, forcing many cinemas to discontinue the advertising. Warner Brothers and Walt Disney, unwilling to anger their customers, prohibit ads before their movies (although enforcement is near impossible). But movie chains

Cineplex Odeon Theaters, which sells big-screen ad time before its movies, promises advertisers "a captive audience."

Thanks to the Commuter Channel, public transit users in many cities are targeted by video monitors mounted over the waiting platform.

admit their allegiance doesn't always lie with the ticket-holders. "People in general are not in love with advertising, wherever it is," said Howard Lichtman, Cineplex Odeon's vice president of marketing. "It becomes a question of what you're used to."[105]

Lichtman may be right. Given no alternative, people become complacent about the disappearance of commercial-free zones. As a result, nothing is sacred. For instance, Michigan-based Privy Promotions intrudes on some of our most private moments by placing ads in bathroom stalls at stadiums and other public arenas. Shamelessly, Privy tells advertisers that "a captive audience of consumers will stand staring at the walls for... three to seven minutes each." Privy also asserts that "people hate to wait in lines without anything to think about."[106] After all, without the stimulation of an advertiser's slogan, what thoughts could we possibly have?

Flying billboards take advantage of large outdoor gatherings, marring the skyline with inescapable advertising.

The Checkout Channel imposed ad-filled video programs on shoppers trapped in the checkout line. Although that particular venture failed, other similar endeavors are in the works.

VideoCart installed large computerized screens on shopping carts. Equipped with electronic sensors, the screens could issue coupons according to a shopper's position in the store. This particular effort failed.

In the preceding chapters, we have dealt with the nature of the commercial approach or the target audiences. We now take a closer look at the specific content of ads that clearly abuse the trust of consumers: advertising that lies and advertising for products that kill. ✳ Officially, the business

Advertising

community condemns dishonest advertising. Industry spokespersons claim that only small, fly-by-night businesses stoop to deceptive marketing practices. But even blue-chip corporations have been caught in out-and-out lies. And if they are caught, the penalty— perhaps a day of bad publicity and a fine of

Lies,

a few thousand dollars—is usually trivial compared to the profits the deception yielded. ✳ The nation's two most popular drugs— tobacco and alcohol—together account for one out of four

Advertising

deaths. Yet, as we explain in Ads That Kill I and II, the makers of those drugs are permitted to advertise as if their products were the elixirs of health and the keys to happiness. Despite the manifest deception in advertising for potentially

Kills

addictive drugs, those who would regulate or legislate such advertising are paralyzed by political pressures.

Ads That Lie

"A Sure Cure for all FEMALE WEAKNESSES" was promised in a late-nineteenth-century ad for Lydia E. Pinkham's Vegetable Compound. This wonder drug, it seemed, could be used to treat everything from PMS to cancer. For kidney disease, the ad boasted, it was "the Greatest Remedy in the World." What, you may ask, was in this magic formula? A few herbs and a whopping shot of booze—the "vegetable" compound contained 19 percent alcohol.

LYDIA PINKHAM WAS CERTAINLY NOT THE FIRST snake-oil peddler to cash in on the credulity and desperation of the general populace. But she may have been the first to tell bald-faced lies in a national advertising campaign. As we'll see, she was not the last.

Most of us regard Lydia Pinkham's primitive ads with an indulgent smile, secure in our belief that merchants have evolved beyond that sort of nonsense. Advertisers still exaggerate, we tell ourselves, but now there are agencies and regulators to prevent them from telling outright lies. Right?

Right and wrong. There are agencies and regulators charged with keeping advertisers honest, but they cannot keep up with the sheer volume of falsehood in the marketplace. The U.S. Office of Consumer Affairs estimates that marketplace fraud costs Americans at least $40 billion a year.[1] From tiny fly-by-night outfits to the nation's largest corporations, countless companies are willing to stoop to deception in order to make a buck.

Lies or "Puffery"?

Much of this book is devoted to ads that lie in subtle ways. When a manufacturer of gas-guzzling

The Food and Drug Administration forced Eggland's Best to discontinue claims on packaging that its eggs do not raise serum cholesterol, but the company continued the falsehood in its advertising. Eventually, the Federal Trade Commission cracked down on the advertising.

automobiles pretends to be a protector of the environment, for example, that's a subtle lie. And innumerable advertisers engage in "puffery"—exaggeration and hyperbole. Claims that a product is the "world's greatest" or "new and improved" often fall into this category. Regulators have spent decades trying to draw the line between puffery and lies in advertising. Some argue that there is no difference at all; if puffery cannot be substantiated, it is a lie. As legal scholar Milton Handler wrote in 1929, "The statements in advertising are either true or false—there is no in-between. Legitimize puffing while forbidding downright falsehood and the door is open to subterfuge, litigation, and argument. No advertiser will ever believe, no less admit, that his untruths rise above the plane of puffs. And more important still, only the bungler among copywriters will resort to positive misstatements capable of contradiction when the same ends may be attained by the shrewd use of exaggeration, innuendo, and subtle half-truth."[2]

Handler was right about advertisers' preference for "subtle half-truth," although his call to erase the distinction between puffery and lies went unheeded. However, he underestimated advertisers' appetite for "positive misstatements." Particularly in a lax regulatory climate, the benefits of lying may actually outweigh the risks.

Food companies, for instance, routinely serve up huge helpings of untruth in their advertisements. A perfect illustration is a 1992 ad for Klondike Lite ice-cream bars that declared the product "93% fat

Nature's Plus's Source of Life, a dietary supplement, makes unsubstantiated claims about its miraculous benefits.

? ? ?
? Did you
know ?
? ? ?

A boneless pork loin chop is lower in fat, calories and cholesterol than the same size skinless chicken thigh.

Come out of the dark.

Information based on USDA Handbook 8 Series.

pork
The Other White Meat.®

America's Pork Producers

In an attempt to give pork an image makeover, the National Pork Producers Council compared lean pork chops to fatty cuts of chicken. This ad claims pork has less fat than chicken, but nutritionists say that when more typical cuts are compared, the opposite is true.

free." An FTC investigation found that the bars actually contained at least 14 percent fat, or twice as much as claimed in the ad. How did the bar's manufacturer justify such a departure from the truth? A close examination of the label reveals that Klondike Lite bars are a "93% Fat Free Frozen Dessert *with chocolate-flavored coating*" (italics added). So, Klondike Lite bars are indeed 93 percent fat-free, as advertised, *if* you peel off their thick chocolate coating. Klondike received a slap on the wrist from the FTC; the company was required to sign an agreement saying that it would not misrepresent the fat content of its products in the future.

Also in this genre is a 1987 television spot for Kraft Singles Cheese Slices, which implied that a young child could get as much calcium from a slice of its processed cheese food as from five ounces of milk. "Imitation slices hardly use any milk," the ad claimed, "but Kraft has five ounces per slice, five ounces so her little bones get calcium they need to grow." A slice of Kraft Singles may well be made with five ounces of milk, but much of the calcium and other nutrients in the milk are lost during manufacturing, so a slice of Kraft Singles has one-third less calcium than five ounces of milk. Again, the ad was pulled, but not before its dishonest claim deceived millions. In fact, the ad continued to run during the FTC investigation, and the case took eight years to resolve.

Food companies often lie about what is (and isn't) in their food. In 1985, McDon-

ald's tried to dupe consumers into believing that its Chicken McNuggets were made of "only delicious chunks of juicy breast and thigh meat." However, McNuggets at that time also contained chunks of cholesterol-laden, artery-clogging chicken skin, deep-fried in saturated beef fat.[3] And ads for Perrier mineral water asserted that the "naturally sparkling" beverage comes straight from a pristine spring. Fact is, Perrier gets its sparkle from machine-injected carbon dioxide, just like inexpensive seltzer water.[4]

In 1990, a company called C.R. Eggs introduced specially produced eggs that it claimed contained less cholesterol than ordinary eggs. Within three months, the Food and Drug Administration (FDA) ordered C.R. to stop selling the eggs because, it said, there was no evidence to support the company's cholesterol claims. Case closed? Not quite. In 1992, C.R. Eggs reincorporated as Eggland's Best and again began marketing its "low-cholesterol" eggs. This time, the company did not make its deceptive claims on packaging, which is strictly regulated by the FDA, but in *advertising*, which is only halfheartedly policed by the FTC. A TV commercial for Eggland's Best announced that "in clinical tests…even twelve a week cause no increase in serum cholesterol." One FDA staff member who read Eggland's clinical studies described them as "amazing" because they showed that Eggland's eggs actually *do* raise serum cholesterol levels, especially in peo-

What gasoline is as clear as island water?

Amoco Oil Company claimed that its more expensive higher octane "Silver" gasoline improved acceleration in cars driven over 15,000 miles, but information from automakers disputed that fact for most models.

ple who have high cholesterol levels to begin with.[5] Only after pressure from consumer groups and the FTC did Eggland's Best discontinue the ads.

Eggland is not the first company to use false or misleading "clinical tests" in ads. Ads for Pfizer Inc.'s Plax medicated mouthwash, for example, asserted that Plax removes "300 percent more plaque than brushing alone." Doubtful competitors asked the Better Business Bureau to investigate, and the BBB found that in the clinical trial the use of Plax was compared to brushing *without toothpaste* for just fifteen seconds. That revelation prompted two TV networks to ban the misleading ad, but Pfizer continued to claim that Plax removes more plaque than brushing alone. Wrong again: Independent studies conducted by the American Academy of Periodontology found that Plax has "no effect on plaque reduction."[6]

Some industries skirt science altogether. Dietary supplements, for instance, have escaped heavy regulation, leading to many bloated claims about the wonders of over-the-counter vitamins, herbs, and similar products.[7] Although some supplements can help prevent certain health conditions, advertisers frequently make wildly unsubstantiated claims. Typical of such exaggerations is an ad for Nature's Plus Source of Life, which promises that "the very first time you try it, you'll feel an incredible burst of energy. Guaranteed." Although the FDA issued regulations in 1994 to control the claims on supplement packaging, claims in *advertising* are only rarely policed.

Visual Lies, Lies of Omission

Some ads lie with pictures rather than words. A 1990 Volvo commercial showed an oversized "monster" truck driving across a line of cars, crushing all but a Volvo station wagon. A marvel of engineering? No, a paragon of perfidy. Volvo later confessed that its wagon had been reinforced with steel and wood and that

the other cars had been weakened by severing their supporting columns.[8]

Often, advertisers tell lies of omission. Northwest Airlines, for instance, offered "incredible vacation fares" in a 1994 television ad. However, vacationers who called the airline discovered that travel and purchase dates were so restricted that the best discounts were only valid for fifteen days (in midweek) out of the four-month period advertised.[9]

Similarly, Colgate-Palmolive boasted in ads that calcium in its Colgate toothpaste helps fluoride penetrate the teeth. But, until it was reprimanded by the American Dental Association, Colgate

neglected to mention that abundant supplies of calcium are also present in human saliva.[10] In the same vein, a 1992 ad for the Discover credit card made much of the fact that it doesn't charge interest on cash advances, just a "small transaction fee." But Discover's transaction fee is anything but small: A consumer who took out a $300 cash advance and paid it back in one month would pay the equivalent of 30 percent interest on the loan.[11]

Diet Industry Takes the Cake

The weight-loss industry deserves a special mention in any discussion of deceptive advertising. In fact, evidence suggests that this $33 billion[12] behemoth is founded on one big whopper of a lie.

The Discover Card advertised that it charged no interest on cash advances paid in full within a month, unlike the card belonging to the man in the commercial. However, Discover's transaction "fee," imposed even on payments made promptly, is often higher than interest would have been.

According to experts on obesity, there is no evidence that *any* weight-loss product or service produces lasting results. The success rate for all diets—commercial or medically supervised—is extremely low. Researchers at a National Institutes of Health conference in 1992 concluded that more than nine out of ten dieters regain most or all of the weight they lose within five years.[13]

Undaunted by that depressing reality, the weight-loss industry continues to hawk its powdered drinks, prepackaged dinners, and behavior-modification programs to the estimated 100 million Americans who are trying to slim down. Its ads feature astonishing before-and-after shots (occasionally featuring paid models who were not even on the advertised diets),[14] actors in lab coats exuding a vaguely medical air, and claims based on "scientific" data.

The weight-loss industry's scientific claims are often fabricated out of whole cloth. Optifast, for example, claimed in its ads that its clients "*maintain* more weight loss, on average, than on any other program. And we have large, published clinical studies to prove it." However, Optifast was unable to produce these clinical studies when it became the target of an FTC investigation. Optifast is not alone: According to Representative Ron Wyden (D-Ore.), head of the congressional subcommittee that investigated the industry's marketing practices, "Not one company has been able to produce one statistic to back their advertising claims."[15]

The diet industry has also been known to deny the risks associated with its products, although such risks can be serious. An ad for Medifast claimed that it had helped "more than 300,000 formerly obese patients without one instance of serious side effect." Yet Medifast and other liquid diets have been implicated in cases of gallbladder disease, among other ailments.

How do they get away with it? Again, regulators are just no match for diet marketers. "There aren't enough of us to go after every single diet product," says Susan Cohn of the FTC's advertising compliance program. "If we took every single attorney in this division and put them on a diet case, we still couldn't cover the whole field."[16] The result, according to Representative Wyden, is that the diet industry "has grown at an extraordinary rate, and it has been left completely unregulated. It's an open field. The cops weren't on the beat and there weren't any rules."[17]

Following the congressional investigation, the FTC, FDA, and the National Association of Attorneys General have joined in a laudable, if overdue, effort to crack down on false and misleading diet advertising. In September 1993, the FTC issued complaints against five of the major diet companies, including Jenny Craig, Weight Watchers, Nutri-System, Physicians Weight Loss Centers, and the Diet Center. Among other charges, the FTC cited failure to support claims that "their customers typically are successful in reaching their weight loss goals or maintaining them long-term." Jenny Craig and Weight Watchers went on to litigate the charges while the other three settled with the FTC out of court, agreeing to discontinue the misleading advertising.[18]

Deceiving the Desperate

As Lydia Pinkham no doubt discovered, desperate people are easy marks for deceptive advertising. The sick, the bald, the overweight, the infertile—many of these have fallen prey to purveyors of advertised "remedies."

Sadly, some of the most outrageous lies in advertising are aimed at the most desperate. A company called International

Airlines often publicize fares without mentioning restrictions. Trans World Airlines advertised a $149 ticket to Puerto Rico, but that price bought only one-half of a round-trip ticket and was only available in conjunction with purchase of hotel accommodations or car rental.

White Cross marketed Immune Plus, a vitamin supplement purported to cure AIDS, in San Francisco. "RESULTS SHOW IMPROVED IMMUNE SYSTEMS!" shouted the headline of one ad, which went on to describe a pilot test in which twenty-six of twenty-eight AIDS patients "showed significant improvement, and no patient remained in the AIDS category." Those who grasped at this straw were summarily bilked out of $300 for a four-month supply of the phony remedy.[19] International White Cross was nabbed by the FTC, but similar scams proliferate wherever there is money to be made off the suffering of others.

Infertile couples are another favorite target for advertised scams. "Yes! You Will Become Pregnant," proclaims the headline of an ad for Rabbit Computers, a device that purports to help women determine their most fertile days. In their fervent hope for a high-tech solution, some infertile couples may have overlooked the fine print, which promises results only if "you're medically able to conceive." That ad was modified after it drew objections from the Council of Better Business Bureaus. But, like B-grade movie monsters, similar ads just keep coming back.

Bald men have long been victimized by ads for fake miracle cures. One recent example is an infomercial for a product called Omexin. "I'd say that nine out of ten patients that I've put on [Omexin] stopped losing hair...." declares a narrator. "To prove that Omexin really works, we've done thorough, extensive testing

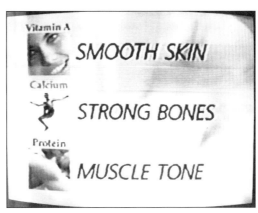

The American Dairy Association (ADA) claimed that Vitamin A in milk helps keep skin smooth, but Americans' skin problems are rarely caused by Vitamin A deficiency. Moreover, exercise—not protein—builds muscles.

In a classic deceptive ad, a Monster Truck roars over a row of cars, crushing all but the Volvo. Unbeknownst to viewers, the Volvo was reinforced to survive the weight of the truck.

using medically sound methods and applying the highest scientific standards." Those claims were completely bogus, says the FTC, which ordered Omexin's manufacturers to pull the ads.[20] The FTC pulled similarly deceptive infomercials for the EuroTrym Diet Patch (a so-called weight-loss aid), Foliplexx (another "cure" for baldness), and Y-Bron (a phony impotence remedy).

Some forms of advertising—such as telemarketing—seem to be particularly well-suited to exploitative scams. Indeed, John Barker of the National Consumers League has observed that "the telephone is fast becoming a slot machine with the odds heavily in favor of the house."[21] Heartbreaking stories of "telemarks" are legion. In 1992, for instance, a woman named Sonya Louis received a call from a Houston company, informing her that she had just won a new car. To collect her prize, all she had to do was pay $599 in "shipping charges." Louis, who suffers from sickle-cell anemia, told the caller she was poor, disabled, and couldn't afford to be ripped off. But the caller insisted that the offer was for real and even asked Louis to pick out the color car she wanted. Louis took the leap of faith. She borrowed the money from her grandmother, who took out a cash advance on her credit card. After taking Louis' money, the Houston firm vanished. Louis is not alone: A recent Harris poll found that nine out of ten Americans had been approached by telemarketers with similar phony prize schemes; three out of ten said they have responded at some time.[22]

What People Have Done

Industry has many kinds of voluntary guidelines for preventing deceptive advertising, but the key word here is *voluntary.* The Council of Better Business Bureaus' National Advertising Division, for example, attempts to hold companies to a code of ethical advertising practices. However, the council has no enforcement provision.

Government agencies have a mixed record on combating lies in advertising. Some state attorneys general have been very active in this area. The Federal Trade Commission is sporadically active, although it was practically dormant throughout the 1980s. Again, because of the huge volume of falsehood that pervades advertising, regulators tend to focus on the most blatant lies while innuendo and puffery often go unchallenged.

The Center for Science in the Public Interest hosts the Annual Hubbard Lemon Awards in which leading consumer organizations "dishonor" the most misleading ads of the year. Named after Harlan Page Hubbard, the creator of Lydia Pinkham's ad campaign, the event draws attention to the prevalence of deceptive ads and the failure of the FTC to effectively stop them. In some instances, Hubbard recipients have been shamed into amending their claims.

Another nonprofit organization, the National Consumers League, runs a National Fraud Information Center (NFIC), which provides information, referral services, and assistance in filing complaints regarding deceptive advertising, telemarketing fraud, or other scams. Founded in 1992, the NFIC filed 10,000 consumer-fraud complaints with federal officials in its first six months.

This ad implies that doctors independently encourage patients to eat more Yoplait custard-style yogurt. The small print says Yoplait surveyed a group of 600 doctors but fails to divulge what exactly they were asked—perhaps: "Would you recommend Yoplait over chocolate ice cream?" Yoplait refused to disclose details of its research.

Ads That Kill I

Tobacco

"Cigarette smoking," says former Surgeon General Dr. C. Everett Koop, "is the chief, single, avoidable cause of death in our society and the most important public health issue of our time."[23] According to the Centers for Disease Control, cigarettes kill 434,000 Americans each year[24]—more than automobiles, fires, accidents, alcohol-related causes, murder, suicide, AIDS, cocaine, and heroin combined.[25]

FOR HALF A CENTURY, THE TOBACCO INDUSTRY has conspired to conceal the deadly effects of its product. Cigarette makers have mounted what the *Wall Street Journal* calls "the longest-running misinformation campaign in U.S. business history."[26] Advertising was—and is—the most potent weapon in the tobacco industry's arsenal of deception. Ads have been systematically deployed to downplay the dangers of smoking, buy the complicity of the media, and seduce new smokers into addiction.

What We Know . . .

Cigarettes cause emphysema, chronic bronchitis, heart disease, miscarriages, and cancer of the lungs, mouth, esophagus, bladder, kidney, pancreas, stomach, uterus, and cervix.[27] An epidemic of lung cancer has followed closely behind the steadily increasing number of smokers. In 1930, 3,000 Americans died of lung cancer; today, the disease kills that many every nine days.[28]

What's more, you don't even have to smoke to be killed by cigarettes. Secondhand, or environmental, tobacco smoke has been classified as a "known human carcinogen" by the Environmental Protection Agency (EPA). A comprehensive study released by the EPA in June 1992 concluded that second-hand smoke causes 3,000 lung-cancer deaths and as many as 50,000 deaths from all causes among non-smokers each year. It also aggravates up to a million cases of asthma and creates up to 26,000 new ones. Secondhand smoke is also linked to pneumonia, bronchitis, reduced lung function, middle-ear problems, and respiratory infections.[29]

Why, you may ask (if you've never been a smoker) does anyone persist in this lethal habit? The answer is simple: Cigarettes are as addictive as heroin, cocaine, or alcohol.[30] The Tobacco Institute (the cigarette industry's Ministry of Propaganda) insists that smoking can be stopped if and when a person decides to do so. But a 1991 Gallup poll showed that 70 percent of smokers disagree, referring to themselves as "addicted."[31] Like other addicts, smokers suffer physical withdrawal symptoms and require steadily increasing dosages until they find a level that keeps withdrawal at bay. Relapse rates are astounding. Each year nearly 20 million Americans try to quit smoking, but only about 3 percent have long-term success. Even among smokers who have lost a lung because of cancer or undergone major cardiovascular surgery, only about 50 percent can resist cigarettes for more than a few weeks.[32] Most smokers *want* to quit, but addiction means not being able to "just say no."

. . .And When Did They Know It?

The hazards of tobacco have been suspected for centuries. Hard evidence began to accumulate around 1900, when medical experts noticed a suspicious increase in the incidence of lung cancer and tobacco juice was first used to induce cancer in a test animal. In 1925, cigarette "tar" was linked to cancer in lab animals.[33] And in 1938, Dr. Raymond Pearl, professor of biology at Johns Hopkins Medical School, released a study showing that smoking reduces life expectancy. "Smoking is associated with a definite impairment of longevity," he wrote. Pearl found that even moderate smokers died younger than nonsmokers, and heavy smokers died younger still.[34]

Like a terminal cancer patient, the tobacco industry's first response to the bad news was denial. (Actually, the denial stage has now lasted for about fifty years.) In the 1940s, cigarette companies responded to growing concern by making grand, specious claims about the health benefits of their products. "More doctors smoke Camels than any other cigarette," read one ad, implying that smoking was endorsed, if not outright prescribed, by the medical profession. Another Camel ad promised smokers "a harmless restoration of the flow of natural body energy," better digestion, and increased manual dexterity. L&M cigarettes were touted as "just what the doctor ordered," and Philip Morris cigarettes were "recognized by eminent medical authorities."[35] According to advertising historian Richard Pollay, between 1940 and 1960 half of all cigarette ads used health as a theme.[36]

The most infamous of these ad campaigns was launched in the early 1950s by Lorillard. For health-conscious smokers, Lorillard introduced Kent cigarettes with miraculous Micronite filters. "Kent offers the greatest health protection in cigarette history," the ads avowed. Micronite was described as a "pure, dust-free, completely harmless material that is so safe, so effective, it is actually used to help filter the air in hospital operating rooms." The magic ingredient in Micronite? Get this: asbestos. Just after researchers linked airborne asbestos with a host of respiratory diseases, including a rare form of lung cancer, Lorillard was encouraging people to put it in their mouths and breathe deeply. The "great-

Photo courtesy of Jane Zenger, Billboards Limited.

Tobacco billboards are abundant in crowded, inner-city neighborhoods, looming over—and sending unhealthy messages to—children every day.

est health protection in cigarette history" actually delivered a lethal double dose of carcinogens. Worse, Lorillard learned from tests in 1954 that asbestos was escaping into the smoke from its cigarettes but kept Micronite-filtered Kents on the market for another three years.[37]

Meanwhile, damning studies continued to pile up. In 1964, the U.S. surgeon general released a landmark report that conclusively linked cigarettes to cancer and respiratory ailments and hypothesized a causal relationship between smoking and heart disease. A second report, published in 1979, found that cigarettes were even more hazardous than was evident in 1964. In the report's introduction, Health Secretary Joseph Califano declared, "[This report] demolishes the claims made by cigarette manufacturers and a few others fifteen years ago and today: that the scientific evidence was sketchy; that no link between smoking and cancer was 'proven.' These claims, empty then, are utterly vacuous now."[38]

"A Very Moralistic Company"

Undaunted by the facts, tobacco companies continued to insist that there is some doubt about whether cigarettes kill. A typical denial was uttered by the chairman of R. J. Reynolds in 1981: "We believe the campaign against tobacco is based on statistical inferences unsupported by clinical findings," he said.[39] A Philip Morris executive interviewed in 1984 displayed an equally determined rejection of reality: "If the company as a whole believed cigarettes were really harmful," he said, "we would not be in the business.

We're a very moralistic company."[40]

Despite the tobacco industry's resolute denial, a few determined lawmakers and regulators managed to get health warnings on cigarette packs. Inevitably, they faced the economic might of the industry, and the wrath of its apologists in Congress—representatives from the tobacco states. In 1965, Congress rejected a proposal by the Federal Trade Commission to mandate detailed warnings on packs and in advertising, choosing instead to require the ambiguous "Caution: Cigarette Smoking May Be Hazardous to Your Health" on packaging only. A similar battle between the FTC and Congress ensued in 1969 and resulted in a somewhat stronger warning. Health warnings in ads were not mandated until 1972, and protracted debates ensued over the size of type needed to meet the law's required "clear and conspicuous display."

In 1969, the Supreme Court ruled that under the Fairness Doctrine, health messages about smoking should be given free time to compete with cigarette commercials.[41,42] That ruling prompted a clever series of TV spots that parodied tobacco ads (a wrinkled old woman on a respirator clasps a cigarette, asking "Aren't I sexy?"; a Marlboro-inspired cowboy bursts through saloon doors, then collapses in a fit of coughing). Those ads were so successful that tobacco companies "voluntarily" removed their commercials from television and radio, thus pulling the plug on televised antismoking messages. In 1971, broadcast ads for cigarettes were officially outlawed under the Federal Cigarette Labeling and Advertising Act.

By the 1980s, the tobacco industry was even more embattled. Dr. C. Everett Koop, President Reagan's surgeon general, spearheaded a crusade against cigarette smoking. As the health risks of secondhand smoke became clear, numerous states passed "clean indoor air" laws. The tobacco industry fought antismoking ordinances as if its life depended on it by launching propaganda campaigns and organizing phony, industry-funded "citizen" groups.[43] But the tide of public opinion was turning. By 1990, the number of smokers in the United States had dropped to 25.5 percent of the population, down from 40 percent in 1964.[44]

Fighting Back with Advertising

Against this backdrop, the tobacco industry launched a massive, two-fisted advertising campaign to keep Americans smoking and enlist new smokers. In 1970, tobacco companies shelled out $361 million for advertising and promotion, more than half of which was spent on TV commercials. By 1994, the total had risen to $4.6 billion, or more than $10 million per *day*—and that's without broadcast ads, mind you.[45] In addition to conventional advertising, such as billboards and print ads, tobacco companies are spending an ever-larger share on promotional tactics including sponsorship of events, direct mail, coupons, premium giveaways, and the like. In constant dollars, there has been a fivefold increase in tobacco advertising and promotional expenditures since 1971, making cigarettes the most heavily advertised consumer product in America.[46]

The marketing realities are chilling. Cigarette companies lose more of their customers each year than do manufacturers of any other product; 434,000 die from smoking-related diseases, and 1.5 million kick the habit. Add to those numbers the smokers who die of other causes, and it's clear that the industry needs to attract at least 2 million new

Kool, a product of Brown and Williamson, violates the industry's own rules against linking cigarette smoking to social prominence, success, or sexual attraction.

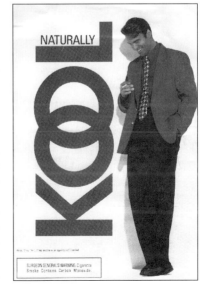

smokers every year just to break even.[47]

The tobacco industry insists that its ads are intended to persuade existing smokers to switch brands, not to recruit new smokers. However, there are only six major cigarette manufacturers in the United States, and two of those (Philip Morris and RJR Nabisco) control 75 percent of the market. So if a smoker changes brands, there is a good chance he or she will switch to another brand of the same parent company.[48] Advertising experts agree that market expansion—attracting new users—is a primary objective of all advertising. Emerson Foote, founder of Foote, Cone and Belding and the former chairman of the board of McCann-Erickson, one of the world's largest ad agencies, scoffed at the notion that cigarette ads are not aimed at expanding the market: "The cigarette industry has been artfully maintaining that cigarette advertising has nothing to do with total sales. This is complete and utter nonsense. The industry knows it is nonsense. I am always amused by the suggestion that advertising, a function that has been shown to increase consumption of virtually every other product, somehow miraculously fails to work for tobacco products."[49]

A Brown and Williamson marketing executive, quoted anonymously in the *Louisville Courier-Journal,* explains what market expansion really means to the tobacco industry: "Nobody is stupid enough to put it in writing, or even in words, but there is always the presumption that your marketing approach should contain some element of market expansion, and market expansion in this industry means two things—kids and women."[50]

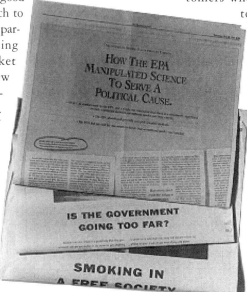

In 1994, reacting to heavy criticism, the tobacco industry launched an aggressive advertising campaign that attacked government regulation and disputed evidence about the dangers of secondhand smoke.

Targeting Teenagers

As the Brown and Williamson executive implied, the best way to recruit new smokers is to get 'em while they're young. Between 85 and 90 percent of all new smokers start before or during their teenage years, so marketing demographics compel cigarette companies to target adolescents if they are to replace customers who die or quit.[51] Naturally, tobacco companies become righteously indignant whenever anyone accuses them of aiming ads at kids. The Tobacco Institute claims to believe that "smoking is an adult custom."[52] But internal marketing documents and cigarette ad campaigns tell a different story.

In 1975, Brown and Williamson hired a market research company to design a marketing strategy for its high-tar Viceroy cigarettes. The strategy plan, which was later subpoenaed by the Federal Trade Commission for hearings on cigarette advertising, contained a chapter devoted to initiating "young starters" to Viceroy:

> In the young smoker's mind a cigarette falls into the same category with wine, beer, shaving, wearing a bra (or purposely not wearing one), declaration of independence and striving for self-identity. For the young starter, a cigarette is associated with introduction to sex life, with courtship, with smoking "pot" and keeping late studying hours. Thus, an attempt to reach young starters should be based, among others, on the following major parameters:
>
> Present the cigarette as one of a few initiations into the adult world.
>
> Present the cigarette as part of the illicit pleasure category of products and activities.
>
> To the best of your ability (considering some legal constraints) relate the product to "pot," wine, beer, sex, etc.
>
> Don't communicate health or health related points.[53]

Mounting evidence that cigarette companies market their product to teens prompted Surgeon General Joycelyn Elders to release a report in 1993 on tobacco use among young people. The report strongly criticized the tobacco industry for targeting youth by linking smoking with attitudes and activities that appeal to the young, including individualism, adventure, and sociability. "Young people are being indoctrinated with tobacco promotion at a susceptible time in their lives," wrote Elders in the report's preface. "[Tobacco promotion] provides a conduit between actual self-image and ideal self-image—in other words, smoking is made to look cool."[54]

Several ad campaigns illustrate the industry's shrewd understanding of how to appeal to teenagers. The best example is the now ubiquitous ad campaign for Camel cigarettes, launched in 1988, when R.J. Reynolds decided to give the ailing brand a facelift. RJR hired an illustrator to redraw its trademark Old Joe camel as a contemporary cartoon. The illustrator gave Old Joe Sean Connery's face, Don Johnson's hair, and dressed him in the coolest of duds.[55] (Old Joe's redesigned face, many critics have noted, bears more than a passing resemblance to male genitalia.) RJR then proceeded to spend $75 million a year to plaster Old Joe on billboards, magazines, t-shirts, jackets, sports arenas, and storefronts across the land.[56]

RJR insists that it chose a cartoon character in order to appeal to adult smokers. But Old Joe has become wildly popular among kids, enabling RJR to cut in on Philip Morris's Marlboro brand, which dominated the youth market before 1988. Even more disturbingly, the camel character is widely recognized by toddlers and young children. Studies in the *Journal of the American Medical Association* found that

almost one-third of three-year-olds associated Old Joe with cigarettes, that Old Joe was as familiar to six-year-olds as Mickey Mouse, and that far more teenagers than adults were able to recognize the cartoon camel. The studies also detected a strong correlation between brand recognition and sales patterns. Before Old Joe appeared in ads, less than 1 percent of smokers under eighteen smoked Camels; after the ad blitz 33 percent of these teen smokers preferred Camels.[57] A similar study by University of California–San Diego researcher John Pierce found a steady decline in adolescent smoking until the birth of Old Joe; the rate then began to climb 0.7 percent every year through 1990.[58]

The *JAMA* authors concluded that although "cigarette companies claim that they do not *intend* to market to children, their intentions are irrelevant if the advertising *affects* what children know. R.J. Reynolds is as effective as The Disney Channel in reaching six-year-old children. Given this fact and the known health consequences of smoking, cigarette advertising may be an important health risk for children."[59]

Even *Advertising Age* thought RJR had gone too far. An editorial accused the company of crossing "the divide between its legal right to advertise and its unique social responsibility." It argued that "Sprightly cartoon ads...subtly encourage youngsters to smoke."[60]

But calls to retire Old Joe have gone unheeded. In March 1992, then-Surgeon General Antonia Novello urged RJR to call off the campaign, to no avail. In 1993, following escalating complaints by antismoking groups and a petition by twenty-seven state attorneys general, the FTC proposed a ban on Old Joe ads.[61] In mid-1994, the FTC (whose five commissioners were all appointed by Presidents

The rugged image of the Marlboro cowboy has endured through the years, helping the brand become America's most smoked cigarette.

Reagan or Bush) decided not to pursue a ban, but observers believe the issue could well be revisited when new commissioners are appointed.

Tobacco companies target kids with other promotional tactics as well. In 1990, RJR division manager J.P. McMahon sent a letter to his employees, urging them to identify convenience stores patronized by young people, especially those "in close proximity to colleges, *high schools,* or areas where there are a large number of young adults" (emphasis added). "The purpose

of this exercise," he explained, "is to be able to identify those stores where we would try to keep premium items...at all times." After the memo was leaked to the *Wall Street Journal,* an RJR spokesman called it "a mistake."[62]

Tobacco advertisers circumvent regulations against TV advertising by planting high-profile logos at televised sporting events.

Tobacco companies encourage heavy smoking by swapping cigarette proofs-of-purchase for merchandise. Marlboro ran a popular "Get More Gear" campaign, offering "adventure wear" for Marlboro's self-proclaimed Adventure Team.

Smoke Your Way to Stardom

Sponsorship of sports events offers tobacco pushers another effective way to reach adolescents, who commonly idolize athletes. Tobacco companies have bribed their way into nearly every sport: They now sponsor the Marlboro Cup (horse racing), Winston Cup Series and Marlboro Grand Prix (auto racing), Vantage Golf Scoreboard, Camel Supercross (motorcycle racing), Salem Pro-Sail races, Newport Ski Weekends, Lucky Strike bowling, Winston Rodeo, Benson & Hedges On Ice, Virginia Slims Tennis, and countless other sports events. Tobac-

co companies spend over $108 million on promotion and advertising at sporting events alone.[63] In 1989, cigarette logos also adorned twenty-two of the twenty-four Major League ballparks.[64]

Ironically, sports sponsorship links cigarettes with activities requiring aerobic and respiratory fitness—the very qualities that smoking destroys. By aligning themselves with prime examples of aerobic health, tobacco companies subliminally refute the health hazards of smoking. The Virginia Slims Tennis logo, for instance, depicts a woman holding a tennis racket in one hand and a cigarette in the other.

Sponsorship also enables tobacco companies to neatly circumvent the ban on broadcast advertising. In sports arenas, cigarette logos are intentionally clustered near the scoreboard and other places where television cameras linger. As a sponsor of the 1989 Championship Auto Racing Teams, Marlboro got three hours, twenty-six minutes of in-focus logo exposure—as well as forty-six brand-name mentions—all for the bargain price of $8.4 million.[65] (A comparable amount of traditional ad time would cost $34.6 million during the Masters golf tournament or a whopping $103.4 million during a popular sitcom like *Roseanne.*[66])

I Smoke, Therefore I Am Free

Women have been the prime target of a sustained tobacco marketing campaign, the success of which can easily be measured in escalating rates of smoking and smoking-related disease. In 1935, the ratio of male to female smokers was three to one. During the late 1970s and mid-1980s, the rate of smoking among girls and young women outpaced that of their male counterparts. By 1985, men and women smoked in roughly equal numbers.[67] That shift directly followed the introduction of the first "women's cigarette" and a deluge of tobacco ads aimed at women.

As the proportion of women who smoke increases, more women get sick and die of smoking-related disease. The incidence of lung cancer in women has increased fivefold since the early 1970s, killing 60,000 women in 1991 and recently overtaking breast cancer as the major cause of cancer death in women.[68] Smoking carries additional health risks for women; tobacco use has been linked to cervical and uterine cancer, osteoporosis, infertility, menstrual irregularity, and early menopause. Women who take birth-control pills run a much higher risk of stroke if they smoke. And smoking among pregnant women may cause up to 4,000 infant deaths each year due to premature delivery and low birth weight.[69]

Higher rates of smoking are disastrous for women, but you'd never know it from looking at ads for women's cigarettes. Indeed, cigarettes are presented as agents of women's progress, and smoking as the very embodiment of liberation. The equation of feminism and smoking is an old ploy: In 1929 the American Tobacco Company orchestrated a parade of ten cigarette-puffing "feminists" down Fifth Avenue in New York to protest the taboo on women smoking in public.[70] A more contemporary example is Philip Morris's "You've Come a Long Way, Baby" ad campaign for Virginia Slims, which won the advertising industry's Clio award in 1968 and has appeared in hundreds of incarnations ever since.

One recent version of the Virginia Slims ad features an antique-looking, sepia-toned photograph of a man and woman dressed in turn-of-the-century garb. While the man lounges in an armchair reading the newspaper, the woman furtively smokes a cigarette behind a curtain. She has erected a life-size, two-dimensional model of herself, which she controls with a string to simulate her presence at the man's side. A caption beneath the photo reads: "In 1904, Mrs. George Hubbard found a clever way to sneak a cigarette while her husband still got the attention he demanded." In the foreground of the ad, a beautiful model poses in full color, smoking a cigarette beside the slogan "You've come a long way, baby."

Virginia Slims ads present smoking as the embodiment of women's liberation.

The manifest message of the ad is that women are now "free" to smoke cigarettes when and where they choose. Back in that dark, sepia-toned past, women were forced to submit to men's silly and tyrannical rules. But now women smoke, therefore they are free. There is also a subliminal message, which is hinted at by the models' costumes. The woman in the "old" photo is buttoned up to the neck in a prim Victorian housedress; the young model wears a revealing black lace evening gown. Black lace, long the fetishized emblem of "bad" girls and prostitutes, is an allusion to women's sexual emancipation. The ad links smoking, by extension, to freedom from sexual repression. However, the leering familiarity of the unseen narrator—who feels free to use the endearment "baby" —reassures the viewer that liberation (and smoking) won't render her unattractive to men.

Capri targets African-American women.

Like many ads aimed at women, cigarette ads often equate feminine beauty with slenderness and make barely veiled references to tobacco's reputation as an appetite suppressant. In the 1930s and

1940s, Lucky Strike made the connection explicitly by urging women to "Reach for a Lucky Instead of a Sweet." Today the reference is implicit in the pervasive use of "Slims" and "Thins" in the names of cigarettes marketed to women. "Unmistakably feminine," purrs an ad for Virginia Slims *Super*slims (an appeal to anorexics, perhaps?). A mail-in coupon urges the reader to "Try the cigarette that's as feminine as it looks." Women get the message: Nearly 40 percent of women who smoke say they do so to maintain their weight.[71]

Working-class women are a favorite target for cigarette advertisers. A marketing plan for RJR Nabisco, which was leaked to the press in 1991, revealed that the company intended to target its new brand of Dakota cigarettes at so-called virile females: hard-partying, poorly educated, low-income women aged eighteen to twenty. The prototypical virile female, according to the market researchers, holds an entry-level job and spends her free time at tractor pulls, or doing "whatever her boyfriend is doing." To lure these women, the plan suggested events such as "Night of the Living Hunks"—male strip shows—and premiums such as washable tattoos and his and her interlocking beer mugs.[72]

In addition to advertising and promoting their products to women, tobacco companies seek to ingratiate themselves by donating money to women's organizations. Tobacco companies have contributed to an impressive array of women's groups, including the National Women's Political Caucus, the American Association of University Women, the National Coalition of 100 Black Women, the Women's Campaign Fund, the Women's Research and Educational Institute, the American Federation of Business and Professional Women's Clubs, Wider

Opportunities for Women, the League of Women Voters Educational Fund, the Center for Women Policy Studies, and Women Executives in State Government.[73] Perhaps not coincidentally, almost none of those organizations have campaigned against women smoking.

RJR Takes a Trip Uptown

African Americans are also heavily targeted with cigarette ads. *Essence* magazine, which calls itself "the magazine for today's black women," gets fully 12 percent of its ad revenues from cigarette companies.[74] Again, demographic considerations dictate marketing strategy: According to *Adweek's Marketing Week,* "Tobacco companies have to target minorities because whites have been kicking the habit at a much faster pace."[75]

The huge volume of tobacco ads aimed at blacks helps reinforce a deadly trend: Black women contract lung cancer 58 percent more often than their white counterparts and have a 50 percent greater rate of heart disease. Black men are stricken with heart disease 20 percent more often than white men.[76] More than 48,000 African Americans a year die of smoking-related diseases—more than die from homicides, AIDS, car accidents, and all illegal drugs combined.[77] Yet only 14 percent of black teens smoke, compared to 25 percent of Hispanic teens and 31 percent of white teens.[78] The tobacco industry undoubtedly sees that statistic as a challenge.

In 1989, RJR Nabisco launched Uptown, a menthol cigarette high in tar and nicotine, in a crass appeal to black smokers. But when RJR test-marketed Uptown in Philadelphia, it drew bitter protests from black community leaders and then-Secretary of Health and Human Services Louis Sullivan, who called the campaign "slick and sinister."[79]

Jay Leno joked that the brand was named Uptown "because the word 'Genocide' was already taken."[80] Momentarily shamed, RJR withdrew the brand. But RJR continues to target African Americans. Market research for Uptown indicated that blacks prefer strong cigarettes with a mild menthol taste. So, in ads for its new Salem Golds, RJR touts "Max Taste. Less Chill."— which is, apparently, tobacco industry pseudo-jive for "strong cigarettes with a mild menthol taste."[81]

Lorillard Tobacco Company's Newport cigarettes, popular among African Americans, targets a truly captive market. In addition to saturating minority neighborhoods with billboards, since the mid-1980s Lorillard has distributed Newport cigarettes to prisons in several states with large populations of African Americans, including the District of Columbia (where black men comprise 90 percent of all inmates), Alabama, and South Carolina. The Newport program allows inmates to trade empty cigarette packages for sporting and electronic equipment or discounted cigarettes.[82]

Tobacco companies also appeal to blacks by contributing to a broad range of African-American organizations. The National Association for the Advancement of Colored People (NAACP), the National Urban League, the National Black Caucus of State Legislators, the Congress of Racial Equality, and the United Negro College Fund have all accepted money from cigarette makers.[83] Tobacco companies earn a substantial return on this investment; evidence suggests that tobacco money has bought the support, or at least the silence, of some black leaders. When the New York City Council proposed tough workplace smoking restrictions in 1987, several tobacco-funded African-American organizations opposed them. A particularly vehement opponent was Hazel Dukes, president of the state NAACP. Dukes argued that because blacks made up a large share of the clerical workforce, they would be disproportionately affected by the ban.

White managers would continue to puff away in their private offices, she said, while black clerical workers would be forced to sneak cigarettes in stairwells or on the street.[84] Dukes failed to acknowledge, however, that the substantial majority of *nonsmoking* black clerical workers stood only to gain from cleaner office air.

Ad targeting, like other increasingly popular forms of "niche marketing," offers an effective way to reach demographic subgroups. This strategy may be unassailable if the product being marketed is a detergent or a brand of underwear; in fact, it may even help identify and accommodate the needs of certain groups. But cigarettes are not detergent or underwear. As Philip Wilbur of the Smoking Control Advocacy Resource Center points out, "Cigarettes kill 30 percent of the people who use them. When [tobacco companies] decide they want to sell to a certain segment of the population, what they are deciding is that they want that segment to die at a higher rate. That may not be their intention, but that's the effect."[85]

Innocence by Association

As public sentiment turns against smoking, tobacco companies seek to buy public favor by presenting themselves as good corporate citizens, dispensers of charity, and defenders of constitutional freedoms. Sponsorship is a key tactic; cigarette companies give freely to arts and cultural organizations, charities, and groups that advocate for women and minorities (see Chapter 5, "Corporate Culture"). These "gifts" make up an increasingly large share of tobacco companies' marketing bud-

"*The unfinished business of the Bill of Rights...*"

Philip Morris Companies Inc.

Many consider Philip Morris's Bill of Rights campaign a thinly veiled attempt to buttress the company's "right" to advertise. Father Theodore Hesburgh of Notre Dame University (above) and Benjamin L. Hooks of the NAACP (opposite page) lent their prestige to the campaign.

gets. The proportion of cigarette advertising dollars devoted to sponsorship and promotional activities rose from one-quarter in 1975 to two-thirds in 1988.[86]

Perhaps most important, sponsorship purchases innocence by association for an industry that *should* be worried about its soul. Philip Morris, in particular, seems almost desperately concerned about its image of moral rectitude. Its "Good people do good things" ad campaign pictured Philip Morris employees who help the handicapped, protect animals, and so on. And in its 1978 annual report, the company claimed that "Good corporate citizenship is not an afterthought but an active concern in everything we do. Our social activities are not pursued solely for the sake of profit. They are mounted simply because that is the kind of company Philip Morris is."

Although it claims to be motivated by pure altruism, Philip Morris goes to great lengths to publicize its good deeds. In Louisville, Kentucky, the company spent an estimated $15,000 on billboards thanking itself for contributions to local charities. Each of the billboards featured the logo of a charity and said "Thank You Philip Morris" in huge block letters.[87]

Newport cigarettes uses playful, active images to support its deceptive slogan, "Alive with Pleasure!" On the right, Doctors Ought to Care (DOC), an anti-smoking activist group, parodied the Newport campaign.

Life, Liberty, and the Pursuit of Lung Cancer

Philip Morris also presents itself as a guardian of civil rights and free speech. In 1989, the company donated $600,000 to the National Archives, in return for which it got to launch a massive promotional campaign linking the company's name with the Bill of Rights. Philip Morris took out a series of television commercials and full-page newspaper and magazine ads that spoke glowingly about political freedom and sponsored a $60 million tour with the Bill of Rights.

Not coincidentally, Philip Morris began championing the Bill of Rights at a time when nonsmokers were vigorously asserting their rights to work and play in smoke-free buildings. By sidling up to the manifesto of democracy, Philip Morris clearly hoped to persuade Americans that smokers have rights, too. In fact, the Bill of Rights campaign coincided with the company's attempts to galvanize a "smokers' rights" movement, which never quite caught fire.[88] The campaign netted public relations benefits as well. As one Philip Morris vice president candidly declared, it was "a way to give the company an identity. We hope people will think better of the company."[89]

But lots of people did not think better of the company. The Bill of Rights ad campaign and tour was assailed by critics and drew protests in several cities. Dr. Sidney Wolfe, director of the Public Citizen Health Research Group, said the deal "smears the Bill of Rights with the blood of all Americans killed as a result of smoking Marlboro and other Philip Morris cigarettes."[90] And Michael Pertschuk of the Advocacy Institute argued that the cigarette company "should be treated like the Medellin drug mafia, not the Founding Fathers." Pertschuk and others also pointed out that Philip Morris's television spots were a clever way to circumvent the ban on broadcast advertising of tobacco. Nonetheless, the campaign may have succeeded in distancing Philip Morris from the horrors of smoking. As a spokeswoman for the National Archives weakly explained, "My understanding was that we were dealing with Philip Morris, the corporation, not a smoking company."[91]

Smoke Gets in Their Eyes

Philip Morris is a great champion of free speech, unless it's used to criticize cigarettes. When Dr. Alan Blum of Doctors

Ought to Care designed a series of public service announcements satirizing the company's ads, Philip Morris slapped him with a lawsuit. Philip Morris brought out its big legal guns to silence Peter Taylor, whose documentary film *Death in the West* showed real-life "Marlboro Men"—cowboys dying from lung cancer and emphysema. Taylor interviewed men like John Holmes, a cattle rancher who smoked for forty-five years and died of emphysema shortly after the film was made. Holmes rode with an oxygen cylinder strapped to his saddle, tubes going up his nose. After the film was broadcast on BBC television,

Philip Morris successfully sued to gain possession of all copies of the film except one, which was to be locked in a vault and never shown again. (Someone, however, leaked a copy to an antismoking group in California.) Philip Morris also tried to impugn the film's credibility by questioning the men interviewed in the film about whether they were *really* cowboys—as if that were the point of the film.[92]

Philip Morris is not the only tobacco company that muzzles free speech, directly or indirectly. Tobacco-dependent newspapers and magazines are often reluctant to antagonize major sources of ad revenue. Remember: Cigarettes are the most heavily advertised products in America. Every year from 1974 to 1992, cigarettes made the Publishers Information Bureau's top ten list of magazine advertisers by revenue. (By 1993, cigarettes had dropped out of the top-ten as companies favored other types of promotion.[93]) According to a 1992 study reported in the *New England Journal of Medicine,* magazines that rely heavily on cigarette ads

are almost 40 percent less likely than others to report on the dangers of smoking. Women's magazines that accept tobacco ads are 50 percent less inclined to warn their readers about cigarettes.[94]

Cosmopolitan editor Helen Gurley Brown defends her magazine's deference to tobacco companies: "Having come from the advertising world myself, I think, 'who needs someone you're paying millions of dollars a year to come back and bite you on the ankle?'"[95] Rather than bite tobacco companies on the ankle, *Cosmopolitan* kisses their feet. In January 1986, *Cosmopolitan* ran an article reporting the findings of a single study that suggested that smokers have a lower rate of endometrial cancer than nonsmokers. Although the article mentioned that smokers face other cancer risks, the emphasis of the article may have left readers with the impression that smoking is less risky than it is often portrayed.[96]

Accounts of magazine self-censorship are common. For example, in 1983 *Newsweek* published its first supplement on personal health, written by the American Medical Association. Although a stated goal of the supplement was to "help [readers] avoid self-induced illnesses," it contained but a single, meek reference to smoking: "If you smoke, you should discuss the risks with your doctor." The AMA authors admitted privately that their original manuscript had included strong warnings about smoking, which were excised by tobacco-sponsored *Newsweek*.[97] The supplement generated a hailstorm of criticism, which prompted *Newsweek* to include warnings about smoking when it published a second health supplement in 1984. But a third supplement, published in 1985, reverted to silence about the dangers of smoking.[98]

In her 1990 article entitled "Sex, Lies, and Advertising," Gloria Steinem explains

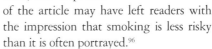

R.J. Reynolds attracts youth with the controversial Joe Camel (above, left). Activist/artist Bonnie Vierthaler in Portland, Maine, created a mock Camel ad (above).

how tobacco advertisers influenced editorial decisions at *Ms.* magazine before the publication went ad-free. The tobacco companies did not insist that *Ms.* run articles touting the health benefits of cigarettes, they merely canceled their ads if editors insisted on detailing the hazards of smoking. As Steinem writes, "By the time statistics in the late 1980s showed that women's rate of lung cancer was approaching men's, the necessity of taking cigarette ads had become a kind of prison."[99]

Advertising-supported publications have good reason to fear the wrath of

Shasta County Tobacco Education Coalition designed an anti-tobacco billboard.

tobacco companies. The big cigarette companies are now huge conglomerates that control vast ad budgets. RJR has merged with Nabisco; Philip Morris owns General Foods. Each company spends more than a billion dollars each year on advertising and promotion. And sometimes the companies turn vindictive. For example, Nabisco canceled its $80 million-per-year contract with the ad agency Saatchi and Saatchi after the agency prepared a series of ads promoting Northwest Airlines' no-smoking policy.[100] And after publishing two critical articles about tobacco in 1978, the editor of *Mother Jones* was told that the magazine "would never get cigarette advertising again."[101] (*Mother Jones* now refuses all tobacco ads.)

As a direct result of the media's pandering to cigarette companies, few people are aware of the magnitude of devastation caused by smoking. Half a century after the first studies showed that cigarettes

kill, 30 percent of the American population did not know that smoking shortens life expectancy, and almost 60 percent were surprised to hear that smoking causes most cases of emphysema. (Among smokers, the percentages were even higher: 41 percent and 63 percent, respectively.[102])

Reams of evidence show that health information *does* have an impact on smoking. For example, in the first two months after the release of the surgeon general's report in 1964, cigarette sales declined by 20 percent.[103] More recently, a campaign of anti-smoking ads in California, paid for with tobacco tax revenue, spurred a drop in smoking. Californians voted to hike cigarette taxes from ten cents to thirty-five cents a pack and spend a quarter of the revenues raised ($115 million in 1991) on tobacco-related health research and antismoking ad campaigns. The program has been a great success: smoking declined by 17 percent between 1987 and 1990, and a third of those who stopped smoking credited the antismoking ads for helping them quit.[104]

Curbing the flow of tobacco money into the media can help as well. Once free of the restrictive ties of tobacco ad revenue, editors take a more active role in making health information available. Garfield Mahood, a Canadian antismoking activist credited with pushing through restrictive legislation on tobacco ads in Canada, said newspapers began to strongly editorialize against tobacco use once advertising revenue was not an issue. "Take my word for it, the minute you get tobacco ads out of the newspapers," he said, "they become advocates. It's hard to do that when your editorial or news story is printed on the back of a full page spot for Player's cigarettes."[105]

What People Have Done

The most effective campaigns to curb smoking have combined bans on cigarette advertising, excise taxes on cigarettes, and public education efforts. A campaign launched in Norway in 1975, for example, incorporated those three elements plus stringent health warnings on cigarette packs. Before 1975, per capita consumption of cigarettes in Norway had increased steadily; in the decade afterward, smoking declined every year but one. Smoking among fourteen-year-olds, which had been on the rise, dropped from 17 percent to 10 percent.[106]

Although the tobacco industry predictably denies it, advertising restrictions *do* influence demand. A survey of thirty-three countries conducted by the American Cancer Society found that countries that severely restricted tobacco promotion experienced the greatest annual declines in tobacco consumption.[107] The study noted that the most effective policy "combines a total ban on tobacco promotion with repeated price rises and continual publicity on the health consequences of smoking" but determined that "the elimination of tobacco promotion appears to be influential in its own right."[108]

Ad bans must be monitored with vigilance because the tobacco industry is notorious for circumventing restrictions. After Belgium banned tobacco advertising, cigarette companies began marketing other products with what looked for all the world like cigarette ads, but weren't. For example, Philip Morris took out ads depicting a standard cowboy scene, "Marlboro" set in huge type along the bottom, and what appeared to be the familiar red-and-white pack rising out of the horizon. But wait— on closer inspection, it wasn't a Marlboro pack, it was a cigarette *lighter*, which is perfectly legal to advertise.[109]

Legislators are beginning to respond to the uproar over cigarette advertising despite heavy pressure from the tobacco lobby. In 1993, Representative Henry Waxman (D–Calif.) introduced a bill that would require tobacco advertisers to devote the top one-fourth of print ads to a health warning. In addition to other restrictions, the bill would ban tobacco

Artist Bonnie Vierthaler created this dark parody of a Merit ad.

advertising in any sports stadium within 2,000 feet of a school attended by students under age eighteen.[110] Several cities, such as Seattle and Baltimore, have also passed laws to limit tobacco advertising.

Another way to curb the volume of cigarette advertising is to reduce the incentive for tobacco companies to advertise. Several members of Congress, including Representative Jim Moran (D–Va.) and Senator Tom Harkin (D–Iowa), have proposed legislation to reduce the tax-deductibility of tobacco advertising.

In Canada, taxes were raised so that an average pack cost $4.72 in U.S. dollars, as opposed to $1.73 in the United States. Canada also prohibits tobacco ads but allows other forms of promotion, such as sponsorship. Perhaps as a result, 16 percent fewer Canadians smoked in 1991 than 1990.[111] Unfortunately, Canadian cigarette taxes were lowered in 1994 because the sharp differences between cigarette prices in the United States and Canada fostered a huge black market.

The antismoking movement is gathering momentum around the world. So many individuals and groups have stood up to the tobacco companies that it is impossible to list them all here. A few creative examples: In 1977, Dr. Alan Blum of Doctors Ought to Care (DOC) pioneered the use of paid counter-advertising as a means of undermining tobacco ads. For example, when RJR came to Houston to test-market Dakota cigarettes, Blum designed a satirical ad that read: "Dakota, DaCough, DaCancer, DaCoffin." Blum's group Doctors Ought to Care has launched a number of counter-advertising campaigns to satirize the lies of the tobacco industry. Similarly, Dr. Arthur Chesterfield-Evans, an Australian surgeon, picked up a can of spray paint and began "improving" cigarette billboards with clever antismoking messages. At his trial for vandalism, Chesterfield-Evans said, "If

I saw someone pouring cholera bacteria from a flask into a water supply, I would try to stop him, even if I had to steal the flask. To paint cigarette billboards is the same thing."[112] (The stories of other "improvers" of tobacco ads appear in Chapter 6, "Litter on a Stick.")

Lots of athletes are protesting tobacco's invasion of sports. Skiers rebelled when RJR tried to underwrite the Canadian Ski Association, and the National Hockey League has banned ads on boards around rinks. Former soccer star Pele refused to be photographed near tobacco ads. And Dr. Alan Blum coined the term "Emphysema Slims" when DOC made a "house call" to the Virginia Slims tennis tournament. DOC uses the "Emphysema Slims" name to sponsor its smoke-free tennis tournaments.

Several magazines have voluntarily banned tobacco ads, including the *New Yorker, Good Housekeeping,* and *Seventeen. Reader's Digest,* which originally did not include advertising of any kind, was among the first to report on the hazards of smoking. When the *Digest* began accepting ads in the 1950s, it specifically excluded tobacco ads. Among African-American magazines, *Heart and Soul* refuses all alcohol and tobacco ads; as a result, it can—and does—candidly discuss the health risks to the black community posed by those products. Taking ads for alcohol and tobacco is "a conflict of interest,"

according to *Heart and Soul* publisher Reginald Ware. "It would be a slap in the face to our readers to promote products that harm the community so much."[113] Some newspapers, which generally receive a much smaller percentage of ad revenue from tobacco than do magazines, also refuse cigarette ads. Prompted by antismoking activists, the *Seattle Times* made headlines in 1993 when it announced a new policy against tobacco advertising, making it the largest newspaper to ban cigarette ads. *Seattle Times* president H. Mason Sizemore bluntly explained that "these ads were designed to kill our readers, so we decided to refuse them." At least twelve smaller newspapers already ban cigarette ads.[114]

Several women's and minority organizations have kicked the tobacco habit. A group called Concerned Black Men, for example, does not accept money from cigarette companies. Nor does the National Organization of Women, whose former director, Molly Yard, once said that it is "contemptible…a form of prostitution to take money for something that's going to kill women."[115]

The tobacco industry is a huge, powerful monolith, but citizen activists have taken it on—and won. Activists helped kick tobacco ads off television, pressured government to require health warnings in ads and on cigarette packs, and limited smoking in public places.

WHAT YOU CAN DO

- *Work to ban cigarette advertising. Several bills have been introduced in the House and Senate but have stalled under pressure from the tobacco lobby. Write to your representatives and tell them that you support a total ban on all cigarette advertising and promotion.*
- *Contact your local antismoking group to find out more about bans and ordinances in your area. State heart, lung, and cancer associations are good places to start. Or you may want to contact one of the activist groups below:*

ACTION ON SMOKING AND HEALTH (ASH)
2013 H ST. NW
WASHINGTON, DC 20006
202-659-4310

STOP TEENAGE ADDICTION TO TOBACCO (STAT)
511 E. COLUMBUS AVE.
SPRINGFIELD, MA 01105
413-732-7828

COALITION ON SMOKING OR HEALTH
1150 CONNECTICUT AVE. NW, SUITE 820
WASHINGTON, DC 20036
202-452-1184

DOCTORS OUGHT TO CARE (DOC)
5510 GREENBRIAR, SUITE 235
HOUSTON, TX 77005
713-798-7729
(DOC has state and local chapters as well)

SMOKING CONTROL ADVOCACY RESOURCE CENTER (SCARC)
1707 L STREET NW, SUITE 400
WASHINGTON, DC 20036
202-659-8475

WOMEN VS. SMOKING NETWORK
1707 L STREET NW, SUITE 600
WASHINGTON, DC 20036
202-659-8475

Ads That Kill II

Alcohol

America has a serious drinking problem. Alcohol, the nation's most popular drug, wreaks more havoc than all illicit drugs combined. As lethal substances go, it is second only to tobacco: Booze is directly responsible for 100,000 deaths each year in the United States.[116] Alcohol causes cancer, liver disease, pancreatitis, neurological disorders, hypertension, and fetal alcohol syndrome— the leading preventable cause of mental retardation.[117]

ON THE NATION'S HIGHWAYS, the carnage from alcohol abuse is astounding. Every year, some 18,000 lives are lost—and countless people are injured—in alcohol-related car crashes.[118] The deadly combination of automobiles and alcohol is one of the top three causes of death among young people.[119] In 1990, alcohol-related automobile accidents took the lives of more than 7,000 fifteen- to twenty-five-year-olds, making it the number one killer of young people for that year. Drunk-driving accidents cost between $10 billion and $15 billion per year, as well as cause an incalculable amount of human suffering.[120]

Most of the 66 percent of American adults who drink are not alcoholics. But nearly half of the population has been touched by the disease of alcoholism: Forty-three percent of Americans have lived with, or are related to, a problem drinker or alcoholic.[121] And nearly everyone helps pay the costs of excessive drinking, an estimated $98.6 billion per year by 1990.[122]

Alcohol, with many of its attendant problems, has been around for thousands of years. Unlike cigarette smoking, which owes its place in American society to aggressive marketing efforts, alcohol use was well entrenched before the advent of advertising. The causes of alcohol abuse are still poorly understood and certainly complex. Parental example, genetic predisposition, and peer pressure are

Miller tries to enlist farmers in its lobbying efforts through a brochure emphasizing that brewers buy large amounts of grain.

major factors. Nonetheless, although alcohol advertising in itself cannot be blamed for America's drinking problem, booze merchants are vigorously fueling the fire. The $95 billion alcohol industry pours $1.1 billion into marketing each year.[123] To get those numbers in perspective, consider that the $315.9 million Anheuser-Busch alone spends to market beer is more than double the budget for federally funded research through the National Institute on Alcohol Abuse and Alcoholism.[124] Moreover, the imperatives of marketing—increasing consumption, targeting particular groups, enlisting a new generation of consumers—undermine every effort to curb alcohol abuse.

A Trip to Liquor Land

Let's step away from the grim statistics for a moment and into the cheery world of alcohol advertising— Liquor Land, we'll call it. The bars here in Liquor Land are spotlessly clean, well lit, and patronized almost exclusively by good-looking young people. They bear little resemblance to the ubiquitous smoky dives so familiar to Americans. Moreover, bar patrons never exhibit any of the unsavory side effects of drinking: slurred speech, obnoxious behavior, fistfights, vomiting, hangovers, or beer bellies. No one ever enters or leaves these wonderfully self-contained establishments, so the thorny issue of drunk driving never arises.

Liquor companies often associate their products with risky activities like surfing, which can be dangerous after a few drinks.

There *is* driving in Liquor Land, however—usually of very fast vehicles. A 1987 ad for Michelob shows speeded-up images of cars zipping through a city at night while a male voice sings: "I move better in the night / I won't stop until the daylight.../ I'm overheating, I'm ready to burn / Got dirt on my wheels, they're ready to turn." In fact, booze ads routinely associate their products with activities that require skill and coordination. A series of ads for Coors Light used action-packed images of surfing and auto racing with the tag line "Won't slow you down." In truth, alcohol is a depressant, which will indeed slow you down by short-circuiting your motor coordination. But here in Liquor Land, no one is bothered by the odd juxtaposition of dangerous activities with a substance that impairs reflexes and judgment.

Liquor Land beckons as a place where our dull lives will be magically transformed. "Absolut Magic," declares a vodka ad. "Paradise Found," "Fairy tales can come true," promise others. In an ad for Piper champagne, drinkers appear in vibrant full color against a backdrop of monochromatic teetotalers—just like Dorothy emerging from black-and-white wreckage into technicolor Oz. "It separates the exceptional from the merely ordinary," reads the headline. And in a TV commercial, an elderly woman approaches the Budweiser fountain of youth and is instantly transformed into a shapely young blonde in a skintight dress.

Hard work and achievement go hand

Sex is often an implied promise in alcohol ads. Canadian Mist Whiskey claims to be "a great first move."

Seagram links its gin to sexual prowess, saying that drinking Seagram's "could turn a 'maybe' into...'again.'"

in hand with alcohol in Liquor Land. Beer is a working man's reward for a job well done: After a tough day at the construction site or steel mill, "This Bud's for you." Drinking is even presented as a tonic for the intellect, as in ads for Guinness Stout that feature photos of great authors, with the tagline: "Guinness helps you get to the bottom of things." And hard liquor is presented as the very embodiment of success and affluence in ads that depict golf courses, mansions, and other trappings of upscale living. "Dewar's Profiles" of hardworking overachievers use clever wordplay to imply that drinking premium alcohol is, in itself, an accomplishment. Never mind that in the real world, heavy drinking is frequently incompatible with holding a job, much less climbing the ladder to success.

In Liquor Land, booze is a foolproof aphrodisiac and romance-enhancer. "[I]t could turn a 'maybe' into 'again!'" leers an ad for Seagram's gin. And St. Ides Malt Liquor offers this blunt advice to the aspiring date rapist: "Why don't ya grab a six-pack and get your girl in the mood quicker, and get your jimmy thicker, with St. Ides malt liquor." In reality, however, drunks do not make better lovers. Although sexual inhibitions may be reduced after drinking, alcohol is a well-known cause of impotence in men: As Shakespeare observed, drink "provokes the desire, but it takes away the performance."[125] Nor does alcohol promote marital bliss. As many as 43 percent of offenders in domestic violence cases are intoxicated, according to a study of police records, and often both the abuser and the victim have been drinking.[126]

Liquor Land, of course, is not reality. Alcohol advertisers, given the run of our culture, quite naturally present their product in the best possible light. We do not expect them to broadcast ads featuring drunk-driving victims or cirrhosis patients. Alcohol manufacturers are merely following the dictates of sound marketing practice. But when used to sell a potentially lethal substance, sound marketing practice can be deadly.

Here's to the Heavy Drinkers

Although they sponsor an occasional ad encouraging moderation, the booze companies *need* alcoholics. Ten percent of the adult population drinks about 60 percent of all alcohol consumed, so alcoholics and binge drinkers literally keep the industry afloat.[127] According to the Alcohol Research and Information Service, if every drinker in the United States consumed the official maximum "moderate" amount (about two drinks a day), the industry would lose 40 percent of its business.[128] No wonder the Miller Brewing Company (a subsidiary of tobacco-monger Philip Morris) feels so grateful to heavy drinkers. Miller dedicated its 1984 book *Lite Reading: The Lite Beer From Miller Commercial Scrapbook* "to that 20 percent of beer drinkers who drink 80 percent of the beer."[129] In another nod to the having-more-than-one crowd, a Miller Lite ad shows a six-pack with the headline, "The Joy of Six." Such ads reinforce the notion of beer-drinking as recreation in itself rather than as an accompaniment to other activities.

Target: Youth

Just like their counterparts in the tobacco industry, alcohol executives say they never target young people. Both industries claim to be sublimely indifferent to the rules of the marketplace, which dictate that even in a "mature," or saturated, market, new consumers must be enlisted to replace those who die or, in the case of alcohol, age out of their peak drinking years. The best way to attract new consumers, of course, is to target the

This Halloween Bud Light will make your profits go Psycho.

Get on the phone and call your Anheuser-Busch wholesaler today and make your Halloween sales scream. Bud Light has a great Fright Night promotion with your customers winning MCA Psycho Home Videos, Fright Night Treats, and an exciting grand prize — a party with Spuds MacKenzie at The Psycho Mansion. They can also take advantage of a special Spuds mug offer. And, best of all, they can pick up plenty of Bud Light . . . the light beer with the first name in taste. Backed by national TV, radio, print and Spuds MacKenzie, heavy consumer response will make your profits go psycho.

BUD LIGHT Everything else is just a light.

Circle No. 13 on Reader Service Card

young. Yet both industries insist, with equally negligible credibility, that they seek only to capture a larger brand share of the existing market.

Their promotional tactics tell a different story. Alcohol companies insert themselves into the landscape of childhood and youth, associating their products with wholesome good times. For example, at Cleveland's North Coast Harbor, a "family-oriented" park, huge inflated replicas of beer cans sometimes hover along the shore, attracting the wondering gaze of toddlers and kids.[130] And in flyers handed out at shopping malls, Anheuser-Busch encourages parents to "Bring the Family" to see its Clydesdale horses "pulling a bright red Budweiser wagon."

Beer logos even appear on kids' toys. Toy racing cars ("for ages 5 and up") are plastered with Miller decals, just like their life-size models. "While the brewer says it does not aim its advertising at children,"

Anheuser-Busch was forced to stop using the dog Spuds MacKenzie to promote Bud Light after protesters said the mascot blatantly appealed to children.

says Dr. John Slade, a specialist in addiction medicine, "the use of Miller trademarks on children's toys suggests an amazing lapse of judgment." He adds that putting logos on toy cars is particularly dangerous because "these toys directly link drinking with driving at high speeds."[131] Miller Brewing also licensed the use of its logo on a battery-operated "dancing" beer can. Although its box contains an inconspicuous disclaimer that the product "is not a toy and is not recommended for children," a reply card inside is more realistic. The card asks where the product was purchased and who will use it; choices include "toy store" and age groups "10 and under," "11–15," and "16–20."

Alcohol companies also launch ad campaigns with direct appeal to children. Just as Old Joe introduced Camel cigarettes to the kindergarten set, Spuds MacKenzie became a mascot for underage drinkers. Spuds, the cute bull terrier who served until recently as spokesdog for Bud Light, pandered shamelessly to kids. In one Christmas commercial, Spuds appeared in a Santa suit with a twelve-pack. And in summer 1990, when Teenage Mutant Ninja Turtle fever gripped elementary schools and day-care centers across America, Spuds frolicked with Ninjas on prime-time TV. The ads were highly effective: One study found that 82 percent of fifth- and sixth-graders could identify Spuds MacKenzie and link the dog with Bud Light. (In contrast, only

Booze ads aimed at college students are about as demeaning and sexist as they get.

10 percent of the kids surveyed were able to link Coca-Cola to the slogan "It's the Real Thing."[132]) In response to public outcry, Budweiser retired Spuds MacKenzie. But Anheuser-Busch has not reformed its ways; Spuds's replacement is the Bud Man, a cartoon character that became an instant hit with kids.

Often, kids watch beer commercials without even knowing it. Brewers employ "product placement" to sneak their brands into Hollywood films, TV shows, and music videos. An in-house videotape produced by Miller Brewing Company in the early 1980s touts the benefits of sneaking its products into music videos: "By placing Miller Brewing Company's products in today's music videos, Miller is able to penetrate the hard-to-reach young adult market. And since music videos enjoy tremendous frequency on network television, local stations, MTV, and VH-1, Miller reaches the all-important entry-level drinker over, and over, and over again."[133]

The Miller videotape went on to reveal that the company had inserted its products in such films as *Back to School*, *Fraternity Vacation*, *Cannonball Run II*, *Gremlins*, *St. Elmo's Fire*, and *Police Academy 2*; such TV programs as *Dallas*, *Miami Vice*, and *The A-Team*; and music videos featuring Madonna, Bruce Springsteen, and Cheech and Chong.[134] Clearly, Miller is reaching a large audience of kids and teenagers, as well as "young adults," with this marketing ploy. Indeed, kids are the real "entry-level drinkers"—the average age at which Americans begin to drink is thirteen.[135]

Booze companies may not really want young children to drink, but they *do* want kids to develop positive attitudes about alcohol. Research indicates that beer ads are achieving this goal. A study conducted at the University of California at Berkeley found a strong correlation between exposure to beer advertising and positive attitudes toward drinking. More than a quarter of the kids surveyed thought beer commercials tell the truth, and half the kids did not think beer commercials make drinking "seem better than it really is."[136] As Lawrence Wallack, the author of the Berkeley study, testified before Congress in 1990 "The more brands the children identify in commercials, the more likely they are to have a positive set of beliefs about the social aspects of using beer" and "the more likely they are to have a higher expectation to drink as an adult."[137]

If brand awareness in kids does indeed prove to be a reliable predictor of adult drinking, then we should prepare for an onslaught of serious boozing. American kids are extremely conscious of alcohol brands: A study by the nonprofit Center for Science in the Public Interest found that eight- to twelve-year-olds in Washington, D.C., could name more types of booze than U.S. presidents. One ten-year-old girl could name only four presidents, but rattled off the names of fourteen brands of alcohol. An eleven-year-old boy breezed through the spelling of Matilda Bay, King Cobra, and Bud Light, but stumbled over presidents "Nickson" and "Rosselvet."[138]

Alcohol ads contribute to an atmosphere in which adolescent drinking is strikingly common. A study done for the Department of Health and Human Services found that 13 percent of eighth-graders and 23 percent of tenth-graders reported drinking five or more drinks in a row in the two weeks prior to the survey.[139] The Department of Health and Human Services has reported that junior and senior high school students drink 1.1 billion cans of beer a year, and that sev-enth- through twelfth-graders consume 35 percent of all wine coolers.[140] Teenagers who testified before the National Commission Against Drunk Driving declared almost unanimously that advertising encourages young people to drink.[141]

Drinking 101

Alcohol companies must be coy about their appeals to children and young teens, but they pursue college students with all the delicacy of a bulldozer. Although many are below the legal drinking age of twenty-one, college students down about $4.2 billion worth of alcoholic beverages each year.[142] In addition to their prodigious thirst for booze, college students are prized as impressionable young consumers, in the process of forming drinking habits that alcohol companies hope will last a lifetime.

Booze companies blitz campuses with ads. Thirty-five percent of college newspaper advertising pushes alcohol.[143] These ads range from plugs for local liquor stores to invitations to "all you can drink" events and "chug-a-lug" contests.[144] Alcohol banners adorn frat house walls, and huge inflatable beer bottles rise like totems in quadrangles across the country. College students wear alcohol advertising in the form of hats, t-shirts, and other premiums offered for free at campus events. And many colleges subtly undercut their own alcohol policies by allowing the school insignia to be used on shot glasses, beer mugs, and other drinking paraphernalia.

Few booze ads could be considered highbrow, but those aimed at college students are about as demeaning and sexist as they get. Alcohol marketers appear to believe that the prototypical college student is (1) male; (2) a nitwit; and (3) interested in nothing but booze and "babes." Take, for example, a spring break college-newspaper insert that features Van Go-Go, a cartoon character, and several buxom females. Here are a few items from Van's daily itinerary:

• 10:35 AM TO 1:00 PM—MILLER LITE PARTY. SCAM BABES.

• 1:00 PM—HEAD TO THE MILLER OASIS. DUMP OFF EMPTIES. GET CLEAN CLOTHES. SCAM BABES…

• 1:05 PM TO 7:00 PM—MILLER GENUINE DRAFT PARTY. SCAM BABES.

• 7:10 PM TO SUNRISE—CRUISE THE BARS. LOTS OF MILLER LITE AND MILLER GENUINE DRAFT BEER. PARTY. SCAM BABES…

Similarly, the cover of the 1987 "Spring Break Guide" (published by brewers and inserted into college papers) features a husky college student, who is holding a huge beer can aloft while grinding lesser males into the sand and attracting adoring, bikini-clad women. These ads, of course, did not *invent* the sexist, sophomoric milieu from which they draw their images and language. But their prevalence, indeed their very existence, gives this milieu a kind of legitimacy. Boys will be boys, say the booze advertisements with a knowing wink.

Every year, thousands of college students head to warm-weather resorts for spring break, and the alcohol industry follows them. Brewers in particular have played a crucial role in turning this traditional getaway into a boozy bacchanalia. In the 1980s, the high-water mark of spring-break debauchery, a two-story inflatable Budweiser six-pack loomed over the festivities while revelers were treated to beer-sponsored beach concerts, the Miller Oasis "hospitality tent," and all manner of souvenir t-shirts and paraphernalia emblazoned with beer-company logos. Advertisements such as the Van Go-Go poster mentioned earlier presented massive overindulgence in alcohol as the recreational activity of choice.

Under pressure from then Surgeon

Miller beer draws up a babe-scamming party schedule for Spring Break.

General Antonia Novello and fed-up resort communities, brewers softened their hard sell during spring break 1992. However, the brewers still maintained a significant presence. At Lake Havasu, an up-and-coming spring-break destination in Arizona, women in bathing suits handed out Bud Paradise t-shirts and other items to bar patrons drinking Budweiser.[145]

Brewers have even hired students to help them infiltrate campus culture. According to a 1989 Miller Brewing Company publication, student representatives serve to "create brand awareness…merchandise, advertise, and market the product line…[and] research potential involvement with annual or special events." In 1983, Miller had 550 student representatives on its payroll; Coors had 182. After fielding criticism from college administrators, the brewing companies withdrew direct support of student representatives. The reps are still there, but their salaries are now paid by local distributors.[146]

Perhaps not surprisingly, college students spend more each year on alcohol—$446 per student—than soft drinks, tea, milk, juice, coffee, and books combined.[147] Alcohol abuse is a serious problem at American colleges and universities. Ninety-five percent of violent crime, 90 percent of reported rapes, and 80 percent of vandalism on campuses are alcohol-related.[148] Forty-two percent of college drinkers are binge drinkers, reporting that they have drunk five or more drinks at a time within the previous two weeks. Among their non-collegiate counterparts the rate is only 33 percent.[149] Twenty-eight percent of those who drop out of college attribute alcohol as the cause. And, ultimately, more undergraduates will die from alcohol-related causes than will receive master's or doctorate degrees.[150]

Take Me Out to the Beer Commercial

One time-tested method of reaching young people is through sports sponsorship. The predominantly young, male sports audience is also a prime market for beer. Brewers have so thoroughly exploited this advertising vehicle that sports and beer are practically synonymous in many people's minds. Boys, especially, get a heavy dose of beer advertising from the time they start watching sports on television.

The union of sports and beer was consummated in 1880, when saloon-keeper Chris von der Ahe bought a piece of the St. Louis Brown Stockings in order to sell beer in the ballpark. Almost a century later, Anheuser-Busch president August Busch employed the same tactic when he purchased the St. Louis Cardinals. Busch was unabashedly motivated by profit, rather than by any sentimental attachment to his home team. As he said in a 1978 interview: "Even though we've had losing seasons, on the balance sheet in recent years, the brewery is still ahead and so am I....The brewery's sales have gone up from fewer than 6,000,000 barrels a year to more than 35,000,000 now, partly because of the baseball association."[151]

Today, according to the magazine *Sports Inc.,* brewers are the single-largest "economic contributors" to the sports economy.[152] In 1990, Anheuser-Busch alone spent nearly $200 million on sponsorship of sports events and sports-related media buys.[153] Brewers are by far the dominant advertisers during televised sports coverage.

Again, regardless of whether they intentionally target kids, brewers can hardly be unaware of the fact that their ads reach millions of children and teenagers. In 1990, Super Bowl coverage on ABC drew 11.7 million viewers age seventeen and under. Twenty percent of the viewing audience during NBA games is seventeen or younger.[154] As young sports fans watch their heroes master the opposition, they can't help but sop up

beer commercials—along with the implicit assumption that alcohol and sports are perfectly compatible.

Like tobacco companies, the alcoholic-beverage industry benefits greatly from its association with athletes in peak physical condition. This connection serves to subliminally refute the increasingly dire warnings about the health effects of alcohol. If star athletes drink, we reason to ourselves, it can't be *that* bad for us. "It's really paradoxical that alcohol and all it stands for should be associated with excellent athletic performance," says Dr. William Beausay, president of the Academy for Sports Psychology. "You cannot have one and the other at the same time. If you're going to perform as a top-grade athlete, you have to cut out alcohol."[155]

Target: Women and Minorities

As alcohol consumption has stagnated among white men, booze merchants are training their sights on women and minorities in an attempt to boost sales.

Women represent a great untapped market. According to an advertiser who handles the Anheuser-Busch account, "The male market has been such an exploited market that there probably would be more opportunities with women. Beer makers are seeing a niche that hasn't really been talked to before."[156] Brewers are now taking the radical step of featuring women in beer ads for purposes other than decoration. Recent examples include spots of fully dressed women riding in rodeos and in professional office settings. Alcohol producers also target

To find out about Black history, ask someone who's lived it.

Coors

Brewers often seek to endear themselves to the African-American community. For instance, Coors, which has been accused of racist hiring practices, hypes Black History Month. Budweiser's Superfest features African-American performers, such as Kool and the Gang and Patti Labelle.

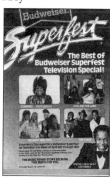

In late 1993, Remy Martin appeared to be targeting African Americans with a cognac ad containing sexually suggestive language. The risque ad (above) was preferentially placed in *Ebony* and other African-American magazines, while a look-alike version with innocous language was run more commonly in *The New Yorker* and other general-circulation magazines.

women with drinks designed for "feminine" tastes. Brewers are now test-marketing "clear beers" and fruit-flavored malt liquors—the alcohol industry's answer to the question, What do women want?

These marketing efforts have provoked the wrath of health advocates. "Beer marketers are endangering the health of women," says a spokesman for the National Council on Alcoholism and Drug Dependence.[157] Health officials and advocates fear, with good reason, that alcohol advertising will undo the gains they have made in educating women about the dangers of fetal alcohol syndrome. This syndrome, which can result when a pregnant woman drinks, is the leading preventable cause of mental retardation and birth defects. One in every 2,700 babies born in the United States suffers from fetal alcohol syndrome.[158] A spokeswoman for the Arc (formerly the Association for Retarded Citizens) points out that many pregnant women "think plain beer and wine aren't as bad as hard liquor," whereas, in fact, beer and wine are "as dangerous as a Manhattan or a Zombie." She adds that fruit-flavored drinks are particularly dangerous, as their sweetness masks the taste of alcohol and could lull women into thinking they are consuming a low-alcohol beverage.[159]

Booze companies also pursue minority groups—African Americans, Hispanics, Native Americans—with a vengeance. As we noted in the previous chapter, target marketing of racial or ethnic groups is not inherently bad. But when it is used to market a potentially lethal product to a particularly vulnerable popula-

tion, the use of target marketing is deeply troubling.

The minority communities that have been singled out for bombardment with booze ads are already reeling from alcohol-related problems. According to the National Institute on Alcohol Abuse and Alcoholism, alcohol abuse is the leading health and safety problem in the African-American community. African Americans consume less alcohol per capita than whites, but poverty and poor health care contribute to disproportionately high rates of alcohol-related disease.[160] And whereas drinking among white men peaks when they are young and then decreases, drinking rates among black men tend to increase as they move into middle age.[161]

Drinking patterns vary widely among Hispanic subgroups, but two of the largest Hispanic populations in the United States—Mexican-Americans and Puerto Ricans—have elevated levels of alcohol problems. "When compared to other ethnic groups in the U.S. population, Hispanic men are among the groups with higher rates of drinking and alcohol problems," says Dr. Raul Caetano, a pioneer in the study of Hispanic drinking patterns.[162]

In the Native-American community, alcohol abuse has reached plague proportions. Native Americans die from alcohol-related diseases at four times the rate for Americans as a whole, and the incidence of fetal alcohol syndrome is thirty-three times higher for Native Americans than for Caucasians.[163]

Against this backdrop, it is questionable whether alcohol companies should target minority groups at all. But compounding the problem is the *type* of appeals used to sell booze in minority communities. When addressing African Americans, Hispanics, and Native Americans, booze companies (especially brewers) flagrantly violate their own codes of ethical advertising guidelines, as well as commonly held notions of decency and good taste. Industry guidelines are often ignored in mass-market ads as well, but the most egregious violators, by far, are ads targeted at minorities.

For example, Brewing Industry Advertising Guideline #8 states: "Advertising should neither state nor carry any implication of alcohol strength."[164] But brewers produce high-alcohol malt liquor beverages specifically to market in minority communities, and their advertisements for these products frequently allude to the products' strength. TV commercials for Colt 45 feature cans "blasting off" or being fired out of a rocket launcher or submarine; Schlitz shows a bull smashing through concrete walls. The slogan for Olde English 800 puts it plainly: "It is the Power" (or "Es La Fuerza" in the Hispanic version). An ad for St. Ides featured rapper Ice Cube chanting, "I usually drink it when I'm out just clowning, me and the home boys, be like downing it / Cause it's stronger but the taste is more smooth / I grab me a forty [ounce bottle] when I want to act a fool." Similarly, ads for King Cobra warn, "Don't let the smooth taste fool you," and promise "The bite that's right." Perhaps the most blatant example is that of Power-Master, a high-test malt liquor introduced in 1991 by the G. Heileman Brewing Company. PowerMaster was marketed solely on the basis of its astonishingly high alcohol content—7.5 percent, or about 60 percent higher than regular beer.

References to "power" in ads aimed at minority communities carry a double meaning. These ads borrow the language

WHAT MAKES A MOMENT

A MEMORY

The industry urges people to mark important events by drinking. In this case, Courvoisier Cognac targets African Americans.

of the civil rights movement and pretend to offer empowerment to the disenfranchised and alienated. It is a cruel bait and switch. "PowerMaster is marketed to primarily low-income, powerless people....We all know that power and masterfulness do not come from a can of malt liquor—they come from study, from discipline," says Reverend Calvin Butts of the Abyssinian Baptist Church in Harlem.[165]

Brewing Industry Advertising Guideline #9 states: "Beer advertising should not portray sexual passion, promiscuity, or any other amorous activity as a consequence of drinking beer." Guideline #10 adds, "Advertisements should not contain suggestive double entendres or any other material that might be considered lewd or obscene." But when advertising to minority men, beer companies completely abandon their (already low) standards on sexual suggestiveness.

Ads for Colt 45 malt liquor, for example, present their product as an absolutely indispensable sexual aid. In a TV commercial for Colt 45, actor Billy Dee Williams declares, "Part one is the lady. Part two is the Colt. Now remember that the Colt is essential. And part three is a little luck. Well, I've got the Colt and I've got my lady. So wish me luck." Another ad in this series shows Williams endeavoring to interpret the body language of women at a party. An attractive young woman fondles her necklace, and Williams observes, "That means she has

A billboard for Champale suggests that alcohol can change a sour, distant couple into a happy, loving one. In reality, alcohol—and alcoholism—often do the opposite.

Ads for malt liquor, marketed most aggressively in inner cities, frequently allude to its high alcohol content, despite Bureau of Alcohol, Tobacco, and Firearms (BATF) rules to the contrary.

Exploiting— and trivializing— the Catholic tradition in the Hispanic community, Felipe II depicts two priests drinking cognac and gazing at the heavens. The billboard states: "Tomarlo no es pecado" (drinking is not a sin).

an interest in the finer things in life." Then the woman fills her glass, and Williams says, "And now she's pouring a Colt 45 and we all know what that means." Williams asks the woman if he may join her, and she replies, "You must have read my mind." The implication—that a woman who drinks is asking to get picked up—is reminiscent of the "she asked for it" defense popular among rapists. Each of these ads concluded with the not-so-subtle tag line: "It Works Every Time." This series of commercials appeared on prime-time television, during family-oriented comedies popular with African Americans.

The list of violators in this category is endless. In the December 1993 *Ebony* magazine, a Remy Martin cognac ad showed a liquor bottle below the words, "Mistletoe gets you a kiss. Imagine what this will bring."[166] An ad for Guinness Stout that ran in Hispanic magazines shows a bare-chested Latino man embracing a woman whose lacy nightgown has fallen from her shoulder, exposing much of her right breast. Translated, the ad copy reads, "Dark, suggestive, and delicious." St. Ides (which also ran the "Get your girl in the mood quicker …with St. Ides malt liquor" spot cited previously) claimed in one ad that its product was "guaranteed to get a big booty undressed." And in an ad for Midnight Dragon, a sexy female model caresses a beer bottle and purrs, "I could suck on this all night."

Brewing Industry Advertising Guideline #2 says: "Beer advertising should neither portray nor encourage drinking by individuals below the legal age of purchase." As we have seen, brewers have circumvented this rule with ads that are seen by millions of kids. But in the minority community, they go one step further. At the sixty-fifth annual White Mountain Apache Reservation parade in 1990, beer distributors dressed as Spuds MacKenzie and the Bud Man tossed rolls of candy, packaged to look like little Budweiser cans, to the children in the crowd. The parade also featured two kindergarten-age Apache girls carrying a twelve-foot Budweiser banner.[167]

Guideline #11 reads: "Advertisements should not associate beer with crime, criminals, or any illegal activity." Yet beer ads aimed at African Americans frequently allude to the inner-city underworld of guns, drugs and gangs. Two brews are named after firearms: Colt 45 and Miller Brewing Company's Magnum (slogan: "High Caliber Taste"). And an ad for St. Ides features this rap song from Ice Cube: "Mmmmm, I need some refreshin' when I finish manifessin' / Too cold to hold / Bold like Smith & Wesson / Ice Cube's in the house don't you know me / Pour out on the curb for the homies."

"Bold like Smith & Wesson" is an obvious reference to the gun of the same name. "Pour out on the curb for the homies" is more obscure, referring to the gang tradition of pouring beer on the street in honor of an absent or deceased gang member.[168] In another such appeal, St. Ides posters showed Ice Cube making a hand sign—thumb, index finger, and pinkie extended—that is associated with inner-city gang members.[169]

In the same vein, Olde English 800 erected billboards in African-American neighborhoods showing suggestively dressed women around a pool table, with the slogan "8 Ball Anyone?" In addition to the crass sexual allusion, those ads contain a play on the street expression for buying an eighth of an ounce of drugs. One Harlem drug dealer had a good laugh when shown the ad. "What Olde English is trying to put over," he explained, "is that this is a cheaper high than drugs."[170] A public service message, perhaps.

Pillars of Society

In addition to using exploitative, hard-sell ad campaigns, alcohol companies insinuate themselves into minority communities by sponsoring local events and organizations. Corona beer boasted of its good works by erecting billboards in Hispanic neighborhoods that showed Corona bottles holding up the roof of an ornate, official-looking building. "Pillars of Society" read the inscription below.

Booze companies also appropriate cultural symbols to appeal to minorities. For instance, Hornell Brewing Company markets "The Original Crazy Horse Malt Liquor," which offended many Native Americans. Legislative efforts to ban the product's name by then-Surgeon General Novello and leaders of Crazy Horse's tribe, the Oglala Sioux, failed.[171]

Sometimes alcohol companies virtually create events in minority communities in order to use them as marketing tools. In southern California, for example, beer companies transformed the annual Cinco de Mayo festival into a beer-drinking extravaganza. Cinco de Mayo, which celebrates the defeat of French invaders by the Mexican army on May 5, 1862, is a decidedly low-key holiday in Mexico. It was a minor holiday for the Mexican-American community, too, until the brewers got their marketing claws on it. "Until ten years ago, Cinco de Mayo was largely ignored by the non-Latin community," said an article in *USA Today*. "Then, perhaps because there are few other spring marketing opportunities or because they just realized what an untapped market Hispanics were, several large beer and soft-drink companies began sponsoring local events. Others soon joined them, eventually turning Cinco de Mayo into a Mexican St. Patrick's Day."[172] In 1989, the beer-sponsored festival in Los Angeles's Lincoln Park degenerated into a drunken

brawl, resulting in six injuries and one shooting death.[173]

In the Native-American community, brewers sponsor more than forty powwows, parades, and other cultural and sporting events each year. In the bizarre world of beer sponsorship, native dancers compete

wearing full tribal dress and placards bearing the Coors insignia. Beer companies also underwrite national conferences of Native-American organizations, at which they provide open bars and logo-covered memorabilia.[174]

According to *Marketing Booze to Blacks,* a 1987 report by the Center for Science in the Public Interest, the number and range of African-American cultural and other events sponsored by major alcohol producers is "staggering." The report notes that just one company, Coors, sponsors such varied

Many women's magazines carry cigarette and liquor ads. *Glamour* tells potential advertisers that its subscribers drink more liquor than the average woman.

Photo by Marilyn Aquirre-Molina.

activities as black rodeo events, broadcasts of black collegiate football games, tennis tournaments, rock concerts, boxing matches, college interview fairs, film workshops, and even a gala concert at the annual meeting of the Congressional Black Caucus Foundation.[175] Marketers expect something in return for their money, and they get it. Sponsorship buys invaluable goodwill in minority communities, which translates into increased market share. At least one alcohol company has tried to buy the services of minority leaders as a kind of public relations SWAT team. The Adolph Coors Company, which had a

One way the alcoholic-beverage industry reaches minority groups is by sponsoring festivals and special events.

Photo by Marilyn Aquirre-Molina.

reputation for racist hiring policies and bad labor practices, sought in 1984 to boost its image by investing heavily in African-American and Hispanic communities. In return, several minority leaders were asked to sign a pledge "to take positive and visible action to help eliminate the misconceptions of Coors."[176]

Just as insidiously, support from booze companies may buy the silence of some minority leaders about alcohol problems in their communities. For example, despite powerful grassroots opposition to alcohol and tobacco billboards in inner-city Detroit, the local chapter of the Urban League refused to take a stand on the issue. The National Urban League, which receives substantial support from Stroh's Brewery, reportedly asked its Detroit chapter to remain silent.[177]

Concern Is Not Paternalistic

Alcohol companies say that those who oppose targeting of women and minority groups are "paternalistic"—that women and minorities are just as capable of resisting the lure of advertising as any other group. Indeed they are. But the fact is, *targeting works*. No group, it seems, is immune to the siren song of sophisticated ad campaigns designed just for them, and using themes that touch their innermost aspirations and desires, by companies that have bribed their way into the community with generous gifts. Targeting works on white male college students as well as it works on women

and minorities. If mass marketing is a shotgun blast that explodes on everything in its path, targeting is a high-powered rifle. An eerie echo of the rifle's report may be heard in statistics on alcohol abuse: African Americans and Hispanics have higher rates of mortality from alcohol-related liver disease than whites, fetal alcohol syndrome is seven times higher among blacks than whites, and alcohol abuse is a factor in the five leading causes of death for Native Americans.[178] The alcohol industry, of course, scoffs at the idea that its advertising contributes to alcoholism, drunk driving, or any of the problems associated with alcohol abuse. The industry often points to the fact that no studies have shown a causal relationship between advertising and alcohol abuse. However, reliable studies are virtually impossible to conduct, and lack of studies certainly doesn't prove that no relationship exists.

The industry line begs an obvious question: If alcohol advertising does not get people to drink, why does the industry spend $1.1 billion a year on it? Certainly, each company wants a bigger slice of the existing market pie. But the net effect of all booze companies seeking a bigger slice is that the pie itself is likely to expand, or at least less likely to contract.

Alcohol advertising will not turn an abstainer into an alcoholic. But the constant barrage of ads will certainly encourage some people to switch brands, others to drink more, and others to give drinking a try. A 1994 study by the National Bureau of Economic Research concluded that highway fatalities could be reduced by 2,000 to 3,000 a year if the government banned all broadcast advertising of beer and wine.[179] And the ubiquity of booze ads helps create what advertising critic Jean Kilbourne calls a "climate of denial," in which heavy drinking is tolerated and the dangers of alcoholism are kept from view.[180]

Finally, alcohol ads are problematic because they are a key source of information about alcohol in our society. Images of Liquor Land dominate the cultural airwaves, and alternative messages are rarely seen. As a result, most Americans think that illegal drugs are the nation's biggest drug problem. Few are aware that alcohol kills more than fifteen times as many people each year as all illicit drugs combined.[181] As former Surgeon General C. Everett Koop noted, "Currently, public-service announcements with pro-health and pro-safety messages are completely overshadowed by alcoholic-beverage advertising. They are not as slick, not as sophisticated, and not as frequently aired as the alcohol advertisements."[182]

What People Have Done

More and more Americans are fighting back against the deluge of booze ads. A Dallas parent group, for example, gave the boot to alcohol companies' "educational" programs in their schools. And in Michigan, alcohol companies are no longer permitted to advertise in college newspapers.

Even the symbiotic union of beer and sports has been called into question by stadium owners fed up with drunken brawls in the stands. At least one athlete beer endorser has turned his back on his sponsor. Bubba Smith, an ex-NFL defensive end, enjoyed a lucrative second career as a spokesman for Miller Lite. But in the fall of 1985, Smith did an about-face when he served as grand marshal of a homecoming parade at Michigan State University. "I was riding in the backseat of this car," he remembers, "and . . . one side of the street was yelling 'Tastes Great!' and the other side was yelling 'Less Filling!' It just totally freaked me out. When I got to the stadium, the older folks are yelling 'Kill, Bubba, Kill!' but the kids are yelling 'Tastes Great! Less Filling!' And everyone in the stands is drunk." Smith quit doing the Miller commercials. "I didn't like the effect I was having on a lot of little people," he said. "When kids start to listen to what you say, you want to tell 'em something that's the truth."[183]

Some of the most effective protests have been launched by minority groups fed up by alcohol-industry targeting. As we noted in Chapter 6 ("Litter on a Stick"),

ABSOLUT NONSENSE.

Adbusters designed a series of fake ads to ridicule Absolut Vodka's marketing campaign. Absolut sued *Adbusters;* although a judge allowed the activist group to carry on, it was forced to add an "e" at the end of Absolut.

there has been a vigorous grassroots movement against alcohol and tobacco billboards in minority neighborhoods. When PowerMaster malt liquor was introduced in 1991, minority leaders organized protests and boycotts across the country. As a result, the Bureau of Alcohol, Tobacco, and Firearms ordered G. Heileman Brewing Company to discontinue using the PowerMaster label. Other groups have decided to "just say no" to alcohol companies bearing gifts of cash. For example, in 1987 the Cherokee nation turned down an offer from Coors to sponsor cultural events, and many other tribes have since followed suit.[184]

In the mid-1980s, advocates led by the Center for Science in the Public Interest fought to require national broadcasters to provide equal time for public service announcements (PSAs) on the dangers of alcohol. (As we

ABSOLUTE ON ICE.

noted in "Ads That Kill I: Tobacco," PSAs on smoking proved so effective that tobacco companies "voluntarily" pulled their TV commercials in order to get rid of them.) Although a Gallup poll found that 75 percent of Americans supported this legislation, the bill was crushed by a powerful lobby of broadcasters and brewers.[185]

In 1988, advocates won a federal law that requires alcohol manufacturers to put health warnings on bottle labels. The battle continues for health and safety messages in alcohol ads. The Sensible Advertising and Family Education Act of 1993 (the SAFE bill) called for warnings similar to those now included in cigarette ads, both in print and in broadcast advertising. But the SAFE bill was opposed by an array of advertising and alcohol-industry forces, including the American Association of Advertising Agencies, the National Association of Broadcasters, the Beer Institute, and the Ad Council, which creates public service ads. The legislation's main advocate, Senator Strom Thurmond (R–S.C.), withdrew the bill days before a scheduled Senate committee vote when it appeared the effort would fail.[186] Another measure, introduced by Representative James Moran (D–Va.), would eliminate the tax deduction for alcohol (and cigarette) advertis-

ing. Yet another proposal by advocates would provide funds for a national health-care plan by raising excise taxes on alcoholic beverages. However, the Clinton administration and Congress, heavily lobbied by the alcohol industry, rejected the recommendation.[187]

Many groups are working at the state level to restrict alcohol advertising. In Washington State, for example, citizens concerned about booze ads demanded a hearing with the state liquor control board. The citizens presented the board with examples of harmful ads and proposed to allow only "tombstone" advertising of alcohol products—black-and-white ads without slogans or models. Although the board approved only a watered-down version of this proposal, the hearing garnered substantial public attention and may serve as a model for organizers in other states.

Occasionally, change is brought about by a single irate citizen with pen and paper. In July 1990, Dion Neese of Saranac Lake, New York, wrote a letter to New York attorney general Robert Abrams, protesting the Coors "Won't slow you down" commercials. Neese's letter encouraged Abrams to launch an investigation, which resulted in Coors pulling the ads and paying $100,000 in investigative fees to the state of New York.

WHAT YOU CAN DO

- If you are a college student, protest booze ads on campus. Work with student government and college administrators to get alcohol ads out of campus media and events.

- If you have children, find out if alcohol companies are "educating" your kids. Talk to your children about the health risks of alcohol and the undesirable aspects of heavy drinking. Do not let advertising and promotional material be their only source of information.

- Write to your senators and representative and tell them you support health warnings in alcohol ads, more PSAs to counter beer and wine ads on TV, and elimination of the tax deduction for alcohol advertising.

- Write to your state legislators and the state liquor authority and tell them you support restrictions on alcohol advertising. Find out if bills or initiatives have been introduced to curb booze ads in your state; your local council on alcoholism may be able to help.

- If you're mad about an ad, complain! Write to your state attorney general; elected officials; the Federal Bureau of Alcohol, Tobacco, and Firearms; and the Federal Trade Commission. Send a copy of your letter to the offending advertiser.

- Contact a nonprofit organization working against alcohol advertising, such as the Alcohol Policy Project of the Center for Science in the Public Interest, 1875 Connecticut Ave. NW, Washington, DC 20009.

CHAPTER EIGHT

Commercialized Holidays and Rituals

If the business year could be likened to a football season, holiday time would be the Super Bowl. Commercialism in America rises to a screaming crescendo every Christmas. Holiday spending sprees have become a tradition: Toy companies and several other industries make half or more of their sales in the last couple of months of the year. In this chapter, we see how advertisers have appropriated—and changed the meaning of—Christmas and other celebrations. ✱ *But Christmas is not the only holiday appropriated by marketers. Advertisers have coopted nearly every religious and civic celebration. And, for those down-times in the marketing year, advertisers have created holidays of their very own. Personal rituals, such as weddings and bar/bat mitzvahs, have also succumbed to commercialism.*

Dreaming of a Noncommercial Christmas

As any anthropologist will tell you, holidays offer revealing glimpses of cultural values and attitudes. Through their accompanying legends, rituals, and heroic figures, holidays reflect and perpetuate the mythologies that form a society's core beliefs. Not surprisingly, the holidays of twentieth-century America testify to the thorough commercialization of our culture. And no holiday says more about the triumph of commercialism than Christmas.

ADMITTEDLY, THE HISTORY OF CHRISTMAS IS not entirely that of a solemn religious holiday profaned by marketers. Rather, one might argue that it is a pagan holiday that was co-opted for several centuries by the church and is now reverting to its origins of excess. Ancient Europeans traditionally celebrated the winter solstice with wild, orgiastic revelries that sometimes lasted for weeks. Early church leaders had trouble putting an end to this custom, so in the ninth century A.D. they simply changed the name and the rationale for the celebration. Christmas is celebrated during the solstice not because Christ was born on December 25, but because the church realized that it was easier to appropriate pagan holi-

ABSOLUT HARMONY.

days than to wipe them out. Over the centuries, many reformers have railed against lingering traces of paganism in Christmas. Early American Puritans, for example, denounced Christmas as a "wanton Bacchanalian feast."[1]

In the United States, Puritan influences (and widespread impoverishment) helped keep Christmas celebrations modest well into the nineteenth century. Gift-giving was not mandatory and usually involved handcrafted items or food. But in the 1870s, businesses discovered the holiday's merchandising potential. Macy's in New York is credited with promoting the first manufactured Christmas gifts, but other department stores quickly joined in.[2] Advertisers vigorously promoted the exchange of store-bought gifts, and a tradition was born.

In the twentieth century, that tradition evolved into a major industry. Virtually every trimming and trapping of Christmas—the traditional ornaments, food, music, and decorations—has been transformed into a salable commodity. Americans spend a fortune on Christmas *stuff:* about $80 billion each year.[3] Department stores typically generate up to 50 percent of their annual profits during the last two months of the year.[4] Few are immune to the media- and advertising-induced Christmas spending frenzy. And every year, marketers tug on our leashes a little earlier. Retailers once waited until after Thanksgiving to unveil their Christmas displays; now the displays are often in place by Halloween.[5] Direct marketers, such as the Metropolitan Museum of Art, start even sooner, mailing Christmas catalogs as early as August.

Some retailers try to jump-start the holiday spirit with extravagant displays or lavish print ads. For instance, in 1993 Absolut commissioned a glossy, foldout insert for its vodka in the *New Yorker*—a four-page, hand-drawn holiday spread that included a series of five greeting

Chocolatiers like Godiva cash in on the season's sweet cravings.

is the peak month for embarking on diets. Christmas is also the time of year when it seems reasonable to blow our hard-earned money on useless baubles and expensive luxury items: For example, more than half of the year's diamond and fur sales take place before Christmas.[8] For those with money to burn, Christmas spending can reach unimaginable heights. Each holiday season, the *Robb Report*, a magazine for the "affluent lifestyle," publishes an annual "Ultimate Gift Guide" with such must-haves as a private, backyard theme park

ONLY 25 SHOPPING DAYS 'TIL CHRISTMAS. TICK, TICK, TICK..... PULSAR WE KNOW WHAT MAKES PEOPLE TICK.

Manufacturers and retailers of consumer goods fan the flames of consumption by counting the days—often months ahead—before Christmas.

Kwanzaa was created to celebrate African-American heritage but may soon fall prey to marketers.

cards and envelopes; each snow-filled scene featured hand-lettered Absolut logos. Even TV Christmas specials serve as advertisements. Toys 'R' Us produced a show for kids called "Nick and Noel" that featured animated stuffed animals only available at the giant toy retailer.[6]

Christmas in the consumer culture is a celebration of overconsumption—a blowout bender of spending, eating, and drinking that would impress even our pagan ancestors. Roughly 20 percent of annual liquor sales occur during the holiday season.[7] Overindulging in food is a traditional holiday pastime; not coincidentally, January

for $20 million; a 220-gallon hot tub for $21,500; and a life-size robotic "body-double" programmed to speak in your own voice—a bargain at $150,000 to $200,000.[9]

And it is not only the wealthy who manage to drop a bundle during the holidays. According to the Conference Board, a business research group, the average American family spent $400 on Christmas gifts in 1992.[10] If you don't have the cash on hand, no matter: An estimated 30 percent of all credit card use is registered between Thanksgiving and New Year's Day, leaving a legacy of interest payments for the new year.[11] To promote holiday spending on credit, American Express commissioned a double-decker bus, painted to look like a credit card, to shuttle shoppers around Chicago during the 1993 holiday season. The ride pass was, of course, an American Express card.[12]

Christmastime consumption also

KWANZAA

1 s t f r u i t

KWANZAA
MUSIC

D A N C E
song

p o e t r y

IT'S A PEOPLE. IT'S A RHYTHM.
1.UNITY 2.SELF-DETERMINATION 3.COLLECTIVE WORK AND RESPONSIBILITY
4.COOPERATIVE ECONOMICS 5.PURPOSE 6.CREATIVITY 7.FAITH (-7 DAYS)

wreaks havoc on the environment, what with excess packing materials, gift-wrapping knickknacks, and purchases of plastic toys and other nonbiodegradable items. "If garbage is a solid-waste stream, Christmas is a tidal wave," says William Rathje, a University of Arizona anthropologist who studies garbage. "There is no question it's the single largest discard event of the year."[13]

The Patron Saint of Shopping Malls

The orgy of Christmas consumption, of course, is hardly in keeping with the anti-materialist philosophy of the man for whom the holiday is named. Indeed, although Christ's birth is the pretext for

MANUFACTURED HOLIDAYS

A number of American holidays have been created or promoted for the express purpose of selling goods. Mother's Day may be the best example. First proposed by a West Virginia woman named Anna Jarvis in 1908, Mother's Day was championed by commercial florists, who naturally believed the day should be commemorated with flowers. Florists launched an aggressive advertising and public-relations campaign to encourage observance of the holiday. As the trade journal *Florists' Review* asked its readers in 1910: "Well, what have you started to help along Mother's Day? Seen the mayor about issuing a proclamation? Called the minister's attention? Spoken to the local newspapers?...We can't expect ready-made flower days—we've got to do something to work them up."[1]

The florists' campaign to promote Mother's Day was so successful that by 1913, *Florists' Review* was moved to announce: "Mother's Day is ours; we made it; we made it practically unaided and alone."[2]

ONLY 9 SHOPPING DAYS 'TIL CHRISTMAS. TICK, TICK, TICK..... PULSAR
WE KNOW WHAT MAKES PEOPLE TICK.

celebrating Christmas, the holiday's dominant mythical figure is the more retail-friendly Santa Claus. Santa, as we know him, is a distinctly American invention. Although he is a descendant of such European figures as the Dutch Sinterklass, the German Christkindlein, the British St. Nicholas, and the French Père Noel, the American Santa departs from these earlier figures in his secularism and emphasis on gift-giving.[14] His predecessors brought nuts, fruits, and homemade toys (if they brought gifts at all); the American Santa arrives bearing Nintendo. A thoroughly commercialized being, Santa frequents

Brand-name products work their way into Christmas ornaments in this catalog of holiday knickknacks.

Anna Jarvis, who had envisioned the day as a quasi-religious celebration of maternal love and sacrifice, fumed about "the mire of commercialism" into which Mother's Day had sunk.[3] Jarvis fought back, urging people to stop buying flowers and other gifts for the occasion, but the florists easily triumphed over her protests. In 1922, the *Florists' Review* joyfully announced that Jarvis's efforts had been "completely squelched!"[4]

Over the years, marketers have tried with varying degrees of success to introduce holidays to the American calendar. Secretary's Day caught on, but Friendship Day—dreamed up by the greeting card industry as a way to fill the August lull in sales—did not. Candy Day, created by the National Confectioners' Association in 1923, was too transparently commercial for most Americans. But, repackaged as Sweetest Day, the manufactured occasion survives in a modest way.

shopping malls and owes much of his popularity to advertising. First given visual form in Thomas Nast's engravings for *Harper's Weekly* in 1863, the American Santa was made ubiquitous by Haddon Sundblom's ads for Coca-Cola in the 1930s.

The mythology of Santa Claus says much about the culture that spawned it. As we all know, Santa rewards good children with presents; bad children get lumps of coal or nothing at all. It is debatable whether the Santa myth encourages consumerism, but it certainly reinforces an un-Christlike view of the poor. If children are told that they get presents for Christmas because they are good and deserving, then poor children whose parents can't afford to buy them presents might naturally conclude that

CELEBRATE CHRISTMAS, NOT COMMERCIALISM

The following statement was released in December 1992 by a coalition of two dozen prominent religious leaders to protest the overcommercialization of Christmas. Convened by the Center for the Study of Commercialism, the coalition included Father Theodore Hesburgh of Notre Dame University, Reverend Joan Brown Campbell of the National Council of Churches, and Reverend Calvin Butts of the Abyssinian Baptist Church. The statement was widely publicized in the mainstream and religious press; local ministers around the country also imparted the message from their pulpits.

We, the undersigned coalition of religious leaders, are deeply concerned about the excessive commercialization of Christmas. For far too long we have witnessed the spiritual yield to the commercial. We have seen the spirit of Christmas reduced to a carnival of mass marketing. Consumption has taken on an almost religious quality; malls have become the new shrines of worship. Massive and alluring advertising crusades have waged war on the essential meaning of the spiritual life, fostering the belief that the marketplace can fulfill our highest aspirations. As religious leaders, we wish to help reclaim the true glory of Christmas and the true spirit of giving.

Regrettably, many people find it ever more difficult to separate Christmas from commerce. Good will towards all, concern for our communities, and love for our families are goals that come from the heart. They cannot be purchased hastily in department stores. And yet, many (with

earnest intentions), prodded by advertising campaigns that now begin as early as Labor Day, engage in obsessive spending as a way to fill the spiritual vacuum left by an over-consumptive society. In the end, the delirium of commercial Christmas devours some, leaves others in ruinous debt, and punishes the poor for whom the joy of Christmas always seems a dollar away.

Christmas giving, in all its forms, is enriched when spiritual and ethical values overshadow the almost chronic compulsions to buy. The advertising lords of Madison Avenue have been successful in developing among many a coerced sense of guilt that drives consumer anxiety (and buying) at Christmas time. At the same time, they have failed to recognize or achieve the ideal of giving.

Making Christmas real means, in part, making giving personal, altruistic, and reflective. For some, this may mean giving the gift of family, baking and breaking bread with old and young alike. It means opening our hearts to family

and friends, and, more, to those we do not know personally but whose needs we recognize. It means expressing community, sharing good will with neighbors. It may also mean giving simple clothes or toys to children because of need, not compulsion.

We call on all people of faith to speak out against the overcommercialization of Christmas in our media and malls. Moreover, as people motivated by compassion, we must be mindful of how our addiction to consumer goods is devastating the planet. Let us instead invest in renewing our own spirits, our relationships, and our natural environment.

We must begin to reorder our priorities. Christmas was never intended to be a crass marketing ploy. Let us restore the spiritual and life-affirming potential of the season—and take it into the new year. We call on all people who share our unyielding faith to join with us in this Christmas effort.

—Religious Coalition to Take Commercialism Out of Christmas

RITES OF CONSUMPTION

As holidays have succumbed to commercialism, so have family celebrations and rituals. In the close competition for most-commercialized ritual, weddings clearly take the cake.

The average American wedding costs a whopping $15,800, not including the honeymoon ($3,000) and, of course, gifts ($6,000 to $8,000).[1] Advertising fuels the wedding-industrial complex; brides-to-be are perhaps the most zealously targeted subgroup of consumers. The February-March 1992 issue of *Bride's and Your New Home magazine* was believed to be the heaviest magazine ever, surpassing the February-March 1990 issue, which was entered in the Guinness Book of Records.[2] Weighing in at 4.2 pounds, *Bride's* 1,046 pages are crammed with ads for gowns, housewares, and vacation destinations. As humorist Dave Barry has noted, each of these ads features "a full-color photograph of a radiant young bride, her face beaming with

that look of ecstatic happiness that comes from knowing, deep in her heart, that her wedding cost as much as a Stealth bomber, not including gratuities."[3]

Bar and bat mitzvahs, the traditional Jewish coming-of-age rituals, have also come loose from their religious moorings and entered the realm of commercialism. *Reform Judaism* magazine reports that bar and bat mitzvahs typically cost from $10,000 to $50,000 or more. "Theme" bar and bat mitzvahs are all the rage—one family held a barbecue hoedown and called it a "barn mitzvah." "I've seen every theme except human sacrifice," one rabbi joked. Another asked despairingly, "What's wrong with the real theme of bar mitzvah: Jewish commitment?"[4] Prompted by such concerns, the Union of American Hebrew Congregations recently issued a resolution declaring that "bar/bat

mitzvah has become an occasion for idolatry and the relentless commercial colonization of our sacred events." The resolution calls instead for celebrations characterized by "family cohesion, authentic friendship, acts of tzedakah [charity] and parties suitable for children."[5]

Bride's and Your New Home *sets the norm for lavish weddings. The 530-page June-July 1992 issue (above) contained 376 full-page ads, in addition to numerous smaller ads and "articles" peppered with brand-names. The ads feature high-priced wedding items and glamorous diamond-clad brides. Rarely do you find tips on planning a simple, inexpensive ceremony and reception.*

they are bad or undeserving.

Poor children are not the only ones who have a difficult time at Christmas. In fact, Christmas represents the annual peak for depression, domestic quarrels, drug overdoses, hotline calls, and emergency medical calls.[15] Although the causes of these problems are legion, some psychologists think that relentless Christmas hype is a contributing factor.

Everywhere we turn during the Christmas season we are confronted with images of prosperous, loving, Ozzie-and-Harriet-type families. They gather round the fire in commercials for Kodak or frolic in the snow in the J. Crew catalog. Their homes are tastefully decorated, their

clothes ironed, their children well behaved. In comparison, our own homes seem squalid and messy, our families hopelessly dysfunctional.

Economic realities also contribute to holiday-time stress. Dr. Elaine Rodino, a Santa Monica psychologist and expert on holiday-time depression, treats many parents who are forced to cut back on expenses. Those parents must face their disappointed children, whose expectations are shaped by commercials for the latest toys and clothes. People of all income levels, unable to resist the pressures to consume, often find themselves in debt, which can increase the risk of depression, according to Rodino.[16]

What People Have Done

Some Americans, hung over from the consumer binges of the 1980s and sobered by the economic realities of the 1990s, are fighting back against the hype and commercialism of Christmas. The *New York Times* reported in 1991 that "Americans with pocketbooks of all sizes [are] expressing boredom, distaste—even disgust—with the spending frenzy of Christmases past."[17] A typical sentiment was expressed by Cathy Tran of Columbus, Ohio: "We have enough toys at home. We really have enough of just about everything, and I'm not just going to buy, buy, buy because it's Christmas. It's gotten to be too much of a circus."[18]

Some people, disturbed by the hollowness of the typical commercial Christmas, are rescuing the benevolent spirit of the holiday by donating to charities instead of buying gifts. As Barbara Grob of San Francisco explained to the *New York Times* in 1990, "The day after Christmas, I began to find myself feeling like there was supposed to be something more,

Disney World hosts extravagant "Fairy Tale Weddings and Honeymoons" on its grounds, turning the wedding ritual into a commercial for Disney. Accessories to the fairy tale include Cinderella's Glass Coach for $1,200 and Disney characters in the ceremony at $395 each.

something that was meaningful. Christmas was becoming a chore." So Grob decided to make donations to the Coalition for the Homeless in the names of everyone on her gift list. Grob's father was so impressed with the idea that the following year he donated his gift budget to Save the Children.[19]

Those who seek a less commercial Christmas have even formed an organization: SCROOGE, or the Society to Curtail Ridiculous, Outrageous, and Ostentatious Gift Exchanges. Founded in 1979, SCROOGE is devoted to "providing good-natured moral support for those who want to change their holiday gift-giving practices—to stop wasting large sums of money on gifts that don't seem to make anybody all that much happier."[20] SCROOGE founder Chuck Langham says that his organization's 1,300 members are all for the Christmas spirit, but are fed up with the holiday's commercial emphasis and compulsory spending. "With all the hype, people feel guilty if they don't spend a fortune on gifts. We offer a little support for those who want to be more sensible." In its annual newsletter, SCROOGE offers tips for a less commercial Christmas, including ideas for truly useful gifts and strategies for inoculating kids against the onslaught of toy ads.

Also working to decommercialize Christmas is Alternatives, a "Christian-based social justice organization that encourages people of faith to examine and challenge our consumer society." Alternatives provides resources and information for those seeking modest, socially responsible holiday celebrations.

WHAT YOU CAN DO

- *Don't be bullied into spending a fortune just because it's Christmas. Try giving homemade gifts (crafts, baked goods, and the like) or donations to charity instead of impersonal store-bought presents. Gifts of time and skill are also much appreciated—give your friends and family "coupons" redeemable for child- or pet-*

sitting, sewing lessons, lawnmowing, or other favors.

- *If you have kids, try to counter the force of toy ads by helping your kids see through the ploys used by advertisers. Instead of lavishing presents on your kids, try giving them one really thoughtful gift and lots of time and attention.*

- *If you need help planning less commercial holiday gatherings, exchanges, and activities, contact*

SCROOGE
1447 Westwood Road
Charlottesville, VA 22903

Alternatives
P.O. Box 429
Ellenwood, GA 30049
404-961-0102

Facing Commercialism

Marketers'
constant
pressure
has kept Americans scurrying, almost
like rats on a treadmill, to buy all the "great," "new,"
"deluxe" things and experiences that money can buy.
We become, first and fore-   *most, consumers. We work*
and spend, always wanting
more than our pocketbooks can manage. ✳ *Granted,*
the material world offers unmistakable pleasures. But the
consumption-oriented lifestyle has
a downside that is rarely
discussed. Thus, Part Two   *of* Marketing Madness
investigates the diverse problems that may be caused, albeit inadver-
tently, by a marketplace-dominated culture. Those
problems turn up in our minds and bodies,
our families,
and our
communities.

CHAPTER NINE

The Impact of Commercialism

Affecting Our Minds, Pocketbooks, and Planet

Each possession you possess helps your spirits to soar/That's what's soothing about excess/Never settle for something less/Something's better than nothing, yes!/But nothing's better than more, more, more.   *—Madonna[1]*

I don't pay attention to advertising.   *—Anonymous millions*

AMERICANS, HAVING GROWN UP IN A SEA OF commercials, are a pretty sophisticated lot, say marketers. Sure, we sometimes are annoyed by commercials, but we are smart enough to sniff out lies, ignore blandishments, even zap ads with our remote control.

Most people would probably agree with that assessment. Perhaps our friends and neighbors are affected by advertising, but we ourselves are tough, cynical, savvy consumers.

But are we really so immune to commercial influences? The nationally advertised products we purchase, the latest fashions in our closets, the outstanding debt on our credit cards, and our encyclopedic knowledge of brand names would suggest otherwise.

Of course, no one would contend that humans are Pavlovian dogs that run immediately to the store or telephone to buy advertised products. And not all advertising is a sinister instrument of thought control—some actually provides useful information.[2] This book certainly does not advocate a ban on marketing, advertising, or commerce. But, like air pollution and acid rain, commercialism has crossed the threshold into the danger zone, and it is time to consider remedial action.

Marketers claim that advertising does not create values or shape our way of life; rather, it simply reflects existing lifestyles. For the sake of argument, let us accept that notion. Even so, advertising would exert a significant influence over the way we live. For advertising reflects, cultivates, and amplifies only certain values and behaviors—preoccupation with one's physical appearance, a belief in happiness as a purchasable commodity, and the like—and not necessarily the values and behaviors that make for fulfilled people, a great nation, and a sound environment. Without the pressure exerted by advertising, the particular values and behaviors it fosters might have remained fragments in the mosaic of human characteristics, rather than the dominant pattern. Even *Advertising Age*, the leading advertising trade publication, has acknowledged that "what used to be a somewhat even battle between the exaggerations and lure of advertising and the prudence of authority figures at home has become dangerously one-sided."[3]

Marketers also claim (at least when responding to critics) that advertising doesn't *create* needs but merely *responds* to consumer demand. That may be true for certain products: Everyone knows that soap and milk exist, and advertising largely serves to lure people from one brand to another.[4] But for new kinds of products, such as compact-disc players and car phones, or new versions of old products, such as new toys or new styles of clothing, advertising certainly alerts people to a new "need." More significantly, advertising touts only what is salable to consumers. As Michael Schudson, professor of sociology and communications at the University of California, San Diego, has written, "First, marketers do not actually seek to discover what consumers 'want,' but what consumers want *from among commercially viable choices.*. .Thus, consumers are not asked if they would prefer public television to advertising-supported television or public transportation to private automobiles or government-supported health care to private physicians."[5]

Some industry cheerleaders claim that advertising is not only harmless but a uniquely beneficent and constructive force. "Advertising," according to *Editor and Publisher* magazine, "is the engine that keeps our economy running. It has been responsible for our high standard of living."[6] The former head of the American Advertising Federation, Howard H. Bell, said, "We need a full-court press...to explain and document the vital role advertising plays in sustaining and fueling our free-market economy, as well as its *pro bono* contributions to our social well-being."[7]

Yet many would argue that other, more powerful engines are driving our economy: scientific research, new technologies, education, investments in the nation's physical and social infrastructure (roads, telecommunications, schools, etc.). In fact, in 1990, despite record-high advertising expenditures of $1.4 *trillion* (1994 dollars) in the preceding decade, the economy plunged into recession.[8] Teachers, mayors, construction workers, and consumers may wonder whether our economy wouldn't have been much better off if a good chunk of that enormous sum had been invested in schools, roads, or day-care centers—or if the marketers simply had advertised less and put their savings into lower prices.

Moreover, even if advertising does keep our economy running, it might be running in the wrong direction. A gross national product (GNP) bloated by overpriced and poorly made products, the costs of cleaning up pollution, and the costs of treating preventable diseases hardly reflects a healthy or sustainable economy.

Commercialism has clear parallels with industrial pollution. Just as modest amounts of waste can be absorbed by the natural environment, so modest amounts of commercialism can be assimilated by our cultural environment. Large amounts, however, can totally overwhelm either environment, and such is the case today.

For decades we failed to recognize, let alone control, the harm caused by industrial practices. In some cases, such as air pollution from coal-burning furnaces, the problems were obvious but were either ignored or justified on the basis of short-term economic gain. In other cases, such as toxic chemicals that pollute the air and water, the dangers were not even recognized. So it is with commercialism: We excuse its obvious defects in the name of economic progress; we don't even try to identify more subtle effects.

Again as with pollution several decades ago, the consequences of excessive commercialism remain unexamined and unproven. Our understanding rests on a handful of often preliminary or inconclusive academic studies. The fact is that, despite the dominance of commercialism in our culture, social scientists have barely begun to explore its nature and its consequences. Moreover, government regulatory programs are inadequate to contain commercialism. Agencies that focus on deceptive advertising have such small budgets—totaling only about one-thousandth as much as what is spent on advertising—that only the most blatantly dishonest advertising can be stopped. Other forms of commercialism go completely unexamined.

What, then, is the impact on our society, when, as *Advertising Age* wrote, "mass-media advertising explodes out of a shotgun and sprays everyone in its path, kids included"?[9] And beyond advertising, what are the effects of living in a culture where even schools, museums, sports, and noncommercial broadcasters have been commercialized? Does commercialism, indeed, turn engaged citizens into mere consumers?

Promoting Materialism

On one effect of commercialism, many critics agree: our hyper-commercialized society, and advertising in particular, promotes materialism.[10] The late Christopher Lasch, in his book *The Culture of Narcissism*, maintained that advertising "manufactures a product of its own: the consumer, perpetually unsatisfied, restless, anxious, and bored. Advertising serves not so much to advertise products as to promote consumption as a way of life. It 'educates' the

TWENTY-SEVEN PROBLEMS WITH ADVERTISING

1 Ads lie about the quality of products and services by touting benefits and hiding drawbacks.

2 Advertising contributes to environmental problems by encouraging wasteful consumption and over-packaging and by defacing the landscape with billboards.

3 Ads increase the prices of many products—both because of the cost of the ads and the higher-value image of products that the ads cultivate.

4 Advertising is subsidized by taxpayers. Ad costs are a fully tax-deductible business expense, thereby depriving state and federal treasuries of billions of dollars annually.

5 Advertising may encourage materialism, greed, and selfishness. That, in turn, may make people less supportive of spending for critical social needs such as schools and health care.

6 Ads encourage a brand-name mentality: buying on the basis of the maker rather than the quality or price of the product.

7 Image advertising can distort the public perception of a company's activities and priorities (for example, by portraying major polluters as environmentally conscious philanthropists).

8 Advertising may encourage people to care more about their own and others' appearances than about their character, talents, and personalities.

9 Advertising fosters dissatisfaction, envy, and insecurity.

10 Advertising projects unrealistic images of our society: You're not cool unless you drive an expensive car; to be adult means drinking alcohol.

11 Advertisers influence the content of many publications and broadcasts.

12 Corporate sponsorship may undermine the objectivity and influence the content of exhibits at science and art museums.

13 Advertisers influence the content of movies and TV shows—and even books and board games—through "product placement" advertising.

14 Advertisers' sponsorship of civic, environmental, and other nonprofit groups discourages those groups from mounting activities that their benefactors don't like (for example, supporting antismoking legislation).

15 Advertising promotes alcohol and tobacco addictions, which kill half a million Americans annually.

16 Commercial advertising has paved the way for political advertising that offers more imagery than substance (for example, the "Morning in America" ads used by Ronald Reagan in 1980).

17 Ubiquitous advertising—on billboards, in the sky, and on the phone—means that we can hardly ever escape the annoyance of commercial messages.

18 Advertising perverts our culture by turning every event into a sales event. Examples include the Federal Express Orange Bowl and the Macy's Thanksgiving Day Parade with Disney-character floats.

19 Commercial messages and corporate logos degrade the dignity of government agencies, museums, and "noncommercial" radio and TV stations.

20 Advertising steals our time. The average American will spend almost three full years of his or her waking life just watching television commercials.

21 Advertising implies that there's an easy solution to everything, from having friends to being healthy.

22 The incessant promotion of shopping and consumption distracts from other activities, such as reading, thinking, and playing.

23 Direct marketers compile detailed electronic portraits of consumers. Those ever-expanding databases present a staggering potential for abuse.

24 Advertising aimed at children intrudes on the parent-child relationship and undermines parental authority.

25 Advertising may erode values—such as sharing, cooperation, and frugality—fostered by families, religious institutions, and schools.

26 Advertising perpetuates racial (African Americans as musicians and athletes), gender (women as sex objects, men as businesspeople), and class (middle-class whites as the social norm) stereotypes.

27 Advertising materials in school undermine objective education.

Photo by Ann Lesley Williams.

The 78-acre Mall of America in Minneapolis is the world's largest indoor shopping gallery, with approximately 350 stores, 13,000 parking spaces, and an amusement park called Knott's Camp Snoopy.

masses into an unappeasable appetite not only for goods but for new experiences and personal fulfillment. It upholds consumption as the answer to the age-old discontents of loneliness, sickness, weariness, lack of sexual satisfaction....it creates new forms of unhappiness—personal insecurity, status anxiety.[11]

Economist John Kenneth Galbraith has charged that advertising is "modern want creation....Wants can be synthesized by advertising, catalyzed by salesmanship, and shaped by the discreet manipulations of the persuaders."[12] Psychologist Paul Wachtel holds that "advertising stirs desires that might otherwise not be there...and in their very ubiquitousness they contribute to the growth state of mind as well."[13] Michael Schudson, a sympathetic analyst of advertising, acknowledges that "advertising not only promotes specific products but also fosters a consumer way of life."[14] Even an article in the *Wall Street Journal*, where editorials trumpet the virtues of wealth and consumption, noted, "Many of us can no longer afford what our fathers could—

a house, an education for our children—but an enormous percentage of us can afford practically anything else, and we buy it. What is more, *we have made the very act of pursuing it almost an end in itself*"[15] (emphasis added).

Perhaps parents are the ultimate experts on whether advertising promotes materialism in children. A 1993 survey of 1,000 parents found that 92 percent "agree" or "strongly agree" that "commercials aimed at children today make them too materialistic."[16] Rarely do surveys detect such virtual unanimity of opinion.

Although scholars and parents may agree that commercialism and advertising promote materialism, there is little empirical evidence on the nature or extent of that link. Clearly, this is a tough area to study. For instance, it is difficult to distinguish the effects of advertising from those of the programs or editorial content with which it is associated. Also, because practically our entire population is steeped in commercialism, there is no suitable subgroup to provide a basis of comparison. Those few people who abstain from the consumer culture, such as Amish farmers and monks, live in subcultures so different from the norm that it is impossible to separate the absence of commercialism from a multitude of other factors that support nonmaterialistic attitudes. Equally flawed are comparisons to citizens of less-commercialized countries because so many other cultural differences exist.

Occasional small studies do provide some empirical evidence of a link between advertising and materialism. One such study, done by Michigan State University researchers, compared the values of high school students who watched Channel One (twelve-minute telecasts that millions of high school students are required to watch daily) to those of similar students whose schools did not have

Channel One. The researchers found that Channel One viewers held more materialistic attitudes. Though Channel One carries only two minutes of advertising a day, the researchers suggested that those ads may be particularly influential because they are shown in a school setting and are implicitly endorsed by the school.[17]

Such a study is hardly definitive, but at the very least it underscores the need for more research on the relationship between commercialism and materialism. Ultimately, however, this matter might be just one of countless social issues that are not amenable to rigorous, quantitative empirical research and where calls for more testing may simply be a smoke screen for inaction. And inaction could affect everything from human happiness to the survival of the global environment.

Destroying Our Planet

The lifestyle of consumerism in a growth-is-everything economy is largely responsible for global environmental problems that threaten our collective future. Resource consumption has been implicated as a cause of climate change (global warming) caused by the accumulation of carbon dioxide in the atmosphere, the depletion of the atmosphere's protective ozone layer due to CFCs (chlorofluorocarbons), the destruction of forests by acid rain, and the poisoning of humans and wildlife by pesticides and other toxic chemicals.

Marketers contribute to environmental problems by promoting the wasteful use of resources. Economist Victor Lebow wrote in 1955, and it remains true today, that "we seek our spiritual satisfaction, our ego satisfaction, in consumption.... We need things consumed, burned up, worn out, replaced, and discarded at an ever-increasing rate."[18] Some industries— the women's fashion industry is the quintessential example—survive on *planned obsolescence*. At the same time they are persuading us to buy this year's fashions, companies are already superannuating

them with the hot new styles and marketing campaigns for next year.

We can also fall victim to *perceived* obsolescence. Makers of computers, stereos, autos, and other products use advertising to tempt us with their newest, fastest, most colorful products, planting seeds of desire and dissatisfaction in consumers' hearts. Decades ago, Charles Kettering, the general director of General Motors' research labs, described the marketers' challenge as "the organized creation of dissatisfaction."[19] Earnest Elmo Calkins, who developed the strategy of rapid planned stylistic change, proclaimed, "The purpose is to make the customer discontented with his old type of fountain pen, kitchen utensil, bathroom, or motor car, because it is old-fashioned, out-of-date....We no longer wait for things to wear out. We displace them with others that are not more effective but more attractive."[20]

America the Gluttonous

The culture of waste fostered by advertising is fundamentally incompatible with basic tenets of environmentalism: recycling, conservation, and reduced consumption. E. F. Schumacher, the economist-author of the classic book *Small Is Beautiful*, said, "It is obvious that the world cannot afford the U.S.A. Nor can it afford Western Europe or Japan....Think of it—one American drawing on resources that would sustain fifty Indians!"[21] The goal, says Schumacher, should be "the maximum of well-being with the minimum of consumption."[22] That is hardly the goal of marketers, whose well-being derives from our maximum consumption of their products.

One measure of consumption is the use of energy and natural resources. The developed countries of the world hold 25 percent of the world's population but consume 75 percent of all energy, 79 percent of all commercial fuels, 85 percent of all wood products, and 72 percent of all steel production. They also generate nearly three-fourths of all carbon dioxide emissions.[23]

Americans—even the poor—consume far more oil, gas, coal, aluminum, iron, water, wood, and other resources than did our ancestors or than do people in both developing and developed nations. Consider the following:

• *Americans consume eighteen times as much commercially produced energy as do Bangladeshis.*[24]

• *Americans consumed more minerals from 1940 to 1976 than did all of humanity up to 1940.*[25]

• *The 2.6 million people added to the U.S. population each year generate 52 million tons of carbon dioxide—15 million tons more than are generated by the 17 million people born in China each year.*[26]

• *Americans consume approximately twice as much energy per capita as the British, French, Swedes, Norwegians, or Japanese.*[27]

To some extent, a high level of consumption contributes to a better quality of life, but Americans clearly are consuming far more than necessary. The danger lies less in running out of resources than in the impact that their extraction, processing, use, and disposal have on the environment.

The environment suffers at every stage of the manufacturing-consumption-disposal chain. Mining and manufacturing result in air and water pollution. Many products require gasoline, batteries, electricity, or other fuel, the production and use of which generate more pollution. Finally, disposal of the product—be it a two-ounce paper bag whose useful life is measured in minutes or a two-ton automobile that lasts for five or ten years—necessitates garbage dumps, leakage from which may contaminate drinking water, or toxin-spewing garbage incinerators.

Solid waste—or garbage—is perhaps the most obvious environmental problem associated with a consumer society. Each year our great industrial machine churns out, per person, one ton of hazardous waste, fifty tons of other solid waste, and a great deal more wastewater, carbon dioxide, and other garbage. In addition, each person produces about a ton of solid waste and thousands of gallons of wastewater. Of the 20,000 U.S. landfills in use in 1979, 15,000 were filled up and closed by 1992. As cities ran out of landfills, they began feeding their garbage into incinerators, which may release into the air such toxic chemicals as mercury, cadmium, and PCBs and leave behind small mountains of toxin-filled ash.[28]

Advertising itself contributes to the garbage problem. Consider the enormous amount of generally unread advertising matter that fills up half of most magazines, turns each Sunday newspaper into a muscle-building weight, and overflows our mailboxes. The one good thing we can say about radio and television commercials is that they don't accumulate in our homes and the environment.

Environment Becomes a Political Issue

Before the first Earth Day (1970), the environment was an issue of interest to few citizens and wasn't even on the political map. In the past twenty-five years, "the environment" has evolved from concern about litter on highways to global problems of climate change, the ozone layer, and acid rain. Increasingly, people have associated environmental problems with lifestyle. And as public concern has broadened and deepened, political leaders around the world have begun understanding the importance of protecting the environment. Former Soviet president Mikhail Gorbachev, for instance, has become an environmental crusader as president of Green Cross International. Gorbachev observed, "If we're going to protect the planet's ecology, we're going to need to find alternatives to the consumerist dream that is attracting the world....America must be the teacher of the world, but not the advertiser of the consumer society. It is unrealistic for the rest of the world to reach the American living standard. The world can't support that."[29]

In his best-selling book *Earth in the Balance*, Vice President Al Gore recognized the need for a revolutionary new relationship to our planet. He attacked the "throwaway mentality" and maintained,

> Our civilization is holding ever more tightly to its habit of consuming larger and larger quantities every year of coal, oil, fresh air and water, trees, topsoil, and the thousand other substances we rip from the crust of the earth, transforming them into not just the sustenance and shelter we need but much more that we don't need: huge quantities of pollution, products for which we spend billions on advertising to convince ourselves we want, massive surpluses of products that depress prices while the products themselves go to waste, and diversions and distractions of every kind.[30]

Gore proposed that protecting the global environment—and ensuring the viability of human beings and other endangered species—should be the new central organizing principle of the post–Cold War world.

Stealing Our Time . . .

Regardless of what one thinks about the effects of consumption, it certainly takes a lot of our time. The act of consuming—driving to the mall, perusing catalogs, debating buying decisions—eats deeply into our day. Compared to people in other lands, Americans are Olympic-caliber shoppers: We spend three to four times as much time shopping as do Western Europeans.[31] And once we bring our purchases home, we spend a great deal of time cleaning, oiling, painting, and otherwise caring for them.

In addition, television commercials and certain other kinds of advertising are nibbling away at our lives. For instance, the commercials with which broadcasters punctuate a two-hour film could easily stretch the film to two and a half hours. That extra half-hour is time directly stolen out of our lives. One reason that baseball games are getting longer is that the commercial breaks between innings have grown from one minute to as much as two and a half minutes, thereby adding almost a half-hour to a game. Football fans are often frustrated by the "TV time-outs" that broadcasters demand. Telemarketers who ring their way into our homes take a little more of our time. Though the newspaper says the film starts at seven, more and more theaters are forcing us to suffer through several minutes of advertising and more minutes of previews before the film actually begins. The thirty-minute network evening newscast on television actually provides only about twenty minutes of real news; the rest is, from the viewer's point of view, time wasted on ads and promotions.

An average person spends almost an hour a day reading, watching, or listening to television and radio commercials, theater advertising, ads at the beginnings of videotapes, direct-mail appeals, or talking to telemarketers. By the time one is seventy-five years old, advertising will have stolen about four years of his or her life.[32]

Perhaps the biggest way in which advertising and a lifestyle of consumption steals our time is by creating the material desires that necessitate our working longer and harder. Ironically, the richer our society gets, the longer we spend on the job, despite opinion polls showing that the vast majority of Americans would like to spend more time with family, friends, and leisure activities.[33] Juliet Schor, author of *The Overworked American* and associate professor of economics at Harvard University, reports that many Americans have traded time for money—working, on average, an additional one full month (163 hours) per year between 1969 to 1987.[34]

To the extent that we could reduce our need to purchase things and experiences, we could reduce greatly the amount of time we work. In theory, a person who takes home $30,000 per year could take off one week from work for every $600 reduction in spending. For instance, just taking home-made lunches to the office, instead of eating out every day, could save enough money to work one less week a year.

...And Taking Our Money

All but forgotten in this "buy till you die" era are the notions of simple living, delayed gratification, and saving. Benjamin Franklin's "A penny saved is a penny earned" guided generations of people who did *not* spend like there was no tomorrow. It was conventional wisdom to save for a rainy day.

Psychoanalyst Erich Fromm observed, "In contrast to the nineteenth century, in which saving was a virtue, the twentieth century has made consumption into the main virtue."[35] David Shi, a social historian at Davidson College, contends that "the advertising industry shrewdly helped undermine the conscientious frugality that progressives had helped revive at the turn of the century."[36] It's gotten to the point that people who try to economize risk being derided as cheapskates.

In the event that consumer appetites outstrip monetary resources, the business world has developed a convenient (and profitable) solution: credit cards. Decades ago, if people wanted to spend more than they had in the bank, they would have to take out a bank loan or (horrors!) defer gratification by either postponing purchases or buying them on a layaway plan. Credit cards provide instant loans. Although often invaluable, credit cards help millions of people buy far more than they can afford. The average cardholder now carries eight to ten credit cards, owes about $2,500, and pays about $450 in interest annually. In 1992, Americans paid some $27 billion just in interest charges.[37] It's not unusual for someone to receive dozens of credit card offers in a year, with the credit lines totaling over $100,000.[38]

College freshmen and even high school students are now being targeted for credit cards. A Texas professor says that students in her classes had as many as ten credit cards, each with a $1,000 limit. "I've seen kids with $50,000 to $70,000 in debt....They spend the money on clothes, pizza, tuition, books, fun travel, presents for girlfriends, shoes, watches, engagement presents, proms, formals. Kids just go haywire."[39]

Visa's and MasterCard's television commercials, filled with happy consumers, keep up a drumbeat of reminders to buy more, charge more. Never do they suggest budgeting your money or paying your bills on time to avoid outrageously high interest rates. Americans listen...and spend: In 1993 Americans charged $422 billion, up 25 percent from 1992. Analysts were projecting another 25 percent increase in 1994.[40] Meanwhile, MasterCard was running "sponsor identifications" on National Public Radio that bragged about its "continuing efforts to help you manage your money." Worse, AT&T encouraged users of its Universal card to run up large interest payments by awarding points (redeemable for discounts and prizes) on the basis of unpaid balances.[41]

Profligate spending is fun until the money runs out. The price many people pay for being spendthrifts is perpetual indebtedness, with no capacity to cope with emergencies. In extreme cases, people must declare bankruptcy, an increasingly common phenomenon: Almost 900,000 people went bankrupt in 1992, almost three times as many as in 1985.[42]

Will Frugality Destroy the Economy?

Just as the credit-card industry is reshaping our perception of money into that of a limitless resource, so too is ubiquitous advertising affecting our attitudes about spending. The tidal wave of advertising messages drowns out the few countervailing calls to be frugal or save for a costly crisis. Other than occasional ads from financial institutions, we are almost never urged to save or invest our money for our family's or our nation's future.

The result, not surprisingly, is a society that lives for the moment and is ill-prepared for financial crises.

Still, some businesspeople tell us that it is our patriotic duty to continue our spending spree, saying that if we spent less, our economy would nosedive into a recession. What they overlook is that money not spent on consumer goods does not just disappear from the economy. The chances are it will be put in the bank, not shoved under the mattress. The bank will invest those funds in commercial or personal loans. Thus, savings are fundamental to economic growth and development.[43]

Regardless of what the spending-spree advocates say about the "macro" effects of saving versus spending, *from the individual's perspective, saving and frugality always make sense.* We all need money in the bank for retirement, a child's education, a medical emergency, or other events that life has in store for us.

The True Costs of Advertising

Advertising not only influences our attitudes about spending, it also directly affects our pocketbook. It is consumers who each year end up paying for the nearly $150 billion—or almost $600 per person—that companies spend on advertising. For instance, when we buy cosmetics, compact discs, and games, 10 percent or more of the price goes for promotional costs.[44]

Amateur buyers are generally at a terrible disadvantage when it comes to dealing with professional sellers. The complexity of modern products and the plethora of brands and models of consumer products and services are not matched by reliable comparative information on quality and value. The end result? Millions of people will waste billions of dollars every year on

unwise choices. The biggest risks come with the big-ticket items such as houses, cars, and securities: We can waste thousands of hard-earned dollars on purchases influenced by misleading advertising.

Still, advertising's defenders argue that it fosters competition and therefore

McDonald's worked its way onto the borders of Canadian stamps by sponsoring the "October is Stamp Month" campaign.

brings down prices. But they become uncommunicative when asked to discuss the potential cost after a heavily promoted brand wipes out the competition. One of the main intents of massive advertising programs is to *reduce* competition and allow higher prices. Small companies, which might have lower-priced, higher-quality products than market leaders, have a tough time breaking into a market dominated by companies that pump tens of millions of dollars into advertising. If a company can't ante up those kinds of dollars, it might as well forget about challenging the likes of McDonald's, Chevrolet, and Nike.[45]

Companies marketing national brands strongly prefer to compete on the basis of advertising, not price. That strategy— which keeps profit margins high—is obvious any time you go to the grocery store. Nationally advertised products, whose perceived quality and value have

violence] boils down to…. Violence sells."[62]

Television contributes to a sense that the world is a dangerous, violent place, according to George Gerbner, dean emeritus of the Annenberg School of Communications at the University of Pennsylvania. People who watch a lot of television tend to suffer from what Gerbner calls "the mean-world syndrome,"[63] a pervasive sense of insecurity and a belief that violence is the answer to many problems.

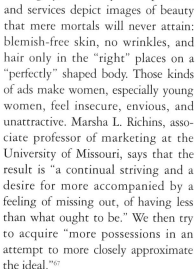

As this order for retouching demonstrates, a photo of actress Michelle Pfeiffer needed extensive revision before it was considered acceptable for publication.

Twisting Our Minds

Advertising's effect on our mental health is even harder to quantify than its effect on our physical health. As a former secretary of the Smithsonian Institution has noted, "The advertising man in some respects is as much a brain alterer as is the brain surgeon, but his tools and instruments are different."[64] Let's examine the postoperative results.

Advertisements seem to be selling cars or toothbrushes, but as environmentalist Alan Durning charges, in fact, "Ads are stitched together from the eternal cravings of the human psyche. Their ingredients are images of sexual virility, eternal youth, social belonging, individual freedom, and existential fulfillment. Advertisers sell not artifacts but lifestyles, attitudes, and fantasies, hitching their wares to the infinite yearnings of the soul."[65]

Marketers purposefully and systematically promote envy, create anxiety, and foster feelings of inadequacy and insecurity to sell us their products. The *Wall Street Journal* has said, "Advertising, crude at first, became subtle, subliminal, a whispered message that we would not smell good enough, be sexy enough, have enough status, unless we bought."[66] Commercial products are recommended to assuage our psyches by "improving" every feature of our anatomies.

Target One: Women's Minds

As we have seen earlier (Chapter 4, "The Iron Maiden: How Advertising Portrays Women" and "Sex as a Commodity"), women are bombarded with propaganda contending that products from cars to cosmetics will make them look more attractive, feel more self-confident, and, most important, enable them to get that man. Ads for perfume, cosmetics, plastic surgery, and many other products and services depict images of beauty that mere mortals will never attain: blemish-free skin, no wrinkles, and hair only in the "right" places on a "perfectly" shaped body. Those kinds of ads make women, especially young women, feel insecure, envious, and unattractive. Marsha L. Richins, associate professor of marketing at the University of Missouri, says that the result is "a continual striving and a desire for more accompanied by a feeling of missing out, of having less than what ought to be." We then try to acquire "more possessions in an attempt to more closely approximate the ideal."[67]

Men as Targets

Ads that promote a rigid ideal of female beauty also harm men—and have a boomerang effect on women. When a company wants to target men, the simplest tactic in the marketing manual is to put a sexy woman in ads. From an early age, images of the "ideal" woman are burned into boys' minds, and, not surprisingly, some of those boys become frustrated men who for years may search in vain for that woman, never satisfied with the ones they meet—who are inevitably too tall or too short or too fat or too skinny or too buxom or too flat-chested or whatever.[68] As Naomi Wolf writes in her book

The Beauty Myth, "When aimed at men, the effect is to keep them from finding peace in sexual love. The fleeting chimera of the air-brushed centerfold, always receding before him, keeps the man in destabilized pursuit, unable to focus on the beauty of the woman—known, marked, lined, familiar—who hands him the paper every morning."[69]

Furthermore, says Donna R. Lenhoff, general counsel of the Women's Legal Defense Fund, the constant barrage of images of sexy women also makes men less able to see women as peers, contributing to sexual harassment and other forms of discrimination in the workplace and in society at large.[70]

Considering advertising's impact on both women and men, it is remarkable that prominent women's groups, such as the National Organization for Women, have not targeted advertisers, ad agencies, and the media for reform.

The Effect on the Poor

Advertising aimed at the middle class and rich is seen by the poor. What was intended to stimulate sales to the haves may promote feelings of inadequacy, envy, and resentment in the have-nots. Nicholas Johnson, former commissioner of the Federal Communications Commission, has observed that, "One of the most vicious of television's predatory habits is its stalking of the poor. The affluent have nothing to lose but their money and control over their own lives and personalities. The poor are not so lucky. They must sit there without even the liberating knowledge that money can't buy happiness and constantly be told that their lack of material possessions is a badge of social ostracism in a nation that puts higher stress on monetary values than moral values."[71] Of course, advertising cannot be aimed exclusively at the wealthy, but we should recognize the special impact that advertising has on people who cannot afford what is advertised.

Florence Rice, an African-American consumer activist in New York City says that many poor people get caught up, to their detriment, in the spending fervor of Christmas. "It is horrendous how much money they

THE THIRTIES ARE BACK:
not the decade, of course, but the era, in a kind of elegant fashion

LUXE
redux

It doesn't take a master of masculine arcana to read the writing on big steak houses make a comeback. Then those support groups sitting around the campfire with their hands on their walking stic ancient as the Iron Age. And last but definitely not least con

REUNION
MENSWEAR

The clothing industry is now encouraging men to become more fashion conscious.

spend on gifts. They go broke and can't pay their phone bills." She blames much of that on television advertising's "terrible impact on poor people. Parents feel lousy, kids feel lousy."[72] Barbara Birdfeather, a welfare mom in Los Angeles, said that all the holiday advertising "tends to make one feel disenfranchised."[73]

All over the country, in fact, poor youths are turning to crime to obtain heavily advertised status symbols.[74] In 1992 a fifteen-year-old robbed and killed a delivery man in Brooklyn in order to buy things for his girlfriend. The girlfriend, who owned gold jewelry and twenty pairs of Nikes and Reeboks, told a reporter, "I'm, like, materialistic."[75] In 1988 a fifteen-year-old Baltimore boy named Michael Thomas disappeared while walking to school in his brand-new $100 Air Jordan sneakers. His body, minus the sneakers, was later found in a nearby field. James David Martin, seventeen, was arrested for the murder. On his feet were Thomas's Air Jordans. Michael Thomas was the *third* Baltimore youngster killed for his clothes in five years.[76] Countless other youths have been robbed of their sneakers, leather jackets, jewelry,

THE AD INDUSTRY'S ETHICAL GUIDELINES

The American Association of Advertising Agencies has what may be the single most ignored ethical code in the corporate world.

The code, in part, calls on ad agencies that belong to the A.A.A.A.:

To extend and broaden the application of high ethical standards. Specifically, we will not knowingly create advertising that contains:

a False or misleading statements or exaggerations, visual or verbal

b Testimonials that do not reflect the real opinion of the individual(s) involved

c Price claims that are misleading

d Claims insufficiently supported or that distort the true meaning or practical applica-

tion of statements made by professional or scientific authority

e Statements, suggestions, or pictures offensive to public decency or minority segments of the population. . . .

We agree not to recommend to an advertiser, and to discourage the use of, advertising that is in poor or questionable taste or that is deliberately irritating through aural or visual content or presentation.

and other status items. Critics pin part of the blame on television commercials, including ones featuring African-American heroes like basketball legend Michael Jordan and movie director Spike Lee, that are deftly targeted to inner-city youths. Thirty-second commercials are certainly not the major cause of urban misery and crime, but it is distressing that they should contribute at all.

The Distortion of Thought: Truth Becomes "Truth"

Despite improvements over the years, much advertising is still characterized by oversimplification, superficiality, and shoddy standards of proof.[77] Heavy exposure to such logic may dull critical thinking in all areas of life. That's one reason it is so disconcerting that Channel One commercials are beamed directly into thousands of schoolrooms.

Advertising is filled with words and phrases, such as "revolutionary," "new," "best seller," and "lowest price," that appear to have a clear meaning. But as Jules Henry explained in his classic book *Culture Against Man*, advertising lingo obeys its own "pecuniary logic." Pecuniary logic "is a proof that is not proof but is intended to be so for commercial purposes."[78] Thus, an "all new" product might simply be a new color; a "best-selling" book might have sold poorly but is the most popular that the publisher has in a particular category.

A steady diet of pecuniary logic could promote fuzzy-minded thinking and dishonesty. Why should the average person be honest when "trusted" corporations (they are national advertisers, after all) routinely twist the truth? What conclusions might children draw when they realize that the adult world accepts television commercials that provide incomplete, misleading, or dishonest information? Might children respond to untruthful advertising by feeling that *they* should not be constrained by the truth? Is lying or deception wrong when one person is talking directly to another person but acceptable when amplified by the mass media and told to millions at a time? Those are all questions that deserve further discussion and research.

When the distorted "logic" of commercial advertising becomes the currency of political, social, economic, and other forms of once-serious discussion, democratic government suffers. That development, says broadcast journalist Bill Moyers, "is wrecking the polity of America, destroying our ability as a cooperative society to face reality and solve our problems."[79]

The Elusiveness of Happiness

The sales pitches imply, if they don't state explicitly, that the more we buy, the happier we'll be. And it would certainly seem logical that acquiring material goods should increase one's level of happiness. After all, who could deny that people gain pleasure from having a fancy new car or compact disc?

Most people would predict they would be happier if they had twice their current income, but that's exactly what has happened to our nation as a whole in recent decades without yielding the anticipated bliss. For instance, per capita income, adjusted for inflation, more than doubled between 1950 and 1993 (though the increases have been negligible in recent years).[80] The ownership of cars, homes, televisions, kitchen and laundry appliances, VCRs, and other things has increased enormously. Yet the percentages of people who say they were "happy" or "very happy" hardly changed at all.[81]

Happiness is elusive in part because it correlates with relative, not absolute, levels of wealth.[82] We compare our lives to our neighbors or to what the media suggest is today's norm, and we may feel deprived if we don't live as well as others. We do not compare our lives to the way people lived in 1950 or 1850 or to the way people live in poorer nations.

We find we "need" all kinds of things that were either considered luxuries or were not yet invented thirty years ago: air conditioners in our house and car, vacations abroad, a cellular telephone and several television sets, and a large house. Our new level of consumption becomes an irreducible minimum standard of living, and the thought of living the simpler life that many environmentalists advocate is psychologically traumatic.

Keeping up with the Joneses was always hard enough, but in today's world marketers are tempting us with an outpouring of expensive high-tech products: computer games, talking toys, car phones, personal communications systems, CD-ROM encyclopedias, interactive 500-channel TV...the list goes on and on. And marketers have led us to believe that owning them all is our birthright.

Academic researchers have begun to explore the relationship between lifestyle and happiness. Russell W. Belk, a business professor at the University of Utah, conducted surveys that found, first, that materialism is associated with feelings of possessiveness, nongenerosity, and envy. He then found that all three of those traits correlated inversely with happiness.[83] In other words, materialism may well lead to unhappiness. That finding doesn't mean that an ascetic lifestyle will guarantee happiness, but it does indicate that having ever more will not necessarily increase one's level of happiness.

Richins, the University of Missouri marketing professor, and Scott Dawson, associate professor of marketing at Portland State University, have found that materialistic people were more likely to buy things for themselves and less likely to give to charities or to relatives. More interesting, the researchers found that materialistic people were also less satisfied with their lives.[84]

Some researchers consider consumption to be an addiction, with all that that term implies: development of "tolerance," which requires ever greater consumption, and "withdrawal" symptoms, which spur continued consumption. As Swarthmore psychology professor Barry Schwartz observed in his book *The Costs of Living*, people addicted to drugs are offered addiction clinics, but people addicted to consumption are vigorously encouraged to maintain their habits by ubiquitous advertising: "Getting and spending is actively promoted, encouraged, advertised, and revered....Until consumption stops being regarded as the national pastime, we can expect only that more and more individuals will develop thing addictions."[85]

Sapping the Community's Strength

In a culture of commercialism run amok, civic-mindedness is an alien concept and community withers. This is the "me only" world where politicians feed the public with disingenuous promises of "no new taxes."

Toward the dusk of the most self-indulgent decade in American history, President George Bush, in his 1989 inaugural address, called on Americans to celebrate "the quieter, deeper successes that are made not of gold and silk but of better hearts and finer souls." Bush's speech came not long after the humbling and reality-awakening experience of "Meltdown Monday"—that October 1987 day when a 508-point Dow Jones drop shocked frenzied speculators and the era of rising expectations began winding down. "The days of the automatic more were over," said Laurence Shames, author of *Searching for Values in an Age of Greed*.[86] A new value, a new notion of "more," Shames said, would soon emerge: "more appreciation of good things beyond the marketplace, more insistence on fairness, more attention to purpose, more determination to choose a life, and not a lifestyle."

Consumption as the Dominant Value

America is still reeling from what Ralph Waldo Emerson labeled as an "imbalance…between materialism and idealism in the pursuit of the good life."[87] The political and commercial leaders of the 1980s led us to believe that materialism and idealism were synonymous, that individual pursuit of material goods was not only pleasurable, but also in the public interest. History has proven them wrong. As the 1980s drew to a close, the nation faced a soaring budget deficit, the savings-and-loan system was bankrupted by spendthrift speculators, thousands of companies were raided and gutted by takeover mania, and a host of social problems were made more urgent by a decade of neglect. All but forgotten in the buy-till-you-die era were many of the key principles on which this nation was founded. One value—consumption—came to dominate all others. It was as if America had lost the ability to order its priorities and was losing touch with its very soul.

Commercialism appropriates our culture's images and ideas—from George Washington to the Bill of Rights—and then associates them with particular products and services. Through some mysterious marketplace alchemy, the meanings of images and ideas are infused into commercial activities, just as the commercial meanings are infused into historic images and ideas.

There is something parasitic about the commercial way. It feeds on the organisms of noncommercial culture—the culture's past and present, ideology and myths, politics and customs, art and architecture, literature and music. Consider how President's Day, July 4th, and other holidays have been stripped of their true meaning and turned into so many more "sale" days. The end result is that much of our culture has been consumed and transformed.

The commercial infrastructure makes it easier and easier to consume. Shops planted everywhere—in high schools, airports, and sports arenas—help us to spend money wherever we are. And whereas once stores were closed most evenings and at least one day a week, more and more are open twenty-four hours a day, seven days a week—they'll always be ready when the urge to shop strikes us. And if going out shopping is too much trouble, mail-order catalogs, home-shopping channels, and 800 or 900 telephone numbers enable us to buy practically anything without getting out of bed.

Few mortals can resist powerful cultural influences; it's only human to bend with the wind. A humanitarian, communitarian, intellectual, or environmental wind would move us one way, a commercial wind another. Should it be a shock, then, that so many Americans focus so much more on consumption than on other means of satisfaction?

Commercialism's Domino Effect

The focus on personal wealth and consumption has profound consequences for the nation as well as for the individual. Recent years have witnessed a decline in public support for programs to benefit the least fortunate. And throughout the 1980s and beyond, politicians have pandered to voters by pretending that America's problems would be solved with tax *cuts*, not increases.

Many people believe they can wall themselves off from the problems that government at times has helped to ameliorate: urban slums, homelessness, illiteracy, and the like. But decay in the community affects everyone, just as a malignant tumor affects the whole body. An executive seeking a secretary discovers that many applicants can't spell or type. Urbanites wary of crime fear visiting whole sections of town. The fanciest cars suffer the pot-hole revenge meted out by poorly maintained roads. And even those in walled-off suburban developments have to worry about dangerous chemicals in their food, water, and air.

A public sector starved for support cannot provide essential services. As Galbraith has noted, "The engines of mass communication…assail the eyes and ears of the community on behalf of more beer but not of more schools.…The inherent tendency will always be for public services to fall behind private production."[88] That situation will persist until voters see that progress-through-selfishness is an oxymoron and agree to invest more in their country's future.

Eroding Religion

One business leader has said, "It's not that people value money more, but that they value everything else so much less; not that they are more greedy, but that they have no other values to keep greed in check."[89] Religion, which traditionally has been a powerful vehicle for conveying social values from one generation to the next, to a great extent has fallen victim to the values of commercialism. Organized religion, instead of zealously protecting and advocating social values, too often provides its remaining followers with empty rituals and vapid sermons.

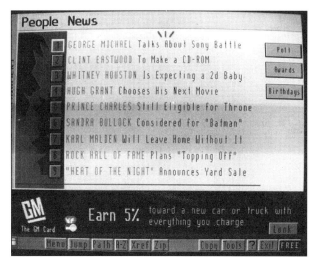

For several years, the Prodigy computer network sold space to advertisers.

Most religious traditions condemn acquisitiveness, selfishness, extravagant wealth—all characteristics that are associated with today's consumer culture. For example, the Bible warns that "it is easier for a camel to go through a needle's eye, than for a rich man to enter into the kingdom of God."[90] It counsels love for one another, justice, concern for the poor, stewardship of the earth, and nonviolence. The impact of those timeless messages is dulled by the ceaseless pressure of commercialism.

Religion's influence on personal and social values may have shrunk, but religious leaders are still among the most persistent and perceptive moral analysts of our society. For instance, in *Economic Justice for All, Pastoral Letter on Catholic Social Teaching and the U.S. Economy*, the National Conference of Catholic Bishops has asked, "Does our economy distribute its benefits equitably or does it concentrate power and resources in the hands of a few? Does it promote excessive materialism and individualism?…Are we able to distinguish between our true needs and those thrust on us by advertising and a society that values consumption more than saving?"[91]

In the meantime, though, commercialism marches on, even transmogrifying the day commemorating the birth of Jesus Christ into an unparalleled orgy of consumption. Santa Claus, our economy's number one pitchman, long ago elbowed

Jesus out of the holiday-time spotlight. Consider: A 1993 survey found that 97 percent of those who celebrate Christmas go Christmas shopping, compared to just 56 percent who attend church services on Christmas Eve or Christmas day.[92]

Robert Parham, director of the Baptist Center for Ethics, sees a schizophrenia of values on display at Christmastime. Many people, he says, place "others before self, the spiritual and ethical before the material, and the community good before the private gain." But then there is "the shadow side of human nature…things like greed, insecurity, pos-

Many taxi owners make extra cash selling billboard space on their cars' roofs and add one more bit of commercial clutter to cityscapes.

sessiveness. And the commercialization of Christmas plays to the shadow side."[93]

Madison Avenue's version of Christmas has also infected Hanukkah, which until recently was a minor Jewish holiday celebrated with token gifts. Hanukkah has become the Big Holiday that children look forward to, not for its religious significance but for the big-ticket gifts they might receive. Likewise, the ceremonies marking a child's coming of age, bar mitzvahs and bat mitzvahs, are often excuses for after-synagogue extravaganzas that may cost as much as $100,000. Some parents even tell of having to get a second mortgage to finance such glitzy affairs so they and their child wouldn't be embarrassed by what friends might say about a simpler celebration.[94]

Commercialism also undercuts the

spiritual side of our lives quite apart from organized religion. It becomes harder to concentrate on such lofty and vital matters as the meaning of life, on Homo sapiens' place in the universe, on justice within and between nations when businesses are pounding away at us to be consumers.

Undermining Civic Institutions

It is the reality of our times: Government spending cuts have forced hungry nonprofits to turn to the business community for funds. Businesses have converted charitable donations into profit-oriented investments, blurring the line between altruism and commerce.[95]

As we have seen (Chapter 5, "Corporate Culture"), museums of art and science offer golden opportunities for marketers to reach wealthy, educated consumers, as well as impressionable children, in what is perceived as a noncommercial environment. The corporate funds that pay for exhibits may seem like a windfall to the institutions, but those funds pay only for exhibits that jibe with the donors' interests. Those who would like to produce controversial, political exhibits need not apply for corporate funding.

Likewise, the general timidity of public broadcasting (Chapter 2, "The Private Life of Public Broadcasting") is due partly to a fear of offending major underwriters. "Good corporate citizens" rarely fund programs that highlight problems related to themselves, major companies in general, or to our economic system.

Businesses Profit from Nonprofits

Organizations that seek to influence

public opinion or public policy and present themselves as independent need to be truly independent if they expect to remain credible. In the early 1980s, the National Council on Alcoholism (NCA—now the National Council on Alcoholism and Drug Dependence) would not advocate restricting alcohol advertising or boosting taxes on alcoholic beverages. Back then, the NCA received significant funding from the beer, wine, and liquor industries, and three of the seven members of the executive committee of its board of directors came from those industries. Ultimately, the organization recognized the limitations imposed by its corporate "friends." As soon as NCA adopted a no-corporate-donations policy and reorganized its committees, it became an aggressive advocacy group that helped pass legislation to put warning notices on every beer, wine, and liquor label.

In contrast, to pick one prominent example, the American Council on Science and Health (ACSH) bills itself as a scientifically balanced "consumer education association," but its list of supporters reads like the membership directory of the Business Roundtable. Except for its forthright opposition to smoking, virtually every position ACSH takes defends business in general and its sponsors' products in particular. In the 1980s the *Washington Post* revealed that an amicus brief ACSH filed in a lawsuit challenging a government ban on formaldehyde was actually written by the plaintiffs, Georgia-Pacific, a leading user of formaldehyde, and the Formaldehyde Institute.[96] That's not the kind of independence that makes for a strong nonprofit sector.

Considering the times, groups like Con-

Alcohol and tobacco companies commonly sponsor minority events to appeal to black and Hispanic communities.

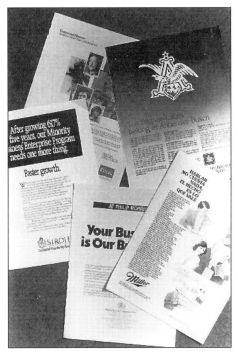

sumers Union and Public Citizen deserve recognition for their "just say no" policy on financial support from corporations.

Schools on the Corporate Dole

Perhaps most important, our society appears willing to trade children's minds for commercial profit. It is far simpler and more lucrative for schools to hawk commercial products than citizenship. Cash-strapped schools are fertile territory for businesses marketing wares to hard-to-reach teens (see Chapter 1, "Schools Go Commercial"). Thus, companies ply teachers and their pupils with brochures, free samples, hallway posters, videos, and ads on Channel One. Not only does such commercialism jeopardize the quality of education, it sends a strong signal to students that commercial values are of paramount importance.

The Benefits and Costs

Something significant is lost when citizens groups and civic institutions become dependent upon corporate funding. Nonprofits may change from institutions wed to the public trust into institutions beholden to private interests. What had been independent voices on America's cultural landscape may be muffled or muzzled with cash. Policymakers, journalists, and educators may be relying on information from groups whose tongues are twisted by corporate contributions. For too long, we have applauded corporate donors and "public-private partnerships" without recognizing the price that such generosity often extracts.

Not all nonprofits are adversely affected by industry funding, but many say they must pander to corporations to survive. At some point, though, one wonders whether survival is worth the price. For instance, Chicago's Museum of Science and Industry may have outlived its educational usefulness by becoming, as discussed earlier, largely a stately showcase for corporate propaganda.

Ultimately, what is at stake here is the preservation of parts of our culture that are free of the tentacles of commercialism. In the past, a vibrant and independent nonprofit sector was an important part of that culture. But when nonprofits become arms of the marketing division of corporate America, culture succumbs to commerce.

Making Pawns of the Press

Advertisers bankroll the media, but they don't give broadcasters and publishers a blank check.[97] They use the power of the wallet in ways ranging from subtly influencing writers to openly prescribing content. Many producers, editors, and publishers alter or pull stories that might offend advertisers, write pieces expressly to appease or attract advertisers, avoid topics that create controversial "environments" for advertising, and gear articles and programs to attract an audience that advertisers crave. In short, they often trade editorial integrity for the almighty ad dollar.

Advertisers have long influenced the media they depend on. A hundred years ago, it was common for marketers to pay newspapers to write favorable articles.[98] In the 1930s and 1940s, the *New York Times*, *Science*, *Redbook*, and dozens of other publications would not accept advertising for *Consumer Reports* magazine for fear of offending advertisers whose products rated poorly in that magazine.[99] For instance, the advertising director of the *New York Herald Tribune* told Consumers Union, the publisher of *Consumer Reports*, "I feel strongly that we are committed to maintaining a marketplace and that we should not take money from owners of brand names and branded products and at the same time take money for the admission into that marketplace of an

organization such as yourselves that seeks to set up final standards in product selection as a substitute for the advertising processes."[100] Women's magazines, according to one report, began tolerating censorship in 1956 when a nylon manufacturers' association bought a $12,000 ad in *Woman*, a British magazine, on the condition that no articles in that issue prominently feature natural fibers.[101]

Advertisers are not secretly plotting to control the media, but in their quest to improve sales they are steadily flexing their muscles and reducing the freedom of the press. That phenomenon has serious ramifications for everything from entertainment to documentaries to newscasts in both print and broadcast media.

Less of the News That Is Fit to Print

Nowhere is the impact of advertisers of greater concern than in the context of the news media. Economic pressures resulting from increased competition and recessionary times have forced some of the news media to compromise traditional standards of journalism in order to attract advertising revenue.

The Center for the Study of Commercialism, in a 1992 report entitled *Dictating Content*, documented more than sixty instances of advertiser censorship. For example, the owners of Minneapolis's KARE-TV killed a story by a veteran consumer reporter on car dealerships for fear of angering car-dealer advertisers.[102] *The Birmingham* (Alabama) *News* fired a columnist of twenty-three years after he criticized the local auto industry's influence over the newspaper's editorial content.[103]

Since *Dictating Content* was published, many additional examples have surfaced. For example,

- *When* Daily Variety *critic Joseph McBride panned Paramount Pictures'* Patriot Games, *Paramount yanked all its advertising.* Daily Variety *editor Peter Bart publicly apologized to Paramount and promised that McBride would never review* another *Paramount movie.*[104]

- *Reporter Sheila Kaplan wrote an article for* Mademoiselle *on women lobbyists, but the editors deleted text that profiled a Philip Morris lobbyist. The editors said that Philip Morris, after previewing the article, threatened to pull its advertising if the section ran. Kaplan was also warned that if she went public with the censorship,* Mademoiselle *would never take another of her stories.*[105]

- *In September 1993, Mercedes-Benz wrote to about thirty magazines requiring them to pull all Mercedes ads from any issue containing articles critical of the company, German products, or even Germany itself. That policy would discourage any magazine hungry for a piece of Mercedes's $14.5 million in annual magazine ad expenditures from running the proscribed articles. Mercedes eventually rescinded its policy after several large publishers complained—but not before half the magazines had already signed and returned the agreement to Mercedes.*[106]

- *When Wal-Mart stores stopped advertising regularly in the* Nashville (Arkansas) News, *the paper reversed its deliberately favorable coverage of the retailer and now throws away Wal-Mart press releases. "I don't give free publicity to companies that don't help pay the light bill around here," said editor Louis Graves to the* Wall Street Journal.[107]

According to a 1992 Marquette University study, virtually all 150 newspaper editors surveyed acknowledged editorial in-

The Iowa Department of Taxation sold ads to financial services in its 1993 tax brochures, possibly compromising its objectivity in overseeing those companies.

terference by advertisers. The most meddling, they reported, were automotive, real estate, construction, and restaurant advertisers. Almost 90 percent of the editors said advertisers tried to influence story content, and 37 percent said they succeeded. More than 70 percent of the editors said advertisers tried to kill stories.[108]

A survey by the Society of American Business Editors and Writers found that 75 percent of respondents were aware of growing pressure by advertisers on editorial content; 55 percent reported that that pressure has influenced their editorial decisions. One wrote, "We no longer cover the auto industry like we should, especially [on] consumer issues, because of dealer pressure."[109]

Women's magazines have been particularly responsive to advertisers' wishes (see Chapter 4, "The Iron Maiden: How Advertising Portrays Women"), and tobacco companies are particularly prone to pressure those magazines and other media in which they advertise (see Chapter 7, "Ads That Kill I: Tobacco").

Even more ominous is advertising's potential effect on news and political coverage. During the Gulf War, advertisers were concerned that images of death and destruction would undermine their upbeat campaigns; they pulled·several million dollars worth of ads in the early days of war coverage.[110] Whether the networks toned down the gloom to avoid advertiser pullouts is impossible to know.

Some analysts believe that advertiser

control of the media threatens the freedom of the press, guaranteed by the First Amendment. The First Amendment was designed to protect an "uninhibited, robust, and wide-open" press from government controls, as Supreme Court Justice William Brennan once put it.[111] Clearly, though, the threat of censorship is no longer limited to state control. Private economic forces have ushered in another kind of censorship, one generally beyond the reach of the First Amendment. Like its government counterpart, censorship by advertisers denies the public access to knowledge that is crucial for making informed political and economic choices.

Journalists Versus Advertisers

Can the American press stand up to Philip Morris, Revlon, Procter and Gamble, and other corporations? Bill Lazarus, a prize-winning reporter who writes for the *Hammond* (Indiana) *Times*, says: "When you write about government, the attitude of [editors] tends to be 'no holds barred.' When you write about business, the attitude tends to be one of caution. And for businesses [that] happen to be advertisers, the caution turns frequently to timidity."[112]

And how cozy is the relationship between the newsroom and the adroom? Do editors and producers actually take *affirmative* steps to produce copy or programming intended primarily to please advertisers? A *Washington Post* business writer responds that "even the most reputable broadcasters and publishers are knocking new holes in the wall that traditionally has separated news and entertainment from their advertising departments."[113]

Granted, economic pressure in the news media is not a new phenomenon, but as the media have extended their reach into our lives, the threat to their integrity has grown. Many in the news industry say their more collaborative arrangement with advertisers is necessary if their publication or station is to survive.

But at what cost to independent journalism? If the "free press" serves its financial backers over the citizenry it informs, then how valuable to the public is its survival?

Double-standard journalism—hard on government but soft on advertisers—mocks the public's right to know. Critical of how some editors have bowed to advertiser pressure, Charles Peters, editor of the *Washington Monthly*, has said: "I think it's extremely important to expose the cowardice that comes from almost all of the press."[114]

But coming forward has its costs, both professional and personal. Editors and publishers frequently dismiss the problem as anecdotal and aberrational or, conversely, as so ingrained in the profession as not to be worthy of mention. Reporters, fearful of losing their jobs, typically don't go public when a story is censored.

Fears of retaliation are understandable: One longtime newspaper reporter was fired in 1991 after he was quoted in the *Washington Journalism Review* about his paper's sensitivity to car advertisers. Financial analyst Graef Crystal, who was writing a column about executive salaries, was fired by *Financial World* after advertisers complained their executives were getting bad coverage.[115] An editor at *Philadelphia* magazine was ousted after clashing with his publisher over the issue of advertiser interference,[116] but he said he would jeopardize his future in the industry if he talked for the record.

If advertiser dollars are able to influence media content, the public will never get the whole story or quality programming. Advertisers—quick to assert their own right to free commercial speech—fail to concede their role in subverting the First Amendment. The press enjoys special constitutional protection for being an instrument of self-rule, an educational tool of democracy, not simply to protect the profits of advertisers and the media. But if the citizenry is only told what suits advertisers, the democratic ideal is left in tatters.

CHAPTER TEN

Call to Action

Taming Commercialism

{A} man is rich in proportion to the number of things which he can afford to let alone. —Henry David Thoreau[1] ✳ *Let us be frank in acknowledgement of the truth that many amongst us have made obeisance to Mammon, that the profits of speculation, the easy road without toil, have lured us from the old barricades. To return to higher standards of living we must abandon the false prophets and seek new leaders of our own choosing. — Franklin Delano Roosevelt*[2]

IN THIS CHAPTER, WE PRE-sent an agenda for action. Our proposals suggest ways that individuals, schools, government, and others could halt the spread of commercialism and return marketing to a smaller, more appropri-ate role in our society. Real-ists that we are, we do not propose grandiose changes in America's economic system; our more modest proposals are challenges enough for now.

To oppose cigarette advertising, Doctors Ought to Care (DOC) commissioned a "Barfboro" van to trail Philip Morris's "Marlboro" van around the country.

Photo by Erik Vidstrand, courtesy of DOC.

Historian David Shi has described the long thread of simple living that runs through America's history from the Puritans and Quak-ers to Thoreau and Emerson to the counterculture of the 1960s. Simplicity, says Shi, "requires neither a log cabin nor a hairshirt but a deliber-ate ordering of priorities so as to distinguish between the necessary and superfluous, useful and wasteful, beauti-ful and vulgar."[4]

Lifestyle changes are more than merely personal choices. Ronald J. Sider, executive di-rector of Evangelists for Social Action, questions whether we can "demand an ever higher standard of living while mil-lions of children starve to death each year?...By spend-ing less on ourselves, we can transform the lives of neighbors who will die unless we care."[5] That trans-formation, to be sure, is not automatic but depends upon personal actions and government policies to shift resources to where they are most needed.

Changing Our Daily Lives

More and more people of every political stripe are realizing that the fruits of our hypercommer-cialized society offer short-term personal pleasure and long-term cultural crisis. Whether it was grazing through fifty (soon to be 500) channels of ad-filled television programs, learning of a company's plan to launch a billboard into space, being subjected to advertising on "noncommercial" radio, or discover-ing that their kids are required to watch advertis-ing in school, many Americans have concluded that commercialism is warping our values and degrad-ing our environment. They have vowed to resist the consumption ethic espoused by marketers and in-stead lead simpler lives focused more around fami-ly, community affairs, and personal growth.[3]

Starting Small

Despite the encompassing presence of commer-cialism and consumerism, every individual can do something to escape from their influences and make his or her community a better place to live. A starting point is to evaluate the extent to which commercialism has crept into your own life. Count the ads, note the product tie-ins, see the corporate logos practically everywhere. Then start decom-mercializing by:

- *Relying more on public radio and TV and on newsletters and magazines that contain little or no advertising.*

- *Declaring yourself an ad-free zone by not wearing clothing that features corporate logos.*

- *Using the buttons on your car radio and your TV's remote control to avoid advertising.*

- *Boycotting companies whose advertising or sales practices offend you (tell them why you stopped buying their products).*

- *Wasting less time reading unwanted advertising circulars and junk mail; get your name removed from many national direct-mail and telemarketing lists (see Chapter 6, "Intrusive Marketing"); tell catalog houses you buy from, nonprofit groups you belong to, and magazines you subscribe to not to rent or trade your name.*

- *Reducing the number of commercial transactions by bartering or exchanging favors with friends.*

Granted, those small, largely symbolic, personal actions will not crush commercialism. But they're still worth doing, because they can be done easily and quickly, send small signals to others, and lay a foundation for larger, more meaningful changes.

We need to examine the extent to which we are living by our own standards and values or letting peer pressure and marketing strategies influence our lives. Once we begin looking at our lifestyles from that perspective, we are ready to contemplate the critical question posed by environmentalist Alan Durning: "How much is enough?"[6] For most Americans, as psychologist Paul Wachtel observes in his insightful book *The Poverty of Affluence*, "'Enough' is always just over the horizon, and like the horizon it recedes as we approach it....Wanting more remains a constant, regardless of what we have."[7] (A California marketing professor said only half-jokingly, "What is enough is when your money runs out."[8]) Serious consideration of the "enough" question should

During a No-TV Week in Andover, Connecticut, grade school children colored flyers, like the one above, and posted them on the front lawns of participants.

get us thinking about how much of our consumption is necessary and how much is wasteful.

Americans are clearly hooked on consuming. According to one 1987 survey, 93 percent of teenage girls deemed shopping their favorite pastime.[9] For some people, shopping is not just a means to an end but an end in itself. In the most extreme cases, a few people feel a compulsion to shop; they need professional help. We would do well to evaluate the role that shopping plays in our lives and to check whether we shop to relieve boredom or loneliness and wind up buying things we don't need.

One kind of shopping that only a Scrooge would criticize is shopping for gifts.[10] But perhaps the most expressive gifts are those that are homemade, such as a loaf of bread, necklace, or scarf, along with a homemade gift card. Or how about giving friends your own personal coupons for babysitting, grocery shopping, or other services? If you're not the artsy-craftsy type, you can buy handmade products from local weavers, jewelers, and carpenters; you'll not only be giving unique gifts but also supporting the creative community.

Keeping Americans focused on consumption is television, the most powerful entertainment medium—and sales device—ever invented. Two leading analysts of television, Robert Kubey of Rutgers University and Mihaly Csikszentmihalyi of the University of Chicago, acknowledge that television is the cheapest, most accessible escape imaginable.[11] But they also warn that for some people, TV-watching is almost an addiction. They recommend that viewers:

- *Plan their viewing, rather than just watching whatever is on.*

- *Turn off the TV when a program is simply a waste of time.*

- *Write a list of enjoyable, constructive non-TV activities and consult it before turning on the television.*

Rediscovering Thrifty Living

The word "frugal" is rarely heard these days—it sounds so frumpy and archaic. We are certainly not encouraged to be frugal, to shop carefully, and to save some of our hard-earned income. Even banks don't encourage savings—they're too busy sending out preapproved credit card applications and urging us to take out home-equity and auto loans.

Joe Dominguez and Vicki Robin, in their best-selling book *Your Money or Your Life*, challenge the normal image of frugality. In their view, being frugal is not synonymous with being a cheapskate, skinflint, or miser. Rather, "frugality *is* balance. Frugality is the Greek notion of the golden mean. Frugality is being efficient in harvesting happiness from the world you live in. Frugality is right-use…the wise stewardship of money, time, energy, space, and possessions….It's that magic word—enough."[12]

Dominguez and Robin urge people to use a combination of frugality, work, simple lifestyle, and conservative investments to achieve "financial independence." They define several stages of "FI." The first is getting free of worry and fears by tracking where your money is going and making better choices. The next stage is getting out of debt and building savings. The final stage is having a big enough nest egg to be able to live on the investment income. To help you get there, Dominguez and Robin provide 110 "sure ways to save money," ranging from eating a proper diet (which cuts medical expenses) to swapping services with family and friends.[13] Here are their first nine tips:

- *Don't go shopping. If you need something, do buy it. But don't just "go shopping" without a specific purpose.*

Former President Jimmy Carter volunteers with and helps raise funds for Habitat for Humanity, a service organization that builds housing for the needy.

- *Live within your means. Far too many people are in hock up to their ears with car payments, mortgages, and credit card bills.*

- *Take care of what you have. Whether it's teeth, toys, or Toyotas, keeping things clean and protected will greatly extend their useful life.*

  - *Wear it out. Postpone buying new clothes, cars, and other things if you can still get use out of your current possessions.*

  - *Do it yourself. Learn to fix your bicycle tires, leaky faucets, missing buttons, and other broken products. But do know your limits.*

  - *Anticipate your needs. Keep an eye out for sales before your tires wear out or you need new shoes. Avoid impulse buying.*

  - *Research value, quality, and durability. Read* Consumer Reports. *It may be worth spending more on products that will last longer.*

- *Get it for less. Use mail-order discounters and discount chain stores.[14] Comparison shop by phone. Bargain with store owners and vendors.*

- *Buy it used. Keep an eye out for thrift shops, garage sales, swap meets, and flea markets. But don't buy junk just because it's cheap.*

Giving Our Planet a Helping Hand

The commercial world makes it tough for Americans to lead environmentally sensitive lives because it vigorously promotes wasteful lifestyles. The mass media are ablaze with the glitzy lifestyles of show-business celebrities, and broadcasters run hundreds of times more product advertisements than public service messages.

We need to guard against buying things just because a company says we need shorter skirts or pastel-colored kitchen appliances. When we feel we need to replace something, we need to consider whether the most economical, ecologically sound action would be to continue using our "outdated" product even if a new model might be a little more efficient, stylish, or convenient. Many people, for instance, buy powerful new computers when all they really need is a bottom-of-the-line model (or even a typewriter) to print out an occasional letter or shopping list. Ideally, prospective buyers of expensive, complex products would have easy access to independent advice to help them match their needs with an appropriate product rather than relying on glossy catalogs or commission-driven salespeople.

Do you recycle cans, bottles, newspapers, and other items as much as you can? Could your family get by with one less car, using a bike or public transportation, or walking instead? Could you live closer to your job or school, saving you time and money? Do you buy more clothes, furniture, and other things than you need? Those are small things, but such individual actions, repeated millions of times a day around the country, would help protect the environment.

Having children may be the most meaningful thing you ever do—but it also will result in greater consumption of natural resources and more pollution than anything else you'll ever do. Can your two-parent family limit itself to having two children? Is adoption for you? If you already have children, do you talk with them about moderating consumption and protecting the environment?

To help citizens do more to protect the environment, cities and towns need to do more to promote "greener" lifestyles. Most communities lack full-fledged recycling systems, and people are forced to throw newspapers, containers, and other products in the garbage. Cities choking on traffic and air pollution should be helping people commute without a car, but bike paths are largely unavailable and bus systems are more primitive than in many Third World countries. Our metropolitan areas desperately need to develop an infrastructure conducive to a "sustainable lifestyle."

Working Less, Enjoying More

Leading a simpler, less materialistic life needn't be the dreary, self-sacrificing experience that one might imagine. Consider the experience of Sloan Wilson, who wrote the best-selling 1950s novel *The Man in the Gray Flannel Suit*. Wilson lived the high life for several years in fancy Connecticut suburbs, but then ambition, divorce, and alcohol took their toll. Now, living with his wife on a modest houseboat in a small Virginia town, Wilson says "The trick is to learn to live simply so you don't need so much money....I've never been so happy."[15]

Or consider Bill and Kathryn, a middle-class couple. They were first motivated to simplify their lives to save money, but they soon found even richer dividends. Kathryn says, "I finally realized things had been running me, instead of me running them." Her husband says, "It isn't about how much or how little; it is reaching a place of contentment....It is not about giving things up, it's about being true to yourself."[16]

Many Americans recognize that purchasing fewer things might make sense. Juliet Schor, author of *The Overworked American*, conducted a survey in 1993 and found that 72 percent of the participants said they could live a more frugal life. About one-fifth of those felt they would be better off, and an additional half felt they would not be worse off, than at present.[17]

Still, we are not suggesting that buying less and living simply is the total formula for happiness. Paul Wachtel urges that while we reduce our materialistic tendencies we also nurture "psycho-ecological" values, which emphasize human relationships and concern for the environment. He says, "The consumer way of life is deeply flawed, both psychologically and ecologically. It fails to bring the satisfactions promised and its side effects are lethal....I would like to see less emphasis on the economic dimension of our lives—growth, productivity, the creation of needs for more and more goods, the 'bottom line'—and more on the psychological: the richness of subjective experience and the quality of human relationships."[18]

The dream of having more leisure time for family or community activities, intellectual interests, or just plain fun has too often been lost in the quest for the money it takes to stay on the consumer treadmill. Do we really have to work as hard as we do? Schor suggests not. If we wanted to, she says, "we could now produce our 1948 standard of living (measured in terms of marketed goods and services) in less than half the time it took in that year."[19] In other words, we could work only *half* as much—four hours a day, six months a year, or one out of every two years. Schor recognizes the impediments to making such a radical change (such as the lack of high-paying part-time jobs and a psychological addiction to our current lifestyle) but suggests that we move gradually in that direction by taking future pay increases in the form of reduced hours, not dollars. That option may not be available to everyone but is worth considering as we reevaluate our lives.

Getting Involved as a Life Choice

The best way to get *unhooked* from the hedonic trap of consumerism is to get *hooked* on activities that we find enjoyable and meaningful. That might mean consciously spending more time with family and friends, further formal education or reading, or exploring new experiences and hobbies. Those activities can meet our real needs for meaning and purpose in a way that the packaged joys of consumerism can only approximate. Environmentalist Donella Meadows describes that as "meeting non-material needs through non-material means."[20]

It is important to build structures into our lives to help sustain our dedication to nonmaterialistic values. Starting or joining a regularly scheduled book club or study group or organizing potluck dinners with discussions could be as valuable for those seeking to lead simpler, more satisfying lives as consciousness-raising groups were for budding feminists in the 1970s. Some community colleges or "free universities" have classes or workshops on simple living.

Serving as a volunteer is one common way of sustaining community-oriented values in a very satisfying way. The 20 percent of American adults who volunteer with public, private, or religious organizations[21] often find themselves surrounded by other people who share their values. Many people become so absorbed in volunteer activities that they lose interest in consumerist attractions. As University of British Columbia marketing professor Richard Pollay says, volunteering can help turn an unsatisfied consumer into a satisfied citizen.

Typically, volunteers feel that they get back far more in satisfaction than they give in time or money. Listen to these two women who volunteer at a homeless shelter in Maryland:

> I got so much out of it that [my husband] could see. I just felt so great....There's nothing to compare it to. Most people work for a paycheck and it doesn't even compare. It's just so good.

> I love doing it....I feel good when I work here. There's just a sense of purpose.[22]

Most cities and counties run volunteer bureaus; call the mayor's office, public library, or United Way to track one down. Or simply call an organization that you would like to assist and ask if it could use someone with your skills.

Even more significant than being a part-time volunteer is to make your career one of public service. Thousands of people are doing so as environmentalists, community organizers, public-interest lawyers, social workers, health activists, and public officials. Their work, and the example they set for others in terms of lifestyle and life goals, strikes a small blow for a more just society and against materialism and commercialism. Such jobs won't pay as much as a Wall Street law firm, but job satisfaction will

**Planned obso-
lescence and
new purchases
can be avoided
by taking
advantage of
shoe-repair
shops and other
mending ser-
vices.**

probably be much greater.

Yet, no matter how much we modify our lives in a less materialistic direction, we encounter social, psychological, and economic roadblocks. Let's turn now to the environment in which we live to identify broader changes that need to be made.

Growing Up Smarter in a Consumer Culture

It is in childhood that we begin developing our notions of what life is all about. Ideas seep in from all directions, and the notion of acquiring goods pours in from everywhere. Children, innocent of the ways of commerce, all too easily fall prey to the constant message of "more."

It Starts with Families

While commercial forces and the mass media attract children as relentlessly as gravity, the most important conveyor of personal and social values is still the family. Parents set the tone. If parents are excited about life and having a positive effect on society through their own job or volunteer activities, children likely will understand that they, too, can contribute to the public welfare and are not merely feckless travelers on a meaningless journey through life. A parent's intellectual life can energize and excite a child. But if parents do not communicate competing worldviews, their children may well adopt the values of the marketplace.

Parents can help their children develop a healthy immunity to exploitative marketers in particular and a materialistic lifestyle more generally. If parents evince skepticism of advertisers, their children will get the message. One approach is for

ANTICOMMERCIALISM HONOR ROLL

- **Rev. Calvin Butts, Rev. Michael Pfleger, and other activists who organized whitewashing campaigns to rid inner-city neighborhoods of cigarette and alcohol billboards.**
- **Dianne Grenier, who organized a highly successful No-TV Week in Andover, Connecticut.**
- **Neil Young, rock musician, for refusing to allow his concerts to be endorsed by breweries. His This Note's For You music video attacks the cooptation of rock music by beer marketers.**
- **The Eagles, a major rock group, which has never endorsed products or had corporate sponsors for tours.**
- **Congressman Edward J. Markey (D–Mass.) for winning passage of legislation that set limits on children's-television advertising and on telemarketing and for introducing a**

bill that would ban advertising in space.
- **Doctors Ought to Care (DOC), a national organization of antismoking physicians and medical students, for sponsoring the Emphysema Slims tennis tournament, anti-smoking ads, and other means of discouraging cigarette smoking.**
- **KSL-TV, the CBS affiliate in Salt Lake City, for discontinuing beer and wine commercials in 1990.**
- **Consumers Union, publisher of Consumer Reports and Zillions, for sponsoring (in cooperation with HBO) holiday-time TV shows for kids that expose dishonest marketing practices.**
- **Adbusters, Extra!, MediaCulture Review, World Watch, In Context, and other nonprofit publications that expose media corruption, the misdeeds of advertisers, and**

environmental destruction and promote a more environmentally aware, less materialistic world.
- **The Tightwad Gazette, the Penny Pincher, and other newsletters that encourage a richer life through frugality.**
- **Gar Mahood, antismoking activist in Canada, who waged a campaign that resulted in a total ban on tobacco advertising in that country.**
- **Ralph Nader, preeminent consumer activist, for devoting his life to championing consumer-protection legislation and training activists.**
- **New York State Department of Education for prohibiting Channel One from the state's public schools.**
- **Arista Technologies for developing The Commercial Eliminator, a device that automatically deletes commercials as a VCR plays back a program.**

parents and children to watch television and read advertisements together. Parents and children can then discuss how programs differ from real life and what some of the subtle, unspoken messages are. They can dissect advertising, figuring out what information is exaggerated or omitted.

But no matter what we do as individuals and as individual families, we cannot totally escape the consumer culture. If we are concerned about that culture, we will need the assistance of larger social institutions, including schools, government, and religion.

Decommercializing Schools

Schools should be playing a vital role in restoring America's civic and moral fabric. They should be helping children think critically about commercialism and many other aspects of life. But whether it's from disinterest, lack of time, or fear of offending some parents, many schools sidestep that task or, worse, become part of companies' sales campaigns.

To many companies, schools are nothing more than a marketing highway to young customers. Although screening out every advertisement might be impossible and unnecessary, teachers and school systems could be doing much more to make schools commercial-free zones. Channel One would be a worthy first target.

Parents should monitor the kinds of supplementary educational materials that teachers are using (see Chapter 1, "Schools Go Commercial"). Many materials produced by companies and trade associations lack objectivity and are little more than thinly veiled advertisements. Parents should ask teachers either not to use misleading materials or to discuss the biases in class. If teachers are not cooperative, parents could ask the PTA or principal to investigate the matter. An alternative would be to ask the state

Citizens for Media Literacy in Asheville, North Carolina, developed a comic book called "Get A Life" to help kids understand the manipulative techniques of advertisers in general, and Channel One in particular.

attorney general to take action against this misleading form of advertising.

The commercialization of schools is occurring at such a rapid pace and on so many fronts that the U.S. Department of Education should conduct a comprehensive review of the potential effects and recommend corrective measures.

Media Literacy

The elimination of corporate propaganda from schools must be complemented by efforts to help students become savvier consumers. Traditionally, schools have focused on the printed word, but they are slowly beginning to recognize that they have a responsibility to educate kids to live in a television-dominated, ad-saturated consumer culture. One vehicle for such education is the new discipline of "media literacy," which is taught in a growing number of schools, especially in Canada and Europe. The Ontario Ministry of Education requires teachers to integrate media literacy into the entire school curriculum to counter mass-media messages.[23]

Media-literacy courses teach students about using and understanding television, radio, movies, newspapers, magazines, and computers and can immunize them against some of the overt or hidden messages in the mass media, including advertising. Most students love such classes because the subject matter is so integral to their daily lives. In their classes, students might create their own video programs and ads, learn how fashion photographs are manipulated, investigate the economics of rock-music stations, consider what might happen if magazines publish articles critical of their advertisers, debate how the physical appearances of actors and models make us feel about ourselves, and discuss how advertisements play upon our insecurities and desires.

Photo by Christine Thelmo.

Participants in Teach for America, a national teacher corps designed to promote equity in education, spend two years teaching school in low-income rural and urban areas. The students recieve added attention and instruction while corps members, usually recent college graduates, learn valuable teaching and advocacy skills. Above, Susan Hendricks helps a fifth-grader.

Kubey and Csikszentmihalyi, authors of *Television and the Quality of Life*, enthusiastically advocate media literacy. They have concluded that "if most children are going to continue to watch 1,000 hours of television every year of their young lives and 1,000 hours every year for the rest of their lives, it is absurd for them not to receive formal education in the medium."[24] Parents and students should insist that their schools teach media literacy and that advertising be an important part of such courses. New Mexico was the first state to adopt a media-literacy requirement.[25]

Economic Literacy

Americans' education about the marketplace is meager and haphazard. Students might learn to balance a checkbook but receive little instruction on money and America's economic system. Schools need to supplement what kids learn at home or from businesses by exploring such topics as the relative merits of saving and spending; what "frugality" means to them; the differences in interest rates, fees, and services of various credit cards; the appropriateness of building a nest egg for college tuition, health crises, and other future expenses; the advantages and disadvantages of buying through catalogs, television shopping channels, and telemarketing; the effects of declaring personal bankruptcy; and differences between savings banks, certificates of deposit, money markets, mutual funds, stocks, and other investment options.

Economics classes could also discuss the role of advertising in our society: who benefits from it, how it seeks to persuade, how informative and honest it is, and how advertising is regulated.

Environmental Literacy

Schools could also spur students to think about how a consumption-oriented lifestyle affects the environment. Students could explore ways in which our economy could be redesigned to promote the general public welfare and protect the planet at the same time it provides jobs.

Every school needs to develop its own environmental program. In fact, schools could even make the environment their "central organizing principle," as Vice President Al Gore has recommended for the nations of the world. Classroom learning could be complemented by making the school itself more ecologically sound (for example, an organic garden to provide food for the lunchroom, solar heating in some rooms, use of recycled paper, and recycling or composting of waste) and by activist projects in the community. Each April, Earth Day offers a perfect occasion to host special events: student-produced programs that could be broadcast on the community-access cable channel, debates between environmentalists and industrialists, and science fairs emphasizing eco-projects.

Students as Citizens

Adolescence is the perfect time to develop lifelong skills, interests, and values and to define one's role in the community. Most teens, though, live in a cloistered world of rock music, stylish clothes, shiny cars, and shopping malls—partly because they have never been introduced to activities that offer deeper satisfactions.

A growing number of public and private high schools are encouraging students to get a taste of community service by volunteering with local environmental groups, battered-women's shelters, nursing homes, and other agencies. The best of the programs promote not just compassion for needy individuals, but an understanding of how social problems have developed and how the levers of power may be used to solve them.

Some of those school programs are totally voluntary, involving a handful of students. Others, including ones in Maryland; Atlanta, Georgia; Rye, New York; Bloomfield Hills, Michigan; and Elizabeth and Bethlehem, Pennsylvania, *require* all high school students to volunteer up to about twenty hours a year. Boston College High School, a Jesuit school, requires all students to spend the last five weeks of their senior year as volunteers.

Allan Luks, executive director of Big Brothers–Big Sisters of New York City, is a strong advocate of mandatory service programs, which, he says, can dissipate the meaninglessness, hopelessness, and boredom that so many students feel. Luks cites studies showing that regular, frequent service (about two hours a week) promotes self-esteem and reduces stress. Says Luks, "Self-esteem grows when someone experiences positive responses from others."[26] One high school girl in Maryland reduced her absences from more than seventy days to just two days from one year to the next. She attributed her turnaround to her school's program that connected her to the Maryland School for the Blind. "It gives me a reason to come to school," she said.[27]

The benefits to the community are incalculable: helping the homeless man find food and a clean bed, befriending the lonely woman in the nursing home, cleaning up the garbage-strewn stream, persuading a youth to forgo drugs. And, in the longer run, community service will create large numbers of people who care about, and have learned to influence, where our society is headed. Luks estimates that service programs cost only $20 per student per year, meaning that 47 million elementary and high school students could be enrolled for under $1 billion.

Some people object to mandatory community-service programs because of the extra burden on students or their cost.[28] But once such programs are adopted, participants (and their parents and teachers) almost always laud them. One Illinois student said, "It's the greatest thing I've ever done. I'm glad they made me. I hope to do it for the rest of my life."[29]

The National Community Service Trust Act of 1993 provides grants to establish service-learning programs in elementary and high schools. The goal of Learn and Serve America is to sharpen students' "academic skills, their sense of civic responsibility, their ability to solve community problems, and their understanding of important concepts such as community, diversity, and citizenship."[30] Every school should have such a program, ideally with students involved in managing it.

Rallying the Religious Community

The sounds of Christmas are heard as early as August with the thuds of mail-order catalogs dropping into our mailboxes.[31] Those sounds should serve to remind religious leaders to renew their efforts to recapture Christmas—and, more important, moral leadership—from the hucksters.

In 1992 and 1993 the National Council of Churches and twenty-five prominent religious figures led the charge by issuing a widely publicized plea to "take the commercialism out of Christmas" (see Chapter 8, "Dreaming of a Noncommercial

Alternative Gift Markets, a California-based organization, coordinates charitable gift-giving to Third World countries. Below, AGM solicits contributions to buy bicycles for a rural community in Mozambique.

Photo courtesy of Alternative Gift Markets, Inc.

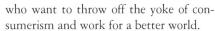

The Media Foundation, an activist group that helped pioneer "culture jamming" and that publishes *Adbusters* magazine, created a series of parodies lampooning Absolut Vodka.

The Neiman Marcus catalog features items ranging from merely frivolous to wildly extravagant, such as a $60,000 mink coat and this $2,000 ready-built lemonade stand.

Christmas"). At the local level, many ministers are nurturing a more spiritual Christmas in their congregations. One minister in Vienna, Virginia, was so upset by what he saw at local shopping malls— "domes and tombs of glamour and glitter"—as well as by pressure from his own children to read Christmas stories faster so they could get to the gifts, that he wrote his own "Call of a Christian in a Consumer Society."[32] Other ministers and lay leaders make use of and publicize such books and booklets as *Celebrating Christmas As If It Matters*, "Whose Birthday Is It Anyway?" and *Unplug the Christmas Machine*.

Many churches sponsor crafts fairs, the profits from which go to help poor people locally or globally. Some churches link up with the nonprofit Alternative Gift Markets (1-800-842-2243), which collects money for specific projects overseas and in the United States. For instance, $90 buys one water buffalo for an Indian villager, $1 buys a fruit tree for a Guatemalan, and $10 pays for one night at a homeless shelter for a woman in San Francisco.

The essential message of Christianity should not, of course, be espoused only at Christmas. As many churches have recognized, fighting for social justice, opposing poverty, and protecting the environment for future generations is not only good in and of itself but also builds strong congregations, especially with young people who are searching for meaning in life. Two inspiring books that relate biblical teachings to today's problems are *Rich Christians in an Age of Hunger* by Ronald J. Sider and *Following Christ in a Consumer Society* by John F. Kavanaugh. They can serve as spiritual, ethical, and practical compasses for those

who want to throw off the yoke of consumerism and work for a better world.

Some Jewish leaders are also responding to the displacement of the spiritual by the material. Numerous synagogues encourage the celebration of bar mitzvahs or bat mitzvahs with charitable donations instead of lavish parties. One bat mitzvah girl in Illinois invited guests to prepare bag lunches and distribute them to homeless Chicagoans. A boy in Omaha, Nebraska, urged his bar mitzvah guests to contribute to his temple's fund that benefits Boys Town; he donated some of the gifts he received to that fund as well. Some youths urge guests to donate to Israeli causes.[33] That same kind of generosity is becoming something of a tradition at Jewish weddings, with the newlyweds donating to charity a fraction of the cost of the event.

Churches and synagogues, which have been so active on hunger and peace issues, could also start study groups on commercialism and materialism. Religious schools and colleges should make those issues a top priority for study and action.

In 1993 the Vatican established a committee to evaluate advertising. American Archbishop John P. Foley, who is president of the Pontifical Council for Social Communications, said, "Because of the importance of advertising in all areas of communications, a number of members thought it was very important to examine the ethics of advertising." A courageous report could send powerful signals to Catholics, the general public, and the advertising community.[34]

Keeping the "Non" in Nonprofit

America's vigorous not-for-profit sector—from local civil rights groups to major metropolitan museums—is becoming increasingly reliant on corporate sponsors. The result is science and art museums whose exhibits are determined by corporations, a "noncommercial" broadcasting system that features product commercials and innocuous programming, and civic organizations whose independence ends where their sponsors' interests begin.

The general public and nonprofits themselves need to craft solutions to revivify what traditionally has been a pillar of American society. The obvious solution—greater funding from government, foundations, and the public—is certainly desirable, but unlikely for the foreseeable future. Three recommendations:

- *A major conference should be held involving funders, grantees, academics, and journalists to promote discussion of the adverse effects of corporate sponsorships.*

- *Nonprofits need to consider constraints imposed by corporate donations. Groups that decide to accept corporate donations should consider how to disclose that potential bias to their members and the public, whether to limit corporate donations to a certain percentage of total income, and how to fend off restrictions on their independence.*

- *The government should recognize corporate support of the Federal Express Orange Bowl, United States Olympic Committee, and similar activities for what it really is: paid advertising. As such, the nonprofit recipients should pay "unrelated business income" taxes on the donations. That would not stop the sponsorships but might put a damper on them. Paying taxes would remind the nonprofit of the role it is serving and would add much needed revenues to the public coffers.*

Businesses Can Do More Than Make Money

The standard of living of even the wealthiest business leaders is reduced by the social discord and environmental blight that are exacerbated by hypercommercialism. Air pollution, for example, does not distinguish between the lungs of the rich and poor. Thus, business executives should recognize their own personal self-interest in restraining commercialism and consumerism.

Every business leader should review his or her company's role in the community and the nature of its promotional campaigns. Does it make generous charitable contributions or has it replaced charitable giving with self-serving marketing programs? Are its ads honest and respectful of every segment of the population? What kinds of programs or publications does its advertising support? Could it cut the volume of its advertising (one ad-industry adage holds that marketers know that half of their advertising is wasted; the trick is knowing which half).

Just as citizens need to be environmentally conscious, so do companies. Smart companies are turning what they once considered waste into profits; they are viewing the production of pollutants as an indicator of inefficiencies. Businesses need to analyze the impact of their manufacturing processes, raw materials, packaging, and products on the environment. The use of more efficient motors in everything from factories to refrigerators would cut energy use. Electric utilities are increasingly looking to solar and other renewable sources of energy to reduce their use of coal, oil, and nuclear power. McDonald's, Wal-Mart, Patagonia, and other companies have been able to incorporate recycled materials into their products or packaging, reducing harm to the environment and saving money at the same time.

Some businesses have focused on making work and the workplace more satisfying to employees. The Body Shop, known for its environmental concerns, also gives employees half a day off, with pay, each week to engage in volunteer activities. Others subsidize mass-transit costs to discourage driving to work, while others have generous family- and medical-leave policies. Xerox is noted for giving employees paid sabbaticals to perform

The Media Foundation, publisher of *Adbusters* magazine, sponsors the annual "Buy Nothing Day"—a "twenty-four-hour continent-wide moratorium on consumer spending."

social-service work.[35] Companies should consider allowing employees to take pay increases in the form of shorter hours.

Other companies have consistently provided charitable contributions. Ben & Jerry's, the ice-cream maker, donates 7½ percent of pre-tax income to nonprofit organizations. In 1992, the biggest corporate donor was IBM, which donated $120 million.[36]

more idealistic younger employees. Feminists, for instance, need to protest the exploitation of women in advertising. Environmentalists should question phony "green marketing" and urge their clients to adhere to policies that really protect the environment. Executives who have children should be especially sensitive to—and oppose—marketing efforts that target young children. Because govern-

COMPENSATION OF TOP CORPORATE EXECUTIVES (1993)

EXECUTIVE, COMPANY	PAY AND STOCK GRANTS (millions)
1. Michael D. Eisner, Walt Disney Corp.	$203.0
2. Sanford I. Weill, Travelers	52.8
3. Joseph R. Hyde III, Autozone	32.2
4. Charles H. Mathewson, International Game Technology	22.2
5. Alan C. Greenberg, Bear, Stearns & Co.	15.9
6. H. Wayne Huizenga, Blockbuster Entertainment	15.6
7. Norman E. Brinker, Brinker International	14.9
8. Roberto C. Goizueta, Coca-Cola	14.5
9. C. Robert Kidder, Duracell International	14.2
10. Thomas S. Hahn, Jr., Georgia-Pacific	13.7

Source: Business Week, April 25, 1994, p. 52

Marketing and public-relations executives, in particular, must reexamine the nature of their "products." Those executives, after all, live in the same media world that everyone else does and may themselves even be offended by the din of advertising. They should consider *Advertising Age*'s plea for restraint: "Shouldn't more advertisers accept a greater responsibility to soften their hedonistic appeals, especially to younger audiences?...This is a time to help 'the other side' by building into selling messages at least some encouragement for those values of prudence and self-denial that we so long sought to overcome. Perhaps advertising can help bring basic values back into fashion. If not us, who?"[37]

Reform could be catalyzed by top marketing executives who don't fear for their jobs. They could set higher standards for their own firms' work products. They could also promote reform on a broader scale by insisting that industry conferences and trade journals debate the effects of ubiquitous marketing. More likely, though, reform will come from

ment has little power to regulate the content of advertising, "conscientious objectors" within the industry are key.

Most nonprofits desperately want to propagate their messages more broadly but lack the skills and money to do so. Just as lawyers have a tradition of donating a portion of their time to indigent and nonprofit clients, marketing and publicity experts could do the same.

Among the thorniest issues for top executives are their own, sometimes lavish, salaries. In 1992, the average compensation (pay and stock benefits) of the top executives at the 200 largest corporations was $3.2 million.[38] In 1993 Michael D. Eisner, chairman of Walt Disney Corp., made $203 million.[39] But even that was small potatoes compared to what George Soros, who manages a Wall Street investment fund, took home: $1.1 billion in 1993, plus investment income of $750 million.[40] His basic pay was greater than the gross domestic product of at least forty-two countries. "Obscene" and "greedy" is how Laurence A. Tisch, chief executive of CBS, Inc., characterized such salaries.[41]

It would take an unrealistic level of self-restraint on the part of high-paid executives to accept lower pay voluntarily. To help them do so, in 1993 Congress enacted a law that taxes companies on salaries of their top five executives that exceed $1 million (normally salaries are considered ordinary business expenses and are not taxed).[42] Going beyond that, some people have suggested simply setting a maximum annual salary of perhaps $1 million.[43] The larger question, which we leave for another time, is figuring out how to distribute the nation's wealth more equitably.

The nonprofit Council for Economic Priorities gently spurs companies to be better corporate citizens. CEP's best-selling book, *Shopping for a Better World* (Ballantine Books), rates corporate citizenship in the areas of environmental protection, production of nuclear weapons, workplace conditions, and other issues.[44] Although *Shopping for a Better World* does not rate advertising practices or product quality, it adds an important social dimension to buying decisions and offers businesses a yardstick against which to measure their social responsibility.

As the ethic of social responsibility slowly permeates the business world, progressive executives are banding together. One example is Businesses for Social Responsibility (BSR), a Washington-based group founded in 1992. BSR's original mission was to lobby Congress for environmental protection, worker welfare, and programs to rebuild inner cities. As BSR's membership soared from dozens to hundreds, the group reduced its emphasis on legislation and began focusing more on day-care programs, philanthropy, and other internal matters over which companies have direct control.[45]

But conventional businesses must serve their stockholders first, and only then, perhaps, the community. "We will ultimately need to build a vast underbrush of new economic institutions more securely anchored in democratic *and* community values, such as co-ops, worker-owned firms, neighborhood corporations, community land trusts, and municipal corporations," says Gar Alperovitz, president of the National Center for Economic Alternatives.[46] He urges that we expand government policies—such as loans and technical assistance—that would sustain such institutions and help achieve an economic system in which the interests of workers and the community were an integral part.

A Special Type of Business: The Mass Media

Publishers and broadcasters, as gatekeepers of information that are given specific constitutional protection, have a special role in our society. While they serve society well in many regards, they have proven to be all too susceptible to advertiser pressure. Advertiser censorship of the media is a serious, almost insoluble problem (see Chapter 9, "Making Pawns of the Press").

Clearly, editors, producers, and others in the news business need to do all they can to maintain the integrity of their media. Sensitivity to this problem should begin in journalism schools, which could ensure that students understand the ethical dilemmas they may face when they start working in advertiser-supported media. But self-policing will go only so far. Outside observers, such as investigative journalists and ad-free media, are needed to uncover and publicize censorship by advertisers.

C. Edwin Baker, a law professor at the University of Pennsylvania, suggests legislation prohibiting advertisers from influencing the content of programs and articles but he acknowledges "this is easier said than done." He also suggests that sponsors not be permitted to dictate during which television programs its commercials would be broadcast; instead, commercials would be more randomly distributed during the day or week. A third suggestion is to bundle commercials in a five- or ten-minute block shown once during the hour, rather than associating them with a particular program.[47]

While some legal limits might be placed

on overt advertiser censorship, *self-censorship* by the media officials themselves poses a far more subtle problem, one that is harder to identify and control. There is no way to stop magazine editors and television producers from crafting articles and programs to please current or potential advertisers. Again, investigative journalists need to publicize blatantly inappropriate examples.

The California Department of Health Services produces and distributes anti-smoking advertising, such as the billboard above.

State or Local Government Can Set the Pace

To brace America's ethical, cultural, and economic backbone, certain areas of life must be declared commercial-free. At a minimum that should include our children, schools, books, museums, public institutions, parks, wilderness, and the heavens.

Reducing Commercialism

Cities, counties, and states have the power to declare certain areas "ad-free." For instance, Oklahoma and Mississippi bar certain kinds of alcohol advertising. Florida, Washington, and several other states have restricted commercial telemarketing. Hawaii, Alaska, Vermont, and Maine have banned all billboards, as have a number of cities. New York State has banned Channel One from public schools. Cigarette and alcohol advertising has been banned by bus and subway systems in Denver, San Francisco (alcohol only), and New York (tobacco only). Some cities have banned unsightly advertising from the tops of taxis. Some communities have strict zoning laws that allow business activities but set limits on the size of buildings and size and content of signs.

Shopping malls, carefully engineered to maximize spending, have become the Main Streets of many communities. Some malls allow selected charities to set up a table and collect donations, but for the most part malls remain private property on which free speech, meetings, and other rights enjoyed on public property are strictly limited. Local governments could require malls to do more for the communities that support them. For instance, every mall could provide free space for a Citizen Involvement Center. Those volunteer-staffed centers could host a community bulletin board, computerized listings of upcoming events and of organizations needing volunteers, leaflets provided by the PTA and other groups, information on regional environmental problems and organizations, and a library of resources. The overall purpose would be to promote involvement in government and in religious, environmental, civil rights, youth, and other organizations.[48]

Opposing the Merchants of Death

Commercialism is at its cruelest when it encourages people—including children—to buy products that may cost them their lives. Makers of alcoholic beverages and cigarettes spend over $5 billion a year on slick, sophisticated inducements to drink and smoke. While it is difficult to achieve a state or local ban on such advertising, a government-sponsored health-promotion campaign is a practical alternative.

Several states, most notably California, have earmarked revenues from increased tobacco taxes to finance mass-media antismoking campaigns. As a result of those campaigns and the higher prices resulting from the new taxes, smoking has declined far faster in California than in the country as a whole. Every state should boost its taxes on cigarettes and alcoholic beverages and use the revenues to wage a war against smoking and drinking, especially among youth.

In 1994 states got even more aggressive, because smoking-related illnesses force state governments (and taxpayers) to pay millions of dollars every year for insurance claims, Medicaid expenses, and other costs. Mississippi sued more than a dozen cigarette manufacturers, wholesalers, and trade associations. It charged that "it is the defendants, not the taxpayers of Mississippi, who should bear the costs of tobacco inflicted diseases." Shortly after Mississippi's suit, Florida legislators unanimously passed a law that provided specific authority to sue the tobacco industry.[49]

Saving Consumers Money

Regardless of how much they simplify their lifestyles and reduce their consumption, people still need to shop. Unfortunately, the marketplace does little to help shoppers get the most value for their money. Shoppers are generally at the mercy of hearsay, advertising, salespeople, and chance. It's almost impossible to obtain objective, reliable comparisons of the quality and cost of everything from food to roofers.

One exception for a wide variety of nationally marketed products is *Consumer Reports* magazine. That magazine, which does not accept advertising, provides independent product ratings and price information. Buying an automobile, washing machine, or other expensive product without checking *Consumer Reports'* ratings is like betting on a

horse race without knowing the odds.

When you are looking for a good dentist, a competent auto-repair shop, or the cheapest and most service-oriented computer store, practically the only helpful resources are the regional guides entitled *Washington Consumers' Checkbook* and *Bay Area Consumers' Checkbook*. They, along with their companion *Bargains* bulletins, are enormously useful buying guides, but only for residents of those two metropolitan areas. *Checkbooks* and *Bargains*, each published twice a year, list prices for and readers' evaluations of a wide variety of local services and retailers. So effective are those publications in promoting price competition that Sony Electronics Corp. told Washington-area retailers not to tell *Checkbook* the prices they charge. According to several dealers, Sony threatened to stop selling to them if they advertised prices below the manufacturer's "minimum advertised prices." Sony's attempt at maintaining high profit margins for its products was called "price fixing" by one retailer.[50]

Local governments could save residents massive amounts of money if they developed a computerized database that compared the prices and qualities (perhaps including ratings compiled by *Consumer Reports*, the Better Business Bureau, and specialty magazines) of local products and services. Such a database could be accessed via free computer terminals at libraries and city office buildings, as well

The ad-free *Bay Area Consumers' Checkbook*, *Washington Consumers' Checkbook*, and *Consumer Reports* provide consumers with independent information on product quality and price.

as by home computers. People could simply dial up the database and compare quickly, for instance, the prices that people recently paid at local dealers for Chevrolet Corsicas with air-conditioning and AM-FM radios or the costs and services offered by area nursing homes, along with the degree of satisfaction of residents and their relatives. As Stephen Brobeck, executive director of the Consumer Federation of America, said, "Without this independent information, consumers make bad product choices that cost them billions of dollars a year."[51]

The Tax Alternative

States could easily generate millions of dollars in revenues to support consumer-information or other programs by taxing advertising. New Jersey, for instance, raises about $20 million annually through a tax on Yellow Pages advertising alone. When legislators propose an ad tax, businesses lobby fiercely against it. When Florida had the temerity to tax advertising in 1986, businesses threatened to move out of state and not to hold conventions in the state, ultimately forcing the legislature to repeal the tax. To overcome such powerful opposition, many states might consider implementing a tax at the same time. Another would be to adopt a national policy on taxing advertising, discussed in the next section.

Washington Should Lead the Charge

National political leaders need to speak out on Americans' preoccupation with consumption and the negative effects of commercialism. In 1978, President Jimmy Carter told Americans: "In a nation that was proud of hard work, strong families, close-knit communities and our faith in God, too many of us now worship self-indulgence and consumption. Human identity is no longer defined by what one does but by what one owns...[but] owning things and consuming things does not satisfy our longing for

meaning. We have learned that piling up material goods cannot fill the emptiness of lives which have no confidence or purpose."[52] Unfortunately, such statements are rarely uttered and even more rarely translated into effective legislative programs. Following is a sampling of some steps that the federal government might take to attenuate commercialism.

Stop Advertising Aimed at Children

In the late 1970s, the Federal Trade Commission (FTC) bravely explored young children's understanding of television commercials and determined that children do not possess the cognitive ability to evaluate television advertising aimed at them. "The only effective remedy would be a ban on all advertisements oriented toward young children," the FTC staff concluded. However, because of massive opposition by the cereal, toy, advertising, and broadcasting industries, the FTC ultimately was forced to acknowledge that "such a ban, as a practical matter, cannot be implemented."[53]

Is it feasible to ban advertising to children? Several European nations have long banned radio and television advertising to kids, and in 1980 the province of Quebec banned advertising to children in Quebec-based media. Perhaps those successes will inspire a new generation of American legislators to try to give children, and their parents, a respite from the advertising deluge.

Restrict Alcohol and Tobacco Advertising

While several states are making incremental progress to restrict the marketing of cigarettes and alcoholic beverages, only congressional action will benefit the entire nation. In 1971 Congress banned cigarette advertising on television and radio, but has done little since. Congress has done nothing to limit alcohol advertising.

In recent years, health-conscious legislators have tried to ban tobacco sponsorship of cultural and sporting events, regulate advertising for cigarettes as tightly as for prescription drugs, require health information in alcohol ads, and require that beer commercials be balanced by public service messages about the health and social impact of alcohol. But so far the cigarette and alcoholic-beverage industries (assisted by convenience stores, broadcasters, magazine publishers, billboard owners, liquor store and tavern owners, and other allies) have successfully blocked the legislation. Meanwhile, Canada has banned *all* cigarette advertising in all media (though a loophole allows certain promotional activities, such as sponsored tennis tournaments, to continue).

Isn't it time that every health official, civic organization, medical school dean, and citizen told Congress to restrict alcohol and tobacco advertising?

In addition to reducing the volume of alcohol and tobacco advertising, the federal government should follow the states' lead by sponsoring massive campaigns to reduce smoking and problem drinking. Higher excise taxes could finance campaigns involving everything from video games for schools to television advertising.

In 1994 the Food and Drug Administration generated unprecedented pressure on the tobacco industry by raising the question of whether cigarettes are actually drugs, because companies manipulate levels of the addictive drug nicotine. At congressional hearings, the FDA explained that if it concluded that cigarettes were drugs, it would have the authority to ban them. FDA commissioner David Kessler, in effect, urged Congress to pass legislation that would result in tighter controls over cigarettes. The Republican takeover of Congress in the 1994 elections, however, made it unlikely that any meaningful laws would be passed.

Restrict Telemarketing and Direct Mail and Protect Privacy

Few forms of marketing anger people as much as telemarketing, with its intrusive calls around dinnertime. The 1991 Telephone Consumer Protection Act provides partial control of the problem, but many people will not notice any reduction in calls, especially by live operators (as opposed to autodialed calls). Ideally, phone companies would periodically ask subscribers whether they wanted sales calls. If not, the phone company would automatically block such calls. The European Union has been considering just such a law.[54] At the least, Congress should strengthen the 1991 law by mandating a single, *national* list of people who do not wish to be called by telemarketers, instead of separate lists maintained by each telemarketer.

Junk mail currently constitutes about half of all mail. To reduce the volume of such mail, the U.S. Postal Service could require companies, magazines, and organizations to ask their customers, subscribers, and members whether they want their name to be rented to other companies or organizations.

Direct marketing via the mail or the phone raises serious privacy issues. We need laws to ensure that, in their zeal to make money by renting their customers' names and providing other information about their customers, companies won't use information in ways that their customers don't expect. Legislation could prevent companies—be they grocers, video stores, or credit bureaus—from disclosing information about individual customers. Great Britain goes much further by forbidding companies to rent or exchange customer lists unless the customer is told prior to purchasing a product that his or her name would be put on the market.[55]

Halt Billboard Blight

Billboards are inescapable. They deface the landscape, push cigarettes and booze to kids and adults alike, and derive their value from publicly funded highways. As the environmental group Scenic America advocates, a law should restrict billboards along highways that are financed in part with federal funds. Such a law would ban construction of new billboards, ban the cutting of trees to make billboards more visible, and give states more power to remove billboards.

Expose Stealth Advertising

To sneak past the public's defenses against advertising, marketers increasingly place commercial messages in formerly ad-free areas. For instance, product placements are now commonplace in movies and sometimes appear in television shows, plays, books, and children's games. Congress should ban paid product placements in children's media and require that all other product placements be disclosed. Audiences could be alerted by a simple, clear notice at the beginning of a movie (or book, television program, or play): "*This film contains paid advertising for the following products. . . .*"

On television, channels are filling up with infomercials, sitcommercials, docu-mercials, and other kinds of "mercials" disguised to look like programs. Infomercials and their ilk should be required to display a continuous notice at the bottom of the screen (for example, "This infomercial sponsored by Volvo" or the word "AD" in a box), just as the major networks put their logos at the lower-right corner of the screen during newscasts. Such a notice might not reduce the number of infomercials, but it would inform viewers immediately that they are watching an ad, not a program.

Another fast-growing form of "stealth" advertising is the corporate-sponsored video news release which is distributed by public relations firms for broadcast during local newscasts. The FTC or state attorneys general could insist, in the interests of honesty in the marketplace, that broadcasters always inform viewers when video footage was prepared by a business interest and not the station or network. Again, text running continuously at the bottom of the screen, along with a verbal announcement by the newscaster, would be appropriate.

Reduce the Volume of Commercial Advertising

The simplest, most comprehensive way to reduce the volume of advertising—and curb commercialism—would be to make advertising more expensive. One way to accomplish that, as we discussed in the previous chapter, would be to revise the tax law that allows companies to treat advertising expenditures as a tax-deductible business expense.[56]

The congressional Joint Committee on Taxation has calculated that allowing companies to deduct only 80 percent of advertising costs in the year when they placed the ads, with the remainder deducted over the next four years, would generate $18 billion in revenues over five years. A simpler plan would be to allow businesses to deduct only 50 percent, 75 percent, or other fixed percentage of their marketing costs. Doing away with the deduction completely would generate as much as $35 billion a year.

Another approach would be to tax advertising budgets that exceed a certain level, such as the average for all companies (about 2 percent). For instance, paper and textile mills and makers of industrial trucks and plastics all devote less than 2 percent of their sales to advertising and would pay no tax. By contrast, jewelry and furniture stores and makers of toys and perfume spend far more on advertising and would be subjected to a tax.[57]

Alcohol and tobacco advertising should be the first to be taxed. Congressman Jim Moran (D–Va.) and others have underscored the idiocy of giving tax deductions for ad campaigns that encourage drinking and smoking, when those habits cost the nation dearly in lives and money. But so far, the alcoholic-beverage and cigarette industries have beaten back the legislation.

Taxing advertising to reduce its overall volume is a development that most people outside of the advertising industry would cheer. The billions of dollars in revenues could be used to fund social programs or reduce the budget deficit. The chances, though, that Congress would trim the advertising tax subsidy are slim. One tax expert said, "The representative or senator who supports the concept faces an overwhelming barrage of opposition from nearly every economic interest in his or her district or state."[58]

A more straightforward way of reducing the volume of advertising than taxing it would be to set specific time limits, particularly in the area of radio and broadcast television, which use publicly "owned" airwaves. The FCC could restrict advertising to a certain number of minutes per hour, or hours per week. In 1993, the FCC began an official proceeding to consider whether the plethora of home-shopping channels, infomercials, and ordinary advertising has made a mockery of broadcasters' requirements to serve the public interest. The United States Catholic Conference, which has long been concerned about media content, urged the FCC to "resuscitate the concept of the public interest obligations of broadcasters, which has taken a back seat in the past decade to marketplace 'regulation' by competition."[59] But both broadcasters and advertisers vehemently oppose any limits. Especially opposed is the infomercial industry, whose thirty-minute ads would be eliminated if advertising were restricted to five, ten, or fifteen minutes an hour.

Revitalize the Federal Trade Commission

At the very least, the government ought to have a cop on the beat who is strong enough to stop dishonest advertisements and marketing schemes. The Federal Trade Commission is supposed to be that cop, but it is so small—during the

1980s its staff was halved—that it poses little threat to marketplace miscreants.[60]

If the FTC is ever to be an effective watchdog of business practices, it must be greatly expanded. Equally important, it needs to act much faster. The agency can take years to halt a single deceptive ad. Typically, as the proceeding creeps along, the ad in question grows stale and is replaced by new ads. FTC lawyers are so busy pursuing ancient improprieties that they cannot deal with current ones.

One effective enforcement measure

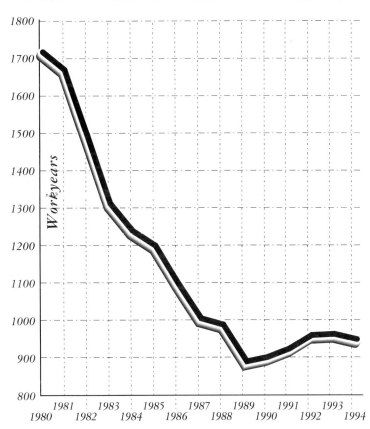

Federal Trade Commission Staff Size

that the FTC should dust off is "corrective advertising." Most companies found to have run dishonest ads are tapped on the wrist and ordered not to repeat the same violation. In the 1970s, but only rarely since then, the FTC sometimes ordered violators to sponsor prominent ads that told the public the truth about previous dishonest claims. The corrective ads enlightened consumers, embarrassed advertisers, and served as a deterrent to future dishonesty.

Anthropologist Jules Henry, in his classic book *Culture Against Man*, proposed sending everyone in the advertising industry to "truth school." That won't happen, but an aggressive chairman of the FTC could create his or her own minischool by telling ad executives that if they don't stop lying—explicitly or subtly—the FTC will crack down. That lesson should be followed up quickly with a flurry of lawsuits.

Protect the Environment

The rich nations of the world, with some help from poor nations, are responsible for today's global environmental crisis. We are despoiling the land, water, and air; generating toxic-waste dumps and mountains of garbage; and killing off species as if there were no tomorrow. But there will be a tomorrow, tainted by today's excesses, that will be home to our children and grandchildren.

While it is beyond the scope of this book to provide a comprehensive agenda for protecting the environment,[61] it is becoming ever clearer that every nation must adopt policies that reorient its economy toward less waste and pollution, greater protection of its natural resources and living species, and a lifestyle that would be sustainable for many generations to come. The United States, as a major industrial nation and the world leader in resource consumption, has a moral obligation to provide leadership for other nations. We Americans need to change both our production and consumption practices. We need to reduce our use of resources and to reuse or recycle those we do use. And we need to reduce marketers' pressure on people to purchase ever more.

The environment will be even more devastated as more and more people in developing nations are able to live the same resource-intensive lifestyle that Americans, Japanese, and Western Europeans are now enjoying. Does that mean that the rich nations should voluntarily modify their lifestyle? Should caps be placed on rich nations' consumption of natural resources and generation of pollutants to enable poorer nations to catch up? And how could population growth be slowed? Those are some of the tough questions that we and future generations will have to grapple with.

Encourage Savings

It's difficult to encourage people to be frugal and save money for future needs when all the media are screaming "Spend!" and national policies actually *discourage* saving. Let's say you scrimped and saved and bought a $10,000 certificate of deposit that pays 5 percent interest. After a year, you will receive $500 in interest. However, if inflation is 4 percent, the value of your CD will be reduced by $400. Moreover, between federal and state income taxes, you will have to pay about $150 in taxes. So your actual return on your hard-earned $10,000 will actually be a *negative* $50! No wonder many people decide to just spend their money.

One simple way of encouraging savings would be to exempt a certain amount of interest income, say $1,000, from taxation. Some people, who see Americans' abysmal rate of savings as a national emergency, have even suggested *requiring* people to salt away a certain percentage of their income. That could be done through payroll deductions that could not be accessed until retirement or a family emergency.[62]

Taxing Individuals and Businesses

John Kenneth Galbraith's *The Affluent Society*, published in 1958, provided a blueprint for strengthening society that still makes sense today.[63] Galbraith contrasted the private sector, where needs are constantly created by advertising, with the public sector, where conspicuous needs for schools, housing, and other services go unfilled: "The community is affluent in privately produced goods. It is poor in public services. The obvious solution is to tax the former to provide the latter—by making private goods more expensive, public goods are made more abundant."[64] Galbraith looked forward to the day when "the opulence of our private consumption will no longer be in contrast with the poverty of our schools, the unloveliness and congestion of our cities, our inability to get to work without struggle, and the social disorder that is associated with imbalance."

Raising taxes at any time is tough, because Americans rebel against paying taxes that are sometimes wasted on ineffective bureaucracies and ill-conceived programs. Granted, money cannot solve every problem, but many problems cannot be solved without more money. At the state and local level, Galbraith urged higher sales taxes.[65] He recommended that new federal funds come, first, from reductions in defense spending, a possibility that the end of the Cold War has made possible, and, second, from tax increases. Changes in tax laws, ranging from limiting deductions for large home mortgages to increasing tax rates for corporations and wealthy individuals, could provide the means for attacking social problems—and cutting tax rates for low- and middle-income families.

Expand Public Broadcasting

America's public TV and radio stations are unique sources of news, educational programming, and entertainment that couldn't survive in the lowest-common-denominator mentality of commercial broadcasting. Unfortunately, the "noncommercial" system increasingly has been forced to rely on advertisers—called "underwriters" in public-broadcasting doublespeak—for revenue. Corporations now provide 30 percent of the national program budget, and audiences must endure an ever-growing number of commercial messages.

Surely a nation with a $1.5 trillion federal budget could find the resources to support a first-class public broadcasting system. Other nations go this route: Japan spends eighteen times as much per person as the United States on public broadcasting, Canada spends thirty-two times as much, and Great Britain thirty-eight times as much, according to a report on public television by the Twentieth Century Fund. That report recommended two strategies to increase federal funding. First, the federal government could auction off, rather than give away by lottery, new parts of the broadcast spectrum, with a portion of the revenues earmarked for public broadcasting. The Commerce Department has estimated that auctioning off frequencies for cellular telephones would have generated at least $49 billion.[66] Another approach would be to charge commercial broadcasters (radio, TV, cable) an annual spectrum usage fee, based on gross advertising revenues, just as mining, timber, and oil companies are charged a small fee for using public lands. A modest usage fee of 5 percent applied to the $40 billion worth of radio and television advertising would generate about $2 billion a year, which could finance the entire public-broadcasting system.[67] A third alternative, of course, would be for Congress simply to provide the necessary funding out of general revenues, but conservatives have prevented that. Aside from providing an adequate funding base, public financing would also largely eliminate the opportunities for commercial sponsors to influence program content.[68]

Public broadcasting also needs to expand its programming beyond the usual cooking shows, nature documentaries, *Barney*, and *Sesame Street*. Broadcasters could be doing much more to spur public understanding of, and involvement in solving, critical problems ranging from school funding to crime to racism. Public radio and television stations are tremendous resources whose potential has barely been tapped.

In theory, the public owns all the airwaves—not just public stations. However, the public doesn't really have access to the airwaves aside from placing an occasional public service message or editorial response to a newscast. Consumer advocate Ralph Nader contends that just having one or two channels of public television, while commercial interests dominate all the others, is totally inadequate. He has called for legislation that would require *every* station to give an hour of prime time every day to the local community. Membership-supported national and community groups (which Nader dubs Audience Network) would air cultural, political, entertainment, scientific, or other programs. Audience Network, which would be funded by individual memberships and by selling back a portion of its allotted air-time to stations, would also serve as an advocacy group representing the public interest before the FCC.[69]

Corporate giants in the telephone, broadcasting, cable, and computer industries, along with the federal government, are now shaping the future of telecommunications. Whatever they decide will have a dramatic impact on public broadcasting and the kind of information people receive. The "information superhighway" promises high-definition, interactive television with an almost unlimited number of channels—but with every service available for a fee and plenty of advertising. Jeff Chester, executive director of the Center for Media Education, says that industry's vision of the superhighway "is nothing more than one virtual electronic shopping mall."[70] Chester and other public-interest advocates are campaigning to ensure that everyone will be guaranteed free or inexpensive access to basic information services and that sufficient channels will be devoted to public service programs.

Promote National Service

Occasionally, a hurricane, flood, or other natural disaster hits a town and everyone pitches in to rescue the needy. Likewise, many Peace Corps volunteers develop a whole new outlook on life as they spend two years assisting people in distant communities. Millions of Americans serve as part-time volunteers for a host of different organizations and causes, but most of us focus our lives largely on our own needs and desires, assuming that someone else is taking care of the community's.

A national service program—VISTA, Earth Corps, NationBuild, call it what you will—simultaneously would attack social problems and help bind us together as a nation. What wonders several million enthusiastic people a year could do: teaching reading, renovating slums, training recent immigrants for jobs, cleaning up trash dumps, and a hundred other activities!

Surveys done by the National Opinion Research Center show broad public support for mandatory national service. Almost two-thirds of the public "probably" or "strongly" favored a program that required all young women to give one year of service to the nation—either in the military forces or in nonmilitary work such as in hospitals or with elderly people. The support rose to three-fourths for such a program for men.[71]

AmeriCorps, the national-service program that was created in 1993, is a small step in the right direction. In 1994, 20,000 college-age people received an $8,000 wage for performing community-service work. After a year, the government will contribute an additional $4,725 toward their college tuition or loans. Eli Segal, director of AmeriCorps, says, "One of our objectives is to create a national ethic of service."[72] The program has its virtues, but critics complain about its small size and the low pay that might attract only poorly educated youths who can't find any other job or rich kids who don't need the money. Universal national service would involve everyone.

Presidential Leadership

Beyond any specific commission or law, we need leadership that can come only from the president of the United States. In 1961 President John F. Kennedy's stirring challenge—"Ask not what your country can do for you; ask what you can do for your country"—energized the nation. Today, our nation, suffused with commercialism and mired in materialism, needs another clarion call. The President could begin by establishing a Presidential Commission on Commercialism and Society analogous to earlier White House conferences on food policies, drug use, and other issues. The commission would investigate how commercialism affects us both as individuals and as a democratic society. It would delve into, and suggest remedies for, such matters as the effects of commercialism on the economy, the environment, personality, violence, justice, and the free press. Such a groundbreaking inquiry, led by respected individuals from universities, civic groups, religion, and government, could provide an agenda for action in future years.

THE FINAL WORD

COMMERCIALISM encompasses ubiquitous, noisy, intrusive, manipulative advertising. But commercialism is also a philosophy that shapes the very way we think and live our daily lives. Thousands of companies, each trying only to increase its own sales, propagate that philosophy and in the process, albeit inadvertently, rip apart the social fabric. Taming America's commercialism is essential if our country's priorities are to be truly geared to the well-being of the public. But reformers face a wall of opposition from marketers, the advertising industry, and advertiser-supported media. Those who profit from commercialism have tremendous political power and oppose every reform effort. Still, just as great progress has been made on certain environmental problems, which also seemed intractable, so can the Hydra of commercialism be tackled. IN ADDITION to shrinking commercialism's influence, it is equally important to cultivate the inherent talents in each and every individual. We need to foster intellectual growth, concern for the environment, civic responsibility, and compassion for others. America, among the richest nations in world history, is beset with tremendous problems that prevent the full flowering of each individual. Solving those problems will depend upon having adequate resources devoted to the social sector. Those resources could come, in part, from our living less materialistic lives and devoting more time and energy to helping our neighbors. As many people know from their own experience, such a lifestyle is a prescription not for deprivation but for enormous personal satisfaction and a better world. AMERICA is at a crossroads. One road is that of continued commercialism and wasteful consumption in a culture overtaken by Marketing Madness. The other road leads to a society more concerned about personal development and the satisfaction of common needs. The choice is ours, both individually and collectively.

NOTES

1. "The American Bazaar," *Fortune,* November, 1947, p. 108.

2. Jonathan Mahler, "LipoSeduction," *Washington Post,* December 26, 1993, p. C1.

3. Quoted in Peter Carlson, "It's An AD AD AD AD World," *Washington Post Magazine,* November 3, 1991, p. 15.

4. Stuart Ewen, *All Consuming Images: The Politics of Style in Contemporary Culture* (New York: Basic Books, 1988), p. 32.

5. See, for example, Kathleen A. Hughes, "Serious Money," *Wall Street Journal,* May 13, 1988, sec. 3, p. 10R.

1. "The American Bazaar," *Fortune,* November, 1947, p. 108.

2. Joseph Goebbels, March 28, 1933; quoted by Volker Köhn in "Theater des Westens' Berlin Cabaret-UFA Revue," *Stagebill,* Kennedy Center (Washington, D.C.), May 1992, p. 29a.

3. Figures, adjusted for inflation, from Robert J. Coen, "Insider's Report," McCann-Erickson, June 1994; Kevin Goldman, "All Signs Point to Greater Ad Spending," *Wall Street Journal,* June 15, 1994. Coen predicted that ad spending would total $157.7 billion in 1995 (Kevin Goldman, "Advertising" *Wall Street Journal,* October 14, 1994, p. B6).

4. Raw data on expenditures from Robert Coen, McCann-Erickson, June 1994; adjusted for inflation according to Consumer Price Index (CPI-U); population data from U.S. Department of Commerce, Bureau of the Census. Data for 1994 are estimates.

5. Cathy Taylor, "Ad Spending to Rebound," *Adweek,* July 25, 1994, p. 6.

6. U.S. Department of Commerce, *Statistical Abstract of the United States* (Washington, D.C.: Government Printing Office, 1993), Table 225.

7. Ibid., Table 514.

8. Ibid., Table 699.

9. Robert J. Coen, "Ad Gain of 5.2% in '93 Marks Downturn's End," *Advertising Age,* May 2, 1994, p. 4.

10. Compiled from *Advertising Age,* September 29, 1993.

11. Ibid.

12. Robert J. Coen, "Estimated Annual U.S. Advertising Expenditures," data summary from 1935 to 1992, McCann-Erickson, May, 1993.

13. Robert Coen, *Insider's Report,* McCann-Erickson, June 1994; *World Watch,* May–

June 1993, p. 15; U.S. Department of Commerce, *Statistical Abstract of the United States, 1993,* Table 4.

14. Leo Bogart, *Strategy in Advertising,* 2d ed. (Lincolnwood, Ill: NTC Publishing Group, 1990), pp. 1–2; see also Leo Bogart, *The American Media System and Its Commercial Culture* (New York: Gannett Foundation Media Center, 1991), p. 6 (a shorter version of this paper, with the same title, appears in *Media Studies Journal,* Fall 1991, p. 13).

15. Ibid.

1. Quoted in Consumers Union Education Services (CUES) "Selling America's Kids" booklet (Mount Vernon, N.Y.: 1990), p. 3.

2. Quoted in Stuart Ewen, *Captains of Consciousness: Advertising and the Social Roots of the Consumer Culture* (New York: McGraw-Hill, 1976), p. 144.

3. James U. McNeal, *Kids as Customers: A Handbook of Marketing to Children* (New York: Lexington Books, 1992), p. ix.

4. 1992 figures from Teenage Research Unlimited, Chicago, Illinois.

5. McNeal, *Kids as Customers,* p. ix.

6. Quoted in Christopher Power, "Getting 'Em While They're Young," *Business Week,* September 9, 1991, pp. 94–95.

7. Quoted in Eric Clark, *The Want Makers: The World of Advertising, How They Make You Buy* (New York: Viking Penguin, 1988), p. 186.

8. Ron Harris, "Children Who Dress for Excess: Today's Youngsters Have Become Fixated with Fashion," *Los Angeles Times,* November 12, 1989, p. A1.

9. James U. McNeal and Chyon-Hwa Yeh, "Born to Shop," *American Demographics,* June 1993, pp. 34, 36–39.

10. Guber and Berry, *Marketing To and Through Kids,* p. 131.

11. *1990 Report on Television* (New York: A.C. Nielsen Company, 1990), p. 8.

12. *TV Monitor* (Children's TV Resource and Education Center) 4, no. 1, 1989, p. 2.

13. EDK Associates, *EDK Forecast: Women Consumers,* New York, December 1993, p. 1.

14. Peggy Charren, personal communication.

15. Edmund L. Andrews, "Broadcasters, to Satisfy Law, Define Cartoons as Education," *New York Times,* September 29, 1993, p. A1.

16. Quoted in Ellen Edwards, "FCC Fines Stations for Excess Ads on Kid Shows," *Washington Post,* October 22, 1993, p. C1.

17. Quoted in Susan Cohen, "Kidvideo Games," by Susan Cohen, *Washington Post Magazine,* April 7, 1991, p. 39.

18. Ibid.

19. Clark, *The Want Makers,* p. 195.

20. Ibid.

21. *ACT Newsletter,* quoted in Clark, *The Want Makers,* p. 196.

22. Quoted in Bruce Horovitz, "New Twist in Tie-Ins," *Los Angeles Times,* November 12, 1992, p. B5.

23. "First Ever Licensing Expo Comes to Las Vegas in 1994," *Playthings,* April 1993, p. 48.

24. Consumers Union, "Zillions TV: A Kid's Guide to the Best Toys and Games," fact sheet, *Consumer Reports* press packet, November 1993.

25. Charis Conn and Ilena Silverman, eds., *What Counts: The Complete Harper's Index* (New York: Henry Holt, 1991), p. 100.

26. Ibid., p. 100.

27. Quoted in Cohen, "Kidvideo Games," p. 37.

28. Marcy Magiera, "Promotional Marketer of the Year," *Advertising Age,* March 21, 1994, p. S1.

29. Kevin Goldman, "Marketers Seek a Successor to Barney, Power Rangers," *Wall Street Journal,* June 10, 1994, p. B3.

30. Quoted in Dan McGraw, "Toyrannosaurus Rex," *Boston Globe,* December 17, 1992.

31. Melissa Ludtke, "How to Neutralize G.I. Joe," *Time,* March 26, 1990.

32. Fara Warner, "Playing Games with Sexual Stereotypes," *Adweek's Marketing Week,* November 18, 1991, p. 9.

33. Quoted in Clark, *The Want Makers,* p. 186.

34. Dorothy G. Singer, Jerome L. Singer, and Diana M. Zuckerman, *The Parent's Guide: Use TV to Your Child's Advantage* (Reston, Va.: Acropolis Books, 1990), p. 154.

35. EDK Associates, *EDK Forecast,* p. 1.

36. Richard A. Easterlin and Eileen M. Crimmins, "Recent Social Trends: Changes in Personal Aspirations of American Youth," *SSR* 72, no. 4, July 1988.

37. Ellen Neuborne, "Teens Keen on Brand Names, 'toon Figures," *USA Today,* September 30, 1993, p. 4B.

38. Quoted in Harris, "Children Who Dress for Excess."

39. Evelyn Nieves, "Back to School, So into the Mall," *New York Times,* September 5, 1993.

40. Harris, "Children Who Dress for Excess," p. A1.

41. Ibid.

42. Quoted in Colman McCarthy, "Protecting Children from the Advertisers," *Wash-*

ington Post, January 29, 1979.

43. In August 1994 Whittle Communications, which needed funds because other parts of the company were in financial trouble, sold Channel One to K-III Communications, publisher of the *Weekly Reader*.

44. UNPLUG, "Should 10th Grade Come with Compulsory Commercials," *New York Times*, op-ed advertisement, April 27, 1994; "Ten Things You Can Do to Unplug Channel One," *With a Growing Voice* (Oakland, Calif.: UNPLUG), Spring 1994; Patrick M. Reilly, "A KKR Vehicle Finds Profit and Education a Rich but Uneasy Mix," *Wall Street Journal,* October 12, 1994, p. 1.

45. Greg Farrell, "The Education of Joel Babbit," *AdWeek*, October 4, 1993, p. 28.

46. Laurie Petersen, "Risky Business: Marketers Make a Beeline for the Nation's Schools," *Adweek's Marketing Week*, May 14, 1990.

47. Quoted in Sheila Harty, *Hucksters in the Classroom* (Washington, D.C. Center for the Study of Responsive Law, 1979), p. 4.

48. Quoted in Lawrence Zuckerman, "Teacher or Trojan Horse?" *Time*, June 19, 1989.

49. UNPLUG, "A National Youth Organization for Commercial-Free Equitable Education," press release, October 19, 1993.

50. Robert Goldberg, "TV: Faustian Bargain with the Schools?" *Wall Street Journal*, March 13, 1989.

51. Institute for Social Research, "Taking the Measure of Channel One: The First Year," Working Paper no. 1 (Ann Arbor, Mich.. University of Michigan, April 1992).

52. Institute for Social Research, "Channel One: The School Factor," Working Paper no. 2 (Ann Arbor, Mich.: University of Michigan, Spring 1993).

53. Susan Chira, "Little Help from a School TV Show," *New York Times*, April 23, 1992, p. A18.

54. C. Tate, "Opinion: On Chris Whittle's School-News Scheme," *Columbia Journalism Review*, May-June 1989; Tim Simmons, "TV News in Classroom Ineffective, Study Finds," *News Observer* (Raleigh, N.C.), March 21, 1989, p. A1.

55. Dennis Niemiec, "No Time for TV: Four Teachers in Trouble for Unplugging Show," *Detroit Free Press*, March 26, 1992.

56. Neil Postman, *Amusing Ourselves to Death: Public Discourse in the Age of Show Business* (New York: Penguin Books, 1985), pp. 146–152.

57. Peggy Charren, "Say No to Ads in Schools" flyer, produced by Action for Children's Television, 1990.

58. Lifetime Learning Systems sales kit, 1991.

59. Ibid.; and Alex Molnar, "Giving Kids the Business: The Corporate Assault on American Public Education," unpublished manuscript.

60. Lifetime Learning Systems sales kit.

61. Molnar, "Giving Kids the Business."

62. Ibid.

63. Lifetime Learning Systems sales kit.

64. Laurie Petersen, "Risky Business: Marketers Make a Beeline for the Nation's Schools," *Adweek's Marketing Week*, May 14, 1990.

65. Ibid.

66. Quoted in Rick Marin, "Release Academy," by Rick Marin, *Premiere*, June 1992, p. 20.

67. Ibid.

68. Weyerhauser Corporation, teacher's guide to *Wood. The Everyday Miracle*, 1988.

69. "Soft Drinks and Nutrition," National Soft Drink Association (Washington, D.C.), undated.

70. Ibid.

71. "Coping With Growth," a unit of the Perspectives series, Reading II, Procter and Gamble, 1984, 1985.

72. Ibid.

73. Learning Enrichment, Inc.,"Critical Thinking About Criticial Issues 92–93," Unit 6, 1993.

74. CBS Television, "Readin', Writin', and Commercials," broadcast on *60 Minutes,* October 10, 1993.

75. Beth Wolfensberger, "Wasting Nothing on the Young," *New England Business*, December 1990; Paul Farhi, "Domino's Pizza Delivers to Public Schools, Dorms," *Washington Post*, September 21, 1990; School Properties USA, Inc. promotional brochure; Leslie Bayor, "Atlanta Schools' Phones Get Ads," *Advertising Age*, July 23, 1990.

76. Yaros Communications, "StudentBody Supports TV Station, Sponsor Marketing Objectives," press release, St. Louis, Missouri, July, 1993.

77. Molnar, "Giving Kids the Business."

78. Ibid.

79. Ibid.

80. "Education Partnerships in Public Elementary and Secondary Schools," report by the National Center of Educational Statistics, U.S. Department of Education, 1989.

81. Alex Molnar, "No Business," *Wall Street Journal*, February 9, 1990, p. R32.

82. Ibid.

83. "Enterprise Village," information packet, September 1990.

84. Laurie Petersen, "Who's Watching Channel One?" *Adweek's Marketing Week*, December 3, 1990.

85. Quoted in Jolie Solomon, "Mr. Vision, Meet Mr. Reality," *Newsweek*, August 16, 1993, p. 62.

SIDEBAR:

National Principals for Corporate involvement in the Schools

1. These principles were developed at a meeting hosted by the School of Education, University of Wisconsin–Milwaukee, November 26–27, 1990.

CHAPTER TWO

The Private and Public Airwaves

1. Robert Coen, "Insider's Report," McCann-Erickson, June 1994.

2. Nielsen Media Research, New York.

3. Patrick Cooke, "TV or Not TV," *In Health,* December 1991–January 1992, p. 39.

4. Robert W. McChesney, "The Battle for the U.S. Airwaves, 1928–1935," *Journal of Communication,* Autumn 1990, pp. 30–31.

5. Ibid., pp. 33–34.

6. Ibid., p. 35.

7. Quoted in Preben Sestrup, *The Electronic Dilemma of TV Advertising* (Aarhus, Denmark).

8. N. R. Kleinfield, "The Networks' New Advertising Dance," *New York Times,* July 29, 1990, sec. 3, p. 1.

9. Erica Gruen, "Advertiser-Produced Shows Still Work in '90s," *Advertising Age,* December 13, 1993.

10. Jeff Silverman, "TV's Creators Face a New Caution," *New York Times,* December 8, 1991, Arts and Leisure sec., p. 1.

11. "'SNL' Hits Brakes," *Entertainment Weekly,* April 3, 1992, News and Notes sec.

12. Quoted in Silverman, "TV's Creators Face a New Caution," p. 31.

13. Frederick Case, "Minds at Risk," *Washington Post,* July 29, 1991, p. C5.

14. Rutgers University, press release announcing the publication of Robert Kubcy and Mihaly Csikszentmihalyi, *Television and the Quality of Life: How Viewing Shapes Everyday Experience,* New Brunswick, N.J., April 30, 1990.

15. Jerry Mander, *Four Arguments for the Elimination of Television* (New York: Quill, 1978), p. 24.

16. American Association of Advertising Agencies, "1992 Executive Summary of the A.A.A.A. Television Production Cost Survey," July 30, 1993.

17. Ibid., pp. 305–306.

18. Charis Conn and Ilena Silverman, eds., *What Counts: The Complete Harper's Index* (New York: Henry Holt, 1991), p. 96.

19. Neil Postman, *Amusing Ourselves to Death: Public Discourse in the Age of Show Business* (New York: Penguin Books, 1985), p. 7.

20. Ibid., pp. 126, 130.

21. Ibid., p. 44. In their more famous debates in the 1858 senatorial campaign, Lincoln and Douglas spoke for an hour and had an additional half hour for rebuttal.

22. Johnnie L. Roberts and Mark Robichaux, "Diller Bets on Home Shopping's Future," *Wall Street Journal,* December 11, 1992, p. B1.

23. Edmund L. Andrews, "TV Shopping Wins a Big Victory in FCC Ruling on Cable Access," *New York Times,* July 3, 1993, p. 1.

24. Ellen Neuborne, "Shopping by TV Goes Upscale," *USA Today,* January 17, 1994, p. 5B.

25. Scott Donaton, "Home Shopping Networks Bring Retailers On Board," *Advertising Age,* April 19, 1993; Gary Strauss, "TV Is New Storefront for Macy's Shoppers," *USA Today,* June 2, 1993.

26. Stephanie Strom, "Mail Order Shifts Its Pitch to Cable," *New York Times,* March 21, 1994, p. D1.

27. Jon Lafayette, "Rivers Quitting Talk for New Shop Show," *Electronic Media,* November 1, 1993.

28. "Axed and Renewed," *USA Today,* June 16, 1994, p. 3D.

29. MTV Networks, "MTV Networks to Test Home Shopping Programming on MTV, VH-1, and Nick at Nite," press release, January 25, 1994; MTV Networks, "MTV Networks and Fingerhut Name Electronic Retailing Test," press release, August 5, 1994.

30. Andrews, "TV Shopping Wins a Big Victory in FCC Ruling on Cable Access," p. 40.

31. Elaine Underwood, "Why I'm a Home Shopper," *Brandweek,* April 19, 1993, p. 26.

32. Donaton, "Home Shopping Networks Bring Retailers on Board," p. S–3.

33. Timothy K. Smith and Thomas R. King, "Madison Avenue, Slow to Grasp Interactivity, Could Be Left Behind," *Wall Street Journal,* December 7, 1993.

34. Quoted in Mark Schapiro, "Public TV Takes Its Nose Out of the Air," *New York Times,* November 3, 1991, p. 31.

35. Public Broadcasting Service, "Facts About PBS," factsheet, October 1993.

36. Schapiro, "Public TV Takes Its Nose Out of the Air."

37. Lewis H. Lapham, "Adieu, Big Bird: On the Terminal Irrelevance of Public Television," *Harper's,* December 1993, p. 38.

38. Cara Appelbaum, "Public Television: The New Kid in Promotions," *Adweek's Marketing Week,* October 28, 1991.

39. Laura Bird, "Public TV's Plugs Getting Closer to Ads," *Wall Street Journal,* August 10, 1992.

40. Laura Shapiro, "Commercially Speaking," *Newsweek,* June 15, 1992.

41. Elizabeth Jensen, "Public TV Prepares for Image Transplant to Justify Existence," *Wall Street Journal,* January 13, 1994.

42. WTTW Chicago, "WTTW/Channel 11 Launches 'Chicago Holiday Gift Exchange,' New Television Venture Featuring Merchandise for Sale from Chicago's Finest Cultural Institutions," press release, October 5, 1993.

43. "In the Matter of Commission Policy Concerning the Noncommercial Nature of Educational Broadcast Stations," public notice, Federal Communications Commission, FC 86-161 36590, April 11, 1986.

44. Elizabeth Jensen, "PBS May Ease Rules As Way to Increase Corporate Support," *Wall Street Journal,* June 1, 1994, p. A3.

45. Peter Carlson, "Is Nothing Sacred?" *Washington Post Magazine,* November 3, 1991.

46. Quoted in Pat Aufderheide, "A Funny Thing Is Happening to TV's Public Forum," *Columbia Journalism Review,* November–December 1991, p. 62.

47. Bird, "Public TV's Plugs Getting Closer to Ads," p. B1

48. Jan Wilson, "Public Television: How It Can Fit Into Your Marketing Plan," *Advertiser,* Winter 1992, pp. 21–22.

49. PBS, "The Public Broadcasting Service: An Overview," factsheet, October 1993.

50. Aufderheide, "A Funny Thing Is Happening," p. 62.

51. National Public Radio, "Sources of Contributed Support by Type; Five Year Average: 1988–1992," graph.

52. "NPR Sponsors: Does Their Money Talk?" *Washington Journalism Review,* June 1990, p. 12.

53. Karen DeWitt, "New Chief Wants to Widen NPR's Financial Base," *New York Times,* March 28, 1994, p. D6.

54. John Carmody, "Deja Vu All Over Again," *Washington Post,* June 10, 1991, p. C8.

55. Quoted in Aufderheide, "A Funny Thing Is Happening," p. 62.

56. "Corporate Friendly Environment," *EXTRA! Update* (New York: Fairness and Accuracy in Reporting), Soundbites sec., December 1993, p. 2.

57. Quoted in Craig Smith, "When Arts Marketers Call the Shots," *Corporate Philanthropy Report,* April 1991, p. 4.

58. Sharon Bernstein, "'PBS' Underwriting Policies Questioned," *Los Angeles Times,* April 2, 1992.

59. Jeff Cohen and Norman Solomon, "Both Sides Missing the Point in Debate About PBS Funding," *Sunday Freeman,* March 29, 1992.

60. Lapham, "Adieu Big Bird," p. 43.

61. *Quality Time: The Report of the Twentieth Century Fund Task Force on Public Television* (New York: Twentieth Century Fund Press, 1993).

62. National Public Radio, "Sources of Contributed Support by Type," 1993.

63. Quoted in Herbert Schiller, *Culture Inc.* (New York: Oxford University Press, 1989), p. 110.

CHAPTER THREE
Hidden Advertising

1. Quoted in Jennifer Lamb-Korn, "VNR=Very Nice Results," *In Motion,* March 1991.

2. Giselle Benatar, "Bad News," *Entertainment Weekly,* May 17, 1991, p. 22; David Lieberman, "Fake News," *TV Guide,* February 22, 1992, p. 10.

3. Cited in Lieberman, "Fake News," p. 16.

4. Joel Bleifuss, "New Angles from the Spin Doctors," *New York Times,* March 20, 1994, p. 13.

5. "Making News," *Consumer Reports,* October 1991, p. 694.

6. Ibid.

7. Ibid.

8. Ibid.

9. Ibid.

10. "Miracle Drugs or Media Drugs," *Consumer Reports,* March 1992, p. 142.

11. Ibid.

12. Quoted in "Fake News."

13. Quoted in "Making News."

14. Chris Swingle, "Captiva Is Polaroid's Photo Finish," *USA Today,* July 21, 1993.

15. Thomas Mosser, "Building Corporate Brands and Reputations with Public Relations," *Advertiser,* Summer 1993, p. 68.

16. Leslie Ellis, "The Infomercial Invasion," *Scene,* September 26, 1992.

17. Patrick R. Parsons and Herbert J. Rotfeld, "Infomercials and Television Station Clearance Practices," *Journal of Public Policy and Marketing* 9, 1990, p. 62.

18. Christopher Stern, "The Sweet Buy and Buy," *Broadcasting and Cable,* October 25, 1993, p. 20.

19. Steven Winzenburg, "Infomercials Flowering on Cable TV," *Advertising Age,* February 22, 1993, p. 18.

20. Ibid.

21. Steve McClellan, "Broadcasters, Cable: The Airing of the Green," *Broadcasting and Cable,* October 25, 1993.

22. McClellan, "Broadcasters, Cable."

23. Debra Aho, "Coming Soon to Your TV: An Infomercial Channel?" *Advertising Age*, November 8, 1993.

24. Kevin Goldman, "CBS to Push Video-taping of Infomercials," *Wall Street Journal*, November 15, 1993.

25. Stern, "The Sweet Buy and Buy."

26. Laurie Ouellette, "The McInfomer-cialization of TV," *MediaCulture Review*, October-November, 1993.

27. Quoted in Debra Aho, "TCI to Create Single-Subject Channels," *Advertising Age*, December 6, 1993, p. 40.

28. Stern, "The Sweet Buy and Buy."

29. Quoted in Rick Marin, "The Stepford Channel," *New York Times*, October 4, 1992, sec. 9, p. 1.

30. Ibid.

31. McClellan, "Broadcasters, Cable."

32. Ibid.

33. Bob Dart, "House Panel Looks at TV Shows That Are Hyped Commercials," *San Francisco Chronicle*, May 19, 1990, p. A3.

34. Gene Silverman, letter to *Advertising Age*, April 1, 1991, p. 22.

35. Laura Bird, "Latest Infomercial: The Situation Comedy," *Wall Street Journal*, November 6, 1992, p. B14.

36. Ibid.

37. Bob Garfield, "Sominex Infomercial Issues a Wake-up Call," *Advertising Age*, November 1, 1993.

38. Quoted in Melanie Wells, "Tums to Offer Half-Hour Calcium 'Docu-mercial,'" *Advertising Age*, November 15, 1993.

39. Quoted in Jon Lafayette, "Mirage Resorts Buys NBC Hour," *Electronic Media*, November 1, 1993.

40. Kevin Goldman, "Some Stars Play Their TV Characters Even While They're Making Commercials," *Wall Street Journal*, November 30, 1992.

41. Joanne Lipman, "'Tonight Show' Sets Eagle Snacks' Live Ads," *Wall Street Journal*, May 8, 1992, p. B4.

42. Laura Bird, "Collagen Corp.'s Video Uses News Format," *Wall Street Journal*, March 29, 1994.

43. Stuart Elliott, "A Newscaster-Turned-Spokeswoman Raises Issues of Credibility," *New York Times*, December 2, 1993, p. D21.

44. Teri Agins, "Is It a TV Show? Or Is It Advertising?" *Wall Street Journal*, August 10, 1994, p. B1.

45. Paul Farhi, "Disney Blurs the Line Between Ballyhoo and Broadcasting," *Washington Post*, July 5, 1994, p. E1.

46. Kevin McManus, "Radio Talk, or Tout?"

Washington Post, December 7, 1992, p. 24.

47. Ibid., p. 25.

48. Quoted in Linda Lawson, *Truth in Publishing: Federal Regulation of the Press's Business Practices, 1880-1920* (Southern Illinois University Press, 1993), p. 106.

49. Ibid., pp. 106–118.

50. Scott Donaton, "Advertorials Are Like a Drug," *Advertising Age*, March 9, 1992, p. S16.

51. Ibid.

52. Quoted in ibid.

53. Julie Steenhuysen, "Custom Publishing Is Catching On," *Advertising Age*, October 11, 1993.

54. Deirdre Donahue, "Drive, Baby, Drive," *USA Today*, October 26, 1993.

55. Silver Screen Placements brochure, September 4, 1990. Emphasis in original.

56. Mark Crispin Miller, *Seeing Through Movies* (New York: Pantheon Books, 1990), p. 193.

57. James Goldston, "Deals on Reels," *Observer* (London), May 5, 1991, as quoted in Sheri Carder, "Product Placement in Film, Advertising Via the Box Office: A Comparison of Marketing Techniques Between the United States and the United Kingdom," University of Southern Mississippi, paper presented at the combined annual conventions of the Southern Speech Communication Association and the Central States Communication Association, Lexington, Kentucky, April 14–18, 1993, p. 15.

58. "Brands on the Screen: Rocky the Salesman," *Economist*, April 20, 1991, as quoted in Carder, "Product Placement in Film," p. 13.

59. Jeremy Schlosberg, "Film Flam Men," *Inside Media*, June 13, 1990.

60. Philip J. Hilts, "Company Spent $1 Million to Put Cigarettes in Movies, Memos Show," *New York Times,* May 20, 1994, p. A16.

61. "The Fine Art of Product Placement," *Harper's*, April 1991; Steven Colford, "Lawsuit Drills Fox, Cato," *Advertising Age*, December 3, 1990.

62. "A Jilted 'Starlet' Sues," *Advertising Age*, December 10, 1990; Colford, "Lawsuit Drills Fox, Cato."

63. "*The Firm* Star Car," *USA Today*, June 22, 1993.

64. Paul Farhi, "The Not-So-Hidden Persuaders," *Washington Post*, January 1, 1989.

65. Numbers of product placements provided by the Center for the Study of Commercialism.

66. Quoted in Lois P. Sheinfeld, "Dangerous Liaisons," *Film Comment*, October 1989.

67. "The Fine Art of Product Placement"; Colford, "Lawsuit Drills Fox, Cato."

68. "Who's Behind Those Ray-Bans?" *USA Today*, July 8, 1993.

69. "A Star Is Brewed as Obscure Beer Scores with Role in Hit Movie," *Wall Street Journal*, July 8, 1993.

70. Marshall Fine, "Lights! Camera! Ads!" *Entertainment Weekly*, August 6, 1993, p. 12.

71. Miller, *Seeing Through Movies*, p. 191.

72. Susan Wloszczyna, "Tom Cruise, Taking Yahoo out of Yoo-Hoo," *USA Today*, December 28, 1992.

73. Jack Valenti, letter to Michael Jacobson, October 23, 1985.

74. Associated Film Productions, promotional brochure, 1983.

75. Janet Maslin, "The Art of Plugging Products in the Movies," *New York Times*, November 15, 1982.

76. "The E.T. Effect: Does Getting Your Product in the Movies Make a Difference?" *Fresh!* (Chicago: Tetra Pak, Inc.), Winter 1993, p. 12.

77. Hajdu, "Why the *'Cheers'* Gang Switched to Stroh's Beer," *TV Guide*, July 30, 1988, p. 30.

78. Joe Mandese, "Video Technology Foils Measurement," *Advertising Age*, March 9, 1992, p. 30.

79. Stuart Elliott, "Advertising," *New York Times,* October 13, 1994, p. D21; Joanne Lipman, "Tour Show to Plug Chrysler Jeep on Stage," *Wall Street Journal*, May 13, 1992, p B9.

80. Joe Queenan, "'Wherefore Art Thou Alfa-Romeo?'" *Wall Street Journal*, February 1, 1989.

81. Miller Brewing Company, promotional video.

82. Randall Rothenberg, "$30,000 Lands Product on Game Board," *New York Times*, February 6, 1989.

83. Entertainment Resources and Marketing Association, "Code of Standards and Ethics," March 1994; Frank Devaney, personal communication, March 11, 1994.

CHAPTER FOUR
Sexism in Advertising

1. Jean Kilbourne, *Still Killing Us Softly*, film distributed by Cambridge Documentary Films, Cambridge, Mass., 1987.

2. Quoted in Stuart Ewen, *All Consuming Images: The Politics of Style in Contemporary Culture* (New York: Basic Books, 1988), p. 87.

3. Ibid.

4. Molly O'Neill, "5 Diet Companies Ask U.S. for Uniform Rules on Ads," *New York Times*, August 25, 1992.

5. Figures given are for both men and women. Naomi Wolf, *The Beauty Myth: How Images of Beauty Are Used Against Women* (New York: William Morrow, 1991), p. 17; Elaine Brumberg, *Save Your Money, Save Your Face* (New York: Harper & Row, 1987), p. xiii.

6. Quoted in Stuart Ewen, *Captains of Consciousness: Advertising and the Social Roots of Consumer Culture* (New York: McGraw-Hill, 1976), p. 39.

7. Susan Brownmiller, *Femininity* (New York: Fawcett Columbine, 1984), p. 51.

8. Ibid., p. 144.

9. Wolf, *The Beauty Myth*, p. 184. Wolf does not specify the years being compared. It is worth noting that the prevalence of overweight among adult women remained fairly constant from 1960 to 1980, but then rose by one-third during the 1980s (Robert J. Kuczmarski et al., "Increasing Prevalence of Overweight Among U.S. Adults," *Journal of the American Medical Association* 272, July 20, 1994, p. 205).

10. Louise Lague and Alison Lynne, "How Thin Is Too Thin?" *People Magazine*, September 20, 1993, p. 74.

11. Quoted in ibid.

12. S. C. Wooley, "Feeling Fat in a Thin Society," *Glamour*, February 1984, p. 198.

13. Alison Bass, "'Anorexic Marketing' Faces Boycott," *Boston Globe*, April 25, 1994, p. 1.

14. Wolf, *The Beauty Myth*, p. 229.

15. Arnold E. Andersen and Lisa DiDomenico, "Diet Vs. Shape Content of Popular Male and Female Magazines: A Dose-Response Relationship to the Incidence of Eating Disorders?" *International Journal of Eating Disorders* 11, no. 3, 1992, pp. 283–287.

16. Wolf, *The Beauty Myth*, p. 185.

17. Wooley, "Feeling Fat in a Thin Society."

18. Wolf, *The Beauty Myth*, p. 215.

19. Ibid., p. 248.

20. Lena Williams, "Woman's Image in a Mirror: Who Defines What She Sees?" *New York Times*, February 6, 1992, p. A1.

21. Cara Appelbaum, "Beyond the Blonde Bombshell," *Adweek's Marketing Week*, June 3, 1991.

22. Wolf, *The Beauty Myth*, p. 83.

23. Kilbourne, *Still Killing Us Softly*.

24. Quoted in Wolf, *The Beauty Myth*, p. 110.

25. Gerald McKnight, *The Skin Game: The International Beauty Business Brutally Exposed* (London: Sidgwick & Jackson, 1989), p. 20.

26. Cara Appelbaum, "Thirteen Going on Twenty-one," *Adweek's Marketing Week*, March 11, 1991.

27. *Media Watch* (Santa Cruz, Calif: Media Watch), Fall 1990, p. 2.

28. Wolf, *The Beauty Myth*, p. 215.

29. Karen McCurdy and Deborah Daro, "Current Trends in Child Abuse Reporting and Fatalities: The Results of the 1993 Annual Fifty State Survey," working paper no. 808, The National Center on Child Abuse Prevention Research, a program of the National Committee to Prevent Child Abuse, Chicago, Ill., April 1994, pp. 3, 7.

30. Kilbourne, *Still Killing Us Softly*.

31. Gloria Steinem, "Sex, Lies, and Advertising," *Ms.*, July-August 1990, p. 19.

32. Ibid., p. 23.

33. England and Gardner, "How Advertising Portrays Men and Women," p. 2.

34. Canadian Advertising Foundation, "Sex Role Stereotyping Guidelines," July 24, 1987.

35. Kim Foltz, "Women Deflate Some Adland Images," *New York Times*, November 17, 1991.

36. Zachary Schiller, Mark Landler, Julia Flynn Siler, "Sex Still Sells, but So Does Sensitivity," *Business Week*, March 18, 1991, p. 100.

37. Stuart Elliott, "Has Madison Avenue Gone Too Far?" *New York Times*, December 15, 1991, sec. 3, p. 1.

38. Leslie Savan, "In the Red Again," *Village Voice*, January 7, 1992, p. 45.

39. Wolf, *The Beauty Myth*, p. 79.

40. Henry J. Reske, "Stroh's Ads Targeted," *ABA Journal*, February 1992. In 1993, however, the court ruled that the ads could not be entered as evidence in the harassment trial ("Ad Can't Be Evidence," *Wall Street Journal*, November 9, 1993).

41. Quoted in Joanne Pohn, "Beer Ads Offend," *MediaWatch Bulletin* (Vancouver, B.C.: MediaWatch) 3, no. 2, Winter 1990, p. 4.

42. Stuart Elliott, "Looking at Male Bodies," *New York Times*, December 15, 1991, sec. 3, p. 6.

43. Elliott, "Has Madison Avenue Gone Too Far?"

44. Anne Swardson, "The Shoe's on the Other Foot?" *Washington Post*, June 30, 1993.

45. Kilbourne, *Still Killing Us Softly*.

SIDEBAR
The Strong Silent Types: Men in Ads

1. Jean Kilbourne, "Sex Roles in Advertising" in Meg Schwarz, ed., *TV and Teens: Experts Look at the Issues* (Reading, Mass.: Addison Wesley, 1982), p. 212.

2. Based on Danish population study, Professor Soren Nielsen, personal communication, January 10, 1994.

3. Jacqueline Stenson, "With Cosmetic Surgery, Men Can Change Everything from Pecs to Private Parts," *Washingtonion*, May 1993.

4. Steve Fishman, "Muscle Bound," *Details*, October 1993.

CHAPTER FIVE
Co-opting Civic Groups, Culture, Sports

1. Bob Garfield, "Beware: Green Overkill," *Advertising Age*, January 29, 1991, p. 26. The Body Shop, whose practices have been lauded by many corporate critics, was the subject of a mild exposé (Jon Entine, "Shattered Image," *Business Ethics,* September-October, 1994, p. 23).

2. John Schwartz, et al., "It's Not Easy Being Green," *Newsweek*, November 19, 1990, p. 51.

3. Janet D. Steiger, chairman of the Federal Trade Commission, speech given at the EPA Environmental Labeling Conference, October 1, 1991.

4. Joseph M. Winski, "Big Prizes, but No Easy Answers," *Advertising Age*, *Green Marketing Special Report*, October 28, 1991, p. GR-1.

5. Kenny Bruce, *The Greenpeace Book of Greenwash* (Washington, D.C.: Greenpeace, 1992), p. 10.

6. Ibid., pp. 10, 11; Council on Economic Priorities, *DuPont: A Report on the Company's Environmental Policies and Practices* (New York: CEP, 1991), p. 1.

7. Catherine A. Dold, "Hold Down the Noise," *Advertising Age*, *Green Marketing Special Report*, October 28, 1991; Schwartz, et al., "It's Not Easy Being Green," p. 51.

8. Judann Dagnoli, "Green Ads Wilt: NAD Chief," *Advertising Age*, January 6, 1992.

9. Earthworks Group, *50 Simple Things You Can Do to Save the Earth* (Berkeley, Calif.: Earthworks Group, 1989), p. 36.

10. Richard Steckel and Robin Simons, *Doing Best by Doing Good: How to Use Public Purpose Partnerships to Boost Corporate Profits and Benefit Your Community* (New York: Penguin Books, 1992), p. 75.

11. Ibid., p. 55.

12. Quoted in Pamela Sebastian, "With Coffers Less Full, Big Companies Alter Their Gifts to Charity," *Wall Street Journal*, November 26, 1993.

13. Steckel and Simons, *Doing Best by Doing Good*, pp. 76–77.

14. Ibid., p. 15.

15. Ibid., p. 21.

16. Colman McCarthy, "Here Comes Santa Cause," *Washington Post*, December 14, 1993, p. D25.

17. Roland Marchand, *Advertising the Amer-*

ican Dream (Berkeley, Calif.: University of California Press, 1985).

18. Susan Faludi, Backlash: The Undeclared War Against American Women (New York: Anchor Books, 1991), p. 72.

19. George A. Hacker, Ronald Collins, and Michael F. Jacobson, Marketing Booze to Blacks (Washington, D.C.: Center for Science in the Public Interest, 1987), p. xiv.

20. American Cancer Society, Cancer Facts and Figures for Minority Americans 1991, factsheet.

21. Julie L. Nicklin, "Philip Morris Boosts Aid to Colleges, but Critics Question Tobacco Company's Motives," Chronicle of Higher Education, October 13, 1993, p. A36.

22. "The Bad Boys of Benetton," Washington Post, Names and Faces section, February 26, 1994.

23. Paula Span, "Colored with Controversy; Outcry over Benetton Ad Showing AIDS Deathbed Scene," Washington Post, February 13, 1992.

24. Ibid.

25. Vicki Goldberg, "Images of Catastrophe as Corporate Ballyhoo," New York Times, May 3, 1992.

26. Personal communication, American Medical Association, Jim Stacey, October 31, 1994, and Dan Maier, November 3, 1994.

27. Susan Calvert Finn, "A Message from the President: Thanks to Our Industry Partners," ADA Courier 32, no. 9, September 1993, p. 2. See also Jane Levine and Joan Dye Gussow, "Consider the Source," New York Times, September 30, 1994, p. A31, for further discussion of links between nutrition organizations and food companies.

28. Kathleen Day, "Genentech, Nonprofit Link Studied," Washington Post, August 16, 1994, p. C1.

29. "National Trends in Consolidated Corporate Contributions to All Causes and Pretax Net Income," table, Corporate Support of Education, 1992 (New York: Council for Aid to Education), September 1993, p. 2.

30. Herbert Schiller, Culture Inc.: The Corporate Takeover of Public Expression (New York: Oxford University Press, 1989), p. 91.

31. Ibid., p. 92.

32. Lee Rosenbaum, "Art's Cozy Relationship with Business," New York Times, September 9, 1990.

33. Ibid.

34. Ibid.

35. Ibid.

36. Ibid.

37. Christopher Hume, "Picturing Santa," Toronto Star, November 9, 1991.

38. Bruce Horovitz, "Well-Heeled Con-

troversy," Los Angeles Times, April 24, 1992.

39. Craig Smith, "When Arts Marketers Call the Shots," Corporate Philanthropy Report, April 1991, p. 9.

40. Paul Goldberger, "Philip Morris Calls in I.O.U.'s in the Arts," New York Times, October 5, 1994, p. 1; "Contributing to Death," Public Citizen Health Research Group, Washington, D.C., October 1993. California wineries have asked charities that want free wine to first write letters supporting the wine industry; those letters may later be used for lobbying purposes (Pamela Sebastian, "Charitable Wineries Ask for More Than Thanks," Wall Street Journal, October 21, 1994, p. B1).

41. National Museum of Natural History, "Newly Renovated O. Orkin Insect Zoo Opens at the National Museum of Natural History," press release, September 9, 1993. Nineteen computer companies gave the Smithsonian $2.3 million for an exhibition on computers (Jacqueline Trescott, "Record Gift Expected," Washington Post, October 23, 1994, p. G10).

42. Russell Mokhiber, Corporate Crime and Violence (San Francisco: Sierra Club Books, 1988), pp. 221–228.

43. Howard Learner, White Paper on Science Museums (Washington, D.C.: Center for Science in the Public Interest, 1979).

44. Michael F. Jacobson, "New Frontiers in Museum-Corporate Partnership," paper presented at the annual meeting of the American Association of Museums, Fort Worth, Texas, May 20, 1993; Michael F. Jacobson, "Museum Exhibits Worrisome Philosophy," Chicago Sun-Times, August 15, 1992.

45. Jacobson, "Museum Exhibits Worrisome Philosophy."

46. Kim Masters and Todd Alan Yasui, "Charges of Commercialism," Washington Post, October 28, 1991.

47. "Philips Interacts with Children's Museums," IEG Sponsorship Report, January 11, 1993.

48. Ibid., p. 1.

49. David A. Adair, "Forge Positive Relationships with Kids Early," Marketing News, March 18, 1991, p. 4.

50. Ibid.

51. "Big Deals," IEG Sponsorship Report, January 11, 1993, p. 8.

52. Pamela Sebastian, "Arts Groups Go After Corporate Sponsors with All the Brashness of the Big Top," Wall Street Journal, February 19, 1992, p. B1.

53. Quoted in Greta Beigel, "What Price the Philharmonic," Los Angeles Times, December 10, 1989.

54. Ibid.

55. Joanne Lipman, "Tour Show to Plug Chrysler Jeep on Stage," Wall Street Journal, March 13, 1992, p. B9.

56. Ibid.

57. Quoted in Marcy Magiera, "Discord on 'Revolution,'" Advertising Age, October 26, 1987, p. 36.

58. Quoted in Jory Farr, "Bringing Music and Lifestyle Together Has Become the Gospel of Marketing," Press-Enterprise (Riverside, Calif.), July 19, 1987.

59. Peter Carlson, "Is Nothing Sacred? The Commercialization of Almost Everything," Washington Post Magazine, November 3, 1991, p. 29.

60. Anita M. Busch and Jeffrey Jolson-Colburn, "Mandrell Ad Link to Album Blasted," Hollywood Reporter, February 8, 1991, p. 56.

61. Kevin Goldman, "Omnicon, Track Marketing Join to Promote Products at Concerts," Wall Street Journal, April 7, 1994.

62. Thom Duffy, "Take It on The Road," AdWeek, November 2, 1992.

63. John Hinge, "A Country Music Star Is Singin' in the Green," Wall Street Journal, February 6, 1991.

64. Paul Grein, "Suds 'n' Bucks 'n' Rock 'n' Roll," Los Angeles Times, July 30, 1989, Calendar sec., p. 8.

65. David Hinckley, "A Tonic to Concert Biz," New York Daily News, September 27, 1991.

66. Jory Farr, "Pop Musicians Sing of Beer and Tobacco for the Big Bucks," Press-Enterprise (Riverside, Calif.), July 19, 1987.

67. "Facts and Information Resources: Underage Drinking," The Healthy Difference Program, Office of Disease Prevention and Health Promotion, U. S. Department of Health and Human Services, Washington, D.C., 1992.

68. David Russell and Martha Russell, "On the McMidway," American Demographics, April 1989, p. 62.

69. Joseph Pereira, "Denmark's Lego Blocks Out Plans for U.S. Theme Park," Wall Street Journal, March 25, 1991, p. B1.

70. Peter Applebome, "How Atlanta's Adman Pushes the City to Sell Itself," New York Times, February 9, 1993.

71. Barbara Harrison, "Two-Card Trick from Visa," London Financial Times, February 4, 1993.

72. Quoted in Applebome, "How Atlanta's Adman Pushes the City to Sell Itself."

73. Charles Truehart, "Corporate Sponsors Welcome at Vancouver Summit," Washington Post, April 2, 1993, p. A22.

74. Albert B. Crenshaw, "Separating Charity From Ads," Washington Post, July 1, 1992,

p. C7; Center for the Study of Commercialism, "Citizens Group to IRS: Tax the Bowl Games and Olympics!" press release, July 21, 1992.

75. Jory Farr, "Pop Musicians Sing of Beer and Tobacco."

76. "An Invidious Video?" *Newsweek*, July 18, 1988, p. 60.

77. Mike Joyce, "Crowes Nest Without Ads," *Washington Post*, August 28, 1992.

78. Horovitz, "Well-Healed Controversy."

79. Julie Liesse and Jeff Jensen, "Whole New Game Without Jordan," *Advertising Age*, October 11, 1993, p. 48.

80. "Advertising Everywhere," *Consumer Reports*, December 1992, p. 753.

81. Barry Schwartz, *The Costs of Living* (New York: Norton, 1994), chap. 4.

82. Joseph M. Winski, "'Impressionism' Makes Its Mark on the National Pastime," *Advertising Age*, August 24, 1992, p. S-2.

83. Paul Farhi, "Take Me out to the Billboard!" *Washington Post*, August 25, 1993, p. F1.

84. Ibid.

85. John Helyar, "Signs Sprout at Sports Arenas As a Way to Get Cheap TV Ads," *Wall Street Journal*, March 8, 1994, p. B1; Paul Farhi, "The Latest Pitch: 'Virtual' Billboards," *Washington Post,* May 17, 1994, p. D1.

86. Dave Sell and George Solomon, "Say Goodbye to the Capital Centre," *Washington Post*, June 17, 1993, p. B1.

87. Larry Weisman and Gordon Forbes, "New Football League a 'Sponsor's Dream,'" *USA Today*, May 3, 1994, p. 1A.

88. "Dos Equis Peddles with Sponsorship," *IEG Sponsorship Report*, May 24, 1993, p. 6.

89. "Olympic Gold," *Wall Street Journal*, July 29, 1992, p. B5.

90. Frank Deford, "Running Man," *Vanity Fair*, August 1993, p. 54.

91. Joanne Lipman, "Product Plugs Dot Olympic Landscape," *Wall Street Journal*, February 11, 1992.

92. Kevin Goldman, "CBS Crams Olympics Coverage with Ads," *Wall Street Journal*, February 13, 1992, p. B3.

93. Stuart Elliott, "A Top Event: NBC's Dash for Ads," *New York Times*, August 6, 1992.

94. Richard B. Meyers, "Thrills, Chills, and Ads," letter to the editor, *USA Today*, February 28, 1994.

95. Gary Strauss, "The Olympics: Brought to You By . . .," *USA Today*, July 21, 1992.

96. Stuart Elliott, "Mass Marketer Jousting Is Newest Olympic Sport," *New York Times*, July 15, 1992, p. D1.

97. Rob Buchanan, "Higher, Faster, Farther," *Adweek*, August 10, 1992.

98. "Perspectives," *Newsweek*, August 10, 1992.

99. Gary Levin, "Olympic Fever Strikes; Marketers Eye '94, '96," *Advertising Age*, July 27, 1992, p. 39.

100. Glenn Ruffenach, "Going for the Gold, Merchandisers and Retailers Promote the Olympics Two Years in Advance," *Wall Street Journal*, December 7, 1993, p. B1.

101. Quoted in Michael Wegs, "Corporate Sponsors: A New Athletic Partnership Unfolds," *AD*, April 1990.

102. Michael J. McCarthy, "College Bowl Sponsors Changing Games' Names," *Wall Street Journal*, December 21, 1990, p. B1.

103. Ibid.

104. Duke Rittenhouse, "Prep Sports, Inc." *Sunday Tribune*, November 3, 1991, p. 8B.

105. Lisa Goulian, "Sports Marketing's Best-Kept Secret," *Sports Inc.*, February 29, 1988.

106. Jeanne Whalen, "Cigarette Interest Flags in Racing," *Advertising Age*, December 6, 1993, p. 28.

107. Michael Novak, *The Joy of Sports* (New York: Basic Books, 1976), p. 276.

108. Christopher Lasch, *Culture of Narcissism* (New York: Warner Books, 1979), p. 217.

109. From interview on ESPN, quoted in "Celtic Calls a Foul on the NBA's Mania for Marketing," *Adweek*, April 19, 1993, p. 19.

SIDEBAR
The Brand of God

1. "Welcome to Burger Heaven," *Newsweek*, August 31, 1992.

2. Michael Janofsky, "In Defense of the Pope's Brand Name," *New York Times*, June 14, 1993; ad for the Miracle Mug appeared in *USA Today*, August 16, 1993.

3. Laurie Petersen, "900 Numbers: A Mixed Blessing for Marketers," *Adweek's Marketing Week*, October 7, 1991.

4. Bob Garfield, "900 Reasons to Hang Up," *Advertising Age*, February 18, 1991.

CHAPTER SIX
Intrusive Marketing

1. Quoted in Michael W. Miller, "Data Mills Delve Deep to Find Info About U.S. Consumers," *Wall Street Journal*, March 4, 1991, p. 1.

2. Larry Tye, "Privacy Lost in High-Tech Era," *Boston Globe*, September 5, 1993.

3. Jill Smolowe, "Read This," *Time*, November 26, 1990, p. 65.

4. Robert J. Coen, "Estimated Annual U.S. Advertising Expenditures 1990–1993," McCann-Erickson, May 1994.

5. Larry Tye, "Proposed 'Bill of Rights' Would Limit Personal Data," *Boston Globe*, September 8, 1993.

6. Michael W. Miller, "Data Mills Delve Deep to Find Information about U.S. Consumers," *Wall Street Journal*, March 14, 1991.

7. Larry Tye, "List-Makers Draw a Bead on Many," *Boston Globe*, September 6, 1993.

8. Ibid.

9. Erik Larson, *The Naked Consumer* (New York: Henry Holt, 1992), pp. 67–70.

10. Tye, "List-Makers," p. 12.

11. Larson, *The Naked Consumer*, p. 66.

12. Ibid, p. 99.

13. Tye, "List-Makers."

14. Larson, *The Naked Consumer*, p. 60.

15. Tye, "Proposed 'Bill of Rights,'" p. 13.

16. David Bender, "The Future of Marketing: Demographic and Technological Influences," paper presented at "Marketing in America: The Consumer Interest," conference sponsored by The Consumer Federation of America, Washington, D.C., October 25, 1991.

17. "Big Brother Watching What You Purchase," *Miami Herald*, November 19, 1991; Joanne Lipman, "Arbitron Pulls the Plug on Scan America," *Wall Street Journal*, September 3, 1992.

18. Quoted in Smolowe, "Read This," p. 66.

19. Larry Tye, "Hidden Assets Are an Open Book to Fla. Firm," *Boston Globe*, September 5, 1993, p. 18.; phone call, Joe Apter, Telephonic-INFO, October 27, 1994. "Permissible purposes" includes collecting money from, employing, or extending credit to an individual.

20. Leonard Sloane, "Credit Reports: The Overhaul Rolls On," *New York Times*, January 4, 1992, p. 48.

21. Tye, "Privacy Lost in High-Tech Era."

22. Larson, *The Naked Consumer*, pp. 204–205.

23. Quoted in ibid., p. 207.

24. Tye, "List-Makers," p. 13.

25. U.S. Department of Commerce, *Statistical Abstract of the United States, 1993* (Washington, D.C.: Government Printing Office, 1993), Table 897.

26. Smolowe, "Read This," p. 63.

27. Paul Hawken, "The Junk Mail Stops Here," *Utne Reader*, November-December 1990, p. 51. Calculation assumes spending 15 minutes a day, six days a week, for fifty years.

28. Will Nixon, "Are We Burying Ourselves in Junk Mail?" *E Magazine*, November-December 1993.

29. Ibid., p. 30.

30. Barry Meier, "Junk Mail to Throw into the Nearest VCR," *New York Times*, January 4, 1992, p. 48.

31. Nixon, "Are We Burying Ourselves in Junk Mail?" p. 30.

32. U.S. Post Office, "Postal Update," newsletter, September 1993.

33. The franking privilege enables federal legislators to use their signatures as postage. Members of Congress send vast amounts of mail to their constituents. During the 1988 election campaign, 805 million pieces of political literature issued from Washington, at a cost to taxpayers of $113 million, according to Jill Smolowe in "Read This." The franking privilege was intended to foster a democratic dialogue; critics say it's used primarily to help incumbents stay in office.

34. Peter Bahouth and André Carothers, "In Defense of Junk Mail," *Utne Reader*, November-December 1990, p. 55.

35. Herb Chao Gunther, "The Difference Between Commercial Mail and Nonprofit Mail," *Utne Reader*, November-December 1990, p. 56.

36. Larry Tye, "German System Puts a Lid on Data," *Boston Globe*, September 7, 1993.

37. Tye, "Proposed 'Bill of Rights.'"

38. Ibid.

39. Michael W. Miller, "Data Mills Delve Deep to Find Information about U.S. Consumers," *Wall Street Journal*, March 14, 1991, p. 2.

40. First example: Lena Williams, "Consumers vs. Callers: The Lines Are Busier," *New York Times*, June 20, 1991; second example: James J. Kilpatrick, "Away with Autodialers," *Washington Post*, August 6, 1991; third example: "Telephone Autodialers Under Fire," *New York Times*, October 31, 1991.

41. Terri Shaw, "Dialing for Your Dollars," *Washington Home*, December 12, 1991; Timothy Gower, "It's None of Your Damned Business," *Boston Phoenix*, July 12, 1991, sec. 2.

42. Ad appearing in "Telemedia," an advertising supplement in *Adweek*, April 10, 1989.

43. Mark Nadel, "Rings of Privacy: Unsolicited Telephone Calls and the Right of Privacy," *Yale Journal on Regulation* 4, no. 99, 1986.

44. "Another Annoying Sales Pitch," *American Demographics*, March 1991.

45. Shaw, "Dialing for Your Dollars," p. 9.

46. Julie Crooker, government affairs director of the Direct Marketing Association, as quoted by Robert Bulmash, Private Citizen (Naperville, Ill.).

47. Jim Klobuchar, "Unwanted Call More Than Irritant," *Star Tribune* (Minneapolis), July 11, 1990.

48. Andrews, "Telephone Autodialers Under Fire."

49. *The New York Times*, May 21, 1988, p. 36. Cited in: Michael F. Jacobson, "Testimony on S.1410 and S.1462," Senate Commerce Committee Subcommittee on Communications, July 24, 1991.

50. U.S. House of Representatives, *Telephone Advertising Regulation Act*, Report 101-633, July 27, 1990.

51. Robert Bulmash, Private Citizen, memo to authors, August 19, 1993.

52. Quoted in Shaw, "Dialing for Your Dollars," p. 12.

53. Louis Brandeis, "The Right to Privacy," *Harvard Law Review* 4, no. 5, December 15, 1890, p. 205.

54. *Carey v. Brown*, 447 U.S. 455, 471 (1980).

55. Figure of $500 billion is from interview with Nadji Tehrani, publisher of *Telemarketing Magazine*, August 19, 1993.

56. Robert Bulmash, Private Citizen, personal communication, July 1992.

57. Memo from Robert Bulmash, August 19, 1993.

58. U.S. House of Representatives, *Telephone Advertising Consumer Rights Act*, report 102-317, p. 16.

59. Ted Schwartz, "What Telemarketing Has Done for America: The Untold Story," promotional materials published by APAC Teleservices, 1992.

60. Miller, "When the 'Junker' Calls," p. 1.

61. Ibid.

62. Quoted in Edward T. McMahon and Patricia A. Taylor, *Citizens' Action Handbook on Alcohol and Tobacco Billboard Advertising* (Washington, D.C.: Center for Science in the Public Interest and Scenic America, 1990), p. 2.

63. Bruce K. Mulock, "Billboards Along Interstate and Federal-Aid Primary Highways: Why No Reliable Estimates of Their Number Exist," *CRS Report for Congress*, Congressional Research Service, 91-115 E, January 28, 1991, p. 1.

64. James Nathan Miller, "The Great Billboard Double-Cross," *Reader's Digest*, June 1985, p. 4; and Coen, "Estimated Annual U.S. Advertising Expenditures."

65. Edward T. McMahon, "Let's Sweep Away 'Litter on a Stick,'" *Preservation News*, National Trust for Historic Preservation, Washington, D.C., March 1990.

66. Quoted in Miller, "The Great Billboard Double-Cross," p. 3.

67. Adam Snyder, "A Potent Washington Lobby," *Adweek's Marketing Week*, July 8, 1991.

68. Ted Williams, "Litter on a Stick," *Audubon*, July 1991.

69. Quoted in ibid., p. 18.

70. Data from the Federal Highway Administration and Congressional Research Service, cited in ibid., p. 18.

71. Ibid.

72. Quoted in Laurie Abraham, "City Balks as Billboards Overrun Poor Areas," *Chicago Reporter*, November 1990, p. 7.

73. Ibid., p. 1.

74. Quoted in Adam Snyder, "Outdoor Forecast: Sunny, Some Clouds," *Adweek's Marketing Week*, July 8, 1991, p. 18.

75. "Companies Make Cuts, but Brands Boost Outdoor Dollars," *Advertising Age*, November 14, 1991.

76. McMahon and Taylor, *Citizens Action Handbook*, p. vi.

77. "Study Warns of Prevalent Youth Drinking," *Detroit Free Press*, December 7, 1988.

78. Olivia Mitchell and Michael Greenberg, "Outdoor Advertising of Addictive Products," *New Jersey Medicine* 88, no. 5, May 1991, p. 332.

79. Terry Wilson, "Acquittal Answers Pfleger's Prayers," *Chicago Tribune*, July 3, 1991, sec. 2, p. 3.

80. Quoted in Williams, "Litter on a Stick," p. 18.

81. Ibid.

82. McMahon and Taylor, *Citizens Action Handbook*, p. 3.

83. "Billions of People a Day to View Mile-Long Space Billboard," *PR Newswire*, April 12, 1993.

84. Center for the Study of Commercialism, "Carl Sagan Condemns Space Billboard," press release, May 14, 1993.

85. Steven Colford, "Blasted Space Ad!" *Advertising Age*, June 7, 1993.

86. Williams, "Litter on a Stick."

87. Alf Siewers, "Priest Freed in Billboard Attack," *Chicago Sun-Times*, July 3, 1991.

88. *Signs of the Times*, July 1982.

89. Quoted in "Public Service Billboards: Signs of an Ulterior Motive," *Scenic America's Sign Control News*, Spring 1992, p. 5.

90. Richard D. Hylton, "An American Icon's New Marching Orders," *New York Times*, June 9, 1991.

91. Scenic America, "Congress Refuses to Allow New Billboards on Scenic Byways," press release, November 22, 1993.

92. Quoted in Scenic America, "Sign Control Helps Tourism," factsheet, n. d.

93. *Metromedia, Inc. v. City of San Diego*, 453 U.S. 490 (1981).

94. Jennifer Lawrence, "Travel Agents to Carry Line of Ad-Backed Videos," *Advertising Age*, January 25, 1993.

95. "Cafe USA Broadcasting to Hungry Shoppers," *Wall Street Journal*, December 21, 1993.

96. Scott Donaton, Kate Fitzgerald, "New Media Concepts Grow," *Advertising Age*, May 14, 1990, p. 4. Laura Bird, "TV Ad Sports at Health Clubs Are Exorcised by Members," *Wall Street Journal*, August 26, 1992.

97. Airport Channel (a division of CNN), information packet, n. d.

98. Metro Vision, Commuter Channel information packet, n. d.

99. Timothy Gower, "Ambush Marketing," *MediaCulture Review*, October-November 1993 (as reprinted from the *Boston Phoenix*); phone call, Wendy Hamer, October 25, 1994.

100. Kevin Goldman, "Turner Bags Checkout Channel, but Rivals Remain Undaunted," *Wall Street Journal*, March 4, 1993.

101. Ibid.

102. Patrick Reilly, "Whittle Communications to Close Down Unprofitable Unit for Doctors' Offices," *Wall Street Journal*, March 1, 1994.

103. Cineplex Odeon, press kit, 1993.

104. Kevin Goldman, "Moviegoers React to Ads on the Big Screen," *Wall Street Journal*, February 18, 1993, p. B11.

105. Martha Moore, "Movie Theaters Take Commercial Break," *USA Today*, October 5, 1992, p. 2B.

106. Privy Promotions, information packet, n. d.

SIDEBAR
The 900-Number Industry: Making the Caller Pay

1. Art Kleiner, "Brave New Audiotex," *Adweek's Marketing Week*, April 10, 1989.

2. Laurie Petersen, "900 Numbers: A Mixed Blessing for Marketers," *Adweek's Marketing Week*, October 7, 1991.

3. National Consumers League, "National Consumers League Advisory: Warning to Be Issued on Outbreak of Recession-Related Phone Scams," press release, April 1991.

4. Christopher Stern, "Expectations Lowered for 900 Numbers," *Broadcasting and Cable*, October 25, 1993.

CHAPTER SEVEN
Advertising Lies, Advertising Kills

1. United States Office of Consumer Affairs, letter to Michael F. Jacobson, August 24, 1993.

2. Milton Handler, as quoted in Jef I. Richards, "A New and Improved View of Puffery," by Jef I. Richards, *Journal of Public Policy and Marketing* 9, 1990, p. 74.

3. Information on misleading health claims obtained from the Center for Science in the Public Interest, Washington, D.C.

4. "A Year of Controversy and Self-Inflicted Wounds," *Adweek's Marketing Week*, December 17, 1990.

5. Bonnie Liebman, Center for Science in the Public Interest, statement at the Annual Harlan Page Hubbard Awards, Washington, D.C., December 9, 1992.

6. Quoted in "Some Facts on Plax," *Consumer Reports*, September 1992, p. 610.

7. In 1994, in the face of massive opposition from the supplement industry, the Food and Drug Administration ordered companies to bring their labels into compliance with the 1990 Nutrition Labeling and Education Act. The FDA, however, does not regulate claims in media advertising.

8. Helen Kahn and Jim Henry, "Volvo Agrees to $150,000 Penalty for 'Monster Truck' Ads," *Automotive News*, August 26, 1991.

9. Aviation Consumer Action Project (Washington, D.C.), "Nomination of Northwest Airlines for Harlan Page Hubbard Lemon Award: Misleading Airline Advertisements," press release, January 27, 1994.

10. "Colgate Corrects Claim," *Wall Street Journal*, April 21, 1992.

11. Gerri Detweiler, director, Bankcard Holders of America, statement at the Annual Harlan Page Hubbard Awards, Washington, D.C., December 9, 1992.

12. Molly O'Neill, "Five Diet Companies Ask U.S. for Uniform Rules on Ads," *New York Times*, August 25, 1992, p. D1.

13. Paul Farhi, "Government Weighs the Claims of Diets," *Washington Post*, May 31, 1992, p. H1.

14. "Pinocchio Awards," *Adweek*, December 3, 1990.

15. Quoted in O'Neill, "Five Diet Companies," p. D2.

16. Quoted in Farhi, "Government Weighs the Claims of Diets," p. H8.

17. Ibid.

18. Federal Trade Commission, "Weight Watchers and Jenny Craig to Face Litigation over FTC Deceptive Advertising Charges," press release, September 30, 1993.

19. *Federal Trade Commission v. International White Cross*, Complaint for Permanent Injunction and Other Ancillary Relief, February 7, 1991.

20. *In the Matter of Patricia Wexler, M.D.*, U.S.A. Federal Trade Commission Docket No. C-3400.

21. Quoted in Jay Mallin, "Dial 900 Industry Wary of Regulation," *Washington Times*, March 1, 1991.

22. Alex Pham, "Poll Finds Phone Fraud Rampant," *Washington Post*, July 7, 1992, p. D1.

23. *The Health Consequences of Smoking: A Report of the Surgeon General* (Atlanta, Ga.: U.S. Department of Health and Human Services, Centers for Disease Control and Prevention, Office on Smoking and Health), 1982.

24. *Preventing Tobacco Use Among Young People: A Report of the Surgeon General* (Atlanta, Ga.: U.S. Department of Health and Human Services, Centers for Disease Control and Prevention, Office on Smoking and Health, 1994), letter of introduction.

25. U.S. Department of Commerce, *Statistical Abstract of the United States: 1993* (Washington, D.C.: Government Printing Office, 1993), tables no. 126, 131, 135; *Sixth Special Report to the U.S. Congress on Alcohol and Health from the Secretary of Health and Human Services* (Washington, D.C.: National Institute for Alcohol Abuse and Alcoholism, 1987).

26. Alix M. Freedman and Laurie P. Cohen, "How Cigarette Makers Keep the Health Question 'Open' Year After Year," *Wall Street Journal*, February 11, 1993, p. A1.

27. *The Health Consequences of Environmental Smoking: Report of the Surgeon-General* (Atlanta, Ga.: U.S. Department of Health and Human Services, Centers for Disease Control and Prevention, Office on Smoking and Health, 1986).

28. David Owen, "The Cigarette Companies: How They Get Away With Murder, Part II," *Washington Monthly*, March 1985, p. 48.

29. Geoffrey Cowley, "Poison at Home and Work," *Newsweek*, June 29, 1992.

30. U.S. Department of Health and Human Services, *Preventing Tobacco Use Among Young People*, p. 31.

31. Ibid.

32. Ibid.

33. Russell Mokhiber, *Corporate Crime and Violence* (San Francisco: Sierra Club Books, 1988), p. 430.

34. Raymond Pearl, "Tobacco Smoking and Longevity," *Science*, March 4, 1938.

35. Cited in Kenneth E. Warner, *Selling Smoke: Cigarette Advertising and Public Health*, (Washington, D.C.: American Public Health Association, 1986), p. 19.

36. Richard W. Pollay, "Themes and Tactics in Cigarette Advertising, 1938–1983: Technical Report on Methods and Measures," working paper, History of Advertising Archives, Vancouver, British Columbia, 1987; Morton Mintz, "Cigarette Ads Said Full of Health Cues," *Washington Post*, March 10, 1988, p. D8.

37. Milo Geyelin and James P. Miller, "Old

Ads May Come Back to Haunt Maker of Kent," *Wall Street Journal*, October 28, 1991.

38. *Smoking and Health: A Report of the Surgeon General* (U.S. Department of Health, Education, and Welfare, Centers for Disease Control and Prevention, Office on Smoking and Health, 1979), pp. i–v.

39. Quoted in Peter Taylor, *The Smoke Ring: Tobacco, Money, and Multinational Politics* (New York: Pantheon Books, 1984), p. 33.

40. Quoted in Peter Taylor, *Death in the West,* film.

41. See Federal Communications Commission, "Applicability of the Fairness Doctrine to Cigarette Advertising," *Federal Register* 32, no. 179, September 15, 1967, for the ruling that led to the court decision.

42. Doris A. Graber, *Mass Media and American Politics* (Washington, D.C.: CQ Press, 1989), p. 117. See Federal Communications Commission, "Applicability of the Fairness Doctrine to Cigarette Advertising," *Federal Register* 32, no. 179, September 15, 1967, for the ruling that led to the court decision.

43. Taylor, *The Smoke Ring,* pp.189–206.

44. "U.S. Smoking Rate Drops to 28%, Survey Says," *New York Times*, November 9, 1991; "Smoking Declines at a Faster Pace," *New York Times*, May 22, 1992.

45. U.S. Department of Health and Human Services, *Preventing Tobacco Use Among Young People,* p. 160; Philip J. Hilts, "Long-Term Decline in Smoking in U.S. Is Apparently Over," *New York Times*, May 20, 1994, p. A16.

46. M. D. Anderson Cancer Center, *Final Report of the Tobacco Use in America Conference*, (Houston, Tex: University of Texas, January 27–28, 1989), p. 29.

47. Ibid., p. 30.

48. Ibid.

49. Ibid., p. 31.

50. Quoted in Warner, *Selling Smoke*, p. 63.

51. M. D. Anderson Cancer Center, *Tobacco Use in America*, p. 31.

52. Tobacco Institute, "Voluntary Initiatives of a Responsible Industry," factsheet.

53. From documents placed in the record of the hearings before the House Commerce Committee Subcommittee on Oversight and Investigations, June 25, 1981, Serial No. 97-66.

54. U.S. Department of Health and Human Services, *Preventing Tobacco Use Among Young People,* p. iii.

55. Laura Bird, "Smooth Sell," *Adweek's Marketing Week*, May 20, 1991.

56. Stuart Elliott, "Camel Cartoon Draws Buyers, Too," *New York Times*, December 12, 1991, p. D1.

57. P. Fischer et al., "Brand Logo Recognition by Children Aged Three to Six Years," *Journal of the American Medical Association* 266, 1991, p. 3145; J. DiFranza et al., "RJR Nabisco's Cartoon Camel Promotes Camel Cigarettes to Children," *Journal of the American Medical Association* 266, 1991, p. 3149; J. Pierce et al., "Does Tobacco Advertising Target Young People to Start Smoking? *Journal of the American Medical Association* 266, 1991, p. 3154.

58. Smoking Control Advocacy Resource Center, Advocacy Institute, "Issue: FTC Considers Taking Action Against 'Joe Camel' Campaign," action alert, Washington, D.C., January 24, 1994.

59. Fischer et al., "Brand Logo Recognition," p. 3148.

60. *Advertising Age*, editorial, January 13, 1992.

61. Paul Farhi, "Push to Ban Joe Camel May Run Out of Breath," *Washington Post*, December 4, 1993.

62. Quoted in Morton Mintz, "Marketing Tobacco to Children," *Nation*, May 6, 1991, front cover.

63. U.S. Department of Health and Human Service, *Preventing Tobacco Use Among Young People,* p. 160.

64. Jason DeParle, "Warning: Sports Stars May Be Hazardous to Your Health," *Washington Monthly*, September 1989.

65. Alan Blum, "The Marlboro Grand Prix: Circumvention of the Television Ban on Tobacco Advertising," *New England Journal of Medicine*, March 28, 1991, p. 914.

66. From Leo Burnett Agency figures, as listed in Martha T. Moore, "Sponsors Pay $900,000 for a Thirty-second Play," *USA Today*, January 31, 1994.

67. Warner, *Selling Smoke*, pp. 4–5; U.S. Department of Health and Human Services, *Preventing Tobacco Use Among Young People,* p. 58.

68. American Cancer Society, *Cancer Facts and Figures 1991* (Washington, D.C.: American Cancer Society, 1991), pp. 8–11.

69. Marjorie Williams, "Feminism's Unaddressed Issue: Health Risks to Women Who Smoke," *Washington Post*, November 14, 1991, p. A1.

70. Stuart Ewen, *Captains of Consciousness: Advertising and the Social Roots of the Consumer Culture* (New York: McGraw-Hill, 1976), p. 160.

71. Naomi Wolf, *The Beauty Myth: How Images of Beauty Are Used Against Women* (New York: William Morrow, 1991), p. 229.

72. Charles Trueheart, "Marketers Test Dakota Cigarettes," *Washington Post*, August 14, 1991.

73. "Many Women's Groups Have Close Ties to Tobacco Industry," *ASH Review* (Washington, D.C.: Action on Smoking and Health, November-December 1991).

74. M. D. Anderson Cancer Center, *Tobacco Use in America*, p. 30.

75. Shaun Assael, "Why Big Tobacco Woos Minorities," *Adweek's Marketing Week*, January 29, 1990, p. 20.

76. Ibid., p. 21.

77. Roger Campbell, "Snuff It Out!" *Heart and Soul*, Spring 1994, p. 45.

78. U.S. Department of Health and Human Services, *Preventing Tobacco Use Among Young People,* p. 61.

79. Dan Koeppel, "In Philadelphia, R.J. Reynolds Made All the Wrong Moves," *Adweek's Marketing Week*, January 29, 1990, p. 20.

80. Quoted in Richard W. Pollay et al., "Separate but Not Equal: Racial Segmentation in Cigarette Advertising," *Journal of Advertising*, March 1992, p. 45.

81. Assael, "Why Big Tobacco Woos Minorities."

82. Tracy Thompson, "Newport's Captive Market," *Washington Post*, June 22, 1994, p. A1.

83. Mark Miller, "A New Tobacco Alliance," *Newsweek*, February 13, 1989; Pollay et al., "Separate but Not Equal."

84. Ibid.

85. Quoted in Trueheart, "Marketers Test Dakota Cigarettes," p. C4.

86. "Cigarette Advertising–United States, 1988," *Morbidity and Mortality Weekly Review* 39, 1990, pp. 261–265.

87. Judith Egerton, "Philip Morris Thanks Itself with Ads Noting Its Good Deeds," *Louisville Courier-Journal*, February 23, 1991.

88. Joanne Lipman, "Philip Morris Curtails Defense of Smoking," *Washington Post*, April 7, 1992.

89. Philip J. Hilts, "Agency Is Assailed on Deal with a Cigarette Company," *New York Times*, November 10, 1989, p. A20.

90. Quoted in ibid.

91. Quoted in ibid.

92. Taylor, *The Smoke Ring*, p. 58.

93. Scott Donaton, "Smoke Gets Out of Publishers' Eyes," December 20, 1993.

94. Kenneth E. Warner et al., "Cigarette Advertising and Magazine Coverage of the Hazards of Smoking," *New England Journal of Medicine* 326, January 30, 1992, p. 307.

95. Quoted in Joanne Lipman, "Media Content Is Linked to Cigarette Ads," *Washington Post*, January 30, 1992.

96. Warner, *Selling Smoke*, p. 82.

97. William L. Weiss and Chauncey Burke,

"Media Content and Tobacco Advertising: An Unhealthy Addiction," *Journal of Communication*, Autumn 1986.

98. Warner, *Selling Smoke*, p. 81.

99. Gloria Steinem, "Sex, Lies, and Advertising," *Ms.*, July-August, 1990.

100. Kenneth E. Warner and Linda M. Goldenhar, "The Cigarette Advertising Broadcast Ban and Magazine Coverage of Smoking and Health," *Journal of Public Health Policy*, Spring 1989; Judann Dagnoli, "Reynolds Smolders: Saatchi Dismissal Prompts Look at All Agencies," *Advertising Age*, April 11, 1988.

101. Warner, *Selling Smoke*, p. 76.

102. Federal Trade Commission, *Staff Report of the Cigarette Advertising Investigation* (Washington, D.C.: FTC, 1981).

103. Weiss and Burke, "Media Content and Tobacco Advertising," p. 65.

104. Michael F. Jacobson, "Your Money or Your Life Style," *Nation*, July 13, 1992.

105. Bischoff, "Smokeless in Seattle," p. 36.

106. Weiss and Burke, "Media Content and Tobacco Advertising."

107. "Government Tobacco Promotion Policies and Consumption Trends in Thirty-Three Countries from 1970 to 1986," *World Smoking and Health* (American Cancer Society) 15, no. 1, Spring 1990.

108. Ibid., p. 19.

109. David Millwood and Helena Gezelius, *Smart Promotion* (Stockholm: National Swedish Board for Consumer Policies, National Board for Health and Welfare, and International Organization of Consumers Unions, 1989), pp. 32–37.

110. Leon Wynter, "Tobacco Ad Proposal," *Wall Street Journal*, November 24, 1993.

111. Ibid.

112. Quoted in Millwood and Gezelius, *Smart Promotion*, p. 15.

113. Reginald Ware, personal communication, January 31, 1994.

114. Bischoff, "Smokeless in Seattle," pp. 35, 36.

115. "Many Women's Groups Have Close Ties to Tobacco Industry," *ASH Review* (Washington, D.C.: Action on Smoking and Health, November-December 1991), p. 3.

116. *Sixth Special Report to the U.S. Congress on Alcohol and Health from the Secretary of Health and Human Services*; David R. Buchanan and Jane Lev, *Beer and Fast Cars: How Brewers Target Blue-Collar Youth Through Motor Sport Sponsorships* (Washington, D.C.: AAA Foundation for Traffic Safety, 1989).

117. Joanne Lipman, "Beer Marketers Brew Controversy with Ads Targeting Women," *Wall Street Journal*, April 6, 1992.

118. Fatal Accident Reporting System (FARS), U.S. Department of Transportation, National Highway Traffic Safety Administration, August 10, 1993.

119. Jim Wright, National Highway Traffic Safety Administration, personal conversation, July 12, 1994.

120. Michael F. Jacobson, Patricia Taylor, and Deborah Baldwin, "Advertising Alcohol: This Brew's for You," *1993 Medical and Health Annual* (Chicago, Ill.: Encyclopædia Britannica, 1992), p. 154; C. Everett Koop, statement at press conference to introduce *Surgeon General's Workshop on Drunk Driving: Proceedings*, U.S. Public Health Service, Washington, D.C., May 13, 1989.

121. "Impact of Alcohol on American Lives," *Washington Post*, December 17, 1991, p. 5.

122. Dorothy P. Rice, Institute for Health and Aging, University of California at San Francisco, letter to the Alcohol Policies Project, Center for Science in the Public Interest, May 21, 1993.

123. "Ad Spending a Mixed Bag in '92," *Impact* 23, no. 15, September 1, 1993, p. 1.

124. "1992 Top Ten Alcoholic Beverage Media Advertisers," table, *Impact* 23, no. 15, September 1, 1993, p. 2; Ann Bradley, National Institute on Alcohol Abuse and Alcoholism, personal communication, July 20, 1994.

125. William Shakespeare, *Macbeth*, II, iii.

126. "The Significant 'Other,'" *Prevention File*, Summer 1992, p. 20.

127. Jacobson, Taylor, and Baldwin, "Advertising Alcohol."

128. Jean Kilbourne, "Deadly Persuasion," *Media and Values*, Spring-Summer 1991, p. 10.

129. Frank DeFord, *Lite Reading: The Lite Beer from Miller Commercial Scrapbook* (New York: Penguin, 1984).

130. North Coast Harbor, personal communication, August 18, 1994.

131. Doctors Ought to Care, "Doctors Protest Miller Beer Trademarks on Children's Toys," press release, April 9, 1991.

132. Lawrence Wallack, Diane Cassady, and Joel Grube, *Beer Commercials and Children: Exposure, Attention, Beliefs, and Expectations About Drinking as an Adult* (Washington, D.C.: AAA Foundation for Traffic Safety, Fall 1990), Figure 12, p. 29.

133. Miller Brewing Company, promotion video on product placement, ca. 1984.

134. Ibid.

135. Jacobson, Taylor, and Baldwin, "Advertising Alcohol," p. 163.

136. Wallack, Cassady, and Grube, *Beer Commercials and Children*, p. 33.

137. Jacobson, Taylor, and Baldwin, "Advertising Alcohol," p. 162.

138. Center for Science in the Public Interest, "Kids Are as Aware of Booze as Presidents, Survey Finds," press release, September 4, 1988.

139. "National Survey Results on Drug Use from the Monitoring the Future Study, 1975–1993," National Institute on Drug Abuse (Washington, D.C.: Government Printing Office, 1994), vol. I, p. 49.

140. Office of the Inspector General, "Youth and Alcohol: A National Survey," *General Reports on Youth and Alcohol* (Rockville, Md.: U.S. Department of Health and Human Services, Office of Substance Abuse and Prevention, National Clearinghouse for Alcohol and Drug Information, 1991., p. i.

141. Koop, statement at press conference to introduce *Surgeon General's Workshop on Drunk Driving: Proceedings*.

142. "Beer Companies Tone Down Campus Promotions," *Prevention File,* Spring 1992, p. 2.

143. Lewis D. Eigen, *Alcohol Practices, Policies, and Potentials of American Colleges and Universities: An OSAP White Paper* (Rockville, Md.: U.S. Department of Health and Human Services; Alcohol, Drug Abuse, and Mental Health Administration, September 1991), p. 43.

144. Ibid., pp. 45–46.

145. "Beer Companies Tone Down Campus Promotions," *Prevention File*.

146. Ibid.

147. Commission on Substance Abuse at Colleges and Universities, *Rethinking Rites of Passage: Substance Abuse on America's Campuses* (New York: Center on Addiction and Substance Abuse at Columbia University, 1994), p. 2.

148. Ibid., p. 4.

149. Ibid., p. 2.

150. Ibid., p. 4.

151. Quoted in Oscar Johnson, "Sports and Suds," *Sports Illustrated*, August 8, 1988, p. 72.

152. Bill Gloede, "What if Beer Were Banned," *Sports Inc.*, September 5, 1988, p. 15.

153. Matthew Grimm, "The Next Crusade? Tobacco, Beer, and Sports," *Adweek's Marketing Week*, May 27, 1991, p. 19.

154. Ibid., p. 22.

155. Quoted in Johnson, "Sports and Suds," p. 78.

156. Lipman, "Beer Makers Brew Controversy," p. B8.

157. Ibid., p. B1.

158. "Fetal Alcohol Syndrome—United

States, 1979–1992," *Morbidity and Mortality Weekly Report* 42, no. 17, May 7, 1993, p. 339.

159. Lipman, "Beer Marketers Brew Controversy," p. B8.

160. George A. Hacker, Ronald Collins, and Michael F. Jacobson, *Marketing Booze to Blacks* (Washington, D.C.: Center for Science in the Public Interest, 1987).

161. *Eighth Special Report to the U.S. Congress on Alcohol and Health from the Secretary of Health and Human Services* (Rockville, Md.: U.S. Department of Health and Human Services, National Institutes of Health, National Institute on Alcohol Abuse and Alcoholism, September 1993).

162. Bruce Maxwell and Michael F. Jacobson, *Marketing Disease to Hispanics* (Washington, D.C.: Center for Science in the Public Interest, 1989), p. 9.

163. Melanie Haiken, "Liquor Ads Targeted at Indians Dismay Some Tribal Leaders," *Washington Post Health*, September 22, 1992, p. 11.

164. United States Brewers Association, "Brewing Industry Advertising Guidelines," pamphlet, December 1984.

165. Keith Greenberg, "Pastor Takes Campaign Back to the Streets," *USA Today,* July 1, 1991, p. 2A; Janet Cawley, "New Brew Fermenting Anger Among Blacks," *Chicago Tribune,* June 20, 1991, p. 2.

166. Remy Martin also sponsored ads with the identical picture, but innocuous words. See illustration elsewhere in this section.

167. Ibid.

168. Annetta Miller, "Do Gang Ads Deserve a Rap?" *Newsweek*, October 21, 1991.

169. Alix M. Freedman, "Malt Advertising That Touts Firepower Comes Under Attack by U.S. Officials," *Wall Street Journal*, July 1, 1991.

170. Ibid.

171. "Crazy Horse Is Free to Roam: Court Rules Name Ban Unconstitutional," *Food and Drink Daily*, April 15, 1993.

172. Quoted in Maxwell and Jacobson, *Marketing Disease to Hispanics*, p. 48.

173. "Cinco de Mayo Cut Short when Crowds Get Rowdy," *Los Angeles Times*, May 8, 1989.

174. Haiken, "Liquor Ads Targeted at Indians Dismay Some Tribal Leaders."

175. Hacker, Collins, and Jacobson, *Marketing Booze to Blacks.*

176. Maxwell and Jacobson, *Marketing Disease to Hispanics*, pp. 67–68.

177. Jacobson, Taylor, and Baldwin, "Advertising Alcohol."

178. National Institute on Alcohol Abuse and Alcoholism, *Alcohol Alert*, no.

23, January 1994, p. 1.

179. "Alcohol-Ad Ban Studied," *Wall Street Journal*, May 31, 1994.

180. Kilbourne, *Calling The Shots*, film distributed by Cambridge Documentary Films, Cambridge, Mass., 1987.

181. Ibid.

182. Koop, statement at press conference announcing the *Surgeon General's Workshop on Drunk Driving: Proceedings*.

183. Quoted in Johnson, "Sports and Suds," p. 79.

184. Haiken, "Liquor Ads Targeted at Indians Dismay Some Tribal Leaders."

185. Jacobson, Taylor, and Baldwin, "Advertising Alcohol."

186. Alicia Mundy, "Team Works," *Adweek*, May 30, 1994, p. 18.

187. Alcohol Policy Project of the Center for Science in the Public Interest, "Booze News," newsletter, Fall 1993.

CHAPTER EIGHT
Commercialized Holidays and Rituals

1. Russell W. Belk, "Materialism and the Making of the Modern American Christmas," unpublished paper, University of Utah.

2. Ibid.

3. Christina Duff and Jeff Bailey, "Sales Talk," *Wall Street Journal*, December 19, 1991.

4. Eben Shapiro, "The War of the Christmas Catalogs," *New York Times*, November 15, 1991, p. D1.

5. "Rushing the Season," *Advertising Age*, October 22, 1990.

6. Howard Rosenberg, "Not Your Standard Christmas Special," *Los Angeles Times*, November 17, 1993.

7. Distilled Spirits Council of the United States, personal communication, July 20, 1994.

8. James S. Henry, "Why I Hate Christmas," *New Republic*, December 31, 1990.

9. Cathy Hainer, "From Lavish Santas Only: A Private Theme Park," *USA Today*, November 17, 1993.

10. Conference Board (New York), "A Bright Christmas Ahead for Retailers," press release, November 20, 1992.

11. Peter Pac, "Credit-Card Use Surges as Consumers Charge Holiday Gifts at Record Pace," *Wall Street Journal*, December 16, 1992, p. A2.

12. "Scattered Shopping; Prevailing Caution," *Advertising Age*, December 13, 1993.

13. Peter Pae and Debbi Wilgoren, "Recycling That Christmas Debris Can Render Holiday Less Wasteful," *Washington Post*,

December 26, 1993, p. B1.

14. Russell W. Belk, "A Child's Christmas in America: Santa Claus as Deity, Consumption as Religion," *Journal of American Culture*, Spring 1987.

15. Ibid.

16. Elaine Rodino, personal communication, December 14, 1993.

17. Stephanie Strom, "Some See Trend in the Low-Key Christmas of '91," *New York Times*, December 24, 1991, p. A1.

18. Ibid., p. D7.

19. "For Many, Donating to Charity Is the Perfect Gift," *New York Times,* December 10, 1990, p. 42.

20. From SCROOGE newsletter, December 1991.

SIDEBAR
Manufactured Holidays

1. National Florists' Association, "Florists' Review," newsletter, April 28, 1910.

2. "Florists' Review," April 24, 1913.

3. Quoted in Leigh Eric Schmidt, "The Commercialization of the Calendar: American Holidays and the Culture of Consumption, 1870–1930," by Leigh Eric Schmidt, *Journal of American History*, December 1991, p. 900.

4. "Florists' Review," May 18, 1922.

SIDEBAR
Rites of Consumption

1. Kelley O'Reilly, *Bride's and Your New Home* magazine, personal communication, August 13, 1993; Kate Fitzgerald, "Catalog Threat Fuels Database Effort at Stores," *Advertising Age, Special Report: The Bridal Market*, January 25, 1993.

2. Ron Alexander, "Bride's Head Revisited: Romance Still Reigns," *New York Times*, June 16, 1992.

3. Dave Barry, *Dave Barry Talks Back* (New York: Crown, 1991), p. 218.

4. Janet Marder, "When Bar/Bat Mitzvah Loses Meaning," *Reform Judaism*, Winter 1992, p. 5.

5. Quoted in ibid., pp. 4–5.

CHAPTER NINE
The Impact of Commercialism

1. Madonna, "More," on *I'm Breathless* album.

2. Though some advertising is clearly informative, Americans are increasingly cynical and suspicious; the percentage of people who believe that advertising is informative plummeted from 37 percent in 1964 to 17 percent in 1989 (Opinion Research Center, *ORC Issue Watch*, February, 1990, p. 2).

3. Editorial, "Ads, Violence and Values," *Advertising Age*, April 2, 1990, p. 12.

4. Even in certain "mature" markets, such as beer and cigarettes, advertising maintains consumption, encourages current drinkers and smokers to consume more, and introduces the products to potential new consumers.

5. Michael Schudson, *Advertising, the Uneasy Persuasion* (New York: Basic Books, 1986), p. 235.

6. Editorial, "They Never Give Up," *Editor and Publisher*, September 18, 1993, p. 8.

7. Howard H. Bell, "Threat to Advertising's Freedom Is Real," *Advertising Age*, December 13, 1993, p. 20.

8 The figure of $1.4 trillion is based on estimates by Robert J. Coen, McCann-Erickson, of annual advertising expenditures; the authors adjusted those figures for inflation, using 1994 dollars.

9. Editorial, "Old Joe Must Go," *Advertising Age*, January 13, 1992, p. 16.

10. Not every concern about material goods is classified as "materialism." Everyone needs shelter, adequate clothing, and other things necessary for a reasonably comfortable life. We do not cast a judgmental eye at wanting food in the pantry and a warm blanket. Rather, our focus is on what some scholars call "terminal" materialism, where consumption serves no goal beyond possession itself and has become a preoccupation.

11. Christopher Lasch, *The Culture of Narcissism* (New York: Warner Books, 1979), pp. 137–138.

12. John Kenneth Galbraith, *The Affluent Society* (Cambridge, Mass.: Riverside Press, 1958), pp. 156–158.

13. Paul Wachtel, *The Poverty of Affluence* (New York: Free Press, 1983), p. 18.

14. Schudson, *Advertising, the Uneasy Persuasion*, p. 238.

15. "The Gimme Generation," *Wall Street Journal*, May 13, 1988, sec. 3, p. 1.

16. "Selling to Kids? First Bow to Parents," *EDK Forecast* (New York: EDK Associates), December 1993, p. 1.

17. Bradley S. Greenberg and Jeffrey E. Brand, "Television News and Advertising in Schools: The 'Channel One' Controversy," *Journal of Communication* 43, 1993, pp. 143–151.

18. Victor Lebow, *The Journal of Retailing*, Spring 1955, p. 7, as quoted in William Witt, *Chicago Tribune*, op-ed, February 18, 1992.

19. Quoted in Juliet B. Schor, *The Overworked American: The Unexpected Decline of Leisure* (New York: Basic Books, 1992), p. 120.

20. Stuart Ewen, *All Consuming Images: The Politics of Style in Contemporary Culture* (New York: Basic Books, 1988), p. 243.

21. E. F. Schumacher, quoted in R. Sider, *Rich Christians in an Age of Hunger* (Dallas: Word, 1990), p. 126.

22. E. F. Schumacher, quoted in John E. Young, *Discarding the Throwaway Society*, Worldwatch Paper 101, Worldwatch Institute, Washington, D.C., January 1991, p. 35.

23. United Nations Population Fund, *Population and the Environment: The Challenges Ahead* (New York: 1991), p. 14.

24. Ibid.

25. Young, *Discarding the Throwaway Society*, p. 8.

26. Paul Harrison, "The United States: Booming with Buyers—and Babies, Too," *Amicus Journal* (New York: Natural Resources Defense Council), Winter 1994, p. 20.

27. U.S. Department of Commerce, *Statistical Abstract of the United States, 1993* (Washington, D.C.: Government Printing Office, 1993), Table 1416.

28. Al Gore, *Earth in the Balance* (New York: Plume, 1993), chap. 8.

29. Colin Greer, "'The Well-Being of the World Is at Stake,'" *Parade*, January 23, 1994, p. 4.

30. Gore, *Earth in the Balance*, p. 221.

31. Schor, *The Overworked American*, p. 107.

32. Based on three hours daily of television (Nielsen Media Research, November 1993), which consists of about one-fifth advertising, or 0.6 hours (36 minutes). (The average adult watches closer to four and a half hours daily, but many people switch channels during ads.) Add another 10 minutes for radio advertising and 5 minutes or so for time spent reading newspaper ads, opening advertising circulars, and dealing with other forms of advertising. That amounts to 51 minutes, or 5 percent of a 16-hour day. Five percent of a 75-year-old person's life is nearly four years.

33. James Allan Davis and Tom W. Smith, *General Social Surveys, 1972–1993* (Chicago: National Opinion Research Center, July 1993; distributed by the Roper Center for Public Opinion Research, University of Connecticut, Storrs), p. 623.

34. Schor, *The Overworked American*, chapter 2. See also Gary Cross, *Time and Money: The Making of a Consumer Culture* (London: Routledge, 1993), for a historical study of Western workers' trading of leisure time for greater pay. Many people are working longer hours for the simple reason that they are getting paid less; average hourly wages decreased by 7.5 percent between 1970 and 1992 (U.S. Department of Commerce, *Statistical Abstract of the United States, 1993*, Table 667). However, since 1970, both per capita income and median family income have increased significantly (Tables 696, 721), partly due to longer hours and two-

earner families; but increases have been meager or non-existent in recent years.

35. Erich Fromm, foreword, in Edward Bellamy, *Looking Backward* (1888) (New York: Signet, New American Library, 1960).

36. David Shi, *The Simple Life: Plain Living and High Thinking in American Culture* (New York: Oxford University Press, 1985), pp. 220–221.

37. "FYI 1993...," pamphlet, Bankcard Holders of America, Herndon, Va., 1993.

38. In 1992, one of the authors (M.F.J.) received thirty-one credit card offers, whose credit lines totaled $131,800; his wife received many additional offers.

39. Cecilia Cassidy, "Chaarrrge!" *Washington Post*, June 25, 1991, p. D5.

40. Anne Willette, "Rewards Are a Big Part of New Appeal," *USA Today*, May 11, 1994, p. 1B.

41. "DM Showcase," *Advertising Age*, July 18, 1994, p. 26.

42. Administrative Office of the United States Courts, Division of Bankruptcy.

43. We wonder if the people who equate spending with patriotism also oppose more durable, energy-efficient cars, refrigerators, and other products on the grounds that they would reduce employment in the auto, mining, oil, and utility industries.

44. "Advertising-to-Sales Ratios, 1992," *Advertising Age*, July 26, 1993, p. 27.

45. Mark S. Albion and Paul W. Farris, *The Advertising Controversy: Evidence on the Economic Effects of Advertising* (Boston: Auburn House, 1981).

46. The product comparisons in almost every issue of *Consumer Reports* reveal that certain house-brand products are as good as, if not better than, nationally advertised brands in terms of both quality and price.

47. Michael F. Jacobson, statement, press conference held by Center for the Study of Responsive Law concerning Frugal Shoppers Week, Washington, D.C., August 31, 1992.

48. Glenn Ruffenach, "Going for the Gold, Merchandisers and Retailers Promote the Olympics Two Years in Advance," *Wall Street Journal*, December 7, 1993, p. B1.

49. "First Ever Licensing Expo Comes to Las Vegas in 1994," *Playthings*, April 1993, p. 48.

50. Abigail Trafford, "U.S. Health Costs to Pass $1 Trillion in 1994," *Washington Post Health*, January 11, 1994, p. 7.

51. Alcohol and tobacco companies, unlike most other companies, maintain that advertising switches people from brand to brand, but does not increase overall sales. That argument must be taken with a grain of salt. Clearly, some consumers respond to advertising by switching brands or by affirming their loyalty to their current brand. However, some consumers are likely to increase their use of the advertised product, and some nonconsumers are likely to be persuaded to take up drinking and smoking. Because per capita drinking and smoking are stagnant or falling, advertising does not appear to have a powerful effect on increasing consumption, but the true test—impossible to conduct—would be to see how rapidly drinking and smoking would decline in the *absence* of any advertising.

52. J. Michael McGinnis and William H. Foege, "The Actual Causes of Death in the United States," *Journal of the American Medical Association* 270, 1993, p. 2207. They attribute between 310,000 and 580,000 deaths annually due to diet and sedentary lifestyle.

53. Nielsen data from November 1993. Youths between twelve and seventeen watched the least television (3 hours per day); adult women watched the most (4 hours, 51 minutes).

54. Larry A. Tucker and Marilyn Bagwell, "Television Viewing and Obesity in Adult Females," *American Journal of Public Health* 81, 1991, p. 908.

55. Marian Burros, "Despite Awareness of Risks, More in U.S. Are Getting Fat," *New York Times*, July 17, 1994, p. 1.

56. William Dietz et al., "Do We Fatten Our Children at the Television Set? Obesity and Television Viewing in Children and Adolescents," *Pediatrics* 75, 1993, p. 807.

57. Robert C. Klesges et al., "Effects of Television on Metabolic Rate: Potential Implications for Childhood Obesity," *Pediatrics* 91, 1993, p. 281.

58. Burros, "Despite Awareness of Risks"; Michael F. Jacobson and Bruce Maxwell, *What Are We Feeding Our Kids?* (New York: Workman Publishing, 1994), pp. 50–51.

59. William Raspberry, "Cut the Act," *Washington Post*, January 28, 1994, p. A23.

60. George Comstock and Haejung Paik, *Television and the American Child* (San Diego: Academic Press, 1991), p. 247.

61. U.S. Department of Commerce, *Statistical Abstract of the United States, 1994*, Table 301.

62. Ellen Edwards, "TV Networks Agree to Use of Monitor," *Washington Post*, January 22, 1994, p. A1.

63. George Gerbner, "Television Violence: The Art of Asking the Wrong Question," *The World & I*, July 1994, p. 385.

64. Leonard Carmichael, *Basic Psychology* (New York: Random House, 1957), quoted in "Advertising Helps Social Sciences," *Advertising Age*, February 11, 1957, p. 12.

65. Alan Thein Durning, "Can't Live With-out It," *World Watch* (Washington, D.C.: Worldwatch Institute), May-June 1993, p. 10.

66. "The Gimme Generation," p. 1.

67. Marsha L. Richins, "Media Images, Materialism, and What Ought to Be: The Role of Social Comparison," in Floyd Rudmin and Marsha Richins, eds., *Meaning, Measure, and Morality of Materialism*, (Provo, Utah: Association for Consumer Research, 1992), pp. 202–206.

68. See, for instance, Douglas T. Kenrick, Sara E. Gutierres, and Laurie L. Goldberg, "Influence of Popular Erotica on Judgments of Strangers and Mates," *Journal of Experimental Social Psychology* 25, 1987, p. 159.

69. Naomi Wolf, *The Beauty Myth: How Images of Beauty Are Used Against Women* (New York: William Morrow, 1991), p. 145.

70. Personal communication, August 3, 1994.

71. Nicholas Johnson, *Test Pattern for Living* (New York: Bantam, 1972), p. 45.

72. Florence Rice, Harlem Consumer Council, in phone interview with Michael Jacobson, February 18, 1994.

73. Barbara Birdfeather on *Marketplace*, National Public Radio, December 9, 1993.

74. Gabriel Escobar, "A Death That 'Wasn't Worth It.'" *Washington Post*, November 14, 1990, p. D1; Isabel Wilkerson, "Challenging Nike, Rights Group Takes a Risky Stand," *New York Times*, August 25, 1990, p. 10.

75. Celia W. Dugger, "Boy in Search of Respect Discovers How to Kill," *New York Times*, May 15, 1994, p. 1.

76. Ron Harris, "Children Who Dress for Excess," *Los Angeles Times*, November 12, 1989, p. 1; "Sneaker-Killing Sentence," *Washington Post*, November 1, 1990, p. B11.

77. Richard L. Lippke, "Advertising and the Social Conditions of Autonomy," *Business and Professional Ethics Journal* 8, 1989, pp. 35–58.

78. Jules Henry, *Culture Against Man* (New York: Random House, 1963), p. 47.

79. "The Public Mind: Leading Questions" (PBS broadcast), November 15, 1989.

80. Disposable personal income was $6,214 in 1950 and $14,330 in 1993. U.S. Department of Commerce, *Statistical Abstract of the United States, 1993* (Washington: Government Printing Office, 1993), Table 696. The 1993 figure is from U.S. Bureau of Economic Analysis, personal communication, April 1994.

81. Tibor Scitovsky, *Human Desire and Economic Satisfaction* (Brighton, Sussex: Wheatsheaf Books, 1986), p. 33; Schor, *The Overworked American*, p. 115 and n. 13.

82. Another reason the general level of happiness has not been rising is that many fam-ilies' incomes have been falling. Between 1977 and 1988 the average income of the poorest fifth of families declined by more than 10 percent (the average income of the wealthiest tenth of families rose by 16 percent). The have-nots are struggling to get by with less; for the haves, surrounded with possessions, each new possession may give only momentary pleasure (Kevin Phillips, *The Politics of Rich and Poor* [New York: Harper-Perennial, 1991], p. 17).

83. Russell W. Belk, "Three Scales to Measure Constructs Related to Materialism: Reliability, Validity, and Relationships to Measures of Happiness," *Advances in Consumer Research* 11, 1984, pp. 291–297.

84. Marsha L. Richins and Scott Dawson, "A Consumer Values Orientation for Materialism and Its Measurement: Scale Development and Validation," *Journal of Consumer Research* 19, 1992, pp. 303–316.

85. Barry Schwartz, *The Costs of Living* (New York: Norton, 1994), pp. 154–162.

86. Laurence Shames, *Searching for Values in an Age of Greed* (New York: Times Books, 1989), p. 258.

87. Quoted in David Shi, *In Search of the Simple Life* (Layton, Utah: Gibbs Smith, 1986), p. 142.

88. Galbraith, *The Affluent Society*, p. 261.

89. Dee Hock, former head of Visa, in Myron Magnet, "The Money Society," *Fortune*, July 6, 1987, p. 26.

90. Luke 18:25. Similarly, "How hardly shall they that have riches enter into the kingdom of God!" (Luke 18:24, Matthew 19:23, Mark 10:23)

91. National Conference of Catholic Bishops, *Economic Justice for All*, pastoral letter on Catholic social teaching and the U.S. economy, Washington, D.C., 1986.

92. Laurie Goodstein, "Growing Movement to Put Christ before the Almighty Dollar," *Washington Post*, December 24, 1993, p. A1.

93. Ibid.

94. Janet Marder, "When Bar/Bat Mitzvah Loses Meaning," *Reform Judaism*, Winter 1992, p. 4.

95. Much of this section was adapted from Michael F. Jacobson and Ronald K.L. Collins, "How Non-Profits Can Stay Clear of Commercialism's Tentacles," *Chronicle of Philanthropy*, July 28, 1992, p. 32.

96. Howard Kurtz, "Council's Brief in Formaldehyde Suit Financed by Chemical Manufacturer," *Washington Post*, June 3, 1984.

97. See Ronald Collins, *Dictating Content: How Advertising Pressure Can Corrupt a Free Press* (Washington, D.C.: Center for the Study of Commercialism, 1992) for a comprehensive discussion of censorship by advertisers.

98. C. Edwin Baker, *Advertising and a Democratic Press* (Princeton, N.J.: Princeton University Press, 1994), p. 50. This book also provides numerous examples of censorship and self-censorship.

99. We are grateful to Richard L.D. Morse for providing us copies of correspondence, contained in the Consumer Movement Archives at Kansas State University Libraries, between Consumers Union and various publications. See Colston E. Warne, *The Consumer Movement*, Richard L.D. Morse, ed. (Manhattan, Kans.: Family Economics Trust Press, 1993), pp. 78–81.

100. We are grateful to Richard L.D. Morse for providing us with a letter from Alfred Stanford to Colston E. Warne, May 9, 1950.

101. Janice Winship, *Inside Women's Magazines* (London: Pandora Press, 1987), p. 40, as cited in Wolf, *The Beauty Myth*, p. 81. We suspect that women's magazines complied with advertisers' concerns about articles long before 1956.

102. Collins, *Dictating Content*, p. 20.

103. Ibid., p. 24.

104. Bernard Weinraub, "Paramount Withdraws Its Ads after a Bad Review in Variety," *New York Times*, June 10, 1992, p. C15.

105. Sheila Kaplan, in phone interview with Karen Brown, July 5, 1993.

106 Scott Donaton, "Mercedes in Full Retreat on Ad Placement Order," *Advertising Age*, September 20, 1993, p. B8.

107. Kevin Helliker, "Small-Town Newspapers Retaliate when Wal-Mart Cuts Advertising," *Wall Street Journal*, October 14, 1992, p. 2.

108. Peg Masterson, "Many Editors Report Advertiser Pressure," *Advertising Age*, January 11, 1993, p. 22.

109. Anne Marie Kerwin, "Behind the Waltzing," *Editor and Publisher*, June 13, 1992, p. 18.

110. James Workman, "Ad Nauseam: Madison Avenue's Anti-War Movement," *New Republic*, February, 18, 1991, p. 10.

111. *New York Times Co. v. Sullivan,* 376 U.S. 254 (1964).

112. Collins, *Dictating Content*, p. 61.

113. Ibid., p. 44.

114. Ibid., p. 15.

115. Alison Leigh Cowan, "Magazine Dropping Column by Expert on Executive Pay," *New York Times*, February, 25, 1992, p. D1.

116. Deirdre Carmody, "Editor Dismissed at Philadelphia Magazine," *New York Times*, July 26, 1991, p. D5.

CHAPTER TEN
Call To Action: Taming Commercialism

1. Quoted in David Shi, *The Simple Life: Plain Living and High Thinking in American Culture* (New York: Oxford University Press, 1985), p. 145.

2. Franklin Delano Roosevelt's acceptance speech at the 1932 Democratic convention, as quoted in ibid., p. 233.

3. The authors' plea for simpler lifestyles is directed primarily to the middle and upper socioeconomic classes, which represent the bulk of Americans. We do not suggest that people with little should have less.

4. Shi, *The Simple Life,* p. 280.

5. Ronald J. Sider, *Rich Christians in an Age of Hunger* (Dallas: Word, 1990), pp. xv, 95.

6. Alan Thein Durning, *How Much Is Enough? The Consumer Society and the Future of the Earth* (New York: Norton, 1992).

7. Paul Wachtel, *The Poverty of Affluence* (New York: Free Press, 1983), p. 17.

8. Marilyn Schwartz, professor of retailing and marketing, College of Marin (Calif.), quoted in Richard Polito, "Deep Stuff," *The News Journal* (Wilmington, Del.), November 1, 1993, p. C1.

9. Durning, *How Much Is Enough?* p. 132.

10. We waste a lot of time and money buying unneeded, unwanted gifts. Yale economics professor Joel Waldfogel estimated that each Christmas Americans waste more than $4 billion on gifts that recipients do not want. Including birthdays, weddings, and other occasions, Waldfogel says the cost of wasted gift-giving "could easily top $10 billion" (Yale University News Release no. 103, December 7, 1993). That's more money than Americans spend on movie tickets or taxicab fares in an entire year (U.S. Department of Commerce, *Statistical Abstract of the United States, 1993* [Washington, D.C.: Government Printing Office, 1993] Tables 398 and 699).

11. Robert Kubey and Mihaly Csikszentmihalyi, *Television and the Quality of Life* (Hillsdale, N.J.: Lawrence Erlbaum Associates, 1990).

12. Joe Dominguez and Vicki Robin, *Your Money or Your Life* (New York: Viking, 1992), p. 169.

13. Ibid., pp. 171–181.

14. But don't forget that you live in a community and that local businesses cannot survive without your patronage. Sometimes it's worth paying a little more to ensure that the corner store stays in business.

15. Jeff Stein, "The Man with No Gray Flannel Suit," *Washington Post Magazine*, December 19, 1993, p. 16.

16. "The Peace of Simple Living," *Simple Living* (Seattle: Simple Living Press) 2, no.

1, 1993, p. 9.

17. Juliet Schor, "Can the North Stop Consumption Growth? Escaping the Cycle of Work and Spend," Harvard University, April 1994.

18. Wachtel, *The Poverty of Affluence*, p. 141.

19. Juliet B. Schor, *The Overworked American: The Unexpected Decline of Leisure* (New York: Basic Books, 1991), p. 2.

20. Quoted in Conn Nugent, memorandum on consumption, Nathan Cummings Foundation, March 5, 1994.

21. U.S. Department of Commerce, *Statistical Abstract of the United States, 1993*, Table 614.

22. Walt Harrington, "Seeing the Light," *Washington Post Magazine*, December 19, 1993, p. 10.

23. Ontario Ministry of Education, *Media Literacy: Intermediate and Senior Divisions* (Toronto), 1989.

24. Kubey and Csikszentmihalyi, *Television and the Quality of Life*, p. 214.

25. *Media Literacy: A Report of the National Leadership Conference on Media Literacy* (Queenstown, Md.: The Aspen Institute, 1993). This report provides an excellent summary of the status of the media-literacy movement.

26. Allan Luks, "Reading, 'Riting, 'Rithmetic—and Required Service," *Sojourners*, September-October 1993, p. 34.

27. Kathleen Kennedy Townsend, "Why Johnny Can't Tell Right from Wrong," *Washington Monthly*, December 1992, p. 29.

28. Students in Chapel Hill, N.C., and Mamaroneck, N.Y., have sued their school systems for requiring community service. Dennis Kelly, "Students Contest Civic Duty Mandates," *USA Today*, April 19, 1994.

29. Luks, "Reading, 'Riting, 'Rithmetic — and Required Service," p. 34.

30. *Federal Register* 59, no. 5, January 7, 1994, p. 1194.

31. One of the authors (M.F.J.) received the Metropolitan Museum of Art's "Holiday Gifts 1994" catalog on August 19, 1994. In 1994 many Hallmark stores started displaying Christmas ornaments in July.

32. Laurie Goodstein, "Growing Movement to Put Christ Before the Almighty Dollar," *Washington Post*, December 24, 1993, p. A1.

33. J. Marder, "When Bar/Bat Mitzvah Loses Meaning," *Reform Judaism*, Winter 1992, p. 4.

34. Michelle McCarter and Judann Dagnoli, "Is Advertising Moral? Vatican Looking into It," *Advertising Age*, September 6, 1993, p. 1.

35. Xerox Corporation, "Between 1971 and 1994, Xerox has given paid leave of up to one year to 400 employees," press release (Stamford, Connecticut), January 24, 1994.

36. James K. Glassman, "American Express Charges Ahead With 'Cause' Marketing," *Washington Post*, December 24, 1993, p. D9.

37. Editorial, *Advertising Age*, April 2, 1990.

38. Andrew E. Serwer, "Payday! Payday! What CEOs Make," *Fortune*, June 14, 1993, p. 102.

39. John A. Byrne, "That Eye-Popping Executive Pay," *Business Week*, April 25, 1994, p. 52.

40. Pierre Belec, "Hedge Fund Managers Top Pay List," *Washington Post*, June 16, 1994, p. B17.

41. David A. Vise, "Billionaire CEOs Join in Criticism of High Pay," *Washington Post*, April 22, 1993, p. A26.

42. A. Byrne, "That's Some Pay Cap, Bill," p. 57.

43. Wachtel, *The Poverty of Affluence*, p. 282.

44. Another good resource is *Ethical Consumer* magazine, which rates the social responsibility of companies and has articles on boycotts, corporate misdeeds, and activist groups. The emphasis is on England, but the magazine reports on events around the world (ECRA Publishing Ltd., 16 Nicholas St., Manchester, England M1 4EJ).

45. See also Lawrence J. Haas, "Corporate Do-Gooders," *National Journal*, August 1, 1992, p. 1775 for a discussion of the more mainstream Committee for Economic Development.

46. *Utne Reader*, September-October, 1993, p. 72.

47. C. Edwin Baker, *Advertising and a Democratic Press* (Princeton, N.J.: Princeton University Press, 1994), pp. 99–111. Baker also suggests that newspapers (and possibly other media) be taxed in proportion to the percentage of their income they receive from advertising; the revenues would be used to subsidize newspapers in proportion to the percentage of their income they receive from readers. That measure would tend to reduce newspapers' reliance on advertising revenues.

48. Some malls do provide resources to the community. For instance, the Clackamas (Ore.) Town Center, a million-square-foot mall, has conference rooms where community groups can meet, a skating rink, and a branch of the Clackamas County Library. It does not, though, promote citizen involvement in the way we have proposed (Susan Orlean, "Figures in a Mall," *New Yorker*, February 21, 1994).

49. "Mississippi Sues Tobacco Companies; Florida Law Empowers State to Sue," *Health Letter* (Washington, D.C.: Public Citizen Health Research Group), July 1994, p. 6.

50. Tony Patane, owner of ApplianceLand, Etc. stores, quoted in Sharon Walsh, "Turned Off by Sony's Tactics," *Washington Post*, November 16, 1993, p. C1.

51. "Consumers Want Independent Product Info," *CFAnews*, December 1993–January 1994, p. 4.

52. Jimmy Carter, statement, July 18, 1978. Quoted in Shi, *The Simple Life*, p. 271. Similarly, in the depth of the depression, President Franklin Delano Roosevelt, in his first inaugural address, reminded Americans that happiness "lies not in the mere possession of money; it lies in the joy of achievement, in the thrill of creative effort" (ibid., p. 233). President George Bush said in his inaugural address: "Are we enthralled with material things, less appreciative of the nobility of work and sacrifice? My friends, we are not the sum of our possessions. They are not the measure of our lives. In our hearts, we know what matters. We cannot hope only to leave our children a bigger car, a bigger bank account. We must hope to give them a sense of what it means to be a loyal friend, a loving parent, a citizen who leaves his home, his neighborhood and town better than he found it.…[We must] celebrate the quieter, deeper successes that are made not of gold and silk, but of better hearts and finer souls."

53. Both quotes from Federal Trade Commission, "FTC Final Staff Report and Recommendation," Washington, D.C., p. 2, March 31, 1981; see also FTC press release, April 2, 1981.

54. "Can the Telemarketers' Autodialers be Controlled at All?" *Privacy Journal* 20, no. 2, p. 1.

55. "UK Strict on Direct Mail," *Privacy Journal* 20, no. 2, p. 4.

56. Tax laws treat advertising much more generously than the purchase of machinery or other capital investments. Businesses can deduct all advertising expenditures in the current tax year rather than over several years, as is the case for capital investments. The rationale for that is that advertising is assumed to provide only short-term benefits. That may largely be the case when a dress shop advertises a sale for the coming weekend only. But much advertising has a long-term impact, such as image ads that promote positive images of a company or the slogans, jingles, and claims that embed themselves in our minds for years. As one prominent industry insider has noted, "Ironically, the advertising establishment, in insisting that advertising was a routine cost of doing daily business, was contradicting its historical position that advertising must be considered an investment whose returns are paid back over the long haul" (Leo Bogart, *Strategies in Advertising*, 2d ed. [Lincolnwood, Ill.: NTC Publishing Group, 1990], p. xxi).

57. "Advertising-to-Sales Ratios, 1992," *Advertising Age*, July 26, 1993, p. 27.

58. Alexander Polinsky, *Taxnotes*, September 27, 1993, p. 1663. See also, hearings of the Subcommittee on Select Revenue Measures, House Committee on Ways and Means, September 8, 1993.

59. Comments to FCC, MM Docket No. 93-254, December 20, 1993.

60. In 1980, the FTC had the equivalent of 1,819 full-time employees; by 1989, that had been reduced to 894. Staffing climbed to 954 in 1994 (Federal Trade Commission, Office of Public Affairs).

61. A good primer on environmental problems and remedies is Al Gore, *Earth in the Balance* (New York: Plume, 1993).

62. Paul Starobin, "Thrift Begins at Home," *National Journal*, October 30, 1993, p. 2592.

63. John Kenneth Galbraith, *The Affluent Society* (Cambridge, Mass.: Riverside Press, 1958). See, especially, chapter 22.

64. Ibid., p. 315.

65. Galbraith recognized that the poor are hit hardest by sales taxes, but he felt that the negative effect was mitigated by the fact that the poor would benefit most from programs made possible by the taxes. Moreover, sales taxes face less political opposition from conservatives, who can usually block more progressive tax increases that specifically target the rich (though federal tax increases in 1993 did focus on the rich). The regressiveness of sales taxes could be corrected partially by tax credits and decreases in income taxes.

66. Twentieth Century Fund, *Quality Time* (New York: Twentieth Century Fund Press, 1993), pp. 28–32. In July 1994, the Federal Communications Commission auctioned off a 120-megahertz band of the radio dial to the "personal communications services" (PCS) industry, netting the government several billion dollars. The revenues, which went to the Treasury, could have been earmarked for public broadcasting (Mike Mills, "The Sky's the Limit," *Washington Post*, June 5, 1994, p. H1).

67. Corporation for Public Broadcasting, "Public Broadcast Income, FY 1993: Preliminary Report by Corporation for Public Broadcasting," June 1994.

68. Baker, *Advertising and a Democratic Press*, pp. 111–115.

69. Ralph Nader, "The Audience Network: Time For the People" (Washington, D.C., undated).

70. Frank Beacham, "Coalition Calls for Equal Access to the Info Highway," *Advertising Age*, November 22, 1993, p. 19.

71. Davis and Smith, *General Social Surveys, 1972–1993*, p. 311.

72. Mary Jordan, "Youth Service Corps Officials Prepare for Recruiting Blitz," *Washington Post*, December 2, 1993, p. A19.

ABOUT THE BOOK AND AUTHORS

I N 1983, REESE'S PIECES MADE THEIR DEBUT ON THE SILVER screen, gobbled up by that lovable alien ET, and sales of the candy shot up instantly by 66 percent. Reebok has sponsored the U.S. Olympic team—and the Russian team, as well! The British Boy Scouts sell space on their merit badges to advertisers.

Michael Jacobson, founder of the Washington, D.C.-based watchdog group, Center for the Study of Commercialism (CSC), and Laurie Mazur have produced *the* book on marketing mania in the United States and the deleterious effects it is having on our ailing culture. Beyond documenting the "unholy alliance" between corporations and Hollywood, the authors take up such disquieting issues as how marketers turn citizens into consumers, the quiet battle between private consumption and social welfare, ads that kill (alcohol and tobacco), the litter of billboards, stealth advertising, corporate interference with public television, the commercialization of Christmas, sex in advertising, marketing in our public schools, and the selling of social issues.

This highly readable book interlocks fascinating illustrations with hard statistics and analysis drawn from years of research conducted under the aegis of the CSC. The result is a powerfully revealing book that informs, astounds, enrages, and instructs. It is a primer on the social ills of commercialism gone rampant, a call to action for all concerned citizens. As the authors contend, "this book documents the problem, analyzes its effects, and empowers the reader by offering 'what you can do' suggestions for personal action."

Michael F. Jacobson is co-founder of the Center for the Study of Commercialism and executive director of the Center for Science in the Public Interest. Jacobson is also author or co-author of *What Are We Feeding Our Kids, Marketing Disease to Hispanics,* and many other books and reports. Laurie Mazur writes on issues of environmental and social justice.

INDEX